Advanced Textbooks in Economics

Series Editors: C. J. Bliss *and* M.D. Intriligator

Currently Available:

Volume 2: *Lectures on Microeconomic Theory* (Second Revised Edition)
E. MALINVAUD

Volume 5: *Applied Consumption Analysis* (Second Revised Edition)
L. PH LIPS

Volume 11: *Collective Choice and Social Welfare*
A. K. SEN

Volume 12: *General Competitive Analysis*
K. J. ARROW and F. H. HAHN

Volume 14: *Distributed Lags* (Second Revised Edition)
P. J. DHRYMES

Volume 17: *Stochastic Methods in Economics and Finance*
A. G. MALLIARIS and W. A. BROCK

Volume 19: *International Trade and Resource Allocation* (Second Revised Edition)
A. D. WOODLAND

Volume 23: *Public Enterprise Economics* (Second Revised Edition)
D. BÖS

Volume 24: *Optimal Control Theory with Economic Applications*
A. SEIERSTAD and K. SYDSAETER

Volume 24: *Capital Markets and Prices: Valuing Uncertain Income Streams*
C. G. KROUSE

Volume 26: *History of Economic Theory*
T. NEGISHI

Volume 27: *Differential Equations, Stability and Chaos in Dynamic Economics*
W. A. BROCK and A. G. MALLIARIS

Volume 28: *Equilibrium Analysis*
W. HILDENBRAND and A. P. KIRMAN

Volume 29: *Economics of Insurance*
K. H. BORCH †; completed by K. K. AASE and A. SANDMO

Volume 30: *Microeconomics: Institutions, Equilibrium and Optimality*
M. C. BLAD and H. KEIDING

Volume 31: *Dynamic Optimization* (Second Revised Edition)
M. L. KAMIEN and N. I. SCHWARTZ †

NOTES AND PROBLEMS IN
APPLIED GENERAL EQUILIBRIUM ECONOMICS

ADVANCED TEXTBOOKS IN ECONOMICS

VOLUME 32

Editors:

C. J. BLISS

M. D. INTRILIGATOR

Advisory Editors:

W. A. BROCK

D. W. JORGENSON

A. P. KIRMAN

J.-J. LAFFONT

J.-F. RICHARD

NORTH-HOLLAND
AMSTERDAM · LONDEN · NEW YORK · TOKYO

NOTES AND PROBLEMS IN APPLIED GENERAL EQUILIBRIUM ECONOMICS

Peter B. DIXON
Brian R. PARMENTER
Alan A. POWELL

Monash University
Melbourne, Australia

Peter J. WILCOXEN

The University of Texas at Austin
U.S.A.

Simulation Software (separately available) by:
K. R. PEARSON
La Trobe University and Monash University

1992

NORTH-HOLLAND
AMSTERDAM · LONDON · NEW YORK · TOKYO

ELSEVIER SCIENCE PUBLISHERS B.V.
Sara Burgerhartstraat 25
P.O. Box 211, 1000 AE Amsterdam, The Netherlands

Distributors for the United States and Canada:

ELSEVIER SCIENCE PUBLISHING COMPANY INC.
655 Avenue of the Americas
New York, N.Y. 10010, U.S.A.

Library of Congress Cataloging-in-Publication Data

Notes and problems in applied general equilibrium economics / Peter B.
   Dixon ... [et al.].
        p.   cm. -- (Advanced textbooks in economics ; 32)
     Includes bibliographical references and indexes.
     ISBN 0-444-88449-1
     1. Equilibrium (Economics)--Mathematical models.   I. Dixon, Peter
   B. II. Series: Advanced textbooks in economics ; v. 32.
   HB145.N67   1992
   339.5'01'1--dc20   91-45877
                                                               CIP

ISBN: 0 444 88449 1
      0 444 89334 2: Simulation Software
      0 444 89379 2: Set

Printed in The Netherlands

Introduction to the Series

The aim of the series is to cover topics in economics, mathematical economics, and econometrics at a level suitable for graduate students or final year undergraduates specializing in economics. There is at any time much material that has become well established in journal papers and discussion series which still awaits a clear, self contained treatment that can easily be mastered by students without considerable preparation or extra reading. Leading specialists will be invited to contribute volumes to fill such gaps. Primary emphasis will be placed on clarity, comprehensive coverage of sensibly defined areas, and insight into fundamentals, but original ideas will not be excluded. Certain volumes will therefore add to existing knowledge, while others will serve as a means of communicating both known and new ideas in a way that will inspire and attract students not already familiar with the subject matter concerned.

The Editors

Preface

Applied general equilibrium modeling has attracted considerable attention in recent years, not only in academic circles but also among economic policy advisers. We hope that this book will prove valuable in initiating graduate and advanced undergraduate students into this field. Moreover, we hope that it will be useful to professional economists who wish to understand model-based analysis better and even to use applied general equilibrium models in their own work.

Reflecting our belief in the models as vehicles for practical policy analysis, we have included a considerable amount of material on data and solution techniques as well as on theoretical structures. Through the efforts of our colleague Ken Pearson, we have been able to provide a companion set of diskettes which will enable users of the book to acquire hands-on experience with computer implementations of the models which we describe (see Chapter 1 for details). We strongly advise readers to obtain copies of the diskettes and to use them with the exercises in the text of the book.

Because of our rather onerous responsibilities in other areas, this book has been a long time in preparation. We are grateful to Michael Intriligator for his encouragement and patience. Victor Ginsburgh and Sherman Robinson provided valuable comments on earlier drafts. As part of the process of disseminating the *ORANI* model, we have, over the last decade, conducted several training courses, attracting more than 150 participants from a large number of public and private organizations. For some years, we have also taught courses in applied general equilibrium economics to graduate students at La Trobe University and at the University of Melbourne. Students of these courses, too numerous to name, gave us vital feedback at all stages of the endeavour. Orani Dixon, Sara Hansen, Frances Peckham, Louise Pinchen, Rosy Qin, Marie Milkovic, Shirley Simmons, Elvine Sullivan and Roger Williams did meticulous work over the years with several word-processing systems in the preparation of a long and difficult typescript. We thank them all.

Peter B. Dixon

B.R. Parmenter

Alan A. Powell

November 1991

Peter J. Wilcoxen

Contents

Introduction to the Series   v

Preface   vii

List of tables   xiv

List of figures   xvi

Chapter 1 INTRODUCTION
  1.1 Preamble   1
  1.2 Background   1
  1.3 Format and Prerequisites   3
  1.4 The Companion Diskettes   3
  1.5 Goals, Reading Guide and References   4

  PROBLEM SET 1:   THE IMPLICATIONS OF TECHNICAL
                  CHANGE IN A WINE-CLOTH ECONOMY   7
    E1.1   What can be produced?   7
    E1.2   What will be produced?   11
    E1.3   Commodity prices and real wages   12
    E1.4   The effects of a change in production techniques   13

Chapter 2 INPUT-OUTPUT DATA AND INPUT-OUTPUT MODELS
  2.1 Introduction   19
  2.2 Goals, Reading Guide and References   20
  PROBLEM SET 2   25
  A. *INPUT-OUTPUT ACCOUNTING*   25
    E2.1   Valuation of transactions: the treatment of
           markups and sales taxes in absorption matrices
           at basic values and purchasers' prices   28

E2.2   Imports: direct and indirect allocation in
       absorption matrices   31

E2.3   Industry by industry tables and secondary production   35

E2.4   Computing import and margin matrices
       from published input-output tables   36

B. *INPUT-OUTPUT MODELS*   38

E2.5   The open static input-output model   38

E2.6   Adding multi-product industries and
       multi-industry commodities   41

E2.7   Adding international trade   45

E2.8   Including markups and sales taxes   49

C. *IMPLEMENTING INPUT-OUTPUT MODELS*   54

E2.9   Calibration of coefficients from input-output data   54

E2.10 Input-output multipliers   65

D. *INPUT-OUTPUT MODELS AS COMPUTABLE
    GENERAL EQUILIBRIUM MODELS*   70

E2.11 Producer optimization   70

Chapter 3 THE JOHANSEN APPROACH

3.1 Introduction   73

3.2 Goals, Reading Guide and References   80

PROBLEM SET 3   87

A. *A STYLIZED JOHANSEN MODEL*   87

E3.1   The theoretical structure for the Stylized
       Johansen model   88

E3.2   The percentage-change form of the Stylized
       Johansen model   94

E3.3   Input-output data and the initial solution   97

E3.4   Input-output data and the evaluation of $A(V^I)$ 98

E3.5   Condensing the Stylized Johansen model   99

E3.6   Two solution matrices for the Stylized Johansen model 103

B. *ELIMINATING JOHANSEN'S LINEARIZATION ERRORS*   109

E3.7   An introductory example of a multi-step
       Johansen computation   110

E3.8   A multi-step computation for the Stylized
       Johansen model   116

C. *ON DERIVING PERCENTAGE-CHANGE FORMS*   124

   E3.9   Linearizing the input demand functions from a
           CES production function   124

   E3.10   Linearizing the input demand functions from a
           CRESH production function   126

   E3.11   Supply response functions with CET and CRETH
           transformation frontiers   128

   E3.12   The translog unit cost function   133

   E3.13   Linearizing the demand functions for separable
           production and utility functions   142

Chapter 4 THE CONSTRUCTION OF A MODEL FOR
             PRACTICAL POLICY ANALYSIS

4.1 Introduction   149

4.2 Goals, Reading Guide and References   150

4.3 Equations, Variables and Notation for
    the DMR Model: An Overview   161

4.4 The Input-Output Database   186

PROBLEM SET 4   191

   E4.1   Final demands in the DMR model: equations (4.3.1) – (4.3.4)   191

   E4.2   Assigning values for the export demand elasticities   195

   E4.3   The commodity composition of an industry's output:
           the derivation of (4.3.5) and (4.3.6)   199

   E4.4   Evaluating the parameters and coefficients
           in the output composition equations   208

   E4.5   Demands for inputs for use in current production:
           the derivation of equations (4.3.7) – (4.3.10)   211

   E4.6   Evaluating the parameters and coefficients in
           the input demand equations   219

   E4.7   The creation of composite commodities: substitution
           between imported and domestic products: equations
           (4.3.11) – (4.3.14)   224

   E4.8   Evaluating the parameters and coefficients in
           the import/domestic substitution equations   229

   E4.9   The zero-pure-profits conditions in the DMR
           model: equations (4.3.15) – (4.3.19)   234

   E4.10   The market-clearing equations: (4.3.20) – (4.3.25)   237

   E4.11   The allocation of the investment budget across industries:
           equations (4.3.26) – (4.3.27)   239

E4.12   The remaining miscellaneous equations: (4.3.28) – (4.3.43)   240

E4.13   Five test simulations for the DMR model under
        the standard ORANI closure   246

E4.14   Finishing the specification: adding GDP, real
        GDP and the GDP deflator   252

E4.15   Simulating a decline in the terms of trade   256

Appendix 4.1   Tabular Listing of the Input-Output Database and
               Parameter File for the DMR Model   268

Appendix 4.2   Listing of Results from the Simulation
               in Exercise 4.15   274

Chapter 5   AN INTRODUCTION TO INTERTEMPORAL MODELING

5.1 Introduction   277
5.2 Goals, Reading Guide and References   278
PROBLEM SET 5   283
A.   *A SIMPLE INTERTEMPORAL MODEL OF INVESTMENT*   283
     E5.1   The value of the firm   283
     E5.2   Conditions for solving the firm's investment problem   286
     E5.3   Earnings functions and investment-cost functions   289
     E5.4   Graphical analysis   292
     E5.5   Analyzing experiments   304
     E5.6   Adding more taxes to the investment model   316
     E5.7   Introducing diminishing returns into the model   325
     E5.8   The stock market and the costate variable   330
B.   *NUMERICAL METHODS*   333
     E5.9   Shooting   334
     E5.10   Multiple Shooting   336
     E5.11   The Fair-Taylor Method   338
     E5.12   Finite Differences   340
     E5.13   Constructing finite-difference formulae   345
C.   *AN INTERTEMPORAL GENERAL EQUILIBRIUM MODEL*   348
     E5.14   The structure of the model   349
     E5.15   Expectations   355
     E5.16   Implementing the model   356
     E5.17   A further implementation test, numerical accuracy and
             grid spacing   361
     E5.18   Some illustrative simulations   367

Appendix 5.1   The Intertemporal Model: Equations,
                    Variables and Trial Data Set   377

   The Equations   377

   (i)   Dynamic Equations   377

   (ii)   Boundary conditions   377

   (iii)   Intraperiod equations   377

   (iv)   Expectations   379

   Variables and Trial Data Set   379

Author Index   385

Subject Index   387

References for:

     Chapter 1   6

     Chapter 2   24

     Chapter 3   85

     Chapter 4   155

     Chapter 5   282

List of tables

E1.1.1	Current Production Techniques: Input-Output Coefficients	8
E1.1.2	Production Techniques after an Improvement in the Technique for Producing Cloth	10
E1.1.3	The Wine-Cloth Economy before and after the Improvement in the Technique for Producing Cloth	14
E2.A	Input-Output Flows (Commodity by Industry) for the Year 19XX with Disaggregated Treatments of Imports, Sales Taxes and Markups ($m) (a) Absorption Matrix: Commodity by Industry (b) Make Matrix: Commodity by Industry	27
E2.1.1	Absorption Matrix (Commodity by Industry) for the Year 19XX at Basic Values with Disaggregated Treatment of Imports ($m)	29
E2.1.2	Absorption Matrix (Commodity by Industry) for the Year 19XX at Purchasers' Prices with Disaggregated Treatment of Imports ($m)	29
E2.2.1	Absorption Matrix (Commodity by Industry) for the Year 19XX at Basic Values with Direct Allocation of Imports ($m)	33
E2.2.2	Absorption Matrix (Commodity by Industry) for the Year 19XX at Basic Values with Indirect Allocation of Competing Imports ($m)	33
E2.2.3	Absorption Matrix (Commodity by Industry) for the Year 19XX at Purchasers' Prices with Direct Allocation of Imports ($m)	34
E2.2.4	Absorption Matrix (Commodity by Industry) for the Year 19XX at Purchasers' Prices with Indirect Allocation of Competing Imports ($m)	34
E2.3.1	Input-Output Flows (Industry by Industry Absorption Matrix) for the Year 19XX with Disaggregated Treatments of Imports, Markups and Sales Taxes ($m)	37
E2.9.1	The Matrices $\mathbf{A}^I$, $\mathbf{B}^I$, Ψ^I, $\Phi^{I\,\prime}$ and $\mathbf{L}^I$	59
E2.9.2	The Matrices $\mathbf{A}_m^I$, $\mathbf{Q}$	59
E2.9.3	Final Demands and Associated Margins	60
E2.9.4	The Matrices Ψ^d, Ψ^E, Ψ^m, Ψ^n, $\Phi^{d\prime}$, $\Phi^{E\prime}$, $\Phi^{m\prime}$ and $\Phi^{n\prime}$	60
E2.9.5	Industry and Commodity Technologies	64
E2.10.1	Multiplier Calculations	68
E3.3.1	Input-Output Data (Flows in dollars)	98
E3.4.1	The Transpose of the Matrix $A(V^I)$ for the Stylized Johansen Model: Incomplete	99
E3.4.2	Answer to Exercise 3.4: The Transpose of the Matrix $A(V^I)$ for the Stylized Johansen Model	100
E3.5.1	Answer to Exercise 3.5(b): The Matrix $A^*(V^I)$ for a Condensed form of the Stylized Johansen Model	102
E3.6.1	Solutions for the Stylized Johansen Model under Alternative Closures	105
E3.7.1	Solutions for V_1 and V_2 in the System (3.1.2) when V_3 is moved from 1 to 2: Calculations based on (3.1.7)	113
E3.8.1	Input-Output Data after 1 Update: (Flow i to j)$_{1,2}$ in Dollars	122
E3.8.2	Input-Output Data after 2 Updates: (Flow i to j)$_{2,2}$ in Dollars	123
4.3.1	The DMR Equations: Levels and Percentage-Change Representations	162

4.3.2	Variables in the DMR Model	169
4.3.3	Other Notation Appearing in the Levels Representation (Equations (4.3.1)(a) – (4.3.43)(a) in Table 4.3.1) of the DMR Model	172
4.3.4	Other Notation Appearing in the Percentage-Change Representation of the DMR Model: The Coefficients and Parameters of the System (4.3.1)(b) – (4.3.43)(b) in Table 4.3.1	173
4.3.5	Two Selections of Exogenous Variables	179
4.3.6	Required Parameters for the Percentage-Change Version of the DMR Model	180
4.3.7	Supplementary Data File for the DMR Model: Variables whose Initial Values are not Implied by the Initial Input-Output Table	181
4.4.1	Schematic Representation of the Input-Output Data Files for the DMR Model	188
E4.2.1	Cronin's Notional Database for Calculating the Export Demand Elasticity for Australian Beef	197
E4.15.1	Macroeconomic Impact of a 10 Per Cent Fall in the World Price of Exportable Commodity 8 under the Standard DMR Closure	258
E4.15.2	Explanation of the Change in Real GDP arising from a 10 per cent Fall in the World Price of Exportable Commodity 8 under the Standard DMR Closure	260
A4.1.1	Key to Industries, Commodities and Occupations	268
A4.1.2	Matrix $\tilde{A}$: Flows of Commodities Used by Industries as Intermediate Inputs ($ million)	268
A4.1.3	Matrix $\tilde{B}$: Flows of Commodities Used by Industries for Capital Formation ($ million)	269
A4.1.4	Matrices $\tilde{E}$ and $\tilde{F}$: Imports and Exports at Different Valuations ($ million)	269
A4.1.5	Matrix $\tilde{G}$: Wage Bill by Occupation and Industry ($ million)	270
A4.1.6	Vector Components of Input-Output Data ($ million)	270
A4.1.7	Scalar Components of Input-Output Data ($ million)	271
A4.1.8	Parameter File: Substitution and Transformation Elasticities	271
A4.1.9	Other Parameters and Initial Values of Coefficients	272
A4.1.10	Supplementary Data — Initial Wage Rates by Occupation and Industry, $\{P_{(n+1,1,k)}^{(1j)}\}$ ($ per year)	273
A4.1.11	Initial Values of Certain Coefficients Based in Part on Supplementary Data	273
E5.14.1	Characteristics of the Sectors	351
E5.17.1	The Effect of Grid Density and Step Number on the Computed Capital Stock of Sector A at Period 10	363
E5.17.2	A Selection of Grid Spacings	364
E5.17.3	The Effect of Grid Choice and Step Number on the Computed Capital Stock of Sector A at Period 10	366
A5.1.1	Variables in the Intertemporal General Equilibrium Model	380
A5.1.2	Parameters in the Trial Data Set	382
A5.1.3	Exogenous Variables	383

List of figures

E1.1.1	Net annual production possibilities under the initial production techniques	9
E1.1.2	Net annual production possibilities after the improvement in the technique for producing cloth	9
E2.11.1	Isoquants of the Leontief production function and isocosts	71
E3.8.1	Flow diagram for a multi-step solution of a Johansen model	118
E3.11.1	The quarter circle production possibilities frontier	130
E3.11.2	Production possibilities frontiers given by (E3.11.4) when $\rho = -1, -2$ and $-\infty$	131
4.3.1	Commodity and factor flows in the DMR model	187
E4.5.1	The input-activity specification in the DMR model: schematic representation of equations (E4.5.2) – (E4.5.3)	217
E5.4.1	Constructing a phase diagram: step one	296
E5.4.2	Constructing a phase diagram: step two	297
E5.4.3	The finished phase diagram	299
E5.4.4	Phase diagram for hypothetical model with two stable paths	301
E5.5.1	Effects of a permanent increase in the dividend tax rate: shifting the loci	307
E5.5.2	Effects of an immediate, permanent increase in the dividend tax rate: finding the dynamic path	307
E5.5.3	Effects of an anticipated, permanent increase in the dividend tax rate: finding the dynamic path	308
E5.5.4	Effects of a surprise increase in the price of output	310
E5.5.5	Effects of an announced increase in the price of output	312
E5.5.6	Effects of a temporary increase in the price of output	313
E5.5.7	Effects of a surprise drop in the price of capital goods	315
E5.6.1	Phase diagram for a model with taxes on dividends, interest and capital gains	321
E5.6.2	Effects of an unexpected decline in the capital gains tax	322
E5.6.3	Effects of an announced decline in the capital gains tax	323
E5.6.4	Effects of a temporary decline in the capital gains tax	324
E5.7.1	Phase diagram for a model with diminishing returns	327
E5.7.2	Effects of a surprise increase in the tax on interest	328
E5.7.3	Effects of an announced increase in the tax on interest	329
E5.14.1	The structure of the model	350
E5.18.1	Effects of an announced increase in the dividend tax	368
E5.18.2	Effects of an announced increase in the sales tax on good A under perfect foresight	370
E5.18.3	Effects of an announced increase in the sales tax on good 2 under perfect foresight	372

Chapter 1

Introduction

1.1 Preamble

This book is about applied general-equilibrium modeling. Both adjectives are crucial. By "general-equilibrium" we refer to an analytical approach which looks at the economy as a complete system of inter-dependent components (industries, households, investors, governments, importers and exporters). It explicitly recognizes that economic shocks impacting on any one component can have repercussions throughout the system and that accounting for these repercussions may be essential in assessing the effects of the shocks — even on the components upon which they impact initially. By "applied" we mean that our primary interest is in systems that can be used to provide quantitative analysis of economic policy problems in particular countries. Hence, as well as a theoretical structure, we require data about the economy of interest and solution methods which allow us to solve the models numerically. *Computable general equilibrium* is an alternative term commonly used to describe such models.

1.2 Background

The heroes and heroines of the book are Leontief, Manne, Johansen, Jorgenson, Adelman, Robinson, Shoven, Whalley and others who have seen that general equilibrium economics can contribute far more than theoretical propositions concerning the existence, uniqueness, stability and optimality of equilibria. With *applied* general equilibrium modeling, they have developed a powerful technique for quantitative analysis of the effects on industries, governments, regions, occupations and households of changes in a myriad of variables, including taxes, trade restrictions, government expenditures, welfare policies, commodity prices, technology and environmental regulations.

Most of our own experience in applied general equilibrium modeling has been in the IMPACT Project and the Institute of Applied Economic and Social Research, both at the University of Melbourne. IMPACT and the IAESR have been responsible for several models, the best known being *ORANI*, an applied general equilibrium model of the Australian economy. *ORANI* has been used extensively in Australia by people in government, business and universities. At last count there were about 300 published *ORANI* applications by many different authors.

The sequence of chapters follows what we see as the historical development of the subject. Chapter 2 deals with Leontief's input-output economics. In the 1930s, Leontief constructed a database for an applied general equilibrium model and implemented the first model. Chapter 3 introduces Johansen's approach. His book, published in 1960, describes a computationally simple general equilibrium model of the Norwegian economy, with price-responsive behavior allowing a satisfactory treatment of substitution possibilities in consumption and production. The Johansen approach is developed further in Chapter 4, where we make a detailed study of a model built in the 1970s by Robinson and others at the World Bank. This model not only generalizes the price responsive behavior specified by Johansen, but also allows for foreign exchange rationing and other common features of Third World economies. Finally, in Chapter 5 we look at the development in the 1980s, by Goulder and others, of applied general equilibrium models with theoretically satisfactory treatments of expectations and forward looking behavior.

Unfortunately, space requirements have prevented us from including an exposition of the mathematical programming approach to applied general equilibrium modelling. This was developed by Manne, Sandee, and others in the 1950s and 1960s, using computational techniques first devised by Dantzig (see Dixon, 1991).

Another contribution of importance in the development of the field but which is not covered in this book is the combinatorial approach to computing equilibria pioneered by Scarf (1967; 1973). Scarf's work provided a bridge in the 1970s between theoretical propositions on the existence of equilibria and the computation of equilibria in numerically specified models. It went a long way towards making applied general equilibrium modeling interesting to theorists. However, it is our view that the combinatorial approach was never the most effective method for doing computations with practical, policy-relevant models[1].

Whatever method was chosen, until quite recently, solving general equilibrium models required large amounts of special-purpose software to be written. The 1980s saw a major change in this situation with the development by Drud, Meeraus, Pearson, Rutherford and others of general-purpose software packages. Each of these packages can handle a wide

---

1   Dixon (1978) argues that, in striving for generality, the combinatorial approach fails to take advantage of special features, almost always present in the mathematics of economic models, which allow the use of computationally simpler and more efficient methods. See also Ginsburgh and Waelbroeck (1981, p. xiv).

range of general equilibrium models, though each places some restrictions on the class of models which it can accommodate. For the classes of models covered, these developments have reduced by an order of magnitude the computing demands on economic modelers. Some of the literature on the packages is cited in the reference list for this chapter and further information can be found on the companion diskettes described below.

1.3 Format and Prerequisites

The book is directed at graduate students and professional economists who may have an interest in constructing or applying general equilibrium models. Its format is similar to that of Dixon *et al.* (1980). Both consist of annotated reading guides and exercises with detailed answers.

Some of the exercises aim to develop the student's skills in manipulating algebraic expressions. Typical of this type of exercise is the derivation of demand functions suitable for applied general equilibrium models from underlying assumptions about behavior, preferences and technology. However, many of the problems go beyond this, requiring the student to confront practical issues in data mobilization, computing and result interpretation.

The formal mathematical prerequisites for using the material are a knowledge of elementary (first-year college level) matrix algebra and calculus, particularly constrained optimization. However, some exercises require considerable perseverance through many steps. The exercises will lose much of their value if students refer to the answers too early. Nevertheless, students should not allow themselves to become bogged down in algebraic detail. A quick glance at our answer will often be very time-saving, while still allowing students to do most of the work required to derive satisfactory answers of their own.

1.4 The Companion Diskettes

The exercises and readings in the book provide a comprehensive introduction to applied general equilibrium modeling. However, mastery of the subject can come only with practical experience and experimentation. This involves computing.

A companion publication to this book is:

> K. R. PEARSON, *Simulation Software for use with 'NOTES AND PROBLEMS IN APPLIED GENERAL EQUILIBRIUM ECONOMICS'* (Amsterdam: North-Holland),

which consists of three, $5\frac{1}{4}$ inch, 360K diskettes. These will allow students to experiment with the models in Chapters 3, 4 and 5 and to carry out all the simulations described there.[2]

1.5 Goals, Reading Guide and References

By the time you have finished this chapter you should have acquired a preliminary understanding of why, in analysing economic issues, it might be important to account for interactions between different industry groups in the context of the overall economic system. You should have become comfortable with studying economics via a structured program of problems and worked solutions. You should be aware of the availability of general-purpose software for the solution of large-scale economic models. Specific goals are to understand:

(1) the representation of industries' production technologies via tables of input-output coefficients and the representation of technical progress via changes in the coefficients;

(2) the concept and construction of an economy's net production possibilities set;

(3) the implications of technical progress for the production possibilities set;

(4) the roles of society's preferences with respect to consumption and of an assumption about the level of employment in determining what will be produced in an economy, given its available technology;

(5) the relationship between real and nominal wage rates;

(6) how technical progress in one industry can affect relative prices, the real wage rate, and output and employment in all industries; and

(7) how technical progress can generate structural change in the economy and what are some of the factors which determine the economy's ability to accommodate structural change.

Reading guide 1 is designed to help you in achieving these goals. It contains abbreviated references which are cited in full in the reference list. This list, which immediately follows the reading guide, also contains other references appearing in the chapter.

---

2   The software runs on IBM-compatible microcomputers using MS-DOS or PC-DOS version 2.10 or higher. You will need at least 512K bytes of memory and either a hard disk or two floppy disk drives.

Reading Guide to Chapter 1

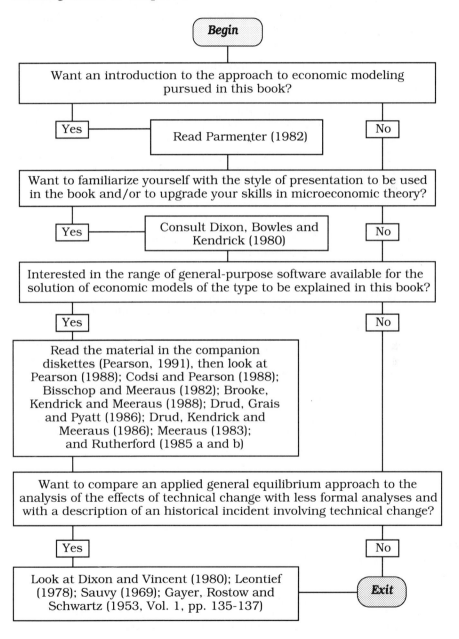

References for Chapter 1

Bisschop, Johannes and Alexander Meeraus (1982) "On the Development of a General Algebraic Modeling System in a Strategic Planning Environment", *Mathematical Programming Study*, Vol. 20, pp. 1-19.

Brooke, Anthony, David Kendrick and Alexander Meeraus (1988) *GAMS: A User's Guide* (Redwood City, California: Scientific Press).

Codsi, G. and K.R. Pearson (1988) "GEMPACK: General-purpose Software for Applied General Equilibrium and Other Economic Modellers", *Computer Science in Economics and Management*, Vol. 1, pp. 189-207.

Dixon, P.B. (1978) "The Computation of Economic Equilibria: A Joint Maximization Approach", *Metroeconomica*, Vol.XXIX, December, pp. 173-185.

Dixon, P.B., S. Bowles and D. Kendrick (1980) *Notes and Problems in Microeconomic Theory* (Amsterdam: North Holland).

Dixon, P.B. and D.P. Vincent (1980) "Some Economic Implications of Technical Change in Australia to 1990-91: An Illustrative Application of the SNAPSHOT Model", *Economic Record*, Vol. 56, December, pp. 347-361.

Dixon, P.B. (1991) "The Mathematical Programming Approach to Applied General Equilibrium Analysis: Notes and Problems", *Impact Project Working Paper* No.I–50, University of Melbourne (April). Available from Impact Information Officer, Industry Commission, P.O. Box 80, Belconnen ACT 2616, Australia.

Drud, Arne, Wafik Grais and Graham Pyatt (1986) "An Approach to Macroeconomic Model Building Based on Social Accounting Principles", *Journal of Policy Modeling*, Vol. 8, pp. 111-145.

Drud, Arne, David Kendrick and Alexander Meeraus (1986) "HERCULES: A System for Development of Multisectoral Economywide Models", World Bank *Discussion Paper* No. DRD169 (April), 12 pp.

Gayer, A.D., W.W. Rostow and A.J. Schwartz (1953) *The Growth and Fluctuation of the British Economy, 1790-1850*, 2 volumes (Oxford: Clarendon).

Ginsburgh, V. and J. Waelbroeck (1981) *Activity Analysis and General Equilibrium Modelling* (Amsterdam: North-Holland).

Leontief, W.W. (1978) "Issues of the coming years", *Economic Impact*, No. 24 (4), pp. 70-76.

Meeraus, Alexander (1983) "An Algebraic Approach to Modeling", *Journal of Economic Dynamics and Control*, Vol. 5, pp. 81-108.

Parmenter, B. R. (1982) "Inter-Industry Analysis", Ch. 5 in L. R. Webb and R. H. Allan (eds), *Industrial Economics* (Boston: George Allen and Unwin), pp.69-110.

Pearson, K.R. (1991) *Simulation Software for use with 'NOTES AND PROBLEMS IN APPLIED GENERAL EQUILIBRIUM ECONOMICS'* (Amsterdam: North-Holland).

Pearson, K.R. (1988) "Automating the Computation of Solutions of Large Economic Models", *Economic Modelling*, Vol. 7, pp. 385-395.

Rutherford, Thomas Fox (1985a) "MPS/GE User's Guide", Department of Operations Research, Stanford University, 72 pp.

Rutherford, Thomas Fox (1985b) "Operating Instructions for CASGEN", Department of Operations Research, Stanford University, 9 pp.

Sauvy, Alfred (1969) *General Theory of Population* (London: Weidenfeld and Nicholson).

Scarf, Herbert (1967) "The Approximation of Fixed Points of a Continuous Mapping", *SIAM Journal of Applied Mathematics*, Vol.15, No.5, pp. 1328–1344.

Scarf, Herbert (1973) *The Computation of Economic Equilibria* (New Haven: Yale University Press).

PROBLEM SET 1: *THE IMPLICATIONS OF TECHNICAL CHANGE IN A WINE–CLOTH ECONOMY*

This warm-up problem set is organized as four exercises. The first describes for a hypothetical economy the net annual production possibilities set, i.e., what *can* be produced with existing techniques and resources in one year. The second introduces consumer preferences to determine what *will* be produced. In the third we discuss prices and real wages. In the last exercise we derive the implications of a change in production techniques.

Exercise 1.1   *What can be produced?*

Consider a society which produces just two products, wine and cloth. The techniques currently in use for the production of these products are described by input-output coefficients in Table E1.1.1. The output of one gallon of wine requires an input of 0.2 yards of cloth and one hour of labor. The output of one yard of cloth requires an input of just one hour of labor. We assume that the society's resource endowment for a year is 100 labor hours.

Table E1.1.1

Current Production Techniques: Input-Output Coefficients

	Outputs	
Inputs	Wine (1 gallon)	Cloth (1 yard)
Wine	*nil*	*nil*
Cloth	0.2 yards	*nil*
Labor	1 hour	1 hour

The society's net annual production possibilities set is shown graphically in Figure E1.1.1. It can be constructed by doing a few calculations. For example, if 50 labor hours were devoted to wine and 50 to cloth, then net annual output would be 50 gallons and 40 yards, the point E_1 in Figure E1.1.1. Notice that the gross output of cloth is 50 yards, but that 10 yards are used up in wine production. If society allocates all its resources (100 labor hours) to cloth production, net annual output would be 100 yards of cloth and no wine (point A in Figure E1.1.1). If all the labor were devoted to wine, we would end up with 100 gallons, but we would have a deficit of 20 yards of cloth (point D in Figure E1.1.1). Perhaps the deficit could be made up by drawing on accumulated stocks or through importing. But for simplicity we will assume that there are no accumulated stocks and that there is no international trade. Thus, the net annual production possibilities available to our society are restricted to the shaded area 0AB in Figure E1.1.1.

(a)   Can our society produce a net annual output of 40 gallons of wine and 60 yards of cloth?

(b)   Can our society produce a net annual output of 40 gallons of wine and 30 yards of cloth?

(c)   Consider the production techniques shown in Table E1.1.2. The only change from those in Table E1.1.1 is that technical progress has taken place which allows a yard of cloth to be produced with only 0.5 hours of labor input rather than one hour. Assume that the society's resource endowment remains at 100 labor hours per year. Construct the new net annual production possibilities set.

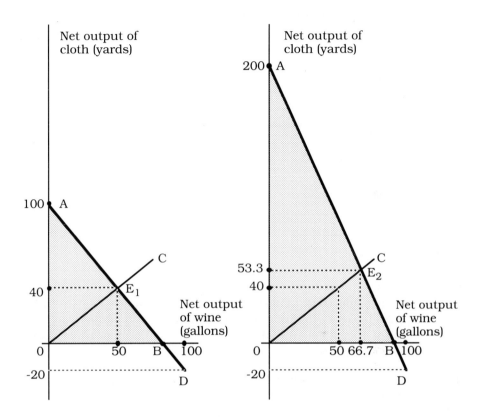

Figure E1.1.1 Net annual production possibilities under the initial production techniques

Figure E1.1.2 Net annual production possibilities after the improvement in the technique for producing cloth

Given the production techniques in Table E1.1.1 and a resource endowment of 100 labor hours, society can produce for final use any combination of wine and cloth shown in the triangle OAB.

Table E1.1.2

Production Techniques after an Improvement

in the Technique for Producing Cloth

	Wine (1 gallon)	Cloth (1 yard)
Wine	*nil*	*nil*
Cloth	0.2 yards	*nil*
Labor	1 hour	0.5 hours

Answer to Exercise 1.1

(a)   No. In terms of Figure E1.1.1, the point 40 gallons, 60 yards lies outside the triangle OAB. Given the production techniques in Table E1.1.1, it would take a gross output of 40 gallons and 68 yards to achieve a net output of 40 gallons and 60 yards. Thus, 108 hours of labor would be required. Only 100 hours are available.

(b)   Yes. In terms of Figure E1.1.1, the point 40 gallons, 30 yards is inside the triangle OAB. Given the production techniques in Table E1.1.1, it would take a gross output of 40 gallons and 38 yards to achieve a net output of 40 gallons and 30 yards. Thus, 78 hours of labor would be required. This is available.

(c)   The new net annual production possibilities set is shown in Figure E1.1.2 as the triangle OAB. It can be constructed by considering the net outputs which would emerge as we vary the allocation of labor between the production of our two commodities. For example, if all the 100 labor hours were devoted to cloth production, then we would obtain 200 yards of cloth and no wine. Hence point A in Figure E1.1.2 is part of the new net annual production possibilities set. If $66\frac{2}{3}$ hours of labor were devoted to wine and $33\frac{1}{3}$ to cloth, then net production would be $66\frac{2}{3}$ gallons of wine and $53\frac{1}{3}$ yards of cloth, point E_2 in Figure E1.1.2. (Notice that the use of $33\frac{1}{3}$ labor hours in cloth generates a gross output of $66\frac{2}{3}$ yards, but that the wine production uses up $13\frac{1}{3}$ (= $0.2 \times 66\frac{2}{3}$ yards.) If 100 labor hours were devoted to wine production, then we would obtain 100 gallons. There would, however, be a deficit of 20 yards of cloth. (See point D in Figure E1.1.2.) Because we rule out both international trade and the existence of accumulated stocks, deficits are not possible. Hence the net annual production possibilities are confined to the triangle 0AB in Figure E1.1.2.

Be sure to compare the new net annual production possibilities set with the old one. As can be seen by looking at Figures E1.1.1 and E1.1.2, technical progress in the cloth industry leads to an expansion of the possibilities set.

Exercise 1.2   *What will be produced?*

Having constructed society's net annual production possibilities set and illustrated it in Figure E1.1.1, our next task is to determine which point in the set will be chosen. This will depend on (i) the level of employment and (ii) consumer preferences for wine and cloth.

Assume that our society achieves full employment, i.e., all of the 100 labor hours are used in production. This contentious assumption is discussed in Exercise 1.4. If we accept the full-employment assumption, then we can restrict our search for the actual net production point to the frontier, AB, of the net annual production possibilities set. It is only on the frontier that we have full employment.

Which point will be chosen on the frontier, AB? This will depend on what society wants to consume. The simplest possible case is to assume that our society always consumes wine and cloth in fixed proportions: 5 gallons of wine to 4 yards of cloth. In terms of Figure E1.1.1, consumption will occur somewhere along the line 0C. In view of our full employment assumption, net production and consumption of wine and cloth will be 50 gallons and 40 yards (point E_1 in Figure E1.1.1).

(a)   At E_1 how many labor hours will be used in the production of wine? How many will be used in the production of cloth?

(b)   Continue to assume that total employment is 100 labor hours and that wine and cloth are consumed in the ratio of 5 gallons to 4 yards. If the production technique for cloth improves to that shown in Table E1.1.2, what will be the new levels for net production and consumption of wine and cloth? How many labor hours will be used in wine production? How many in cloth production?

Answer to Exercise 1.2

(a)   At E_1, the *gross* outputs are 50 gallons of wine and 50 yards of cloth. Hence 50 labor hours are used in wine production and 50 in cloth production.

(b)   In Figure E1.1.2, the consumption line 0C crosses the frontier of the net annual production possibilities set at E_2. The levels for net production and consumption of wine and cloth are $66\frac{2}{3}$ gallons and $53\frac{1}{3}$ yards. Employment is $66\frac{2}{3}$ hours in wine and $33\frac{1}{3}$ hours in cloth.

Exercise 1.3   **Commodity prices and real wages**[3]

Suppose that the nominal wage rate is $1 per hour. Then under the production techniques shown in Table E1.1.1, the price of cloth would be $1 per yard. This is because it takes one hour of labor to make a yard of cloth. The price of a gallon of wine would be $1.2, i.e., the cost of one hour of labor plus the cost of 0.2 yards of cloth. The hourly wage ($1) would be just sufficient to buy a commodity bundle containing 0.5 gallons of wine and 0.4 yards of cloth.

(a)   If the wage rate were $10 per hour, what would be the prices of wine and cloth? Would the wage for an hour's labor still buy a commodity bundle containing 0.5 gallons of wine and 0.4 yards of cloth? In determining the *real* hourly wage rate, does it make any difference whether we assume the nominal hourly wage is $1 or $10?

(b)   Assume that the wage rate is $1 per hour and that the production techniques are those shown in Table E1.1.2. What will be the prices of wine and cloth? Check that the wage for an hour's labor can now buy a commodity bundle containing 0.67 gallons of wine and 0.53 yards of cloth.

Answer to Exercise 1.3

(a)   If the wage rate were $10 per hour, the price of cloth would be $10 per yard and the price of wine would be $12 per gallon. The real wage rate would be unaffected by an increase in the wage rate from $1 per hour to $10 per hour. In both cases, the wage for an hour's labor would buy a bundle of commodities containing 0.4 yards of cloth and 0.5 gallons of wine.

---

3   The real hourly wage rate is measured by a quantity of commodities that can be purchased in return for one hour's labor.

(b) The price of cloth will be $0.5 per yard and the price of wine will be $1.1 per gallon. At these prices, a commodity bundle containing 0.67 gallons of wine and 0.53 yards of cloth would cost $1, i.e., the wage for one hour of labor would buy a bundle containing 0.67 gallons of wine and 0.53 yards of cloth.

Exercise 1.4   *The effects of a change in production techniques*

In Table E1.1.3 we have listed everything that we have found out about our wine-cloth economy. Column I shows commodity outputs, employment in each industry, commodity prices and the real wage rate in the initial situation (i.e., when the production techniques are those in Table E1.1.1). Column II shows the corresponding results when the production techniques are those in Table E1.1.2. By comparing columns I and II, we can see the economy-wide effects of the improvement in the production technique for cloth. The halving of the labor input coefficient for cloth production has allowed consumption and net production of both wine and cloth to increase by $33\frac{1}{3}$ per cent, real wage rates to increase by $33\frac{1}{3}$ per cent, the price of cloth to fall sharply relative to that of wine and $16\frac{2}{3}$ per cent of the labor force to be reallocated from the cloth industry to the wine industry.

This analysis is quite similar to that used by economists concerned with quantifying the effects of technical change in the real world. For example, in their study of the Australian economy, Dixon and Vincent (1980) assembled two tables of input-output coefficients, one showing production techniques as they were in 1971/72 and the other showing the production techniques forecast for 1990/91. They then made some comparisons. Their central computation was designed to answer the following question: how much difference do the projected changes in production techniques make to one's picture of how the economy will be in 1990/91. In terms of Figures E1.1.1 and E1.1.2, Dixon and Vincent computed the points E_1 and E_2, where E_1 refers to the levels which would be achieved in 1990/91 for commodity outputs, prices, real wages, etc., if production techniques remained as they were in 1971/72 and E_2 refers to the situation which will emerge if production techniques are consistent with the forecasts. The comparison between E_1 and E_2 was, therefore, the basis for a discussion of the implications of technical change.

Dixon and Vincent considered many details which were not included in our wine-cloth economy. They divided the economy into 109 sectors, rather than 2. They included capital, not just labor as a primary factor of production and they divided labor into 9 occupational groups.

Table E1.1.3

*The Wine-Cloth Economy before and after the Improvement
in the Technique for Producing Cloth*

	I. Before	II. After
Net annual output and consumption		
Wine	50 gallons	$66\frac{2}{3}$ gallons
Cloth	40 yards	$53\frac{1}{3}$ yards
Employment		
Wine	50 hours	$66\frac{2}{3}$ hours
Cloth	50 hours	$33\frac{1}{3}$ hours
Prices (assuming that the wage rate is $1 per hour)		
Wine	$1.2 per gallon	$1.1 per gallon
Cloth	$1.0 per yard	$0.5 per yard
Real wage rate		
The wage for	0.5 gallons	0.67 gallons
one hour's	*plus*	*plus*
labor buys	0.4 yards	0.53 yards

They considered the role of investment, not just consumption. They allowed for international trade, government expenditure and numerous taxes, tariffs and subsidies. Nevertheless, in essence, their approach consisted of the steps outlined in this problem set: (i) the derivation of alternative net annual production possibilities sets corresponding to alternative assumptions about production techniques, and (ii) the imposition of the full employment assumption and the consideration of consumer preferences leading to the calculation of the net production points.

What did Dixon and Vincent conclude from their study? Given the preliminary nature of their work and a number of deficiencies which they were careful to emphasize, they were cautious. They did, however, offer the following:

"The overwhelming impression . . . . is that the occupational composition of the workforce at the 9-order level in 1990/91 is unlikely to be radically different from that in 1971/72 and that it will be determined largely independently of technical change. Certainly, the present simulations do not pinpoint any likely difficulties in the areas of labor mobility and manpower training." [Dixon and Vincent (1980, p. 358)]

and

"Subject to the qualifications expressed throughout the paper, our results indicate that rapid technical progress is particularly important for the future well-being of those Australian industries which are closely connected with international trade. At the macro level, our results support the view that technical progress is vital for securing increased GDP, increased consumption and higher real wages. Technical progress may also affect macroeconomic management. In the absence of technical progress, we found that the 'full-employment' level of real wages would decline. Under such conditions, it is difficult to imagine that Australia could achieve even a tolerable approximation to full employment." [Dixon and Vincent (1980, p. 359)]

The calculations by Dixon and Vincent and our own analysis of the wine-cloth economy present technical change in a favourable light. Only its role as a source of increased material welfare is emphasized. But this is not the aspect of technical change which has always been emphasized in popular discussions. Sometimes, the principal concern has been with job replacement. Newspapers frequently report fears expressed by various groups in the community concerning the employment effects of new machines: word-processors, automatic bank tellers, point-of-sale terminals, vending machines and robots.

Let us re-examine our wine-cloth story from the point of view of the employment implications of technical change. The critical assumption in the story is that technical change is not an important determinant of the aggregate level of employment. It is assumed that aggregate employment is 100 labor hours both before and after the improvement in the production technique for cloth. There is no need to assume that employment of 100 labor hours is literally full employment. Perhaps 105 hours of labor are available. Our assumption then is that 5 per cent unemployment is just as likely with technical progress as without it.[4]

This assumption should not be too surprising to readers with some knowledge of conventional macroeconomic theory. That theory stresses demand management, fiscal and monetary policy and the real wage rate in relation to labor productivity as the major determinants of aggregate employment. The rate of technical change rarely rates even a mention. This will not be very reassuring to readers who are sceptical about conventional economic theory. They will want us to spell out the process by which workers, displaced by technical change, will find new jobs.

In terms of our wine-cloth economy, the problem is to explain the transition from E_1 to E_2 (Figures E1.1.1 and E1.1.2). Starting at E_1, the halving of the labor input coefficient for cloth will mean that only 25 labor hours (rather than 50) are required in the industry. Cloth now will be cheaper and the real incomes of employed workers will expand. These workers will demand more wine and cloth, thus providing employment for the previously displaced workers. This will set us on the path to E_2.

What about adjustment problems along the path from E_1 to E_2? Recall that the shift from E_1 to E_2 involved the transfer of $16\frac{2}{3}$ per cent of the labor force out of cloth and into wine. What if the skills required of wine workers differ from those of cloth workers? Then might not the move from E_1 to E_2 cause excessive periods of unemployment for surplus cloth workers? Certainly this is a possibility. It is important, therefore, in comparing E_1 and E_2 to consider the feasibility of the implied rates of shift of resources between different activities. This is what Dixon and Vincent did in their analysis of the implications of technical change to 1990/91. They concluded that technical change to 1990/91 could be accommodated without rapid transfers of labor between the nine broadly defined occupational groups. It is possible, however, that technical change to 1990/91 may render redundant certain very specific skills. This does not necessarily imply any serious difficulties. In many countries, workers exhibit a high degree of occupational mobility.

We conclude this exercise with two stories about horses, and a question.

---

4   This assumption may be overly generous to the situation with no technical progress. With no technical progress there is unlikely to be scope for increases in real wages without reductions in employment.

Horse story number one[5]

Maynard, the employer, and his worker, Milton, produce 20 bushels of wheat per year from 5 acres of land. Maynard pays Milton a wage of 10 bushels and retains a profit of 10 bushels for himself.

One day, Maynard makes a remarkable technical improvement. He captures and trains a horse. Using the horse, Maynard can produce 20 bushels of wheat per year without Milton's help. Since the horse consumes only 7 bushels of wheat, Maynard sacks Milton and lives happily ever after consuming 13 bushels of wheat per year.

But what of poor Milton? He leaves the farm and starves to death.

Horse story number two[6]

Anyone who doesn't believe in the possibility of permanent unemployment arising from technical change should think about what happened to employment prospects for horses at the beginning of this century.

Have either of these horse stories any relevance to the analysis of the implications of technical change in a modern economy? Both imply the possibility of an unhappy outcome from technical change. What are the key differences in the assumptions underlying our wine-cloth analysis and the assumptions underlying the horse stories?

Answer to Exercise 1.4

The key differences between the assumptions underlying the horse stories and those underlying the wine-cloth story concern human adaptability to change. In the wine-cloth story, the displaced cloth workers can move into wine production. By contrast, horse story number one depicts the displaced worker, Milton, as having no viable alternative to working for Maynard. One wonders why Milton does not capture a horse and work some land of his own. Perhaps society has advanced to the stage where all the arable land is occupied. But then it is surprising that Milton does not go to a town and work in an urban occupation. Horse story number two also depicts the possibility of the displaced workers being left with nothing to do, the displaced workers this time being horses. We should note, however, that the horses which lost their jobs at the turn of the century had a very limited range of skills compared with human workers.

---

5   This story is adapted from Sauvy (1969, p. 113).
6   This story is adapted from Leontief (1978).

Chapter 2

Input-Output Data and Input-Output Models

2.1 Introduction

The prototype for modern applied general equilibrium models is Leontief's input-output model. It emphasises interdependencies between different industries and between industries and households which arise from their roles as each other's customers: the purchase of material inputs by one industry from others or of labor and capital inputs from households, and the purchase of consumer goods by households from industries.

As we shall explain in subsequent chapters, modern applied general equilibrium models include a range of interdependencies which is wider than just those arising directly from the flows between agents in the economy. In particular, they include interdependence arising from the constraints which bind the economy as a whole. Resource-endowment and balance-of-payments constraints are examples. Through these, demands for labor, capital, foreign exchange and other resources in one part of the economy affect all other parts via movements in factor prices and in the exchange rate and via induced changes in the costs of all goods and services.

Models which attempt to capture all these interdependencies require two types of data: input-output tables and behavioural parameters. Input-output tables record, for one period in time, the commodity flows which took place between components of the economy. Behavioural parameters summarize how agents respond to changes in activity variables and prices: for example, how producers adjust their demands for inputs in response to changes in their output levels and input prices, or how households adjust the level and composition of their consumption in response to changes in their incomes and consumer prices. Input-output models, because they include only direct interdependencies between components of the economy, require as data only input-output tables.

Input-output models are of historical interest. They are also of practical interest because of their continuing popularity as tools for policy analysis. In this chapter, we use a discussion of input-output models to introduce a number of issues which are crucial to applied general equilibrium modeling. Most important is the use of input-output data in setting values for the coefficients of the equations which describe the theoretical structure of the model.

2.2 Goals, Reading Guide and References

By the time you have finished this chapter you should have developed a thorough understanding of input-output data and of how the data can be used to assign values for the coefficients of input-output models. You should also understand how to obtain and interpret solutions from input-output models. Specific goals are:

(1)   to understand absorption and make matrices in input-output accounts;

(2)   to understand the basic-values and purchasers'-prices valuation conventions in input-output tables;

(3)   to understand the direct and indirect allocation of imports in input-output tables;

(4)   to understand the difference between commodity by industry and industry by industry input-output tables;

(5)   to understand the fixed-coefficient technology which underlies input-output models;

(6)   to understand how multi-product industries and multi-industry products, imports and exports, markups and sales taxes can be included in input-output models;

(7)   to be able to manipulate the equations of input-output models to obtain algebraic solutions;

(8)   to be able to use input-output data to set values for the coefficients of the equations in input-output models;

(9)   to be able to calculate input-output multipliers and to understand their limitations as guides to economic policy;

(10)   to understand how the basic open static input-output model can be derived from explicit assumptions about producer optimization; and

(11)   to be familiar with applications of input-output economics to international economics, regional analysis, environmental problems and development economics.

Reading guide 2 is designed to help you in achieving these goals. It contains abbreviated references to readings which are cited in full in the reference list. This list, which immediately follows the reading guide, also contains other references appearing in the chapter.

Reading Guide to Chapter 2

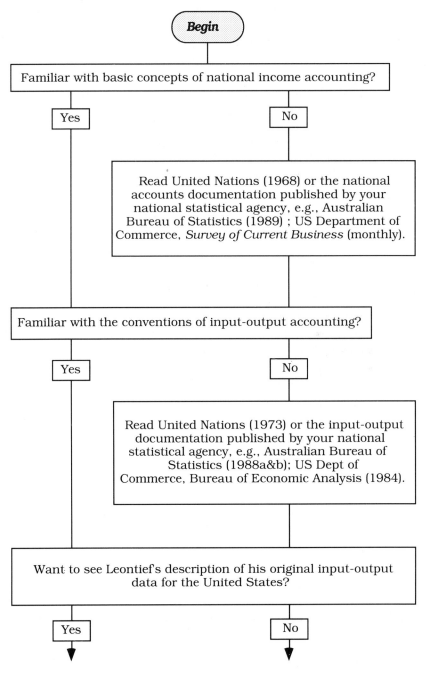

Begin

Familiar with basic concepts of national income accounting?

Yes   No

Read United Nations (1968) or the national accounts documentation published by your national statistical agency, e.g., Australian Bureau of Statistics (1989) ; US Department of Commerce, *Survey of Current Business* (monthly).

Familiar with the conventions of input-output accounting?

Yes   No

Read United Nations (1973) or the input-output documentation published by your national statistical agency, e.g., Australian Bureau of Statistics (1988a&b); US Dept of Commerce, Bureau of Economic Analysis (1984).

Want to see Leontief's description of his original input-output data for the United States?

Yes   No

Reading Guide to Chapter 2 *(continued)*

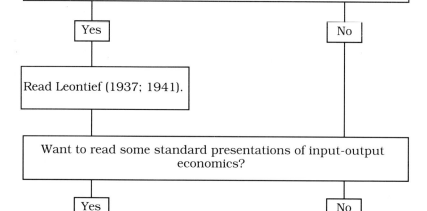

Reading Guide to Chapter 2 (continued)

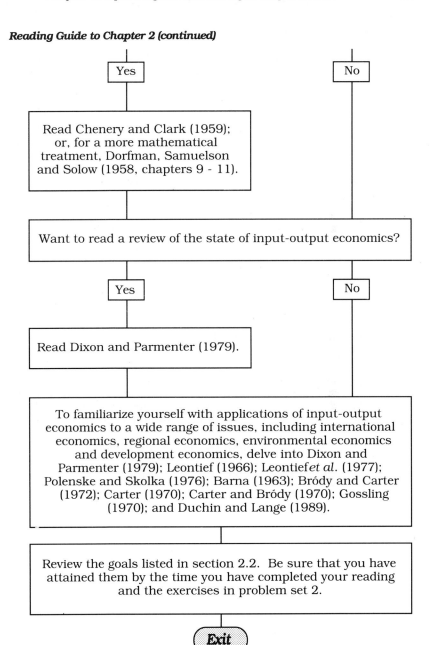

References for Chapter 2

Australian Bureau of Statistics (1988a) *Australian National Accounts — Input-Output Tables 1981-82 and 1982-83*, Catalogue No. 5209.0, Canberra: Australian Bureau of Statistics.

Australian Bureau of Statistics (1988b) *Australian National Accounts — Input-Output Tables Commodity Details 1981-82 and 1982-83*, Catalogue No. 5215.0, Canberra: Australian Bureau of Statistics.

Australian Bureau of Statistics (1989) *Australian National Accounts — Concepts, Sources and Methods*, Catalogue No. 5216, Canberra: Australian Bureau of Statistics.

Barna, T. (ed) (1963) *Structural Interdependence and Economic Development*, London: MacMillan.

Bródy, A., and A.P. Carter (eds) (1972) *Input-Output Techniques*, Amsterdam: North-Holland.

Carter, A.P. (1970) *Structural Change in the American Economy*, Cambridge, Mass.: Harvard University Press.

Carter, A.P., and A. Bródy (eds) (1970) *Input-Output Techniques — Vol. 1: Contributions to Input-Output Analysis* and Vol. 2: *Applications of Input-Output Analysis*, Amsterdam: North-Holland.

Chenery, H.B., and P. Clark (1959) *Interindustry Economics*, New York: John Wiley.

Dixon, P.B., and B.R. Parmenter (1979) "Advances in Input-Output Modeling: A Review Article", *Journal of Policy Modeling*, Vol. 1 (2), pp. 271-285.

Dorfman, R., P.A. Samuelson and R.M. Solow (1958) *Linear Programming and Economic Analysis*, New York: McGraw-Hill.

Duchin, F. and G.M. Lange (1989) "Strategies for Environmentally Sound Development: An Input-Output Analysis", unpublished progress reports #1 and #2, Institute for Economic Analysis, New York University.

Gossling, W.F. (ed) (1970) *Input-Output in the United Kingdom*, London: Cass.

Hadley, G (1961) *Linear Algebra*, Reading, Mass.: Addison-Wesley.

Leontief, W.W. (1936) "Quantitative Input and Output Relations in the Economic System of the United States", *Review of Economics and Statistics*, Vol. 18, pp. 105-125.

Leontief, W.W. (1937) "Interrelation of Prices, Output, Savings and Investment", *Review of Economics and Statistics*, Vol. 19, pp. 109-132.

Leontief, W.W. (1941) *The Structure of the American Economy, 1919-1929*, New York: Oxford University Press.

Leontief, W.W. (1966) *Input-Output Economics*, New York: Oxford University Press.

Leontief, W.W., A.P. Carter and P.A. Petri (1977), *The Future of the World Economy*, New York: Oxford University Press.

Polenske, K.R. and J.V. Skolka (eds) (1976) *Advances in Input-Output Analysis*, Cambridge, Mass.: Ballinger.

United Nations (1968) *A System of National Accounts,* New York: United Nations.

United Nations (1973) *Studies in Methods, Input-Output Tables and Analysis,* Series F, No. 14, rev. 1, New York: United Nations.

United States Department of Commerce (monthly) *Survey of Current Business.*

United States Department of Commerce, Bureau of Economic Analysis (1984) "The Input-Output Structure of the U.S. Economy, 1977", *Survey of Current Business,* May, pp. 42-79.

PROBLEM SET 2

A   *INPUT-OUTPUT ACCOUNTING*

Input-output tables provide the major part of the data for the construction of applied general equilibrium models. For people working in the applied general equilibrium area, familiarity with input-output accounting is required. The exercises in this section provide an introduction to input-output conventions concerning the valuation of transactions, the treatment of imports and the handling of secondary production.

The exercises are built around Table E2.A. This shows input-output data for a hypothetical economy in which there are three domestic industries, three domestically produced commodities, one category of final demand and one category of factor payments. Part (a) of the table is an *absorption matrix* showing the usage of commodities and factors in domestic industries and in final demand. Part (b) is a *make matrix* showing the commodity composition of output in the three industries.

Published input-output tables for real economies often contain more than one hundred industries and several categories of final demands (e.g., household consumption, investment, government expenditure and exports) and of factor payments (e.g., wages and gross operating surplus). However, in two respects the absorption matrix presented in part (a) of Table E2.A is more disaggregated than in conventional input-output tables.

The first is the treatment of imports. In Table E2.A these are fully disaggregated by commodity and user. The commodity dimension (rows) shows four types of imports. The first three are commodities 1, 2 and 3. These are said to be *competing imports* because they are judged to be good substitutes for the corresponding domestic commodities. The fourth type, *non-competing*, are judged to have no close substitutes produced in the domestic economy. For the USA, an example of a non-competing import is coffee, while imported cars are an example of competing imports. The user dimension (columns) identifies the destination of the imports: industries (for use as intermediate inputs) or final demand. In most input-output tables, the disaggregation of imports is either by commodity or by user but not by both.

The second respect in which Table E2.A is more disaggregated than a conventional input-output table is in its treatment of *sales taxes* and *markups*. Examples of markups are transport, wholesale and retail services used in the transfer of domestic commodities from producers to users and in the transfer of imported commodities from ports of entry to users. In Table E2.A it is assumed that there is only one type of markup service, domestically produced commodity 3. Input-output data for a real economy will normally identify several types. However, unlike Table E2.A, input-output tables normally do not show the sales taxes and markups associated with each individual commodity flow. What they do show is the topic of Exercise 2.1.

With sales taxes and markup usage identified separately, all commodity flows in Table E2.A are shown at *basic* values, that is excluding sales taxes and markups. The basic value of a unit of a domestic commodity is the price received by the producer. For an imported commodity, the convention is that the basic value is the price at the port of entry, including duty.[1]

The make matrix in part (b) of Table E2.A shows that industries 1 and 2 both produce commodities 1 and 2 but industry 3 specializes completely in the production of commodity 3. Note that the first two row totals of the make matrix are identical to the totals of the first two rows of the absorption matrix. Both pairs of totals show the aggregate output levels (at basic values) of the first two domestic commodities. In the absorption matrix, the aggregate sales of domestic commodity 3 are the direct sales (the total of the third row in the domestic-commodities submatrix, i.e., 119) *plus* all the markup services[2] (the sum of the row sums of the markup submatrices, i.e., 81). In the make matrix aggregate sales of commodity 3 appear as the third row sum (i.e., 200 = 119 + 81).

The column totals of the make matrix are identical to the totals of the first three columns of the absorption matrix. Both sets of totals show the basic values of the outputs of domestic industries. From the absorption matrix, these are computed by summing the costs of the industries.

---

[1]   We must be careful to distinguish duty on imports from other indirect taxes levied on their sales in the domestic economy. In Table E2.A, the former are included in the imports rows and the latter are shown separately in the tax rows. For a presentation of input-output data in which import duty is shown explicitly, see Table 4.4.1 in Chapter 4.

[2]   The difference between direct and markup purchases is illustrated by the case of transport. Freight services are markups but taxi fares are direct purchases.

Table E2.A

Input-Output Flows (Commodity by Industry) for the Year 19XX with Disaggregated Treatments of Imports, Sales Taxes and Markups ($m)

(a) Absorption Matrix: Commodity by Industry

		Intermediate demand by industries			Final demand	Total usage
		1	2	3		
Sales of:						
domestically	1	10	20	10	40	80
produced	2	15	15	10	80	120
commodities:	3	18	8	58	35	119
imported	1	0	5	10	10	25
commodities:	2	0	6	0	24	30
(competing)	3	0	0	0	0	0
non-competing imports		5	10	4	11	30
Usage of domestic commodity 3 as markup on sales of:						
domestic	1	1	4	3	8	16
commodities:	2	3	5	2	30	40
	3	0	0	0	0	0
competing	1	0	1	3	2	6
imports:	2	0	2	0	9	11
	3	0	0	0	0	0
non-competing imports		1	2	1	4	8
Taxes on sales of:						
domestic	1	1	4	1	10	16
commodities	2	3	3	2	20	28
	3	0	0	0	5	5
competing	1	0	2	2	5	9
imports	2	0	5	0	5	10
	3	0	0	0	0	0
non-competing imports		0	0	0	2	2
Factor Payments		33	18	94		145
Total Demand		90	110	200	300	

(markup block braced: 81)

(b) Make Matrix: Commodity by Industry

		Produced by domestic industries			Total supply of domestic commodities
		1	2	3	
Domestic	1	60	20	0	80
commodities	2	30	90	0	120
	3	0	0	200	200
Total output of domestic industries		90	110	200	

Exercise 2.1   ***Valuation of transactions: the treatment of markups and sales taxes in absorption matrices at basic values and purchasers' prices***

Rather than showing markups as matrices, as in Table E2.A, conventional input-output tables show the usage of markup services together with non-markup usage of such services in the rows corresponding to the commodities to which the services are classified. Similarly, sales taxes are shown as a single row rather than as matrices.

(a)   Show how the data in part (a) of Table E2.A would be presented in an absorption matrix with transactions at basic values and with single rows for the usage of commodity 3 and for sales taxes. What do the entries in these rows represent?

(b)   Show how the data in part (a) of Table E2.A would be presented in an absorption matrix with transactions at purchasers' prices with single rows for the usage of commodity 3 and for sales taxes. What do the entries in these rows represent?

Answer to Exercise 2.1

(a)   In Table E2.1.1 the first two rows of the domestic-commodities matrix and the whole of the imports matrix are identical to the corresponding parts of Table E2.A. They contain flows of the domestic non-markup commodities (1 and 2) and of all imports at basic values.

Row 3 of the domestic-commodities matrix in Table E2.1.1 contains each user's direct purchases of the markup commodity (shown as row 3 of the domestic-commodities matrix in Table E2.A) *plus* the aggregate basic value of markup services required to deliver all the purchases made by each user. The latter components are the users' column sums of the markup matrices in Table E2.A. For example, according to Table E2.A, industry 1 purchases 18 million dollars worth of domestic commodity 3 directly and 5 million dollars worth of markup services are required in the delivery of domestic commodities and imports to the industry ($1m for domestic commodity 1, $3m for domestic commodity 2 and $1m for non-competing imports). Hence, purchases of domestic commodity 3 by industry 1 in Table E2.1.1 are shown as $23m (= 18 + 5).

The sales-tax row of Table E2.1.1 contains aggregate sales taxes payable on each user's purchases. These are the column sums of the sales-tax matrices in Table E2.A.

(b)   The first two rows of the domestic-commodities matrix and the whole of the imports matrix in Table E2.1.2 contain the flows of domestic non-markup commodities and of imports at purchasers'

Table E2.1.1

*Absorption Matrix (Commodity by Industry) for the Year 19XX
at Basic Values with Disaggregated Treatment of Imports*
($m)

Commodities		Intermediate demand by industries			Final demand	Total usage
		1	2	3		
Domestic	1	10	20	10	40	80
commodities	2	15	15	10	80	120
	3	23	22	67	88	200
Competing imports	1	0	5	10	10	25
	2	0	6	0	24	30
	3	0	0	0	0	0
Non-competing imports		5	10	4	11	30
Sales taxes		4	14	5	47	70
Factor payments		33	18	94		145
Total demand		90	110	200	300	

Table E2.1.2

*Absorption Matrix (Commodity by Industry) for the Year 19XX at
Purchasers' Prices with Disaggregated Treatment of Imports*
($m)

Commodities		Intermediate demand by industries			Final demand	Markup and sales taxes on imports	Total usage
		1	2	3			
Domestic	1	12	28	14	58		112
commodities	2	21	23	14	130		188
	3	40	42	58	40	25	205
Competing	1	0	8	15	17		40
imports	2	0	13	0	38		51
	3	0	0	0	0		0
Non-competing imports		6	12	5	17		40
Sales taxes		19	25	5	0	21	70
Factor payments		33	18	94			145
Total demand		131	169	205	300		

prices (i.e., basic value *plus* markup *plus* sales tax). For example, according to Table E2.A, final demand for imported commodity 2 is $24m at basic values. Associated with this are markup services worth $9m and sales taxes of $5m. Hence, in Table E2.1.2 the purchasers' value of final demand for imported commodity 2 is shown as $38m (= 24 + 9 + 5).

Row 3 of the domestic-commodities matrix in Table E2.1.2 contains the purchasers' value of each user's direct usage of commodity 3 plus, in the first 3 columns, the estimated value[3] of the markup services associated with each industry's sales.[4] Markup associated with sales of imports is shown in the penultimate column.

For industries 1 and 2, we estimate the markups associated with their sales by allocating the row totals of the domestic-commodities-markup matrix of Table E2.A in proportion to the shares of the industries in the production of the commodities. For example, Table E2.A(b) shows that industry 1 produces 75 per cent of commodity 1 and 25 per cent of commodity 2. Hence, we assume that $12m (i.e., 0.75×16) of markup is required for industry 1's sales of commodity 1 and $10m (i.e., 0.25×40) for its sales of commodity 2. According to Table E2.A(a), the value of industry 1's direct purchases of domestic commodity 3 is $18m. Hence, the entry in row 3, column 1 of the domestic-commodities matrix in Table E2.1.2 is 40 (= 18 + 12 + 10).

Table E2.1.2 includes a row containing the aggregate sales tax payable on each industry's sales (columns 1 to 3) and on imports (penultimate column). Aggregate sales taxes payable on sales of domestic commodities are shown in the row totals of the domestic-commodities-sales-tax matrix in Table E2.A(a). As in the case of markups, we allocate these sales taxes to domestic industries in proportion to the shares of the industries in the outputs of the commodities. Hence, in Table E2.1.2, $19m of sales tax is allocated to industry 1, of which $12m(i.e., 0.75×16) is tax on its sales of commodity 1 and $7m (i.e., 0.25×28) is tax on its sales of commodity 2.

Note that in Table E2.1.2 markups and sales taxes are double counted in the sense that they appear both added to the basic value of

---

3   Note that we assume that the delivery of markup services requires no markup and attracts no sales tax. Hence, the basic value and purchasers' price of markup services are identical.

4   This latter component is zero for industry 3. Table E2.A shows that no markups are required in selling commodity 3, the sole output of industry 3.

the commodity flows on which they accrue and in aggregate in the row for domestic commodity 3 or sales taxes. Because of this, the industry column totals of the table show the *purchasers' value* of each industry's output. The row totals of the table show the purchasers' value of the aggregate sales of each commodity. Hence, for example, the *column* total for industry 2 is equal to 25 per cent of the purchasers' value of commodity 1 plus 75 per cent of the purchasers' value of commodity 2 (i.e., $169 = 0.25 \times 112 + 0.75 \times 188$). The row total for domestic commodity 3 in Table E2.1.2 shows the purchasers' value of direct sales of the commodity, i.e., \$124m (basic value of \$119m *plus* \$5m sales tax on sales to households, see Table E2.A) *plus* the value of markup (i.e., \$81m, which can be read from the row totals of the markup matrices in Table E2.A).

A third valuation basis sometimes used for input-output tables is *producers' prices*. Producers' prices *include* sales taxes but *exclude* markups. Hence, in a producers'-prices table, sales taxes are treated as in Table E2.1.2, but markups are treated as in Table E2.1.1.

Exercise 2.2   *Imports: direct and indirect allocation in absorption matrices*

Rather than showing imports in a matrix as in Tables E2.A, E2.1.1 and E2.1.2, conventional input-output tables either allocate competing imports *directly* in a single row to domestic users or employ an *indirect allocation* method.

(a)   Show how the data in Table E2.1.1 would be presented in a basic-values input-output table with direct allocation of all imports.

(b)   Show how the data in Table E2.1.1 would be presented in a basic-values input-output table with indirect allocation of competing imports.

(c)   Show how the data in Table E2.1.2 would be presented in a purchasers'-prices input-output table with direct allocation of all imports.

(d)   Show how the data in Table E2.1.2 would be represented in a purchasers'-prices input-output table with indirect allocation of competing imports.

Answer to Exercise 2.2

(a)   Table E2.2.1 is a conventional, commodity by industry, input-output table at basic values with imports allocated directly to users. The only difference between it and Table E2.1.1 is that, instead of showing separately the flows to each user of each imported commodity, only the value of each user's aggregate purchases of imports is shown.   For example, in the imports row of Table E2.2.1, the final-demand category is shown as purchasing imports worth $45m at basic values.   From the imports rows of Table E2.1.1 we see that this comprises $10m for commodity 1, $24m for commodity 2 and $11m for non-competing imports.

(b)   In Table E2.2.2, usage of competing imports is aggregated with usage of the domestic commodities with which they compete.   For example, final demand for commodity 2 is shown as $104m at basic values. As can be seen in Table E2.1.1, this consists of $80m of domestic supplies and $24m of imports.   The aggregate basic values of competing imports of each type are shown in the penultimate column of Table E2.2.2.   (Note that the entries in this column are identical to the entries in the competing-imports rows of the total-usage column of Table E2.1.1.)   Subtraction of this column from the total-usage column in Table E2.2.2 yields the aggregate basic values of domestic supplies by commodity. These are shown in the final column of the table. (Note that the entries in this column are identical to the entries in the domestic-commodities rows of the total-usage column of Table E2.1.1.) Non-competing imports are treated in the same way in Table E2.2.2 as they are in Table E2.1.1, i.e., allocated directly to the users.

(c)   Table E2.2.3 is identical to Table E2.1.2 except that, instead of showing the purchasers' value of each user's imports disaggregated by commodity, it has a single imports row.   The entries in this row show the aggregate values, inclusive of markup and sales taxes, of each user's purchases of imports.   For example, industry 3 is shown as using imports with a total purchasers' value of $20m.   From Table E2.1.2 this can be seen to consist of $15m for commodity 1 and $5m for non-competing imports.

(d)   Table E2.2.4 has the same relationship to Table E2.1.2 as does Table E2.2.2 to Table E2.1.1.   In Table E2.2.4, the first four columns of the rows labelled "Domestic commodities plus competing imports" are obtained by adding the competing-imports matrix from Table E2.1.2 to its domestic-commodities matrix.   The last two columns of Table E2.2.4 show, respectively, aggregate competing imports by commodity at purchasers' prices (equal to the entries in the total-usage column in the competing-imports rows of Table E2.1.2) and aggregate supplies of domestic commodities at purchasers' prices (equal to the entries in the domestic-commodity rows of the total-usage column in Table E2.1.2).

Table E2.2.1

Absorption Matrix (Commodity by Industry) for the Year 19XX at Basic Values with Direct Allocation of Imports
($m)

Commodities		Intermediate demand by industries			Final demand	Total usage
		1	2	3		
Domestic	1	10	20	10	40	80
Commodities	2	15	15	10	80	120
	3	23	22	67	88	200
Imports		5	21	14	45	85
Sales taxes		4	14	5	47	70
Factor payments		33	18	94		145
Total demand		90	110	200	300	

Table E2.2.2

Absorption Matrix (Commodity by Industry) for the Year 19XX at Basic Values with Indirect Allocation of Competing Imports
($m)

Commodities		Intermediate demand by industries			Final demand	Total usage	Less competing imports	Domestic commodity supplies
		1	2	3				
Domestic	1	10	25	20	50	105	25	80
commodities *plus* competing	2	15	21	10	104	150	30	120
imports	3	23	22	67	88	200	0	200
Non-competing imports		5	10	4	11	30		
Sales taxes		4	14	5	47	70		
Factor payments		33	18	94		145		
Total demand		90	110	200	300			

Table E2.2.3

Absorption Matrix (Commodity by Industry) for the Year 19XX at Purchasers' Prices with Direct Allocation of Imports
($m)

Commodities		Intermediate demand by industries			Final demand	Markup and sales taxes on imports	Total usage
		1	2	3			
Domestic	1	12	28	14	58		112
commodities	2	21	23	14	130		188
	3	40	42	58	40	25	205
Imports		6	33	20	72		131
Sales taxes		19	25	5	0	21	70
Factor payments		33	18	94			145
Total demand		131	169	205	300		

Table E2.2.4

Absorption Matrix (Commodity by Industry) for the Year 19XX at Purchasers' Prices with Indirect Allocation of Competing Imports
($m)

Commodities		Intermediate demand by industries			Final demand	Markup and sales taxes on imports	Total usage	Less competing imports	Domestic commodity supplies
		1	2	3					
Domestic commodities	1	12	36	29	75		152	40	112
plus competing	2	21	36	14	168		239	51	188
imports	3	40	42	58	40	25	205	0	205
Non-competing imports		6	12	5	17		40		
Sales taxes		19	25	5	0	21	70		
Factor payments		33	18	94			145		
Total demand		131	169	205					

Exercise 2.3   *Industry by industry tables and secondary production*

So far we have discussed only commodity by industry input-output tables. An alternative is the industry by industry basis on which many published tables are compiled. The typical (ij^{th}) element of the domestic-supplies matrix of an industry by industry table shows the value of purchases by user j from industry i.

Statistical agencies usually define an industry as a collection of establishments producing the same principal product. For example, the "steel" industry might be defined as the collection of establishments whose principal activity is steel making. However, such establishments might also engage in *secondary production* of commodities other than steel, commodities which are the principal products of other industries. Consequently, we can expect some industries to produce more than one commodity and some commodities to be produced by more than one industry. In these circumstances, industry by industry input-output tables differ from commodity by industry tables.

Conversion from commodity by industry data to industry by industry input-output tables requires an assumption about users' sourcing of those commodities which are produced in more than one industry. One such assumption is that all users draw their supplies from industries in proportion to the industries' shares in total output of the commodity in question. Show how, using this assumption, Table E2.A (a) can be converted into an industry by industry table.

Answer to Exercise 2.3

The required sourcing shares can be computed from the make matrix, Table E2.A(b): industry 1 produces 75 per cent of commodity 1, 25 per cent of commodity 2 and none of commodity 3; industry 2 produces 25 per cent of commodity 1, 75 per cent of commodity 2 and none of commodity 3; industry 3 produces none of commodities 1 and 2 but all of commodity 3. Using these as the sourcing shares for all users of domestically produced commodities, the industry by industry table corresponding to Table E2.A (a) is Table E2.3.1.

The first three rows of Table E2.3.1 contain the basic values of sales made by domestic industries. For example, in column 2 industry 2 is shown as purchasing inputs worth $18.75m from industry 1. This consists of 75 per cent of industry 2's purchases of domestic commodity 1 ($20m according to Table E2.A) and 25 per cent of its purchases of domestic commodity 2 ($15m).

Markups and sales taxes on sales of domestically produced commodities are treated in a similar way. For example, Table E2.A shows that sales of domestic commodities 1 and 2 to industry 2 require markups worth $4m and $5m respectively. Hence, Table E2.3.1 shows markup worth $4.25m (= 0.75 × 4 + 0.25 × 5) associated with industry 2's purchases from industry 1. Note that the first two row totals of Table E2.3.1 are identical to the first two column totals: both sets of totals showing the aggregate basic values of the outputs of industries 1 and 2. The treatment of factor payments and of imports and their associated markups and sales taxes is the same in Table E2.3.1 as in Table E2.A.

Exercise 2.4   **Computing import and margin matrices from published input-output tables**

It should be clear from Exercises 2.1 and 2.2 that import matrices and matrices of margins (i.e., markups plus sales taxes) are computable from published tables of the form E2.2.1 to E2.2.4.

(a)   Which tables would be necessary for computation of a matrix of competing imports at basic values? How could such a matrix be computed?

(b)   Which tables would be required for computation of a margins matrix? How could such a matrix be computed?

Answer to Exercise 2.4

(a)   The matrix of competing imports at basic values is obtained by subtracting the matrix formed by the first 3 rows and 5 columns of Table E2.2.1 from the first 3 rows and 5 columns of Table E2.2.2. To check this, perform subtraction and compare the answer with the competing-imports matrix in Table E2.A.

(b)   The matrix of margins on flows of domestic commodities 1 and 2 and on each user's total purchases of imports is obtained by subtraction of the entries in rows 1, 2 and 4 of columns 1 to 4 in Table E2.2.1 from the corresponding entries in Table E2.2.3. Subtraction of the entries in rows 1, 2 and 4 of columns 1-4 of Table E2.2.2 from the corresponding entries in Table E2.2.4 gives the matrix of margins on sales of domestically produced and imported commodities 1 and 2 and on sales of non-competing imports. Note that operations of this sort are not capable of revealing margins on sales of the markup commodity (commodity 3 in our data).

Table E2.3.1

Input-Output Flows (Industry by Industry Absorption Matrix) for the Year 19XX with Disaggregated Treatments of Imports, Markups and Sales Taxes ($m)

Commodities		Intermediate demand by industries			Final demand	Total usage
		1	2	3		
Supply from	1	11.25	18.75	10	50	90
domestic	2	13.75	16.25	10	70	110
industries	3	18	8	58	35	119
Competing	1	0	5	10	10	25
imports	2	0	6	0	24	30
	3	0	0	0	0	0
Non-competing imports		5	10	4	11	30
Markup on sales	1	1.5	4.25	2.75	13.5	22
from domestic	2	2.5	4.75	2.25	24.5	34
industries	3	0	0	0	0	0
Markup on	1	0	1	3	2	6
competing	2	0	2	0	9	11
imports	3	0	0	0	0	0
Markup on non-competing imports		1	2	1	4	8
Sales taxes on	1	1.5	3.75	1.25	12.5	19
supplies from	2	2.5	3.25	1.75	17.5	25
domestic	3	0	0	0	5	5
industries						
Sales taxes on	1	0	2	2	5	9
competing	2	0	5	0	5	10
imports	3	0	0	0	0	0
Sales taxes on non-competing imports		0	0	0	2	2
Factor payments		33	18	94		145
Total demand		90	110	200	300	

81

B. INPUT-OUTPUT MODELS

Exercise 2.5   *The open static input-output model*

In its simplest version, Leontief's open static input-output model depicts the production side of an economy without international trade. The economy contains n producers each of which produces a unique commodity which can be used as an *intermediate* input by other industries or absorbed into final demand. Producers use intermediate inputs and primary factors in their production processes. The underlying technological assumption is that all inputs are required in fixed proportions to output. Final demand is exogenous.

Algebraically, the demand equations for intermediate inputs in the model are

$$X_{ij} = A_{ij}X_j, \qquad i=1,...,n; \ j=1,...,n, \qquad (E2.5.1)$$

and those for primary inputs are

$$F_{kj} = L_{kj}X_j, \qquad k=1,...,m; \ j=1,...,n, \qquad (E2.5.2)$$

where X_{ij} and F_{kj} are, respectively, the quantities of intermediate input i (the commodity produced by industry i) and primary factor k used by industry j; X_j is the output level of industry j; and A_{ij} and L_{kj} are technological coefficients showing, respectively, the quantities of intermediate input i and primary factor k required per unit of output in industry j.

As well as the demand equations (E2.5.1) and (E2.5.2), the model includes equations which equate the supply of commodities and primary factors to the demand for them:

$$X_i = \sum_{j=1}^{n} X_{ij} + Y_i, \qquad i=1,...,n, \qquad (E2.5.3)$$

and

$$F_k = \sum_{j=1}^{n} F_{kj}, \qquad k=1,...,m, \qquad (E2.5.4)$$

where Y_i is final demand for commodity i and F_k is the supply, or total employment, of factor k. Equation (E2.5.4) assumes that there is no final demand for primary factors.

Although prices play very little role in the model, in particular they have no effect on demand, we could add commodity-pricing equations to (E2.5.1) – (E2.5.4). These could follow from the assumption that prices are set equal to unit costs of production, i. e.,

$$P_j = \sum_{i=1}^{n} P_i A_{ij} + \sum_{k=1}^{m} W_k L_{kj} , \quad j=1,\ldots,n, \qquad (E2.5.5)$$

where the P_i and W_k are, respectively, the prices of commodities and primary factors.

Equations (E2.5.1) – (E2.5.5) constitute an open static input-output model. There are $(n^2+nm+2n+m)$ equations in $(n^2+nm+3n+2m)$ variables. The variables are: X_{ij}, $i,j=1,\ldots,n$; F_{kj}, $k=1,\ldots,m$, $j=1,\ldots,n$; X_j, Y_j and P_j, $j=1,\ldots,n$; and F_k and W_k, $k=1,\ldots,m$.

Suggest a closure for the model, i.e., a choice of exogenous variables, which would allow us to compute:

(i)   the supplies of commodities and the employment of primary factors compatible with a given vector, **Y**, of final demands,

and

(ii)   the commodity prices compatible with a given vector, **W**, of primary-factor prices.

Suggest a solution method to obtain these results. Show that the solutions imply that the aggregate value of final demand (i.e., gross national product measured from the expenditure side) is equal to aggregate payments to primary factors (i.e., gross national product measured from the income side).

Answer to Exercise 2.5

Comparing the number of equations with the number of variables, we see that $(n+m)$ exogenous variables are required. In view of what is to be computed, it is clear that the exogenous variables must be the n components of the final-demand vector (**Y**) and the m factor prices (**W**). These are natural choices as exogenous variables. The model includes no theory about the determination of final demands or factor prices. Setting factor prices exogenously is equivalent to assuming perfectly elastic factor supplies, i.e., that there are no binding supply constraints. In this case, we interpret the variable F_k as the endogenously determined employment of factor k, not as its supply.

To consider the question of a solution method, it is convenient to eliminate the input demands, X_{ij} and F_{kj}, by substituting (E2.5.1) and (E2.5.2) into (E2.5.3) and (E2.5.4), yielding:

$$X_i = \sum_{j=1}^{n} A_{ij} X_j + Y_i , \qquad i=1,\ldots,n \qquad (E2.5.6)$$

and
$$F_k = \sum_{j=1}^{n} L_{kj} X_j, \qquad k=1,\ldots,m. \qquad (E2.5.7)$$

These substitutions condense the model to a system of the $(2n+m)$ equations $[(E2.5.6), (E2.5.7) \text{ and } (E2.5.5)]$ in $(3n+2m)$ variables. Next, we rewrite these equations in matrix notation as:

$$\mathbf{X} = \mathbf{AX} + \mathbf{Y}, \qquad (E2.5.6)'$$

and
$$\mathbf{F} = \mathbf{LX}, \qquad (E2.5.7)'$$

$$\mathbf{P'} = \mathbf{P'A} + \mathbf{W'L}, \qquad (E2.5.5)'$$

where the bold characters denote vectors or matrices of the variables and parameters denoted by the corresponding unbolded symbols.

From equation $(E2.5.6)'$, the vector of commodity supplies $(\mathbf{X})$ can be obtained as:

$$\mathbf{X} = (\mathbf{I} - \mathbf{A})^{-1}\mathbf{Y}. \qquad (E2.5.8)$$

The ij^{th} element of the Leontief inverse matrix, $(\mathbf{I} - \mathbf{A})^{-1}$, shows the amount of commodity i directly and indirectly required to supply a unit of commodity j to final demand. The direct requirements are captured by the technological coefficients in the matrix $\mathbf{A}$. By accounting for the indirect requirements, we recognize that other inputs directly required in the production of commodity j may themselves require inputs of commodity i, etc.

Factor employment levels $(\mathbf{F})$ can next be computed by substituting $(E2.5.8)$ for $\mathbf{X}$ in $(E2.5.7)'$, yielding:

$$\mathbf{F} = \mathbf{L}(\mathbf{I}-\mathbf{A})^{-1}\mathbf{Y}. \qquad (E2.5.9)$$

The kj^{th} element of the matrix $\mathbf{L}(\mathbf{I}-\mathbf{A})^{-1}$ gives the direct and indirect usage of factor k required to satisfy a unit of final demand for commodity j.

Finally, from $(E2.5.5)'$, the solution for the price vector $(\mathbf{P})$ is:

$$\mathbf{P'} = \mathbf{W'L}(\mathbf{I} - \mathbf{A})^{-1}. \qquad (E2.5.10)$$

Equation $(E2.5.10)$ reveals that commodity prices are weighted sums of factor prices where the weights account for the direct and indirect requirements of the factors in the production of the commodities. The ith column of the matrix $\mathbf{L}(\mathbf{I} - \mathbf{A})^{-1}$ contains the weights applicable to the m factor prices in the computation of the price of commodity i. These weights reveal the factor intensity of commodity i after all direct and indirect factor requirements are taken into account. For example, they could recognize as quite labor intensive a commodity which uses very little labor directly (i.e., for which the labor coefficient in the direct-requirements matrix **L** is small) but which uses as intermediate inputs, directly or indirectly, commodities which have large labor coefficients in the direct-requirements matrix.

To see that the model conforms to the national income accounting identity, premultiply (E2.5.9) by **W'** and postmultiply (E2.5.10) by **Y**. From this we see that:

$$\mathbf{W'F} = \mathbf{W'L(I - A)}^{-1}\mathbf{Y} = \mathbf{P'Y} . \qquad (E2.5.11)$$

The left hand term of (E2.5.11) is national income measured from the income side. The right hand term is the corresponding expenditure-side measure.

Exercise 2.6   *Adding multi-product industries and multi-industry commodities*

In Exercise 2.5 we dealt with a square model in which the number of domestically produced commodities is identical to the number of domestic industries and in which each commodity is produced by just one single-product industry. An implication of this is that each commodity is produced using only one technology. In this exercise, we break the one-to-one relationship to consider multi-product industries and commodities which are produced in more than one industry. There is no need in such a model for the number of industries to equal the number of commodities, although this was a feature of the data given in Section A (see Table E2.A).

In the models to be considered in this exercise, the assumption of fixed-coefficient technology, analogous to (E2.5.1), must be applied either at the commodity level or at the industry level. When applied at the commodity level, the assumption is that any commodity i is produced with the same technology (i.e., input structure) in all industries. This means that the mix of industries in which commodities are produced is irrelevant in determining the relationships between final demands (**Y**), commodity supplies (**X**) and factor requirements (**F**), and between commodity prices (**P**) and factor prices (**W**). These relationships can be determined from the model:

$$\mathbf{X} = \mathbf{A}^C \mathbf{X} + \mathbf{Y} , \qquad (E2.6.1)$$

and

$$\mathbf{F} = \mathbf{L}^C \mathbf{X} , \qquad (E2.6.2)$$

$$\mathbf{P'} = \mathbf{P'A}^C + \mathbf{W'L}^C , \qquad (E2.6.3)$$

where **X**, **Y** and **P** are, as before, (n × 1) vectors of commodity supplies, final demands and prices, and the columns of the technology matrices **A**^{C} and **L**^{C} describe unique technologies for producing the commodities.

In Exercise 2.9, we explain how input-output data, such as that illustrated in Section A, can be used to calibrate input-output models. The data usually shows the structure of industries' inputs, i.e., they provide an observation of industry-specific technologies, not commodity-specific technologies. (Only under restricted conditions will it be possible to infer unique commodity technologies from such data, see Exercise 2.9). For this reason, we prefer the assumption of industry-specific, rather than commodity-specific, technology. This leads, instead of (E2.6.1) and (E2.6.2), to:

and
$$\mathbf{X} = \mathbf{A}^I \mathbf{Z} + \mathbf{Y}, \tag{E2.6.4}$$
$$\mathbf{F} = \mathbf{L}^I \mathbf{Z}, \tag{E2.6.5}$$

where $\mathbf{Z}$ is an $(h \times 1)$ vector of industry outputs and $\mathbf{A}^I$ and $\mathbf{L}^I$ are fixed $(n \times h)$ and $(m \times h)$ matrices describing the technologies of industries.

To complement (E2.6.4) and (E2.6.5), we require a relationship between outputs by industry and outputs by commodity. Our preferred option is to add an equation defining indexes of outputs by industry in terms of outputs by commodity:

$$\mathbf{Z} = \mathbf{Q}\mathbf{X}, \tag{E2.6.6)(a)}$$

where $\mathbf{Q}$ is an $(h \times n)$ matrix the ij^{th} element of which shows the share of industry i in the total output of commodity j. These shares are assumed to be constant. Note that, combined with the assumption that $\mathbf{A}^I$ and $\mathbf{L}^I$ are constant, this assumption implies that the composition of an industry's outputs can change with no change in the composition of its inputs. The same assumption of input-output separability is used in some applied general equilibrium models (see Chapter 3).

An alternative to (E2.6.6)(a), is to assume that industries produce commodities in fixed proportions, i.e., to assume

$$\mathbf{X} = \mathbf{R}\mathbf{Z}, \tag{E2.6.6)(b)}$$

where $\mathbf{R}$ is a $(n \times h)$ matrix of fixed coefficients, the ij^{th} of which shows the share of commodity i in the total output of industry j.

Treat final demands $(\mathbf{Y})$ and factor prices $(\mathbf{W})$ as exogenous variables. What are the solutions for commodity supplies $(\mathbf{X})$, factor demands $(\mathbf{F})$, industry outputs $(\mathbf{Z})$ and commodity prices $(\mathbf{P})$ in the commodity-technology model {(E2.6.1) – (E2.6.3) and (E2.6.6)(a)}? What are the solutions for $\mathbf{X}$, $\mathbf{F}$ and $\mathbf{Z}$ in the industry-technology model {(E2.6.4),(E2.6.5) and (E2.6.6)(a)}? Is it possible to define unique commodity prices in the latter model? Is the assumption that the matrix $\mathbf{Q}$ is constant reasonable in the context of industry technology?

Assumption (E2.6.6)(b) is theoretically more appealing than (E2.6.6)(a) but using it can we solve for **X**, **F**, **Z** and **P**?

Answer to Exercise 2.6

For the case of commodity technology, the solutions, using (E2.6.6)(a), are:

$$\mathbf{X} = (\mathbf{I} - \mathbf{A}^C)^{-1}\mathbf{Y}, \tag{E2.6.7}$$

$$\mathbf{F} = \mathbf{L}^C(\mathbf{I} - \mathbf{A}^C)^{-1}\mathbf{Y}, \tag{E2.6.8}$$

and
$$\mathbf{Z} = \mathbf{Q}(\mathbf{I} - \mathbf{A}^C)^{-1}\mathbf{Y}, \tag{E2.6.9}$$

$$\mathbf{P'} = \mathbf{W'L}^C(\mathbf{I} - \mathbf{A}^C)^{-1}. \tag{E2.6.10}$$

For the case of industry technology, the solutions are:

$$\mathbf{X} = (\mathbf{I} - \mathbf{A}^I\mathbf{Q})^{-1}\mathbf{Y}, \tag{E2.6.11}$$

and
$$\mathbf{F} = \mathbf{L}^I\mathbf{Q}(\mathbf{I} - \mathbf{A}^I\mathbf{Q})^{-1}\mathbf{Y}, \tag{E2.6.12}$$

$$\mathbf{Z} = \mathbf{Q}(\mathbf{I} - \mathbf{A}^I\mathbf{Q})^{-1}\mathbf{Y}. \tag{E2.6.13}$$

Solutions (E2.6.7) – (E2.6.10) are a straightforward extension of (E2.5.8) – (E2.5.10) and raise no new economic issues. From an algebraic point of view, derivation of (E2.6.11) – (E2.6.13) is also straightforward. However, it is worth noting that in (E2.6.11) – (E2.6.13) we have, in effect, introduced matrices defining unique technologies for producing commodities. These are the matrices $\mathbf{A}^I\mathbf{Q}$ and $\mathbf{L}^I\mathbf{Q}$. The ith columns of these contain the commodity and factor inputs required per unit output of commodity i, calculated as weighted averages of the columns of the industry-technology matrices $\mathbf{A}^I$ and $\mathbf{L}^I$. The weights are industries' shares in the production of commodity i, i.e., the ith column of $\mathbf{Q}$.

In general, if we are assuming both that industry technologies are fixed (i.e., that $\mathbf{A}^I$ and $\mathbf{L}^I$ are constant) and that given commodities can be produced in several industries, then we cannot expect to be able to determine the vector of commodity outputs (**X**) associated with any given final-demand vector (**Y**) unless we make an explicit assumption concerning the mix of industries in which the commodities are produced. Our assumption that $\mathbf{Q}$ is fixed plays this role. It fixes the pattern of industry participation in the production of commodities, allowing us to define commodity technologies as the weighted averages of industry technologies. Now that we have commodity technologies, we can define unique commodity prices in the industry-technology model via (E2.6.3). The solution is

$$\mathbf{P'} = \mathbf{W'L}^I\mathbf{Q}(\mathbf{I} - \mathbf{A}^I\mathbf{Q})^{-1}. \tag{E2.6.14}$$

A problem with this solution is that prices determined according to (E2.6.14) would not render the production of commodities equally profitable in all the industries (each with a different technology) in which they could be produced. Hence, we might expect producers with the most profitable technology for a given commodity to drive out producers with less profitable technologies. That is, the assumption that Q is constant is implausible.

The assumption that R is constant in (E2.6.6)(b) is not subject to this objection. It can be interpreted just as an assumption about technology, analogous on the output side to the Leontief assumption of fixed input coefficients. Moreover, with R constant, the assumption of input-output separability does not arise. However, with (E2.6.6)(b), complete solutions to the input-output model will not generally be obtainable. The problem is that (E2.6.6)(b) need not allow us to solve for Z, given X, i.e., the matrix R need not be invertible — it need not even be square.

With (E2.6.6)(b) replacing (E2.6.6)(a), solutions for commodity and factor supplies and for commodity prices can still be generated in the commodity-technology model via (E2.6.7), (E2.6.8) and (E2.6.10). However, (E2.6.9) has to be replaced by

$$RZ = (I - A^C)^{-1} Y . \qquad (E2.6.15)$$

In general, this will not supply a solution for Z.

For the industry-technology model, a solution like (E2.6.11) for commodity supplies will not generally be available. Instead, we have

$$(R - A^I)Z = Y , \qquad (E2.6.16)$$

with $(R - A^I)$ not generally invertible, nor even square. With no solution for Z, we can solve for neither X nor F. Since the inclusion of (E2.6.6)(b) instead of (E2.6.6)(a) does not allow the definition of unique commodity technologies, solutions for commodity prices are also unavailable.

The starkest intuitive illustration of the problem is to take the case in which there are n commodities but only one industry. In this case, the commodity composition of output is fixed by the assumption that R is constant. It is clear that the model will be unable to provide solutions for arbitrary changes in the commodity composition of final demand.

It is the passive role of prices in input-output models which limits the flexibility with which multi-product industries and multi-industry products can be handled. As you will see in later chapters, modern applied general equilibrium models are able to incorporate more satisfactory treatments by allowing the commodity compositions of industries' outputs and of final demands to be functions of the relative prices of commodities.

Exercise 2.7   *Adding international trade*

The input-output models described above are closed-economy models, i.e., they do not explicitly include international trade. In adding exports and imports to input-output models, it is usual to assume that exports are exogenous and that imports are either not substitutable at all for domestically produced commodities (i.e., non-competing) or perfectly substitutable (i.e., competing).

(a)   Extend the model described by (E2.6.4) – (E2.6.6)(a) to include a vector of n exogenous exports (**E**), a vector of n competing imports (**M**) and a vector of r non-competing imports (**N**). Assume that imports are used both as intermediate inputs and in final demand. Specify intermediate demand for imports via matrices $\mathbf{A}_{\mathbf{m}}^{I}$ and $\mathbf{B}^{I}$, where the ijth element of $\mathbf{A}_{\mathbf{m}}^{I}$ shows the input of competing import i required per unit of output in industry j and the ijth element of $\mathbf{B}^{I}$ shows the input of non-competing import i required per unit of output in industry j. Show how the extended model can be solved for the vectors of commodity outputs (**X**), industry outputs (**Z**), factor demands (**F**) and demands for imports (**M** and **N**).

(b)   In applications of the extended model, $\mathbf{A}_{\mathbf{m}}^{I}$ and $\mathbf{B}^{I}$ are usually treated as parameters. Is this satisfactory?

(c)   Derive pricing equations for the extended model. First assume that the vectors of domestic prices (**P**) and competing-import prices (**Pm**) are distinct. However, it seems sensible to assume that **P** and that **Pm** are equal. Why? What difficulties arise if such an assumption is made?

Answer to Exercise 2.7

(a)   We extend (E2.6.4) to

$$\mathbf{X} = \mathbf{A}^{I}\mathbf{Z} + \mathbf{Y} + \mathbf{E} - \mathbf{M}, \qquad (E2.7.1)$$

where $\mathbf{A}^{I}$ is interpreted as a matrix of technological coefficients, the ijth of which shows the aggregate input of commodity i (domestically produced and imported) required per unit output of industry j and the typical element, Y_i, of the vector **Y** shows the aggregate flow of commodity i to domestic final demand (i.e., final demand excluding exports).

Underlying (E2.7.1) is the assumption that the imports in the vector **M** are perfect substitutes for the domestically produced commodities in the vector **X**. If this is not so, then the subtraction in (E2.7.1) is no more meaningful than subtraction of apples from pears.

Next, we define import-demand equations:

$$\mathbf{M} = \mathbf{A_m^I} \, \mathbf{Z} + \mathbf{Y_m} \qquad (E2.7.2)$$

and

$$\mathbf{N} = \mathbf{B^I} \, \mathbf{Z} + \mathbf{Y_n} \, , \qquad (E2.7.3)$$

where **Y_m** and **Y_n** are vectors of final demands for competing and non-competing imports of dimensions n × 1 and r × 1 respectively.

The solution to the extended model, analogous to (E2.6.11), is obtained, after substitution of (E2.6.6)(a) and (E2.7.2) into (E2.7.1), as

$$\mathbf{X} = [\mathbf{I} - (\mathbf{A^I} - \mathbf{A_m^I})\mathbf{Q}]^{-1}(\mathbf{Y} - \mathbf{Y_m} + \mathbf{E}) \, . \qquad (E2.7.4)$$

Substitution of (E2.7.4) into (E2.6.6)(a) yields

$$\mathbf{Z} = \mathbf{Q}[\mathbf{I} - (\mathbf{A^I} - \mathbf{A_m^I})\mathbf{Q}]^{-1}(\mathbf{Y} - \mathbf{Y_m} + \mathbf{E}), \qquad (E2.7.5)$$

analogous to (E2.6.13). Substitution of (E2.7.5) into (E2.6.5) yields

$$\mathbf{F} = \mathbf{L^J} \, \mathbf{Q}[\mathbf{I} - (\mathbf{A^I} - \mathbf{A_m^I})\mathbf{Q}]^{-1}(\mathbf{Y} - \mathbf{Y_m} + \mathbf{E}), \qquad (E2.7.6)$$

analogous to (E2.6.12). Finally, substitution of (E2.7.5) into (E2.7.2) and (E2.7.3) yields solutions for the vectors of competing and non-competing imports:

$$\mathbf{M} = \mathbf{A_m^I} \, \mathbf{Q}[\mathbf{I} - (\mathbf{A^I} - \mathbf{A_m^I})\mathbf{Q}]^{-1}(\mathbf{Y} - \mathbf{Y_m} + \mathbf{E}) + \mathbf{Y_m} \qquad (E2.7.7)$$

and

$$\mathbf{N} = \mathbf{B^I} \, \mathbf{Q}[\mathbf{I} - (\mathbf{A^I} - \mathbf{A_m^I})\mathbf{Q}]^{-1}(\mathbf{Y} - \mathbf{Y_m} + \mathbf{E}) + \mathbf{Y_n} \, . \qquad (E2.7.8)$$

Instead of (E2.7.2), input-output models sometimes specify the demand for competing imports as

$$\mathbf{M} = \hat{\alpha} \, \mathbf{X}, \qquad (E2.7.9)$$

where the diagonal matrix $\hat{\alpha}$ is treated as fixed. The ith diagonal element of $\hat{\alpha}$ is the ratio of imports of commodity i to domestic production of commodity i. Formulation (E2.7.9) ignores differences across users in the sourcing of commodities. Using (E2.7.9), the solution for commodity supplies, analogous to (E2.7.4), is

$$\mathbf{X} = [\mathbf{I} - \mathbf{A^I} \, \mathbf{Q} + \hat{\alpha}]^{-1}(\mathbf{Y} + \mathbf{E}) \, , \qquad (E2.7.10)$$

with corresponding amendments necessary for solutions (E2.7.5) to (E2.7.8).

(b) The treatment of competing-imports (**M**) and domestic outputs (**X**) as *perfect* substitutes is in tension with the assumption that $\mathbf{A}_{\mathbf{m}}^{\mathrm{I}}$ (or $\hat{\alpha}_{\mathbf{m}}$ in the alternative treatment) is a matrix of parameters. If imports and domestic commodities are close substitutes, then these coefficients, and the split of the vector **Y** between $\mathbf{Y_m}$ and $\mathbf{Y} - \mathbf{Y_m}$, should be very sensitive to relative prices. When a formulation such as (E2.7.1) is incorporated into a linear programming model or into a general equilibrium model in which users are assumed to minimize costs, the "flip-flop" problem arises, with import shares tending to alternate between zero and one according to relative prices. As illustrated in Chapter 3, a more satisfactory approach is to treat imports and domestic commodities as imperfect substitutes in a model which allows an active role for relative prices in determining import shares.

(c) With import prices and the prices of domestically produced commodities distinct, the latter can be defined, analogously to (E2.6.3), as

$$\mathbf{P}' = \mathbf{P}'(\mathbf{A}^{\mathrm{I}} - \mathbf{A}_{\mathbf{m}}^{\mathrm{I}})\mathbf{Q} + \mathbf{P}_{\mathbf{m}}'\mathbf{A}_{\mathbf{m}}^{\mathrm{I}}\mathbf{Q} + \mathbf{P}_{\mathbf{n}}'\mathbf{B}^{\mathrm{I}}\mathbf{Q} + \mathbf{W'L}^{\mathrm{J}}\mathbf{Q} \qquad (E2.7.11)$$

yielding a solution analogous to (E2.6.14):

$$\mathbf{P}' = (\mathbf{P}_{\mathbf{m}}'\mathbf{A}_{\mathbf{m}}^{\mathrm{I}}\mathbf{Q} + \mathbf{P}_{\mathbf{n}}'\mathbf{B}^{\mathrm{I}}\mathbf{Q} + \mathbf{W'L}^{\mathrm{J}}\mathbf{Q})[\mathbf{I} - (\mathbf{A}^{\mathrm{I}} - \mathbf{A}_{\mathbf{m}}^{\mathrm{I}})\mathbf{Q}]^{-1}. \qquad (E2.7.12)$$

According to (E2.7.12), in the amended model commodity prices are weighted sums not only of factor prices but of the prices of competing and non-competing imports as well. The amended pricing equation accounts for direct and indirect import costs as well as for direct and indirect primary-factor costs. Note that, because input coefficients for imports separate from domestic supplies are not explicitly defined under (E2.7.9), the pricing equation cannot be used with this alternative formulation.

As we remarked above, (E2.7.1) implicitly assumes that competing imports and domestically produced commodities are perfect substitutes for each other. For this reason, it seems appropriate to assume that their prices are identical. At least this is the appropriate assumption if commodities from domestic and foreign sources are simultaneously used by any domestic agent.

It is tempting, therefore, to add to the model the equation

$$\mathbf{P} = \mathbf{P_m}. \qquad (E2.7.13)$$

Substituting (E2.7.13) into (E2.7.11), the price solution analogous to (E2.7.12) is

$$\mathbf{P'} = (\mathbf{P'_n B}^I \mathbf{Q} + \mathbf{W'L}^I \mathbf{Q}) [\mathbf{I} - \mathbf{A}^I \mathbf{Q}]^{-1}. \tag{E2.7.14}$$

However, under the natural closure of the model, in which $\mathbf{P_m}$, $\mathbf{P_n}$ and $\mathbf{W}$ are all exogenous, the prices of domestically produced commodities ($\mathbf{P}$) are overdetermined. The system (E2.7.13) and (E2.7.14) contains 2n equations but only n endogenous variables ($\mathbf{P}$). The problem could be relieved by allowing $\mathbf{P_m}$ to be endogenous. But the interpretation of the model is then not very plausible, especially for a small country. It is that the world prices of commodities are determined by domestic costs.

A preferable approach, which is sometimes available, is to have domestic prices determined by exogenous world prices in (E2.7.13) and to make this compatible with (E2.7.14) by endogenizing the prices of n domestic primary factors. This may be satisfactory in models with n commodities and n industries, if each industry has an industry-specific factor (capital).

An approach which is more generally available in models in which domestic prices are determined by world prices involves

(i)   dropping equations such as (E2.7.2),

(ii)   recognizing explicitly that all prices and quantities must be non-negative,

(iii) treating the whole of the vector $\mathbf{W}$ as endogenous and the whole of the vector $\mathbf{F}$ as exogenous, and

(iv)   replacing equations such as (E2.6.5) and (E2.7.11) with conditions such as

$$\mathbf{L}^I \mathbf{Z} \leq \mathbf{F}, \tag{E2.7.15}$$

$$\mathbf{W'(F} - \mathbf{L}^I \mathbf{Z}) = \mathbf{0}, \tag{E2.7.16}$$

and
$$\mathbf{P'} \leq \mathbf{P'A}^I \mathbf{Q} + \mathbf{P'_n B}^I \mathbf{Q} + \mathbf{W'L}^I \mathbf{Q}, \tag{E2.7.17}$$

$$[\mathbf{P'} - \mathbf{P'A}^I \mathbf{Q} - \mathbf{P'_n B}^I \mathbf{Q} - \mathbf{W'L}^I \mathbf{Q}]\mathbf{X} = \mathbf{0}. \tag{E2.7.18}$$

Under (E2.7.15) and (E2.7.16), demands for factors are less than or equal to supplies and factors in excess supply have zero prices. Under (E2.7.17) and (E2.7.18), the prices of domestic commodities are less than or equal to their production costs and commodities with prices less than costs are not produced domestically.

Exercise 2.8   *Including markups and sales taxes*

So far, in discussing input-output models, we have made no reference to sales taxes or to the usage of domestically produced commodities as markups associated with the delivery of domestically produced and imported inputs to their users (industries and final demanders). Explicit consideration of sales taxes and markups was given in the discussion of input-output data in Section A. To include markups and sales taxes in input-output models, we require assumptions describing their relationships to the direct commodity flows with which they are associated. Extending the assumption of fixed-coefficient technology which underlies input-output models, we assume that the quantities of markup services and the sales taxes required to facilitate commodity flows are proportional to the flows. Extend the model described by (E2.6.5), (E2.6.6)(a), (E2.7.1) – (E2.7.3) and (E2.7.11) to include such a treatment of markups and sales taxes.

Answer to Exercise 2.8

The direct commodity flows in the model are:

X_{qj} (q=1,...,n; j=1,...,h)   the flow of domestically produced commodity q to industry j;

M_{qj} (q=1,...,n; j=1,...,h)   the flow of competing import q to industry j;

N_{qj} (q=1,...,r; j=1,...,h)   the flow of non-competing import q to industry j;

E_q (q=1,...,n)   exports of domestically produced commodity q (we assume that no imports are re-exported without processing in a domestic industry);

$(\mathbf{Y_d})_q$ (q=1,...,n)   the flow of domestically produced commodity q to domestic final demand;[5]

$(\mathbf{Y_m})_q$ (q=1,...,n)   the flow of competing import q to domestic final demand; and

$(\mathbf{Y_n})_q$ (q=1,...,r)   the flow of non-competing import q to domestic final demand.

With each of these direct flows, we associate the usage of domestically produced commodities as markup services required to facilitate the direct flow. Typical markup commodities are wholesale, retail and transport services. We assume that all markup services associated with flows in the domestic economy are domestically produced. It is

---

5   We have not previously used the notation $\mathbf{Y_d}$. In terms of the notation of Exercise 2.7, $\mathbf{Y_d} = \mathbf{Y} - \mathbf{Y_m}$.

important to note that for exports and imports the model, and the input-output data, accounts only for flows within the domestic economy, i.e., export flows from domestic producers to ports of exit and import flows from ports of entry to domestic users. Correspondingly the markups on exports and imports with which the model and the data deal are just those required to facilitate flows between the domestic producers or users and the ports of exit or entry, not those required to facilitate international flows. As well as markup services, we also associate with each direct commodity flow a sales tax or a tariff.

Under the assumption that usage of markups (**U**) and tax collections (**T**) are proportional to the direct flows with which they are associated, we obtain:

$$U_{iqj}^X = \psi_{iqj}^X X_{qj}, \qquad\qquad i,q=1,...,n;\ j=1,...,h, \qquad \text{(E2.8.1)(a)}$$

$$T_{qj}^X = \phi_{qj}^X X_{qj}, \qquad\qquad q=1,...,n;\ j=1,...,h, \qquad \text{(E2.8.1)(b)}$$

$$U_{iqj}^M = \psi_{iqj}^M M_{qj}, \qquad\qquad i,q=1,...,n;\ j=1,...,h, \qquad \text{(E2.8.2)(a)}$$

$$T_{qj}^M = \phi_{qj}^M M_{qj}, \qquad\qquad q=1,...,n;\ j=1,...,h, \qquad \text{(E2.8.2)(b)}$$

$$U_{iqj}^N = \psi_{iqj}^N N_{qj}, \quad i=1,...,n;\ q=1,...,r;\ j=1,...,h, \qquad \text{(E2.8.3)(a)}$$

$$T_{qj}^N = \phi_{qj}^N N_{qj}, \qquad\qquad q=1,...,r;\ j=1,...,h, \qquad \text{(E2.8.3)(b)}$$

$$U_{iq}^E = \psi_{iq}^E E_q, \qquad\qquad i,q=1,...,n, \qquad \text{(E2.8.4)(a)}$$

$$T_q^E = \phi_q^E E_q, \qquad\qquad q=1,...,n, \qquad \text{(E2.8.4)(b)}$$

$$U_{iq}^{Yd} = \psi_{iq}^{Yd} (\mathbf{Yd})_q, \qquad\qquad i,q=1,...,n, \qquad \text{(E2.8.5)(a)}$$

$$T_q^{Yd} = \phi_q^{Yd} (\mathbf{Yd})_q, \qquad\qquad q=1,...,n, \qquad \text{(E2.8.5)(b)}$$

$$U_{iq}^{Ym} = \psi_{iq}^{Ym} (\mathbf{Ym})_q, \qquad\qquad i,q=1,...,n, \qquad \text{(E2.8.6)(a)}$$

$$T_q^{Y_m} = \phi_q^{Y_m} (\mathbf{Y_m})_q, \qquad\qquad q=1,...,n, \qquad\qquad (E2.8.6)(b)$$

$$U_{iq}^{Y_n} = \psi_{iq}^{Y_n} (\mathbf{Y_n})_q, \qquad\qquad i=1,...,n; \ q=1,...,r, \qquad (E2.8.7)(a)$$

$$T_q^{Y_n} = \phi_q^{Y_n} (\mathbf{Y_n})_q, \qquad\qquad q=1,...,r. \qquad\qquad (E2.8.7)(b)$$

The definitions of the variables and coefficients appearing in these equations are sufficiently obvious for us not to require a complete list. However, a few examples may be helpful.

U_{iqj}^{X} is the amount of domestically produced commodity i used as a markup in facilitating the flow of domestically produced commodity q to industry j.

U_{iq}^{E} is the amount of domestically produced commodity i used as a markup in facilitating the flow of exports of commodity q from domestic producers to ports of exit.

$T_q^{Y_m}$ is the tax collected on competing imports of commodity q used in final demand.

ψ_{iqj}^{X} is the coefficient showing the requirement of markup i per unit of domestic commodity q delivered to industry j.

$\phi_q^{Y_n}$ is the coefficient showing the tax per unit of non-competing import q delivered to final demand.

Note that our specification allows for the possibility that any of the n domestically produced commodities may be used as a markup. For commodities which in fact are not used as markups, the appropriate coefficients will be zeros.

Direct commodity flows to industries have been eliminated from (E2.7.1) – (E2.7.3) using equations of the form

$$X_{qj} = (\mathbf{A}^I - \mathbf{A_m^I})_{qj} \, Z_j , \qquad\qquad q=1,...,n; \ j=1,...,h, \quad (E2.8.8)$$

$$M_{qj} = (\mathbf{A_m^I})_{qj} \, Z_j \qquad\qquad q=1,...,n; \ j=1,...,h \qquad (E2.8.9)$$

and

$$N_{qj} = (\mathbf{B}^I)_{qj} \, Z_j , \qquad\qquad q=1,...,r; \ j=1,...,h. \quad (E2.8.10)$$

Using these to eliminate direct commodity flows from (E2.8.1)(a) – (E2.8.3)(b) and summing over all commodities used directly by industry j, we conclude that the aggregate markup usage of commodity i required by industry j in obtaining all its produced inputs is

$$U_{ij} = \left\{ \sum_{q=1}^{n} \left[\psi_{iqj}^{X}(\mathbf{A^I})_{qj} + (\psi_{iqj}^{M} - \psi_{iqj}^{X})(\mathbf{A_m^I})_{qj} \right] + \sum_{q=1}^{r} \psi_{iqj}^{N}(\mathbf{B^I})_{qj} \right\} Z_j,$$

$$i=1,...,n; \ j=1,...,h \qquad (E2.8.11)$$

and that the aggregate sales tax on the inputs used by the industry is

$$T_j = \left\{ \sum_{q=1}^{n} \left[\phi_{qj}^{X}(\mathbf{A^I})_{qj} + (\phi_{qj}^{M} - \phi_{qj}^{X})(\mathbf{A_m^I})_{qj} \right] + \sum_{q=1}^{r} \phi_{qj}^{N}(\mathbf{B^I})_{qj} \right\} Z_j,$$

$$j=1,...,h. \qquad (E2.8.12)$$

According to (E2.8.11) and (E2.8.12), industries' demands for markup services and their sales-tax liabilities both are proportional to their outputs, just as are their direct demands for produced inputs and primary factors. In matrix notation, we can write

and

$$\mathbf{U^I} = \mathbf{\Psi^I \ Z}, \qquad (E2.8.13)$$

$$\mathbf{T^I} = \mathbf{\Phi^I \, ' \ Z}, \qquad (E2.8.14)$$

where $\mathbf{U^I}$ is the $n \times 1$ vector of demands for markups to facilitate commodity flows to industries, $\mathbf{T^I}$ is the aggregate sales tax on industries' purchases, and $\mathbf{\Psi^I}$ and $\mathbf{\Phi^I}$ ' are, respectively the $n \times h$ matrix and the $1 \times h$ vector of the coefficients contained in the curly brackets on the right hand sides of (E2.8.11) and (E2.8.12).

Equations (E2.8.4)(a) to (E2.8.7)(b) can be rewritten in a similar matrix notation as

$$\mathbf{U^E} = \mathbf{\Psi^E \ E}, \qquad (E2.8.15)(a)$$

$$\mathbf{U^i} = \mathbf{\Psi^i \ Y_i} \ , \qquad i = \mathbf{d, \ m, \ n,} \qquad (E2.8.16)(a)$$

and

$$\mathbf{T^E} = \mathbf{\Phi^{E'} \ E} \qquad (E2.8.15)(b)$$

$$\mathbf{T^i} = \mathbf{\Phi^{i'} \ Y_i} \ , \qquad i = \mathbf{d, \ m, \ n,} \qquad (E2.8.16)(b)$$

where the vectors $\mathbf{U^i}$ are of dimension $n \times 1$ and contain markups on flows of exports ($\mathbf{i = E}$) and of domestic commodities ($\mathbf{i = d}$), competing imports ($\mathbf{i = m}$) and non-competing imports ($\mathbf{i=n}$) to domestic final demand; the scalars $\mathbf{T^i}$ are the corresponding aggregate sales-tax collections on flows and the $\mathbf{\Psi^i}$ and the $\mathbf{\Phi^{i'}}$ are respectively matrices and vectors of coefficients showing the requirements of markups or sales taxes per unit of direct flows of commodities to final demand. Note that the $\mathbf{\Psi^i}$ are of dimension $n \times n$ for $\mathbf{i = E, \ d}$ and $\mathbf{m,}$ and $n \times r$ for $\mathbf{i = n.}$ Similarly, the dimensions of the $\mathbf{\Phi^{i'}}$ are $1 \times n$ except for $\mathbf{i = n}$ when the dimension is $1 \times r$.

We are now ready to include the vector (**U**) of demands for markups on the right hand side of the domestic-commodity-balance equation (E2.7.1). It will also be convenient to split **Y** into its domestic and competing-import components. We then obtain:

$$\mathbf{X} = \mathbf{A^I Z} + \mathbf{U} + \mathbf{Y_d} + \mathbf{Y_m} + \mathbf{E} - \mathbf{M},$$ (E2.8.17)

where

$$\mathbf{U} = \sum_{i=I,d,m,n,E} \mathbf{U^i}.$$ (E2.8.18)

Note that with markups included explicitly in the model, the coefficients in **A^I** refer to *direct* usage only. Similarly, **Y_d** and **E** refer to *direct* demands for domestically produced commodities, not to markup demands.

No modifications to equations (E2.6.5), (E2.6.6)(a), (E2.7.2) or (E2.7.3) are required in extending the model to include markups and sales taxes. However, modifications to the pricing equation are required. Instead of (E2.7.11), we write

$$\mathbf{P'} = \mathbf{P'(A^I} - \mathbf{A_m^I} + \mathbf{\Psi^I)Q} + \mathbf{P_m' A_m^I Q} + \mathbf{P_n' B^I Q} + \mathbf{WL^I Q} + \mathbf{\Phi^{I\prime} Q}.$$ (E2.8.19)

Equation (E2.8.19) defines the basic-value prices of domestically produced commodities. Consistent with (E2.6.6)(a), in (E2.8.19) we assume that the matrix of markups required to deliver the inputs needed to make a unit of each commodity is $\mathbf{\Psi^I Q}$, i.e., the markup usage of commodity i required to deliver the inputs needed to produce a unit of commodity k [$(\mathbf{\Psi^I Q})_{ik} = \sum_{j=1}^{h} (\mathbf{\Psi^I})_{ij} \mathbf{Q}_{jk}$] is a weighted average of the markup usage of commodity i required to deliver the inputs needed to produce units of output in all the industries which produce commodity k. The weights, from the kth column of **Q**, are the industries' shares in the total production of commodity k. Similarly, we assume that the vector of taxes paid on inputs used in the production of a unit of each commodity is $\mathbf{\Phi^{I\prime} Q}$.

Finally, we add to the extended model an equation defining aggregate tax collections:

$$\mathbf{T} = \sum_{i=I,d,m,n,E} \mathbf{T^i}.$$ (E2.8.20)

Our extended model is now complete. It consists of (E2.8.17), (E2.8.18), (E2.6.5), (E2.6.6)(a), (E2.8.13), (E2.8.14), (E2.8.15)(a) – (E2.8.16)(b), (E2.7.2), (E2.7.3), (E2.8.19) and (E2.8.20). A natural selection of exogenous variables is **Y_d**, **Y_m**, **Y_n**, **E**, **P_m'**, **P_n'** and **W'**. With this selection, we solve the model by substituting from (E2.8.18), (E2.8.13),

(E2.8.15)(a), (E2.8.16)(a), (E2.6.6)(a) and (E2.7.2) into (E2.8.17) to obtain

$$\mathbf{X} = \mathbf{A^I} \, \mathbf{Q} \, \mathbf{X} + \mathbf{\Psi^I} \, \mathbf{Q} \, \mathbf{X} + \mathbf{\Psi^E} \, \mathbf{E} + \mathbf{\Psi^d} \, \mathbf{Y_d} + \mathbf{\Psi^m} \, \mathbf{Y_m} + \mathbf{\Psi^n} \, \mathbf{Y_n} + \mathbf{Y_d} + \mathbf{E} - \mathbf{A^I_m} \, \mathbf{Q} \, \mathbf{X}$$

(E2.8.21)

This gives

$$\mathbf{X} = \Theta^{-1} \Omega,$$

(E2.8.22)

where Θ is an $n \times n$ matrix of coefficients given by

$$\Theta = [\mathbf{I} - (\mathbf{A^I} - \mathbf{A^I_m} + \mathbf{\Psi^I}) \mathbf{Q}],$$

(E2.8.23)

and Ω is an $n \times 1$ vector formed by combining exogenous variables to give

$$\Omega = (\mathbf{I} + \mathbf{\Psi^d}) \mathbf{Y_d} + \mathbf{\Psi^m} \mathbf{Y_m} + \mathbf{\Psi^n} \mathbf{Y_n} + (\mathbf{I} + \mathbf{\Psi^E}) \mathbf{E}.$$

(E2.8.24)

Equation (E2.8.22) can now be substituted into (E2.6.6)(a), (E2.6.5), (E2.7.2), (E2.7.3), (E2.8.18) and (E2.8.20), to obtain solutions for other endogenous variables:

$$\mathbf{Z} = \mathbf{Q} \Theta^{-1} \Omega,$$

(E2.8.25)

$$\mathbf{F} = \mathbf{L^I} \mathbf{Q} \Theta^{-1} \Omega,$$

(E2.8.26)

$$\mathbf{M} = \mathbf{A^I_m} \, \mathbf{Q} \Theta^{-1} \Omega + \mathbf{Y_m},$$

(E2.8.27)

$$\mathbf{N} = \mathbf{B^I} \mathbf{Q} \Theta^{-1} \Omega + \mathbf{Y_n},$$

(E2.8.28)

$$\mathbf{U} = \mathbf{\Psi^I} \, \mathbf{Q} \Theta^{-1} \Omega + \mathbf{\Psi^E} \, \mathbf{E} + \sum_{i=d,m,n} \mathbf{\Psi^i} \, \mathbf{Y_i}$$

(E2.8.29)

and

$$\mathbf{T} = \mathbf{\Phi^I} \, \mathbf{Q} \Theta^{-1} \Omega + \mathbf{\Phi^{E'}} \, \mathbf{E} + \sum_{i=d,m,n} \mathbf{\Phi^{i'}} \, \mathbf{Y_i} \, .$$

(E2.8.30)

The solution for commodity prices, obtained after manipulation of (E2.8.19), is

$$\mathbf{P'} = (\mathbf{P'_m} \mathbf{A^I_m} + \mathbf{P'_n} \mathbf{B^I} + \mathbf{W'L^I} + \mathbf{\Phi^{I'}}) \, \mathbf{Q} \, \Theta^{-1}$$

(E2.8.31)

C. IMPLEMENTING INPUT-OUTPUT MODELS

Exercise 2.9   *Calibration of coefficients from input-output data*

The usual source of values for the coefficients of the equations in an input-output model is a single observation of the structure of the economy in the form of a set of input-output accounts. The accounts show the dollar values of commodity and primary-factor flows. In using them to calibrate a model (i.e., to assign values to the coefficients), the convention is adopted that basic prices of commodities and factor prices are $1. With this convention, the accounts can be read as showing both value and quantity flows, with all quantities being measured in dollars worth.

In Section A, we dealt with input-output accounting. A published set of input-output accounts typically includes a make matrix and absorption matrices in basic and purchasers' prices with direct and indirect allocation of imports, i.e., tables like E2.A(b) and E2.2.1 to E2.2.4. These tables can often be supplemented with tax information, for example, information of the type appearing in the sales-tax entries of the final-demand column of Table E2.A(a). In many countries, such information is published by government budgetary authorities.

(a) List the coefficient matrices and vectors in the model specified by (E2.8.17), (E2.8.18), (E2.6.5), (E2.6.6)(a), (E2.8.13), (E2.8.14), (E2.8.15)(a) – (E2.8.16)(b), (E2.7.2), (E2.7.3), (E2.8.19) and (E2.8.20).

(b) Evaluate these coefficients using Tables E2.A(b) and E2.2.1 to E2.2.4, assuming that you have the following two items of supplementary information on taxes:

(i) that there are no taxes on usage by industries of commodity 3 either as a direct input or as a markup service in the delivery of inputs; and

(ii) that the tax collections on sales to final demand are as shown in the tax components of the final-demand column of Table E2.A(a).

Note that the data do not separate export demand (**E**) from domestic final demand for domestically produced commodities ($\mathbf{Y_d}$). We can deduce ($\mathbf{Y_d} + \mathbf{E}$) from the data but not the component vectors separately. This creates a problem in calculating the corresponding markup and tax coefficient matrices. Overcome this problem by assuming that $\Psi^{\mathbf{d}} = \Psi^{\mathbf{E}}$ and that $\Phi^{\mathbf{d}} = \Phi^{\mathbf{E}}$. Finally, you should note that only commodity 3 is used as a markup service, and that there are no imports of this commodity.

(c) In the model studied in parts (a) and (b), we allow commodity k to be produced with different technologies in different industries. However, as explained in Exercise 2.6, for the economy as a whole we obtain unique commodity technologies by assuming that $\mathbf{Q}$ is constant. In addition, we used this assumption in (E2.8.19) to allow the specification of coefficients showing the markups and taxes associated with inputs to the production of each commodity. Algebraically, we have

$$\mathbf{A}^{CQ} = \mathbf{A}^{I}\,\mathbf{Q}, \qquad\qquad\qquad\qquad\text{(E2.9.1)}$$

$$\mathbf{A}_{m}^{CQ} = \mathbf{A}_{m}^{I}\,\mathbf{Q}, \qquad\qquad\qquad\qquad\text{(E2.9.2)}$$

$$\mathbf{B}^{CQ} = \mathbf{B}^{I}\,\mathbf{Q}, \qquad\qquad\qquad\qquad\text{(E2.9.3)}$$

$$\mathbf{L}^{CQ} = \mathbf{L}^{I}\,\mathbf{Q}, \qquad\qquad\qquad\qquad\text{(E2.9.4)}$$

and
$$\Psi^{CQ} = \Psi^{I}\,\mathbf{Q}, \qquad\qquad\qquad\qquad\text{(E2.9.5)}$$

$$\Phi^{CQ'} = \Phi^{I'}\,\mathbf{Q}. \qquad\qquad\qquad\qquad\text{(E2.9.6)}$$

$\mathbf{A}^{CQ}$, $\mathbf{A}_{m}^{CQ}$, $\mathbf{B}^{CQ}$ and $\mathbf{L}^{CQ}$ are matrices showing input and factor requirements per unit output of *commodities*, estimated as weighted averages of requirements per unit of *industries'* outputs, with the weights reflecting industries' shares in commodity outputs. Similarly, Ψ^{CQ} and $\Phi^{CQ'}$ show markups and taxes on inputs per unit of the production of *commodities*, again estimated as weighted averages of markups and taxes on inputs per unit of industries' outputs.

As mentioned in Exercise 2.6, the assumption of a constant $\mathbf{Q}$, which allows the derivation for the economy of commodity technologies via (E2.9.1) – (E2.9.6), is theoretically unconvincing. If commodity k is produced with different technologies in different industries, then we would expect industry shares in the production of the k to be sensitive to variations in input prices. Such variations would change the relative profitabilities of producing k in different industries.

Now assume that commodity k is produced with the same technology in each industry and that the markups and taxes on inputs to the production of a unit of k are also invariant across industries. Under this assumption, using the data in Section A, could you derive commodity matrices $\mathbf{A}^{CS}$, $\mathbf{A}_{m}^{CS}$, $\mathbf{B}^{CS}$, $\mathbf{L}^{CS}$, Ψ^{CS} and $\Phi^{CS'}$ where the S superscript indicates the assumption that for any given commodity k, the production technology and markups and taxes per unit of output are the *same* in all industries?

Rather than deriving all these matrices, derive $(\mathbf{A}^{CS} + \Psi^{CS})$, $\mathbf{B}^{CS}$, $\mathbf{L}^{CS}$ and $\Phi^{CS'}$ This can be done using only the make matrix, given in Table E2.A(b), and the absorption matrix at basic values with indirect allocation of imports, given in Table E2.2.2.

Answer to Exercise 2.9

(a)   The coefficient matrices to be evaluated are: $\mathbf{A}^l$; $\mathbf{A}^I_m$; Ψ^i and $\Phi^{i'}$ for $\mathbf{i} = \mathbf{I}$, $\mathbf{E}$, $\mathbf{d}$, $\mathbf{m}$ and $\mathbf{n}$; $\mathbf{L}^l$; $\mathbf{Q}$ and $\mathbf{B}^l$.

(b)   The matrix $\mathbf{A}^l$ contains coefficients showing industries' requirements for direct commodity inputs (domestic *plus* imports but excluding markups) per unit output. For commodities 1 and 2 these can be calculated directly from the submatrix comprising the first two rows of the industry columns of Table E2.2.2. The first two rows of each column of $\mathbf{A}^l$ are formed by dividing the corresponding elements in the submatrix of Table E2.2.2 by the column total from the table. For example $(\mathbf{A}^l)_{11}$ is 10/90 = 0.1111.

To calculate the third row of $\mathbf{A}^l$, we must separate direct usage from markup usage. In row 3 of Table E2.2.2 direct usage and markup usage are added together. To make the separation we follow an approach similar to that in Exercise 2.4(b).

By comparing Tables E2.2.2 and E2.2.4, we see that the total margins on the delivery of commodities 1 and 2 (domestic and imported) and non-competing imports to industry 1 is $9 million (i.e., 12 – 10 + 21 – 15 + 6 – 5). Of this, $4m. is taxes (see the tax row of Table E2.2.2 and recall that there are no taxes on usage by industries of commodity 3). This leaves $5m. as the usage of commodity 3 as a markup service on the delivery of inputs to industry 1. (We assume that no markup services are used in the delivery of the markup commodity to any industry, i.e., that there are no markups on markups). From Table E2.2.2, we find that direct usage of commodity 3 in industry 1 plus usage as a markup on inputs is $23m. Now we can deduce that direct usage is $18m. Similarly, we find that direct usage of commodity 3 in industries 2 and 3 is $8m. and $58m. respectively. This gives $(\mathbf{A}^l)_{31} = 18/90$, $(\mathbf{A}^l)_{32} = 8/110$ and $(\mathbf{A}^l)_{33} = 58/200$. The complete $\mathbf{A}^l$ matrix is in Table E2.9.1.

As already mentioned, markup usage of commodity 3 in the delivery of inputs to industry 1 is $5m. The corresponding figures for industries 2 and 3 are $14m. and $9m. This information is required in the evaluation of Ψ^I. As we saw in (E2.8.11), the elements of Ψ^I are the ratios of the markups associated with industries' total inputs to their total outputs. (These can be regarded as fixed coefficients because the commodity structure of each industry's direct inputs is fixed under the model's assumed technology.) With the present data, only the third row of Ψ^I contains non-zero entries because only commodity 3 is used as a markup. Thus, Ψ^I is as shown in Table E2.9.1, with $(\Psi^I)_{31} = 5/90$, $(\Psi^I)_{32} = 14/110$ and $(\Psi^I)_{33} = 9/200$.

The matrices $\mathbf{B}^I$, $\Phi^{I'}$ and $\mathbf{L}^I$ are computed by dividing the non-competing imports, sales-taxes and factor-payments rows of the first three columns of Table E2.2.2 by the column totals. $\mathbf{B}^I$ and $\mathbf{L}^I$ contain straightforward input coefficients for non-competing imports and primary factors. From (E2.8.12), it can be seen that the elements of $\Phi^{I'}$ are the ratios of the sales tax payable on industries' total inputs to their total outputs. As with Ψ^I, these can be regarded as fixed coefficients because the commodity structure of each industry's direct inputs is fixed under the model's assumed technology. $\mathbf{B}^I$, $\Phi^{I'}$ and $\mathbf{L}^I$ are included in Table E2.9.1.

To calculate the input coefficients $(\mathbf{A}_m^I)$ for competing imports, we must first separate the import flows from the flows of the corresponding domestically produced commodities. The generation of the required competing-imports matrix was the subject of Exercise 2.4 (a). The elements of $\mathbf{A}_m^I$ are then calculated by dividing the industry columns of the competing-imports matrix by the column totals of Table E2.2.1. The complete matrix is in Table E2.9.2.

The matrix $\mathbf{Q}$ contains industries' shares in the total outputs of commodities. These can be calculated from part (b) of Table E2.A by dividing the rows of the table by the row totals. For example, $\mathbf{Q}_{12}$, the share of industry 1 in the total output of commodity 2, is $30/120 = 0.25$. The complete matrix is given in Table E2.9.2.

Only the coefficients of markups and sales taxes on final demand (Ψ^i and $\Phi^{i'}$ for $i = d$, E, m and n) remain to be calculated. In doing this, we start by deducing the vectors of final demands $(\mathbf{Y_d} + \mathbf{E})$, $\mathbf{Y_m}$ and $\mathbf{Y_n}$ shown in column 1 of Table E2.9.3. $(\mathbf{Y_d} + \mathbf{E})_i$ and $(\mathbf{Y_m})_i$ for $i=1$ and 2 can be obtained by comparing the final-demand columns in Tables E2.2.1 and E2.2.2. $\mathbf{Y_n}$ can be read directly from Table E2.2.2 and $(\mathbf{Y_m})_3$ is zero because there are no imports of commodity 3. From Table E2.2.3 (or E2.2.4) we see that direct final-demand usage of commodity 3 is \$40m. in purchasers' prices. (In a final-demand column of a table in purchasers' prices, all entries must reflect direct usage.) Now using the tax information in the final-demand column of Table E2.A(a) and assuming that there are no markups on markups, we find that $(\mathbf{Y_d} + \mathbf{E})_3$ = \$35m. (i.e., 40 – 5).

Next, we calculate the margins associated with each component of final demand (column 2 of Table E2.9.3). Comparison of Tables E2.2.1 and E2.2.3 shows that the margins associated with flows of domestically

Table E2.9.1
The Matrices $\mathbf{A}^I$, $\mathbf{B}^I$, Ψ^I, $\Phi^{I'}$ *and* $\mathbf{L}^I$

Matrix	Values		
	0.1111	0.2273	0.1000
$\mathbf{A}^I$	0.1667	0.1909	0.0500
	0.2000	0.0727	0.2900
	0.0000	0.0000	0.0000
Ψ^I	0.0000	0.0000	0.0000
	0.0556	0.1273	0.0450
$\mathbf{B}^I$	0.0556	0.0909	0.0200
$\Phi^{I'}$	0.0444	0.1273	0.0250
$\mathbf{L}^I$	0.3667	0.1636	0.4700

Table E2.9.2
The Matrices $\mathbf{A}_{\mathbf{m}}^{I}$, $\mathbf{g}$

Matrix	Values		
	0.0000	0.0455	0.0500
$\mathbf{A}_{\mathbf{m}}^{I}$	0.0000	0.0545	0.0000
	0.0000	0.0000	0.0000
	0.75	0.25	0.0
$\mathbf{g}$	0.25	0.75	0.0
	0.0	0.0	1.0

Table E2.9.3
Final Demands and Associated Margins

		(1) Final demand at basic values	(2) Margins	(3) Taxes	(4) Markup usage of commodity 3
Domestically	1	40	18	10	8
produced	2	80	50	20	30
commodities	3	35	5	5	0
Competing	1	10	7	5	2
imports	2	24	14	5	9
	3	0	0	0	0
Non-competing imports		11	6	2	4

Table E2.9.4
The Matrices Ψ^d, Ψ^E, Ψ^m, Ψ^n, $\Phi^{d'}$, $\Phi^{E'}$, $\Phi^{m'}$ and $\Phi^{n'}$

Matrix	Values		
Ψ^d (= Ψ^E)	0.0 0.0 0.2000	0.0 0.0 0.3750	0.0 0.0 0.0
Ψ^m	0.0 0.0 0.2000	0.0 0.0 0.3750	0.0 0.0 0.0
Ψ^n	0.0 0.0 0.3636		
$\Phi^{d'}$ (= $\Phi^{E'}$)	0.2500	0.2500	0.1429
$\Phi^{m'}$	0.5000	0.2083	0.0
$\Phi^{n'}$	0.1818		

produced goods 1 and 2 to final demand are $18m. and $50m. Comparison of Tables E2.2.2 and E2.2.4 shows that the margins associated with flows of goods 1 and 2 (domestic and imported) to final demand are $25m. and $64m. This implies that the margins associated with the flows of imported goods 1 and 2 to final demand are $7m. and $14m. From Tables E2.2.2 and E2.2.4 we see that the margins on final demand for non-competing imports are $6m. With no imports of commodity 3, the margins on imported commodity 3 must be zero, and with no markups on commodity 3 we know that the margins on domestic commodity 3 directly used in final demand are just the taxes of $5m.

Column 3 of Table E2.9.3 is the tax information from the final-demand column of Table E2.A(a). The last column of Table E2.9.3 shows the markup usage of commodity 3 associated with each component of final demand. It is the difference between columns 2 and 3.

Using the information in Table E2.9.3, we can now calculate the remaining coefficient matrices and vectors. These are shown in Table E2.9.4. Each coefficient in the third row of a Ψ matrix is the ratio of the entries in columns 4 and 1 of the relevant row of Table E2.9.3. Similarly, the coefficients in the Φ matrices are ratios of entries in columns 3 and 1.

(c)   We let $\mathbf{X^A}$ be the 6×3 matrix given in the industry columns of Table E2.2.2 and $\mathbf{X^M}$ be the 3×3 make matrix given in Table E2.A(b). Then, under the assumption that commodity technologies and associated commodity markup and tax coefficients are the same across industries, we have

$$X_{ij}^{A} = \sum_{k=1}^{3} \left[\mathbf{A}^{CS} + \Psi^{CS} \right]_{ik} X_{kj}^{M}, \quad i, j=1,...,3, \quad (E2.9.7)$$

$$X_{4j}^{A} = \sum_{k=1}^{3} B_{k}^{CS} X_{kj}^{M}, \quad j=1,...,3, \quad (E2.9.8)$$

$$X_{5j}^{A} = \sum_{k=1}^{3} \Phi_{k}^{CS} X_{kj}^{M}, \quad j=1,...,3, \quad (E2.9.9)$$

and

$$X_{6j}^A = \sum_{k=1}^{3} L_k^{CS} X_{kj}^M, \qquad j=1,...,3. \quad (E2.9.10)$$

The left hand side of (E2.9.7) is the usage of commodity i (domestic and imported) by industry j both as a markup service associated with its inputs and as a direct input. The right hand side is the sum of industry j's requirements for commodity i, directly and as a margin service, in its production of commodities 1, 2 and 3. The kth component of this sum is industry j's production of commodity k (X_{kj}^M) multiplied by the coefficient ($A_{ik}^{CS} + \Psi_{ik}^{CS}$), showing the direct and markup requirement for commodity i per unit output of commodity k. Equation (E2.9.8) specifies industry j's usage of the non-competing import as the sum of its requirements in the production of the three commodities. Equations (E2.9.9) and (E2.9.10) are similar to (E2.9.8) and give industry j's tax liability associated with its inputs, and its requirements for inputs of the primary factor.

In matrix notation we can rewrite (E2.9.7) – (E2.9.10) as

$$\mathbf{X}^A = \begin{bmatrix} \mathbf{A}^{CS} + \Psi^{CS} \\ \mathbf{B}^{CS} \\ \Phi^{CS} \\ \mathbf{L}^{CS} \end{bmatrix} \mathbf{X}^M. \qquad (E2.9.11)$$

Given $\mathbf{X}^A$ and $\mathbf{X}^M$, can we deduce the 6×3 matrix of coefficients on the right hand side of (E2.9.11)? This depends on whether $\mathbf{X}^M$ has an inverse. If there were different numbers of industries and commodities, then $\mathbf{X}^M$ would not be invertible and we would not be able to deduce the coefficients. However, in the present example, there are 3 commodities and 3 industries and we find that $\mathbf{X}^M$ has an inverse given by

$$(\mathbf{X}^M)^{-1} = \begin{bmatrix} 60 & 20 & 0 \\ 30 & 90 & 0 \\ 0 & 0 & 200 \end{bmatrix}^{-1} = \begin{bmatrix} 0.01875 & -0.00417 & 0 \\ -0.00625 & 0.01250 & 0 \\ 0 & 0 & 0.005 \end{bmatrix}. (E2.9.12)$$

From here, we can compute the required coefficients as

$$\mathbf{x^A}(\mathbf{x^M})^{-1} = \begin{bmatrix} 10 & 25 & 20 \\ 15 & 21 & 10 \\ 23 & 22 & 67 \\ 5 & 10 & 4 \\ 4 & 14 & 5 \\ 33 & 18 & 94 \end{bmatrix} \begin{bmatrix} 0.01875 & -0.00417 & 0 \\ -0.00625 & 0.01250 & 0 \\ 0 & 0 & 0.005 \end{bmatrix}. \quad \text{(E2.9.13)}$$

The result of the multiplication on the right hand side of (E2.9.13) is given in panel III of Table E2.9.5. Panels I and II show industry-coefficient matrices taken from Table E2.9.1 and commodity-coefficient matrices derived by the constant-**Q** method.

Several features of Table E2.9.5 are worth nothing. First, each of its column sums is 1.0. This reflects our choice of quantity units. Under this choice, the column sums show the number of base-period dollars worth of inputs and taxes required to produce one base-period dollars worth of output of either an industry or commodity.

Second, the last column is the same in each of the three panels. This reflects a property of the make matrix. Because commodity 3 is produced only in industry 3 and industry 3 produces only commodity 3, the technology of industry 3 is the technology of commodity 3 under both methods of deriving commodity technologies.

Third, column 1 in panel II lies between columns 1 and 2 in panel I. Under the constant-**Q** method, the coefficient column for commodity 1 is computed as a weighted average of the coefficient columns for industries 1 and 2, with weights of 0.75 and 0.25. Similarly, column 2 in panel II lies between columns 1 and 2 in panel I. Again, the commodity-coefficient column is computed as a weighted average of the coefficient columns for industries 1 and 2, this time with weights of 0.25 and 0.75.

On the other hand, the coefficient columns for commodities 1 and 2 in panel III both lie outside the range encompassed by the columns for industries 1 and 2 in panel I. This is because these industry columns are weighted averages of the commodity columns. With two thirds of industry 1's output being commodity 1 and one third being commodity 2, we see that the coefficients for industry 1 in panel I are weighted averages of the coefficients for commodities 1 and 2 in panel III with the weights being 0.667 and 0.3333. Similarly, the coefficients

Table E2.9.5
Industry and Commodity Technologies

	I Industry technologies			II Commodity technologies: average of industry technologies			III Commodity technologies: same in all industries		
	Industries			Commodities			Commodities		
	(1)	(2)	(3)	(1)	(2)	(3)	(1)	(2)	(3)
	$(\mathbf{A}^I + \Psi^I)$			$(\mathbf{A}^{C9} + \psi^{C9})$			$(\mathbf{A}^{CS} + \Psi^{CS})$		
Domestic and imported commodities	0.1111	0.2273	0.1	0.1402	0.1983	0.1	0.0312	0.2708	0.1
	0.1667	0.1909	0.05	0.1728	0.1849	0.05	0.1500	0.2	0.05
	0.2556	0.2000	0.335	0.2417	0.2138	0.335	0.2938	0.1792	0.335
Non-competing imports	$\mathbf{B}^I$			$\mathbf{B}^{C9}$			$\mathbf{B}^{CS}$		
	0.0556	0.0909	0.02	0.0644	0.0821	0.02	0.0312	0.1042	0.02
Sales taxes	$\Phi^{I'}$			$\Phi^{C9'}$			$\Phi^{CS'}$		
	0.0444	0.1273	0.025	0.0652	0.1066	0.025	-0.0125	0.1583	0.025
Factor payments	$\mathbf{L}^I$			$\mathbf{L}^{C9}$			$\mathbf{L}^{CS}$		
	0.3667	0.1636	0.47	0.3159	0.2144	0.47	0.5063	0.0874	0.47
Total	1.0	1.0	1.0	1.0	1.0	1.0	1.0	1.0	1.0

for industry 2 in panel I are weighted averages of the coefficients for commodities 1 and 2 in panel III, with the weights reflecting the commodity composition of industry 2's output: two elevenths commodity 1 and nine elevenths commodity 2.

Finally, we note that one coefficient, $\Phi_1^{CS'}$, in panel III is negative. Even when $\mathbf{X^M}$ is invertible, computations based on equations such as (E2.9.11) cannot be guaranteed to produce satisfactory estimates of commodity coefficients. In particular, there is no guarantee that the resulting coefficients will be non-negative.

The occurrence of negative coefficients normally can be taken as evidence that the data in $\mathbf{X^A}$ and $\mathbf{X^M}$ is inconsistent with the assumption that for any commodity k, the coefficients associated with its production are the same in all industries. In the present example, we see from panel I of Table E2.9.5 that sales taxes on inputs per unit of output are large in industry 2 compared with those in industry 1 (0.1273 compared with 0.0444). Given that industry 2 produces mainly commodity 2 and that industry 1 produces mainly commodity 1, we are forced, under the assumption that commodity coefficients are the same across industries, to assign a relatively high value to the tax rate on inputs to commodity 2. However, when we assign a tax rate to commodity 2 high enough to explain the tax collection in industry 2, we are left with too much tax collection in industry 1. (Remember that industry 1 also produces commodity 2). To reduce the tax collection in industry 1 to the observed level, we are forced to assign an unrealistic negative value to the tax rate on inputs to commodity 1. We can conclude that, contrary to our assumption, the data reflects a situation in which taxes on the inputs per unit output of commodities differ across industries.

Exercise 2.10   *Input-output multipliers*

One of the most popular applications of input-output models is multiplier analysis. Multiplier analysis is concerned with the effects of stimulating specific sectors of the economy. The questions which are addressed by multiplier analysis are often of the sort: how much output and employment would be created both inside and outside an industry if we were to generate an extra $1m. of final demand for the industry's products. Answers, showing impressive amounts of output stimulation and employment creation, are often tendered as supporting evidence by industry associations arguing for protection against imports, subsidies for their exports, favoured treatment against foreign competitors for government contracts and other measures which would allow them to expand their activities.

This exercise requires you to do some multiplier analysis with the model developed in Exercise 2.8 and calibrated in Exercise 2.9. Using equations (E2.8.22) to (E2.8.24) and (E2.8.26), calculate the vectors of commodity outputs ($\mathbf{X}$) and primary inputs ($\mathbf{F}$) required to support a unit of final demand for each domestically produced commodity. Notice that the word unit can be interpreted in different ways. For example, in calculating the $\mathbf{X}$ and $\mathbf{F}$ vectors associated with an unit of domestic demand for domestic commodity k, you could:

(i)   set the kth component of $\mathbf{Y_d}$ at 1, with its remaining components and all components of $\mathbf{Y_m}$, $\mathbf{Y_n}$ and $\mathbf{E}$ at zero;

(ii)   set the kth component of $\mathbf{Y_d}$ at r_k, the ratio in the base-period data of the basic value of final demand for domestically produced commodity k to its purchasers' value, again with all other exogenous demand variables at zero; (Note from Table E2.A that $r_1 = 40/58$, $r_2 = 80/130$ and $r_3 = 35/40$.)

(iii) replace $(\mathbf{I} + \Psi^{\mathbf{d}})\mathbf{Y_d}$ in (E2.8.24) by $\mathbf{Y_d^*}$, treat $\mathbf{Y_d^*}$ as exogenous and set its kth component at 1, with its remaining components and all of $\mathbf{Y_m}$, $\mathbf{Y_n}$ and $\mathbf{E}$ at zero. (Note, that $\mathbf{Y_d^*}$ is the vector of direct and markup demands for domestic commodities by domestic final users.)

For each of these three interpretations, calculate the output multipliers associated with units of domestic final demand for domestic commodities 1 to 3. An output multiplier is the effect on gross output (the sum of the components of the $\mathbf{X}$ vector) of a unit demand expansion. Also calculate the effects of unit demand expansions on primary factor usage. Discuss the limitations of multiplier analysis.

Answer to Exercise 2.10

The required calculations under the three interpretations are in panels (i) to (iii) of Table E2.10.1.

The easiest place to start the explanation of the table is with panel (iii). In the kth column of this panel, we have the increases in commodity outputs and factor usage which would be necessary to satisfy an additional demand by domestic final users for a quantity of commodity k worth $1m. in base-period basic values. These increases have been calculated without allowing any change in either the direct or markup usage of any other commodity by final users. Implicitly, we have assumed that the extra quantity of commodity k is transferred from producers to final users without requiring markup services. This unsatisfactory assumption underlies the many multiplier studies in which it is assumed that components of the vector $\mathbf{Y_d^*}$ can be varied independently of each other.

On looking at the output multipliers in panel (iii), we see only minor variations between commodities. The multiplier for commodity 3 (1.806) is a little smaller than those for the other two commodities, reflecting commodity 3's comparatively low reliance on domestically produced inputs. As can be calculated from the $\mathbf{A}^I$, ψ^I, $\mathbf{A}_m^I$ and $\mathbf{Q}$ matrices in Tables E2.9.1 and E2.9.2, 43.5 per cent of the costs of producing commodity 3 are accounted for by domestically produced inputs. The corresponding figures for commodities 1 and 2 under the constant-$\mathbf{Q}$ assumption are 53.0 per cent and 52.2 per cent.

Output multipliers, such as those in Table E2.10.1, calculated as sums of gross outputs suffer from the defect that their values depend on rather arbitrary aspects of the input-output tables from which they are derived. For example, the output multiplier for commodity k can be strongly influenced by the value adopted for the coefficient showing the input of commodity k required per unit of output of k. Such coefficients depend on the levels recorded for intra-industry sales. These reflect definitions of what constitutes a single enterprise within an industry.

A measure which is better than output multipliers for showing the economic activity generated by a unit of final demand is the effect on primary-factor usage (e.g., employment). In panel (iii), stimulation of final demand for commodity 3 is shown to be more effective in generating primary-factor usage than is stimulation of final demand for either of the other commodities. Primary factors, used both directly and indirectly through produced inputs, account for 80.3 per cent of the cost of creating a unit of commodity 3 for final demand, whereas for commodities 1 and 2 the corresponding percentages are 69.2 and 58.4. The explanation can be found by looking at the coefficients in Tables E2.9.1 and E2.9.2. There we see that industry 3 (the sole producer of commodity 3) has comparatively low import and tax coefficients.

In panel (i) of Table E2.10.1, we have made an attempt to correct the problem identified in panel (iii). The kth column of panel (i) shows the effects of an additional direct demand by domestic final users for a quantity of domestically produced commodity k worth $1m. at base-period basic prices, allowing not only for increased production of commodity k and associated inputs but also for the production of the markup services required to transfer this quantity of commodity k from producers to final users. This does not make any difference to the column for commodity 3 because no markup services are required in

Table E2.10.1
Multiplier Calculations

	(i) Effects of unit increases in domestic final demands for domestically produced commodities			(ii)			(iii)		
	Extra final demands worth $1m. in basic values			Extra final demands worth $1m. in purchasers' prices			Extra final demands worth $1m. in basic values but inducing no increase in markups on final demands		
	Commodities			Commodities			Commodities		
	(1)	(2)	(3)	(1)	(2)	(3)	(1)	(2)	(3)
		$\Theta^{-1}(I + \psi d)$			$\Theta^{-1}(I + \psi d)\hat{r}$			Θ^{-1}	
Outputs of commodities 1	1.249	0.305	0.112	0.862	0.188	0.098	1.227	0.263	0.112
2	0.282	1.289	0.113	0.194	0.793	0.099	0.259	1.246	0.113
3	0.845	1.089	1.581	0.583	0.670	0.383	0.529	0.500	1.581
Output multiplier (sum of rows 1–3)	2.376	2.683	1.806	1.639	1.651	1.580	2.015	2.005	1.806
		$L'g\Theta^{-1}(I + \psi d)$			$L'g\Theta^{-1}(I + \psi d)\hat{r}$			$L'g\Theta^{-1}$	
Usage of primary factor	0.852	0.885	0.803	0.588	0.545	0.703	0.692	0.584	0.803

transferring units of commodity 3 to final demand. However, the entries in the other two columns are bigger in panel (i) than in panel (iii), reflecting extra usage of markup services.

An objection to panel (i) is that the sizes of the final-demand stimulations differ across columns. When we take account of markup services, we find that the increase in final demand in column 1 valued in basic prices is $1.2m ($1m. of commodity 1 and $0.2m. of commodity 3, see Ψ^d in Table E2.9.4). Calculated in a similar way, the increases in columns 2 and 3 are $1.375m. and $1m. It is not surprising that commodity 2 emerges in panel (i) as having the largest output multiplier and the largest primary-factor usage effect.

In panel (ii), we have tried to improve comparability between the three columns by imposing in each a final demand increase with the same *purchasers'* value. The kth column shows the effects of an additional direct demand by domestic final users for a quantity of domestically produced commodity k worth $1m. at base-period purchasers' prices. Unlike the situation in panel (i), in panel (ii) commodities with large markup requirements in final demand no longer derive any advantage in multiplier calculations.

Commodity 3 is shown in panel (ii) in the most favourable light. It generates the largest increase in primary factor usage per unit of additional final demand. This is similar to the result in panel (iii) and reflects commodity 3's comparatively low import and tax coefficients. The primary-factor-usage results are smaller in panel (ii) than the corresponding results in panel (iii) because the panel-(ii) calculations include taxes on final demands as part of the $1m. demand increases. In panel (iii), these $1m. increases are net of taxes on final demands.

As we mentioned in the introduction to this exercise, multiplier computations, such as those in Table E2.10.1 are often used as indicators of the effects on the economy of projects which expand final demand for domestic commodities, investment projects, for example, perhaps leading to export sales. Output multipliers have also been used as the basis for the identification of "key sectors", that is, sectors in which additional final demand will have particularly powerful expansionary effects in the economy. The usual inference is that sectors with large multipliers are suitable targets for stimulation through government policy.

The validity of this approach is doubtful because of both the demand-side and the supply-side assumptions implicit in it. On the demand side, no attention is paid to the value to economy of the commodities produced as a consequence of the stimulatory policies; neither to the importance attached to the commodities in household preferences nor to the economy's comparative advantage in supplying them in international trade. On the supply side, multiplier computations implicitly assume that additional output in one sector can occur without crowding out production in other sectors. This is not appropriate if, for example, the economy is subject to any constraints on the supplies of primary factors nor if it faces a balance-of-payments constraint.

D. INPUT-OUTPUT MODELS AS COMPUTABLE GENERAL EQUILIBRIUM MODELS

Exercise 2.11   *Producer optimization*

A modern applied general equilibrium model is usually formulated as a set of behavioural equations and identities which describe the economic behaviour of the agents identified in the model and the technological and institutional constraints facing them. The behavioural equations are usually derived as the solutions to explicit constrained-optimization problems assumed to drive the economic behaviour of a typical, or representative, agent from each component of the model economy, e.g., a typical household of given socioeconomic or demographic characteristics, a typical producer in a given industrial sector, or a typical importer or exporter.

Subsequent chapters in this book rely heavily on this method-ology. To illustrate it in the context of input-output models, we return to the simplest version of the open static model, i.e., the model described in Exercise 2.5. It identifies the following agents:

. producers in each of n industries,

. suppliers of each of m types of primary inputs, and

. a single purchaser of final output.

There is no foreign trade. There is a one-to-one correspondence be-tween industries and commodities, i.e., industry j produces only commodity j and is the sole producer of that commodity.

In the style of modern applied general equilibrium modelling, we can derive the input-output model by assuming that producers in the jth industry are price takers and that they choose produced inputs (X_{ij}) and primary inputs (F_{kj}) to minimize production costs (C_j):

$$C_j = \sum_{i=1}^{n} P_i X_{ij} + \sum_{k=1}^{m} W_k F_{kj} , \quad j=1,...,n, \quad (E2.11.1)$$

subject to a fixed-coefficients or Leontief production function:

$$X_j = \min \left\{ \frac{X_{1j}}{A_{1j}} , ... , \frac{X_{nj}}{A_{nj}} , \frac{F_{1j}}{L_{1j}} , ... , \frac{F_{mj}}{L_{mj}} \right\} , \quad j =1,...,n. \quad (E2.11.2)$$

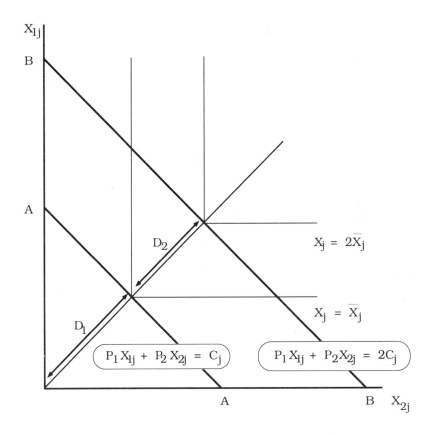

Figure E2.11.1 Isoquants of the Leontief production
function and isocosts

Note: Constant returns to scale implies that the distances
D_1 and D_2 are equal.

As a basis for commodity-pricing equations, we assume that competition
prevents producers from earning pure profits, i.e.,

$$P_j X_j = \sum_{i=1}^{n} P_i X_{ij} + \sum_{k=1}^{m} W_k F_{kj} \quad (= C_j) \ , \quad j=1,\dots,n. \quad \text{(E2.11.3)}$$

Sketch isocosts and isoquants corresponding to (E2.11.1) and
(E2.11.2) for a two-input case, assuming that all prices are positive.
Derive producers' demand functions for produced and primary inputs

from (E2.11.1) and (E2.11.2). Comment on the demand functions in light of the diagram.

From (E2.11.3), derive a relationship between output and input prices. What feature of the production functions (E2.11.2) implies that output prices are independent of quantity variables?

Answer to Exercise 2.11

Figure E2.11.1 shows isocosts and isoquants for the case of two produced inputs, X_{1j} and X_{2j}. It is clear that cost-minimizing producers will use only the minimum amount necessary of each input, so long as input prices are positive. Hence, the demand functions for produced inputs and primary factors are identical to (E2.5.1) and (E2.5.2). These indicate that input demands are independent of relative input prices. In terms of Figure E2.11.1, only the vertices of the right-angled isoquants can be optimal points, whatever the slope of the isocost line. They also reflect the constant returns to scale assumed in the production functions (E2.11.2). In Figure E2.11.1, the expansion path is a ray through the origin, the scale of output associated with successive isoquants cut by this ray being proportional to their distances from the origin.

To derive a relationship between output and input prices, first, use (E2.5.1) and (E2.5.2) to eliminate input demands from the right hand side of (E2.11.3), yielding:

$$P_j X_j \; = \; \sum_{i=1}^{n} P_i A_{ij} X_j \; + \; \sum_{k=1}^{m} W_k L_{kj} X_j \, , \qquad j=1,....,n. \qquad \text{(E2.11.4)}$$

Next, divide through by X_j, concluding that (E2.5.5) is the appropriate pricing equation.

According to (E2.5.5), the price of output in industry j is a weighted sum of input prices, the weights being the technology coefficients from the production function (E2.11.2). The elimination of X_j was a consequence of constant returns to scale, which implies that unit costs are independent of the scale of production.

Chapter 3

The Johansen Approach

3.1 Introduction

In this chapter we consider a class of general equilibrium models in which an equilibrium is a vector, V, of length n satisfying a system of equations

$$F(V) = 0, \qquad (3.1.1)$$

where F is a vector function of length m. We assume that F is differentiable and that the number of variables, n, exceeds the number of equations m. Via (3.1.1) consumer demands will be viewed as arising from budget-constrained utility maximization, zero pure profits will apply, and demands will equal supplies. Preferences and technologies are represented in (3.1.1) by differentiable utility and production functions.

Linearization will play a key role. We will be concerned with the approach pioneered by Johansen (1960). Because system (3.1.1) can be very large and involve a wide variety of nonlinear functional forms, from a computational point of view it might be quite intractable. Johansen's approach is to derive from (3.1.1) a system of linear equations in which the variables are changes, percentage changes or changes in the logarithms of the components of V.

Since system (3.1.1) contains more variables than equations we assign exogenously given values to (n–m) variables and solve for the remaining m, the endogenous variables. In applications of Johansen models, many different allocations of the variables between the exogenous and endogenous categories can be made. For example, if we are analyzing the effects of a change in the tariff on footwear, then this variable is exogenous. On the other hand, if we want to calculate the change in the tariff which would be required to ensure a given level of footwear employment, then the footwear tariff is an endogenous variable and footwear employment is exogenous.

For the purpose of introducing Johansen's computational approach, we can make some illustrative computations with a small system devoid of economic content. We will assume that system (3.1.1) consists of 2 equations and 3 variables and has the form

$$V_1^2 V_3 - 1 = 0 \qquad \text{and} \qquad V_1 + V_2 - 2 = 0. \qquad (3.1.2)$$

For our illustrative computations with (3.1.2), we will assume that the exogenous variable is V_3 and the endogenous variables are V_1 and V_2.

With this assignment of the variables to the exogenous and endogenous categories, we can express the endogenous variables as functions of the exogenous variable as follows:

$$V_1 = V_3^{-1/2} \qquad \text{and} \qquad V_2 = 2 - V_3^{-1/2} \qquad (3.1.3)$$

where we assume (as is often the case in economic models) that only positive values for the variables are of interest. With a solution system such as (3.1.3), we have no difficulty in evaluating the effects on the endogenous variables of shifts in the exogenous variable. For example, assume that initially we have

$$V^I = (V_1^I, V_2^I, V_3^I) = (1,1,1), \qquad (3.1.4)$$

a situation which satisfies (3.1.2). Then we want to evaluate the effects on V_1 and V_2 (employment and prices, say) of a shift in V_3 (the level of protection) from 1 to 1.1. By substituting into (3.1.3), we find that the new values for V_1 and V_2 are 0.9535 and 1.0465. We conclude that a 10 per cent increase in V_3 induces a 4.65 per cent reduction in V_1 and a 4.65 per cent increase in V_2.

Johansen-style computations make use of an initial solution, V^I, with results being reported usually as percentage deviations from this initial solution. The initial solution (i.e., the set of initial values for prices, quantities, tariffs, etc.) is known from the input-output data used in setting many of the parameters of the model (see Exercise 3.3). However, the computations for a Johansen model differ from the simple approach using (3.1.3) because the complexity and size of the system (3.1.1) normally rule out the possibility of deriving from it explicit solution equations. Instead, in the Johansen approach we solve a linearized version of (3.1.1).

To obtain the linearized version, we first derive from (3.1.1) a differential form

$$A(V)v = 0, \qquad (3.1.5)$$

where $A(V)$ is an $m \times n$ matrix whose components are functions of V. The $n \times 1$ vector v is usually interpreted as showing percentage changes or changes in the logarithms of the variables V. However, in some models v is interpreted as the vector of changes in V. In the former case, $A(V)$ is chosen so that (3.1.5) can be used in evaluating elasticities of endogenous variables with respect to exogenous variables. In the latter case, (3.1.5) can be used in evaluations of derivatives. In either case, the linearized (and approximate) version of (3.1.1) used in a Johansen-style computation is generated by replacing the variable matrix $A(V)$ on the LHS of (3.1.5) by a fixed matrix, usually $A(V^I)$.

The derivation of (3.1.5) is by total differentiation of either (3.1.1) or a transformed version of it. The procedure can be illustrated in the context of (3.1.2). We totally differentiate the LHSs of (3.1.2) and set these total differentials to zero recognizing that if (3.1.2) is to continue to be satisfied after a disturbance in the exogenous variables, then the changes in the LHSs must be zero. Thus, we write

$$\begin{bmatrix} 2V_1V_3 & 0 & V_1^2 \\ 1 & 1 & 0 \end{bmatrix} \begin{bmatrix} dV_1 \\ dV_2 \\ dV_3 \end{bmatrix} = 0. \tag{3.1.6}$$

This is a system of the form (3.1.5) where v is interpreted as the vector of changes in the variables V. To obtain a system where v is a vector of percentage changes, we transform (3.1.6) into[1]

$$\begin{bmatrix} 2 & 0 & 1 \\ V_1/2 & V_2/2 & 0 \end{bmatrix} \begin{bmatrix} 100(dV_1)/V_1 \\ 100(dV_2)/V_2 \\ 100(dV_3)/V_3 \end{bmatrix} = 0 \ . \tag{3.1.7}$$

If we replace the (dV_i/V_i)s in (3.1.7) by $(dlnV_i)$s then, on dividing all equations by 100, we obtain a system of the form (3.1.5) in which v is the vector of changes in the logarithms of V:

$$\begin{bmatrix} 2 & 0 & 1 \\ V_1/2 & V_2/2 & 0 \end{bmatrix} \begin{bmatrix} dlnV_1 \\ dlnV_2 \\ dlnV_3 \end{bmatrix} = 0 \ . \tag{3.1.8)[2]}$$

---

[1]   The first equation in (3.1.7) is derived by dividing the first equation in (3.1.6) by $V_1^2V_3$. In the second equation in (3.1.7) we have divided through by 2. It is customary to use share coefficients in the linear-percentage-change system. Notice that $V_1/2$ and $V_2/2$ are the shares of V_1 and V_2 in the sum of V_1 and V_2.

[2]   More formally, we can derive (3.1.8) by first transforming (3.1.2) into

$$2lnV_1 + lnV_3 = ln(1), \quad \text{and} \quad exp(lnV_1) + exp(lnV_2) = 2.$$

Then by total differentiation, we obtain

$$2dlnV_1 + dlnV_3 = 0, \quad \text{and} \quad V_1\,dlnV_1 + V_2\,dlnV_2 = 0,$$

leading to (3.1.8). You will find later in this section that although the A(V) matrices in the percentage-change and log-change versions of (3.1.5) are identical, the two versions give different approximations for the effects on the endogenous variables of finite changes in the exogenous variables.

In a Johansen computation, a system of the form (3.1.5) effectively replaces (3.1.1) as the model. In computations of how far the endogenous variables will move from their initial values in response to given movements in the exogenous variables, $A(V)$ is evaluated at $V = V^I$. Then (3.1.5) is rewritten as

$$A_\alpha(V^I)\, v_\alpha + A_\beta(V^I)\, v_\beta = 0, \qquad (3.1.9)$$

where v_α is the $m \times 1$ subvector of endogenous components of v, v_β is the $(n - m) \times 1$ subvector of exogenous components and $A_\alpha(V^I)$ and $A_\beta(V^I)$ are appropriate submatrices of $A(V^I)$, i.e., $A_\alpha(V^I)$ is the $m \times m$ matrix formed by the columns of $A(V^I)$ corresponding to the endogenous variables and $A_\beta(V^I)$ is the $m \times (n - m)$ matrix formed by the columns corresponding to the exogenous variables. Finally, (3.1.9) is solved for v_α in terms of v_β giving[3]

$$v_\alpha = -A_\alpha^{-1}(V^I)\, A_\beta(V^I)\, v_\beta, \qquad (3.1.10)$$

or more compactly

$$v_\alpha = B(V^I)\, v_\beta, \qquad (3.1.11)$$

where $B(V^I)$ is defined by the right hand side of (3.1.10). If v is a vector of percentage changes or changes in logarithms, then the typical element, $B_{ij}(V^I)$, of $B(V^I)$ is the elasticity evaluated at V^I of the ith endogenous variable with respect to the jth exogenous variable. If v is a vector of changes, then $B_{ij}(V^I)$ is a derivative rather than an elasticity.

Computations (3.1.9) – (3.1.11) can be illustrated via systems (3.1.6) to (3.1.8). With $V = V^I = (1,1,1)$, (3.1.6) becomes

$$\begin{bmatrix} 2 & 0 & 1 \\ 1 & 1 & 0 \end{bmatrix} \begin{bmatrix} dV_1 \\ dV_2 \\ dV_3 \end{bmatrix} = 0. \qquad (3.1.12)$$

On choosing variable 3 to be exogenous, we can rewrite (3.1.12) as

$$\begin{bmatrix} 2 & 0 \\ 1 & 1 \end{bmatrix} \begin{bmatrix} dV_1 \\ dV_2 \end{bmatrix} + \begin{bmatrix} 1 \\ 0 \end{bmatrix} dV_3 = 0. \qquad (3.1.13)$$

---

3   We assume that the relevant inverse exists. If this is not true, then the Johansen method will fail. However, if $A_\alpha(V^I)$ is singular, then it is likely that our classification of endogenous and exogenous variables is illegitimate. That is, it is unlikely that system (3.1.1) implies that V_α is a function of V_β in the region of V^I. In this case, any solution method should fail. See Dixon *et al.* (1982, section 35).

That is
$$\begin{bmatrix} dV_1 \\ dV_2 \end{bmatrix} = - \begin{bmatrix} 2 & 0 \\ 1 & 1 \end{bmatrix}^{-1} \begin{bmatrix} 1 \\ 0 \end{bmatrix} dV_3 \ . \qquad (3.1.14)$$

Hence
$$\begin{bmatrix} dV_1 \\ dV_2 \end{bmatrix} = \begin{bmatrix} -0.5 \\ 0.5 \end{bmatrix} dV_3 \ . \qquad (3.1.15)$$

It is reassuring to note from (3.1.3) that when $V_3 = 1$,

$$\begin{bmatrix} \dfrac{\partial V_1}{\partial V_3} \end{bmatrix} = -\frac{1}{2}(V_3)^{-3/2} = -0.5 \ , \quad \text{and} \quad \begin{bmatrix} \dfrac{\partial V_2}{\partial V_3} \end{bmatrix} = \frac{1}{2}(V_3)^{-3/2} = 0.5.$$

We see that the 2×1 matrix of derivatives of the endogenous variables with respect to the exogenous variable evaluated at V^I is correctly revealed on the right hand side of (3.1.15). If we set $V = V^I$ in either (3.1.7) or (3.1.8), we can derive

$$\begin{bmatrix} v_1 \\ v_2 \end{bmatrix} = - \begin{bmatrix} 2 & 0 \\ 0.5 & 0.5 \end{bmatrix}^{-1} \begin{bmatrix} 1 \\ 0 \end{bmatrix} v_3 \ ,$$

that is,
$$\begin{bmatrix} v_1 \\ v_2 \end{bmatrix} = \begin{bmatrix} -0.5 \\ 0.5 \end{bmatrix} v_3 \ , \qquad (3.1.16)$$

where (v_1, v_2, v_3) can be interpreted as either a vector of percentage changes or a vector of changes in logarithms. Again we can check our result by using (3.1.3) which gives

$$\eta_{1,3} = -\frac{1}{2}(V_3)^{-\frac{1}{2}} / V_1 \quad \text{and} \quad \eta_{2,3} = \frac{1}{2}(V_3)^{-\frac{1}{2}} / V_2 \ ,$$

where $\eta_{1,3}$ and $\eta_{2,3}$ are the elasticities of variables 1 and 2 with respect to variable 3. With $V = V^I$, we see that $\eta_{1,3} = -0.5$ and $\eta_{2,3} = 0.5$, confirming the result in (3.1.16).

Johansen's computational approach is an example of displacement analysis.[4] It allows us to evaluate derivatives or elasticities of endogenous variables with respect to exogenous variables without

---

4   Many of you will be familiar with displacement analysis from derivations of the properties of demand elasticities in the utility maximizing model of consumer behaviour and the cost minimizing model of producer behaviour. See, for example, Dixon, Bowles and Kendrick (1980, Exercises 2.6 and 4.16).

having to obtain explicit forms for the solution equations [(3.1.3) in our example]. All that is required are some simple matrix operations. It should be emphasized, however, that these operations give us the values of the derivatives or elasticities only for the initial values, V^I , of the variables. When we move away from V^I, the derivatives or elasticities will change.

A little experimentation with (3.1.15) and (3.1.16) indicates that the Johansen approach is satisfactory for computing the effects on the endogenous variables of small changes in the exogenous variables. For example, by using (3.1.16) with the v_is interpreted as percentage changes we would say that a 10 per cent increase in V_3 would induce a 5 per cent reduction in V_1 and a 5 per cent increase in V_2. This is close to the answers (–4.65 and 4.65) which we found earlier by substituting into (3.1.3). Even greater accuracy is obtained in this particular example if we interpret the v_is as changes in logarithms. Then the exogenous shock is

$$dlnV_3 = ln(1.1) - ln(1) = 0.095310.$$

On applying this shock in (3.1.16) we obtain

$$dlnV_1 = -0.047655 \quad \text{and} \quad dlnV_2 = 0.047655, \quad (3.1.17)$$

implying that V_1 and V_2 change by –4.65 and 4.88 per cent respectively.[5] However, when we make large changes in V_3, (3.1.16) may not give a satisfactory approximation to the effects on V_1 and V_2. Assume, for instance, that we increase V_3 by 100 per cent (i.e., from 1 to 2). Then the percentage-change version of (3.1.16) implies that V_1 will fall by 50 per cent to 0.5 and V_2 will increase by 50 per cent to 1.5. The correct values, derived from (3.1.3), are that V_1 will fall by 29.29 per cent to 0.7071 while V_2 will increase by 29.29 per cent to 1.2929. With the logarithmic version of (3.1.16), the shock is

$$dlnV_3 = ln(2) - ln(1) = 0.693147.$$

This produces $dlnV_1 = -0.346574$ and $dlnV_2 = 0.346574$. leading to the conclusion that the 100 per cent increase in V_3 reduces V_1 by 29.29 per cent and increases V_2 by 41.42 per cent. Although the logarithmic implementation of (3.1.16) has generated considerably greater accuracy

---

5   The solution for the effect on V_1 of a change in V_3 is free from linearization error. This is because the solution function, (3.1.3), for V_1 can be written as $lnV_1 = -0.5lnV_3$. Thus, no error is introduced by evaluating the change in lnV_1 as –0.5 times the change in lnV_3 .

than the percentage change version, there is still an uncomfortably large error in the result for V_2.

When faced with a large change in the exogenous variables, one approach is to make a sequence of Johansen-style computations. For example, if we want to evaluate the effects of a 100 per cent increase in V_3, we can first use (3.1.16) to generate the effects of a 50 per cent increase. This would take us from the initial situation $(V = V^I)$ to one where $V = V^I + \Delta V_{50}$ with ΔV_{50} denoting our estimate of the change in V arising from the increase in V_3 from 1 to 1.5. Then we can reevaluate the elasticity matrix, B, at $V = V^I + \Delta V_{50}$ and use the reevaluated matrix in computing the effects of moving V_3 from 1.5 to 2. Where greater accuracy is required, we break the change in the exogenous variable into a larger number of smaller steps.

This extended or multi-step Johansen method is the subject of Exercises 3.7 and 3.8. It has been used by Dixon *et al.* (1982, sections 8 and 47). Their experience suggests that the original Johansen method is normally satisfactory. This finding is supported by Bovenberg and Keller (1981). It appears that in policy-oriented work, the changes in the exogenous variables are likely to be sufficiently small that no serious errors are introduced by treating the B matrix as a constant. In situations where it was necessary to allow the B matrix to move, Dixon *et al.* (again supported by Bovenberg and Keller) found that highly accurate solutions were obtained by applying their extended Johansen method with very few steps.

A final issue for this section concerns the interpretation of the changes, percentage changes or log changes in the linearized Johansen system. Johansen (1960) interpreted the variables of his linearized system of equations as growth rates. As described by Taylor (1975, p.100),

> "Basically, he proceeds by logarithmically differentiating the equations characterizing a Walrasian competitive equilibrium *with respect to time* in order to get a simultaneous system of equations which are linear in all growth rates."
> (Emphasis added)

Johansen was concerned mainly with forecasting; with making predictions about the development of the Norwegian economy over future periods. Nowadays, the more common use of Johansen models is in policy analysis in which the main concern is not the future state of the economy but how that state will be affected by, for example, the adoption of a proposal to increase protection against imports. Whereas the time-derivative interpretation of the variables is appropriate in forecasting, it is not appropriate for policy projections.

In forecasting, the initial solution (V^I) is interpreted as the actual state of the economy at time T where T is the current date or a recent date in history. Then the forecasts are made of growth rates in the exogenous variables relying on information from outside the model. For instance, demographic information might be used to forecast the growth of the labor force. Forecasts of movements in the foreign currency prices of imports and exports might be supplied by experts on particular commodity markets. For many exogenous variables, simple extrapolations from past trends might be used. Once a complete set of forecasts has been made for the exogenous variables for the period T to T + 10, say, the growth rates for the period in the endogenous variables can be forecast from the model.

Compared with forecasting, policy projections require little information on the vector of exogenous shocks, v_β. The appropriate values for the components of v_β are usually suggested in a straightforward way by the particular application at hand. For example, if we are interested in the effects of a 5 per cent increase in the real wage rate, then the percentage change in the real wage is set exogenously at 5 while all other components of v_β are set at zero. The model is then used to compute how different the endogenous variables would be from their levels in the vector V^I if the wage rate were 5 per cent higher; i.e., it is used to provide a comparison between two possible states of the economy at a given point of time, one with the real wage rate 5 per cent higher than the other.

3.2   Goals, Reading Guide and References

By the time you have finished with this chapter, we hope that you will have developed the basic skills required for constructing and using a Johansen-style general equilibrium model. In particular, we hope that you will

(1)   be able to describe the four essential parts of the theoretical structure;

(2)   understand the derivation of the linearized system from the nonlinear structural form;

(3)   be familiar with the role of input-output tables in providing both the share coefficients for the linearized system and an initial solution for the nonlinear structural form;

(4) be able to distinguish the interpretation of the variables of the linearized system in forecasting applications from the interpretation which is appropriate for policy projections;

(5) be able to discuss the advantages and disadvantages of condensing the linearized system;

(6) be aware of various solution strategies for handling large sparse systems of linear equations;

(7) appreciate the flexibility inherent in being able to adopt different closures (choices of exogenous variables);

(8) be prepared to interpret solution matrices and to trace out the relationships between solution matrices computed for different closures;

(9) understand the source of the linearization errors occurring in Johansen computations;

(10) know how these linearization errors can be reduced to insignificance by a multi-step Johansen procedure supplemented by Richardson's extrapolation; and

(11) have a facility for deriving linearized demand and supply functions, suitable for use in a Johansen model, from a wide variety of utility maximizing, cost minimizing and revenue maximizing models.

Reading guide 3 and the problem set contain material which will help you to achieve these goals. The readings are referred to in abbreviated form. Full citations are in the reference list which also includes other references appearing in the chapter. The problem set is presented in three parts. Part A uses a small model to illustrate the basics of the Johansen approach. We suggest that you complete the problems in this part before doing any reading. Part B is concerned with linearization errors and their elimination. Part C will give you some practice in deriving linearized demand and supply functions. Exercises on more specialized aspects of Johansen models (e.g., the treatment of international trade, tariffs, taxes and investment) are included in Chapter 4.

Reading Guide to Chapter 3*

Johansen models employ the familiar technique of displacement analysis, i.e., a system of diferential equations is used to describe the displacement of equilibrium caused by the movements in exogenous variables. We suggest that you review a few applications of displacement analysis. Among the more famous are Meade's (1955) analysis of trade and welfare, Harberger's (1962) study of the effects of taxing capital, Frisch's (1959) and Houthakker's (1960) derivations of the restrictions on household demand functions flowing from the adoption of an additive utility function, and Jones' (1979) collected essays in the theory of international trade. Textbook treatments of displacement analysis include Intriligator (1971, particulary sections 7.4 and 8.3), Lancaster (1968, particulary chapters 4 and 8), and Dixon, Bowles and Kendrick (1980, particulary E2.5, E2.6 and E2.17).

Finished with the Stylized Johansen model of part A in the problem set and would now like to work through a more realistic illustrative model?

Yes

No

Read Dixon, Parmeter, Sutton and Vincent (DPSV) (1982, sections 3-7). Section 6 will be helpful if you want more examples of how the flexibility of a model is increased by making allowance for different closures. Also see Taylor *et al.* (1980, pp. 49-60) for a discussion of different closures in the context of an illustrative log change macro model.

Reading guide to Chapter 3 (continued)

No

Read Powell (1981) for a view of where Johansen models fit into the general field of economy-wide modeling. This paper also contains comments on why we build models, on forecasts versus policy projections and on many other modeling issues.

The classic work on Johansen models is of course Johansen (1960). You should at least glance through the whole book and read chapter 3.

Four modern examples of Johansen models are Taylor and Black (1974), Staelin (1976), Keller (1980) and DPSV (1982). Taylor and Black analyse the effects of changes in protection in Chile under a variety of production function specifications. Staelin's study is also a model of protection, this time applied to the Ivory Coast with an emphasis on noncompetitive pricing behavior. Keller presents a very carefully explained model of tax incidence in the Netherlands while DPSV describe a large multi-purpose model of Australia. We suggest that you review at least one of these models or any other operational Johansen model that interests you. Be sure to find out (i) how the model is used (forecasts or policy projections), (ii) how the share coefficients and other parameters are estimated, (iii) what closures are adopted, (iv) what is done about linearization errors and (v) what special features there are in theoretial structure and why they are included.

Reading guide to Chapter 3 (continued)

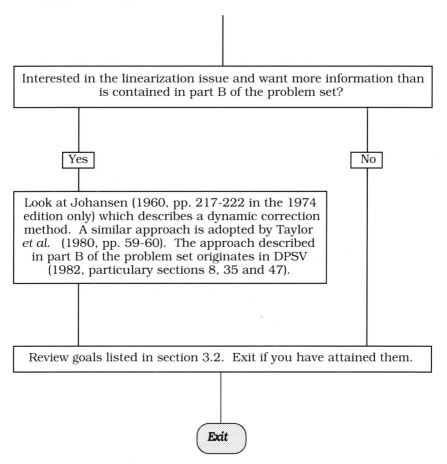

Interested in the linearization issue and want more information than is contained in part B of the problem set?

Yes

No

Look at Johansen (1960, pp. 217-222 in the 1974 edition only) which describes a dynamic correction method. A similar approach is adopted by Taylor *et al.* (1980, pp. 59-60). The approach described in part B of the problem set originates in DPSV (1982, particulary sections 8, 35 and 47).

Review goals listed in section 3.2. Exit if you have attained them.

Exit

* For full citations, see the reference list for this chapter.

References for Chapter 3

Armington, P.S. (1969) "The Geographic Pattern of Trade and the Effects of Price Changes", *IMF Staff Papers*, Vol. 16, July, 176-199.

Armington, P.S. (1970) "Adjustment of Trade Balances: Some Experiments with a Model of Trade Among Many Countries", *IMF Staff Papers*, Vol. 17, November, 488-523.

Arrow, K.J., H.B., Chenery, B.S. Minhas and R.M. Solow (1961) "Capital-Labor Substitution and Economic Efficiency", *Review of Economics and Statistics*, Vol. 43, August, 225-250.

Berndt, E.R. and D.W. Jorgenson (1973) "Production Structure", Chapter 3 in D.W. Jorgenson and H.S. Houthakker (eds), *U.S. Energy Resources and Economic Growth*, Washington D.C., Energy Policy Project.

Berndt, E.R. and D.O. Wood (1975) "Technology, Prices and the Derived Demand for Energy", *Review of Economics and Statistics*, Vol. 56 (3), August, 259-268.

Bovenberg, A.L. and W.J. Keller (1981) "Dynamics and Nonlinearities in Applied General Equilibrium Models", Department for Statistical Methods, Centraal Bureau voor de Statistiek, P.O. Box 959, 2270 Voorburg, The Netherlands, April (mimeo).

Codsi, G. and K.R. Pearson (1988) "GEMPACK: General-purpose Software for Applied General Equilibrium and Other Economic Modellers", *Computer Science in Economics and Management*, Vol. 1, 189-207.

Cohen, A.M. (1973) *Numerical Analysis*, John Wiley and Sons, New York.

Conte, S.D. and Carl de Boor (1980) *Elementary Numerical Analysis: An Algorithmic Approach*, 3rd edition, McGraw-Hill, New York.

Dahlquist, G., A. Bjorck and N. Anderson (translator) (1974) *Numerical Methods*, Prentice-Hall, Englewood Cliffs, N.J..

Deaton, A. and J. Muellbauer (1980) *Economics and Consumer Behaviour*, Cambridge University Press, New York.

Dixon, P.B., S. Bowles and D. Kendrick (1980) *Notes and Problems in Microeconomic Theory*, North-Holland, Amsterdam.

Dixon, P.B., B.R. Parmenter, J.M. Sutton and D.P. Vincent (DPSV) (1982) *ORANI: A Multisectoral Model of the Australian Economy*, North Holland, Amsterdam.

Frisch, R. (1959) "A Complete Scheme for Computing All Direct and Cross Elasticities in a Model with Many Sectors", *Econometrica*, Vol. 27, April, 177-196.

Hanoch, Giora (1971) "CRESH Production Functions", *Econometrica*, Vol. 39, September, 695-712.

Harberger, A.C. (1962) "The Incidence of the Corporation Income Tax", *Journal of Political Economy*, Vol. 70, (3) 215-240.

Houthakker, H.S. (1960) "Additive Preferences", *Econometrica*, Vol. 28, April, 244-257.

Houthakker, H.S. (1957) "An International Comparison of Household Expenditure Patterns, Commemorating the Centenary of Engel's Law", *Econometrica*, Vol. 25, 532-551.

Hudson, E.A. and D.W. Jorgenson (1974) "U.S. Energy Policy and Economic Growth", *Bell Journal of Economics and Management Science*, Vol. 5 (2), Autumn, 461-514.

Intriligator, M.D. (1971) *Mathematical Optimization and Economic Theory*, Prentice-Hall, Englewood Cliffs, N.J..

Johansen, L. (1960) *A Multisectoral Study of Economic Growth*, North-Holland, Amsterdam (second edition 1974).

Jones, R.W. (1979) *International Trade: Essays in Theory*, North-Holland, Amsterdam.

Jorgenson, D.W. (1984) "Econometric Methods for Applied General Equilibrium Modeling", Chapter 4 in H.E. Scarf and J.B. Shoven (eds), *Applied General Equilibrium Analysis*, Cambridge University Press, New York, 139-202. Also available as *Discussion Paper* no. 967, Harvard Institute for Economic Research, Harvard University, February 1983.

Katzner, D.W. (1970) *Static Demand Theory*, Macmillan, New York.

Keller, W.J. (1980) *Tax Incidence: A General Equilibrium Approach*, North-Holland, Amsterdam.

Lancaster, Kelvin (1968) *Mathematical Economics*, Macmillan, New York.

Meade, J.E. (1955) *Trade and Welfare, Mathematical Supplement* (Supplement to Volume II of *The Theory of International Policy*), Oxford University Press, Oxford.

Phlips, L. (1974) *Applied Consumption Analysis*, North-Holland/American Elsevier, Amsterdam/New York.

Powell, A.A. (1974) *Empirical Analytics of Demand Systems*, Lexington Books, D.C. Heath and Company, Lexington, Massachusetts.

Powell, A.A. (1981) "The Major Streams of Economy-wide Modeling: Is Rapprochement Possible?", Chapter 9 in J. Kmenta and J.B. Ramsey (eds) *Large-Scale Macro-Econometric Models: Theory and Practice*, North-Holland, Amsterdam, 219-264.

Powell, A.A and F.H. Gruen (1967) "The Estimation of Production Frontiers: The Australian Livestock/Cereals Complex", *Australian Journal of Agricultural Economics*, Vol. 11, June, 63-81.

Powell, A.A and F.H. Gruen (1968) "The Constant Elasticity of Transformation Frontier and Linear Supply System", *International Economic Review*, Vol. 9, 315-328.

Staelin, C.P. (1976) "A General Equilibrium Model of Tariffs in a Noncompetitive Economy", *Journal of International Economics*, Vol. 6 (1), 39-63.

Taylor, Lance (1975) "Theoretical Foundations and Technical Implications", 33-109 in C. Blitzer, P. Clark and L. Taylor (eds), *Economy-wide Models and Development Planning*, Oxford University Press for the World Bank, New York.

Taylor, Lance, Edmar L. Bacha, Eliana A. Cardoso and Frank J. Lysy (1980) *Models of Growth and Distribution for Brazil*, Oxford University Press for the World Bank, New York.

Taylor, Lance and S.L. Black (1974) "Practical General Equilibrium Estimation of Resource Pulls under Trade Liberalization", *Journal of International Economics*, Vol. 4 (1), April, 37-58.

Tewarson, Reginald P. (1973) *Sparse Matrices*, Academic Press, New York.

Vincent, D.P., P.B. Dixon and A.A. Powell (1980) "The Estimation of Supply Response in Australian Agriculture: The CRESH/CRETH Production System", *International Economic Review*, Vol. 21, February, 221-242.

Young, David M. and Robert Todd Gregory (1972) *A Survey of Numerical Mathematics*, Volume 1, Addison-Wesley, Reading, Massachusetts.

PROBLEM SET 3

A. *A STYLIZED JOHANSEN MODEL*

The implementation of a Johansen model typically includes the following steps:

(I)   the development of a *theoretical structure* consisting of

   (i)   equations representing household and other final demands for commodities,

   (ii)   equations for intermediate and primary-factor inputs,

   (iii)   pricing equations relating commodity prices to costs, and

   (iv)   market clearing equations for primary factors and commodities;

(II)   a *linearization* of the model equations to generate a system which is linear in percentage changes of the variables and in which most of the parameters are cost and sales shares;

(III)   the use of *input-output* data to provide estimates for the relevant cost and sales shares; and

(IV)   the development of *flexible computer programs* for condensing and manipulating linear systems.

In Exercises 3.1 – 3.6 we use a simple Johansen model to give you an overview of the four steps. We refer to this model as the Stylized Johansen model.

Exercise 3.1   *The theoretical structure for the Stylized Johansen model*

In this exercise, we ask you to derive the equations for a simple Johansen model. The model has two commodities, two primary factors and one final user (the household sector). We use the subscript 0 to refer to the final user. Subscripts 1 and 2 denote the two commodities and the two industries which produce them. Subscripts 3 and 4 refer to the primary factors labor and capital. We assume that:

(i)   the household sector chooses its consumption levels of goods 1 and 2 (X_{10} and X_{20}) to maximize the Cobb-Douglas utility function

$$U = X_{10}^{\alpha 10} X_{20}^{\alpha 20}$$ (E3.1.1)

subject to the budget constraint

$$P_1 X_{10} + P_2 X_{20} = Y,$$ (E3.1.2)

where Y is the household expenditure level, and P_1 and P_2 are the prices of goods 1 and 2. α_{10} and α_{20} are positive parameters summing to one.

(ii)   industry j, for j = 1 and 2, chooses its inputs X_{1j}, X_{2j}, X_{3j} and X_{4j} to minimize

$$C_j = \sum_{i=1}^{4} P_i X_{ij}$$ (E3.1.3)

subject to

$$X_j = A_j X_{1j}^{\alpha 1j} X_{2j}^{\alpha 2j} X_{3j}^{\alpha 3j} X_{4j}^{\alpha 4j},$$ (E3.1.4)

where the X_{ij}s are the purchases of good 1, good 2, labor and capital by industry j; X_j is the output of good j by industry j; and A_j and the α_{ij}s are positive parameters with

$$\sum_{i=1}^{4} \alpha_{ij} = 1.$$

Thus, we assume that whatever industry j's output level might be, the industry will minimize the costs of producing that output. In (E3.1.4) we assume that j's production technology is Cobb-Douglas.

(iii)   our model accounts for all costs so that in each industry the value of output equals the value of the inputs. That is,

$$C_j = P_j X_j = \sum_{i=1}^{4} X_{ij} P_i \text{ , for j = 1,2 .} \qquad \text{(E3.1.5)}$$

(iv) output levels for goods 1 and 2 (X_1 and X_2) and employment levels for labor and capital (X_3 and X_4) satisfy

$$\sum_{j=0}^{2} X_{ij} = X_i \text{ , i = 1,2,} \qquad \text{(E3.1.6)}$$

and

$$\sum_{j=1}^{2} X_{ij} = X_i \text{ , i = 3,4.} \qquad \text{(E3.1.7)}$$

Equation (E3.1.6) implies that demands equal supplies for goods 1 and 2. For primary factors, we simply assume that demands are satisfied, i.e., total employment of labor (X_3) is the sum of the demands for labor by the two industries. Similarly, the employment of capital (X_4) is the sum of the demands for capital by the two industries.

(v) the household budget (Y) equals factor income, that is

$$Y = P_3 X_3 + P_4 X_4 \text{ .} \qquad \text{(E3.1.8)}$$

Now do the following:

(a) Show that the household demand functions are
$$X_{i0} = \alpha_{i0} Y / P_i, \qquad i = 1,2 \text{ .} \qquad \text{(E3.1.9)}$$

(b) Prove that the production function (E3.1.4) exhibits constant returns to scale.

(c) Show that the input demand functions for industries 1 and 2 are given by

$$X_{ij} = (\alpha_{ij} \Theta_j X_j \prod_{t=1}^{4} P_t^{\alpha_{tj}}) / P_i \text{ ,} \qquad i=1, ..., 4, \qquad j=1,2 \quad \text{(E3.1.10)}$$

where

$$\Theta_j = \left[\prod_{t=1}^{4} (\alpha_{tj})^{-\alpha_{tj}} \right] / A_j \text{ .} \qquad \text{(E3.1.11)}$$

(d) Show that α_{ij}, for i = 1, ..., 4 and j = 1,2, is the share of total costs in industry j represented by inputs of i.

(e)   Derive from (E3.1.5) and (E3.1.10) the equations

$$P_j = Q_j \prod_{t=1}^{4} P_t^{\alpha_{tj}}, \qquad j = 1,2 . \tag{E3.1.12}$$

What feature of the production functions (E3.1.4) is important in explaining why the zero-pure-profit conditions (E3.1.5) may be rewritten as relationships between prices with no quantity variables?   That is, what allows us to eliminate the X_js and X_{ij}s in going from (E3.1.5) to (E3.1.12)?

(f)   Show that once we have made assumptions (i) – (iv), then it is unnecessary to also include (v).   In fact, (E3.1.8) is derivable from (E3.1.9) and (E3.1.5) – (E3.1.7).   Thus, (E3.1.8) may be omitted from our description of the economy.

(g)   Examine the system of equations (E3.1.9), (E3.1.10), (E3.1.12), (E3.1.6) and (E3.1.7).   Assume that these equations are satisfied by

$\bar{X}_{i0}$, i=1,2; $\bar{X}_{ij}$, i=1, ..., 4, j=1,2; $\bar{X}_i$ and $\bar{P}_i$, i=1, ..., 4; and $\bar{Y}$.

Show that they continue to be satisfied when we modify this solution by multiplying all monetary variables (i.e., $\bar{P}_i$, i=1,...,4; and $\bar{Y}$) by any $\delta > 0$ while leaving all real variables unchanged.

(h)   The system of equations (E3.1.9), (E3.1.10), (E3.1.12), (E3.1.6), (E3.1.7) and (E3.1.23)[6] is the structural form for our Stylized Johansen model.   It corresponds to the system (3.1.1) in Section 3.1.   How many variables do we have in our structural form?   How many equations?   Discuss possible closures.   Would the model be adequately closed if we set P_3 and P_4 exogenously?

Answer to Exercise 3.1

(a)   On putting the ratio of the marginal utilities of the two goods equal to the ratio of their prices, we find that

$$\alpha_{10} X_{10}^{\alpha_{10}-1} X_{20}^{\alpha_{20}} \Big/ \alpha_{20} X_{10}^{\alpha_{10}} X_{20}^{\alpha_{20}-1} = P_1 / P_2 .$$

This equation can be simplified and rearranged as

$$\alpha_{10} P_2 X_{20} = \alpha_{20} P_1 X_{10} .$$

---

6   (E3.1.23) is found in the answer to part (g) of this exercise.

Now we substitute $P_1 X_{10}$ out of the budget constraint (E3.1.2) to obtain

$$\left((\alpha_{10}/\alpha_{20}) + 1 \right) P_2 X_{20} = Y .$$

On recalling that $\alpha_{10} + \alpha_{20} = 1$, we establish (E3.1.9).

Notice that the αs are budget shares. Under a Cobb-Douglas utility function, the share of household expenditure going to each good is independent of commodity prices and the level of total expenditure.

(b) Imagine an initial situation in which the input levels are $\bar{X}_{ij}$, i = 1, ..., 4, giving an output of $\bar{X}_j$. Now assume that all input levels are multiplied by $\delta > 0$ leading to a new output level, $\bar{\bar{X}}_j$. (E3.1.4) implies that

$$\bar{X}_j = A_j \prod_{i=1}^{4} \bar{X}_{ij}^{\alpha_{ij}} \tag{E3.1.13}$$

and

$$\bar{\bar{X}}_j = A_j \prod_{i=1}^{4} \left(\delta \bar{X}_{ij} \right)^{\alpha_{ij}} \tag{E3.1.14}$$

Since $\sum_i \alpha_{ij} = 1$, we can rewrite (E3.1.14) as

$$\bar{\bar{X}}_j = \delta A_j \prod_{i=1}^{4} \bar{X}_{ij}^{\alpha_{ij}} . \tag{E3.1.15}$$

Hence,

$$\bar{\bar{X}}_j = \delta \bar{X}_j . \tag{E3.1.16}$$

Equation (E3.1.16) shows that the new output level is δ times the old one. This establishes that (E3.1.4) exhibits constant returns to scale.

(c) The first-order conditions for industry j's cost minimization problem are

$$\alpha_{ij}(X_j/X_{ij}) = P_i/\lambda \quad \text{for } i=1, ..., 4 \tag{E3.1.17}$$

and

$$X_j = A_j \prod_{t=1}^{4} X_{tj}^{\alpha_{tj}} . \tag{E3.1.18}$$

where λ is the Lagrangian multiplier. To go from these five equations to the four input demand functions, we must eliminate λ. Our strategy is to obtain an expression for λ in terms of input prices and output. Then we substitute this expression back into (E3.1.17).

We start by rearranging (E3.1.17) as

$$X_{ij} = \lambda \alpha_{ij} X_j / P_i \ , \quad i=1, \ldots, 4. \tag{E3.1.19}$$

Now we substitute from (E3.1.19) into (E3.1.18). On simplifying the resulting equation by taking into account that the αs sum to one, we find that

$$\lambda = Q_j \prod_{t=1}^{4} P_t^{\alpha_{tj}} \ , \tag{E3.1.20}$$

where Q_j is defined in (E3.1.11). Finally we substitute from (E3.1.20) into (E3.1.17) to obtain (E3.1.10).

(d)   We could work from the input demand functions, (E3.1.10). However, it is simpler to use (E3.1.17), from which we have

$$P_i X_{ij} / \sum_t P_t X_{tj} = \lambda \alpha_{ij} X_j / \sum_t \lambda \alpha_{tj} X_j \ . \tag{E3.1.21}$$

Since the αs sum over the first subscript to one, the right hand side of (E3.1.21) simplifies to α_{ij}. Thus α_{ij} is the share of j's costs represented by inputs of i. Just as in part (a) we found that the Cobb-Douglas utility function implies constant budget shares, here we find that the Cobb-Douglas production function implies constant cost shares.

(e)   By substituting from (E3.1.10) into (E3.1.5) we obtain

$$P_j X_j = \sum_{i=1}^{4} \alpha_{ij} Q_j X_j \prod_{t=1}^{4} P_t^{\alpha_{tj}} \ , \quad j=1,2. \tag{E3.1.22}$$

Because the αs sum to one, (E3.1.22) simplifies to (E3.1.12).

The key to the elimination of the X's is the constancy of returns to scale in the production functions (E3.1.4). Equation (E3.1.5) says that the value of output equals the cost of inputs. Equivalently, we could say that average revenue per unit of output, P_j, equals the average cost per unit output. With a constant-returns-to-scale production function, the minimum average cost per unit of output can be calculated from the input prices. It is independent of the scale of output. Consequently, P_j is independent of the scale of output. The average cost curve is flat.

(f)   On multiplying the ith members of (E3.1.6) and (E3.1.7) through by P_i, and adding the resulting equations, we obtain

$$\sum_{i=1}^{2} P_i X_{i0} + \sum_{j=1}^{2} \sum_{i=1}^{4} P_i X_{ij} = \sum_{i=1}^{4} P_i X_i \ .$$

Next we substitute from (E3.1.9) and (E3.1.5). This gives

$$Y + \sum_{j=1}^{2} P_j X_j = \sum_{i=1}^{4} P_i X_i .$$

That is,

$$Y = P_3 X_3 + P_4 X_4 .$$

This is an example of Walras' law. Once we have assumed that the total value of commodity outputs is equal to the total value of commodity demands (intermediate plus household) and that it is also equal to total costs (intermediate plus primary-factor), then we have implied that total household expenditure equals total payments to primary factors.

(g) When we use the modified solution to evaluate the left and right hand sides of (E3.1.9) we find that

$$LHS = \bar{X}_{i0} \quad \text{and} \quad RHS = \alpha_{i0} \delta \bar{Y} / \delta \bar{P}_i = \alpha_{i0} \bar{Y} / \bar{P}_i .$$

Since the original solution satisfies (E3.1.9), we know that

$$\bar{X}_{i0} = \alpha_{i0} \bar{Y} / \bar{P}_i .$$

Thus the modified solution satisfies (E3.1.9). We can establish similar results for (E3.1.10), (E3.1.12), (E3.1.6) and (E3.1.7).

We conclude that in the system (E3.1.9), (E3.1.10), (E3.1.12), (E3.1.6) and (E3.1.7), the absolute level of prices is indeterminate. It is often convenient to remove the indeterminacy by setting one of the prices at unity. We assume that

$$P_1 = 1 . \tag{E3.1.23}$$

Thus, good one becomes the numeraire or measuring stick. P_i will be the worth of good i in terms of units of good 1.

(h) Our structural form consists of 17 equations with 19 variables. To close the model we set values for two variables exogenously. One possible choice for the pair of exogenous variables is the primary factor employment levels, X_3 and X_4. This choice would be appropriate if, for example, we were interested in estimating the change in factor prices which would be required to allow a 10 per cent increase in the employment of labor over a period in which the capital stock in use was expected to increase by 5 per cent. Another possibility for the exogenous variables is P_3 and X_4. Here we might be interested in the effects of changes in wages, P_3, on the employment of labor, X_3, in the short run, i.e., a period sufficiently short for us to assume that the economy-wide capital stock, X_4, is determined independently of changes in wages.

A selection of exogenous variables which will not work is P_3 and P_4. This can be explained in at least two ways. First, look at the two-equation system (E3.1.12). This contains four variables P_1, P_2, P_3 and P_4. In part (g) we argued that P_1 can be set at unity and we added equation (E3.1.23) to our model. If we set P_3 and P_4 exogenously, we see that (E3.1.12) is a two equation system determining just one variable, P_2. Only by chance will there be a value for P_2 which is consistent with (E3.1.12), (E3.1.23) and exogenously given values for P_3 and P_4.

A second way to see that our model will not be closed adequately with P_3 and P_4 as exogenous variables is to think about what determines the size of the economy. If we did happen to have a solution for our model in which all of the Xs and Y were endogenous variables, then we would be able to generate further solutions simply by multiplying the Xs and Y by any $\delta > 0$. We would have nothing to tie down the absolute size of the economy. With P_3 and P_4 as our exogenous variables, we have over-determined the price side of our model and under-determined the real side.

Exercise 3.2   The percentage-change form of the Stylized Johansen model

Derive the percentage-change version of the structural form (E3.1.9), (E3.1.10), (E3.1.12), (E3.1.6), (E3.1.7) and (E3.1.23).

Answer to Exercise 3.2

In deriving the percentage-change form, we apply three rules:

The Product Rule, $R = \beta PQ \Rightarrow r = p + q$,

The Power Rule, $R = \beta P^\alpha \Rightarrow r = \alpha p$,

and

The Sum Rule, $R = P+Q \Rightarrow r = pS_P + qS_Q$,

where r, p and q are percentage changes[7] in R, P and Q, α and β are parameters and S_P and S_Q are the shares of P and Q in P+Q, i.e.,

$$S_P = P / (P+Q) \quad \text{and} \quad S_Q = Q / (P+Q) \ .$$

---

7   They can, equally well, be interpreted as changes in logarithms.

Each of these rules is derived by totally differentiating the levels expression. In applying the rules, we must be careful not to divide by zero. Percentage-change or log-change forms are unsuitable for variables which have initial values of zero. To overcome this difficulty, it is sometimes convenient to work with transformed variables. For example, we might include in a model the power of a tariff (one plus the *ad valorem* rate) rather than the *ad valorem* rate. If the initial value of the *ad valorem* rate is zero, then the initial value of the power of the tariff is one. We will be able to calculate percentage changes or changes in the logarithm of the power of the tariff but not in the *ad valorem* rate.

In our Stylized Johansen model, we will assume that there are no variables whose initial values are zero. Therefore, we can apply our three rules directly to the structural form (E3.1.9), (E3.1.10), (E3.1.12), (E3.1.6), (E3.1.7) and (E3.1.23). We obtain

$$x_{i0} = y - p_i \ , \quad i = 1,2, \qquad \text{(E3.2.1)}$$

$$x_{ij} = x_j - (p_i - \sum_{t=1}^{4} \alpha_{tj} \, p_t) \ , \quad i = 1, ..., 4, \, j = 1,2, \qquad \text{(E3.2.2)}$$

$$p_j = \sum_{t=1}^{4} \alpha_{tj} \, p_t \ , \quad j = 1,2, \qquad \text{(E3.2.3)}$$

$$\sum_{j=0}^{2} x_{ij} \, \beta_{ij} = x_i \ , \quad i = 1,2, \qquad \text{(E3.2.4)}$$

$$\sum_{j=1}^{2} x_{ij} \, \beta_{ij} = x_i \ , \quad i = 3,4, \qquad \text{(E3.2.5)}$$

and

$$p_1 = 0 \ , \qquad \text{(E3.2.6)}$$

where the lower case xs and ps can be interpreted either as percentage changes or log changes in the corresponding upper case variables, and

$$\beta_{ij} = X_{ij}/X_i \ , \quad i = 1, ..., 4, \quad j = 0,1,2.$$

That is, the β_{ij}s are sales shares.

It is worth pausing to examine the system (E3.2.1) – (E3.2.6). Often the assumptions underlying a model are more clearly interpretable from the percentage-change form than from the original structural form. In the present model we see from equation (E3.2.1) that all household expenditure elasticities have the value 1, all own price elasticities are –1 and all cross price elasticities are zero. In anything beyond an illustrative model, a more realistic specification would be required, especially for the expenditure elasticities. Engel's law implies that expenditure elasticities for food are usually less than one, while those for clothing and consumer durables are usually greater than one — see Houthakker (1957). Consequently, for practical work we need more general descriptions of preferences than the Cobb-Douglas utility function (E3.1.1). Perhaps the most popular choice in applied general equilibrium modeling is the Klein-Rubin or Stone-Geary utility function leading to the linear expenditure system (see Dixon, Bowles and Kendrick, 1980, E2.3).

Equation (E3.2.2) says that in the absence of changes in relative prices, industry j will change the volumes of all its inputs by the same percentage as its output. This is a consequence of assuming constant returns to scale. On the other hand, if the percentage increase in the price of input i is greater than the percentage increase in a particular index of all input prices, then industry j will substitute away from input i. Its demand for input i will expand by less than its output. The weights used in the index of input prices are the cost shares, i.e., the αs. Finally in (E3.2.2), notice that the price-substitution term could have been written as $\sigma_j(p_i - \Sigma_t \alpha_{tj} p_t)$, where $\sigma_j = 1$. In other words our price-substitution term has an implied coefficient of one. This reflects the well-known property of Cobb-Douglas production functions that the elasticity of substitution between any pair of inputs is unity. Ideally, we should for applied work adopt more general production functions so that the coefficients on the substitution terms can vary according to the input substitution possibilities available in different industries. Production specifications are discussed further in Exercises 3.9 – 3.13.

Equation (E3.2.3) says that the percentage change in the price of good j is a weighted average of the percentage changes in input prices, the weights being cost shares. Equation (E3.2.4) says that the percentage change in the supply of commodity i is a weighted average of the percentage changes in various demands for i, the weights being sales shares. Similarly, (E3.2.5) equates the percentage change in the employment of factor i to a weighted average of the percentage changes in the industrial demands for i. The weights are the shares in the total employment of i contributed by each industry. The last equation, (E3.2.6), reflects our choice of good 1 as the numeraire.

Exercise 3.3 *Input-output data and the initial solution*

(a) Use the input-output data shown in Table E3.3.1 to evaluate the parameters of the structural form (E3.1.9), (E3.1.10), (E3.1.12), (E3.1.6), (E3.1.7) and (E3.1.23). That is, evaluate α_{i0} for i = 1,2; α_{ij} for i = 1, ..., 4 and j = 1,2; and Q_j for j = 1,2.

Hint: In evaluating the Q_js, assume that the quantity units underlying the flows in Table E3.3.1 are defined so that all prices are unity.

(b) Having evaluated the parameters of the structural form, we can check any suggested set of values for prices and quantities for consistency with our model. Check that the structural form equations are satisfied by the values in the input-output table, i.e., check that the model is solved by P_i = 1 for i = 1, ..., 4, X_{11} = 4, X_{21} = 2, X_{31} = 1, X_{41} = 1, X_1 = 8, X_{12} = 2, X_{22} = 6, X_{32} = 3, X_{42} = 1, X_2 = 12, X_{10} = 2, X_{20} = 4, Y = 6, X_3 = 4 and X_4 = 2.

Answer to Exercise 3.3

(a) From (E3.1.9) we know that the α_{i0}s are budget shares. For consistency with Table E3.3.1, they should be fixed at

$$\alpha_{10} = 2/6 = 0.\underline{3} \quad \text{and} \quad \alpha_{20} = 4/6 = 0.\underline{6} ,$$

where we use the notation $0.\underline{3}$ and $0.\underline{6}$ to denote 0.33... and 0.66... .

From (E3.1.10) we know that the α_{ij}s for i = 1, ..., 4 and j = 1,2 are cost shares. The values implied by Table E3.3.1 are

$$\begin{bmatrix} \alpha_{11} & \alpha_{12} \\ \alpha_{21} & \alpha_{22} \\ \alpha_{31} & \alpha_{32} \\ \alpha_{41} & \alpha_{42} \end{bmatrix} = \begin{bmatrix} 0.5 & 0.1\underline{6} \\ 0.25 & 0.5 \\ 0.125 & 0.25 \\ 0.125 & 0.08\underline{3} \end{bmatrix}$$

To evaluate the Q_js, we need to be able to tie down the A_js; see (E3.1.11). From (E3.1.4), it is clear that the values of the A_js depend on the units chosen for quantities of inputs and outputs. We adopt the convention that one unit of good or factor i is the amount which costs 1 dollar in the base period, i.e., the period to which our input-output data refer. Thus, without explicitly evaluating the A_js, we can conclude from (E3.1.12) that

$$Q_j = 1 \text{ for } j = 1,2.$$

Table E3.3.1

Input-Output Data (Flows in dollars)

		Industry		Households	Total Sales
		1	2		
Commodity	1	4	2	2	8
	2	2	6	4	12
Primary Factors	Labor 3	1	3		4
	Capital 4	1	1		2
Production		8	12	6	

(b)   To check that the structural form equations are satisfied by the suggested values, we can substitute into left and right hand sides. For example, for i = 1, we have

LHS (E3.1.9) = 2   and   RHS (E3.1.9) = $(0.\underline{3}) \times 6/1 = 2$.

Notice that our input-output data satisfy an important balancing condition. The total value of inputs for each industry equals the total value of sales. Where the share parameters[8] of a general equilibrium model are set to be consistent with a balanced input-output table, we can always use the table to deduce an initial solution to the structural form equations. The initial solution contains information which can be valuable in computing new solutions, especially if the exogenous shocks under consideration are not too large. It is a strength of the Johansen approach that it makes full use of the initial solution as a starting point for finding new solutions.

Exercise 3.4   Input-output data and the evaluation of A(V^I)

Complete the representation in Table E3.4.1 of the linearized system formed from (E3.2.1) – (E3.2.6) when the coefficients are evaluated using the input-output data from Table E3.3.1. That is, evaluate the A(V^I) matrix.

---

[8]   In the Stylized Johansen model, the share parameters of the nonlinear structural form (the αs) are simple cost and budget shares. When we move beyond Cobb-Douglas functions, then the share parameters (e.g., the δ's in the CES form, see Exercise 3.9) are less readily interpretable. It remains true, nevertheless, that when their values are set for consistency with a balanced input-output table, then the table reveals an initial solution to the structural form.

Table E3.4.1

The Transpose* of the Matrix $A(V^I)$ for the Stylized Johansen Model: Incomplete

	(E3.2.1)		(E3.2.2)									(E3.2.3)	(E3.2.4)	(E3.2.5)	(E3.2.6)
y	−1	−1													
x_{10}	1														
x_{20}		1													
x_{11}			1												
x_{21}															
x_{31}															
x_{41}															
x_{12}															
x_{22}															
x_{32}															
x_{42}															
x_1			−1												
x_2															
x_3															
x_4															
p_1	1		.5												
p_2		1	−.25												
p_3			−.125												
p_4			−.125												

* For typographical convenience we have listed the columns of $A(V^I)$ as rows.

Answer to Exercise 3.4

See Table E3.4.2.

Exercise 3.5   Condensing the Stylized Johansen model

In a detailed Johansen model, the dimensions, m and n, of A(V) may be very large. For example, in the *ORANI* model of the Australian economy both m and n are several million. Therefore, before we try to

Table E3.4.2

Answer to Exercise 3.4: The Transpose of the Matrix $A(V^I)$ for the Stylized Johansen Model*

	(E3.2.1)		(E3.2.2)								(E3.2.3)		(E3.2.4)	(E3.2.5)	(E3.2.6)
y	−1	−1													
x_{10}	1												−.25		
x_{20}		1												−.3̲	
x_{11}			1										−.5		
x_{21}				1										−.1̲6̲	
x_{31}					1									−.25	
x_{41}						1								−.5	
x_{12}							1						−.25		
x_{22}								1						−.5	
x_{32}									1					−.75	
x_{42}										1				−.5	
x_1			−1	−1	−1	−1							1		
x_2							−1	−1	−1	−1			1		
x_3														1	
x_4															1
p_1	1		.5	−.5	−.5	−.5	.83	−.1̲6̲	−.1̲6̲	−.1̲6̲	.5	−.1̲6̲			1
p_2		1	−.25	.75	−.25	−.25	−.5	.5	−.5	−.5	−.25	.5			
p_3			−.125	−.125	.875	−.125	−.25	−.25	.75	−.25	−.125	−.25			
p_4			−.125	−.125	−.125	.875	−.083̲	−.083̲	−.083̲	.916̲	−.125	−.083̲			

*   For typographical convenience we have listed the columns of $A(V^I)$ as rows. Numbers of the form .8̲3, .1̲6, etc. are to be read as .8333..., .1666..., etc.

implement a solution of the form (3.1.10), it may be necessary to condense the linearized version of the model by eliminating some equations and variables. That is, starting from the m × n system

$$A(V)v = 0 \quad,$$

we derive a system of the form

$$A^*(V)v^* = 0$$

where A* has the dimensions $(m-r) \times (n-r)$, v* is a $(n-r)$ subvector of v and r is the number of eliminated variables.

(a)   Condense the system (E3.2.1) – (E3.2.6) by eliminating household demands, x_{i0}, $i = 1,2$, and input demands, x_{ij}, $i = 1, ..., 4$, $j = 1,2$. That is, derive a seven equation system in the nine variables, x_i, p_i, $i = 1, ..., 4$ and y.

(b)   Using the data from Table E3.3.1, compute the coefficient matrix $A^*(v^I)$ of the condensed system.

(c)   In condensing a Johansen model, what criteria would you apply in selecting the variables to be eliminated?

Answer to Exercise 3.5

(a)   We substitute the right hand sides of (E3.2.1) and (E3.2.2) into (E3.2.4) and (E3.2.5). The resulting 7×9 condensed system consists of (E3.2.3), (E3.2.6), plus

$$(y-p_i)\,\beta_{i0} + \sum_{j=1}^{2} [x_j - (p_i - \sum_{t=1}^{4} \alpha_{tj}\,p_t)]\,\beta_{ij} = x_i, \quad i = 1,2, \quad \text{(E3.5.1)}$$

and

$$\sum_{j=1}^{2} [x_j - (p_i - \sum_{t=1}^{4} \alpha_{tj}\,p_t)]\,\beta_{ij} = x_i, \quad i = 3,4, \quad \text{(E3.5.2)}$$

(b)   See Table E3.5.1.

(c)   First, we would avoid eliminating variables which we might want to set exogenously in some applications of the model. For example, we would not normally eliminate tax and tariff rates. In our Stylized Johansen model, we would not choose factor supplies or factor prices for elimination. Eliminated variables are necessarily endogenous.

Second, we would avoid eliminating key endogenous variables, those which are likely to be of interest when we are analyzing and presenting results. This criterion is not as important as the first. Eliminated variables can usually be recovered quite simply by back–solving. For example, if we used the condensed system (E3.2.3), (E3.2.6), (E3.5.1) and (E3.5.2) in computing solutions for our Stylized Johansen model, then by substituting values for x_i, p_i, $i = 1, ..., 4$ and y into (E3.2.1) and (E3.2.2) we could extend our solution to include the

Table E3.5.1
Answer to Exercise 3.5(b): The Matrix A*(V^I) for a Condensed Form of the Stylized Johansen Model

Equation Number	Variable								
	y	x_1	x_2	x_3	x_4	p_1	p_2	p_3	p_4
(E3.2.3)						.5	−.25	−.125	−.125
						−.16	.5	−.25	−.083
(E3.5.1)	−.25	.5	−.25			.7083	−.25	−.125	−.083
	−.3	−.16	.5			−.16	.7083	−.14583	−.0625
(E3.5.2)		−.25	−.75	1		−.25	−.4375	.78125	−.09375
		−.5	−.5		1	−.3	−.375	−.1875	.89583
(E3.2.6)						1			

ten eliminated variables x_{i0}, i = 1,2 and x_{ij}, i = 1, ..., 4, j = 1,2. Nevertheless, back solving involves extra coding and computer time and it should be avoided if possible. Thus, we would include industry outputs and industry employment levels in the condensed system, whereas we might exclude intermediate input flows.

Third, we would try to keep the algebra simple. Ideal targets for elimination are variables which appear in no more than one or two equations and for which we have explicit expressions in terms of variables which are to be included in the condensed system. Commodity flows to households and input flows to industries often meet this criterion. For example, in the Stylized Johansen model, (E3.2.1) and (E3.2.2) provide simple explicit expressions for x_{i0}, i = 1,2 and x_{ij}, i = 1, ..., 4, j = 1,2 in terms of variables to be included in our condensed system. In addition, each of the x_{i0} and x_{ij} appear in only one other equation of the system (E3.2.1) – (E3.2.6), namely, in the relevant market-clearing equation.

How much condensing should we do? This depends on the programs we have available for solving linear systems. For example, with the *GEMPACK* software package[9], systems containing up to 1,000

---

9   See Codsi and Pearson (1988).

equations can be solved on commonly available personal computers. Hence, condensation is often unnecessary. Even for very large models still requiring condensation, *GEMPACK* removes the algebraic drudgery, users simply being required to specify which equations are to be used to eliminate which variables. These automated condensation procedures are less prone to error than use of pencil and paper.

Exercise 3.6 *Two solution matrices for the Stylized Johansen model*

In Exercise 3.3, we saw how the input-output data in Table E3.3.1 provide an initial solution, V^I, for our Stylized Johansen model. Then in Exercise 3.4, we evaluated the coefficients of the system (E3.2.1) – (E3.2.6) at V^I. This allows us to represent the model in the linearized form

$$A(V^I)v = 0, \qquad\qquad (E3.6.1)$$

where $A(V^I)$ is the 17×19 matrix whose transpose is shown in the body of Table E3.4.2 and v is the 19×1 vector of variables listed in the left margin of the table.

To solve the model we first choose two variables to be exogenous and we rearrange (E3.6.1) as in (3.1.9). Then, as in equations (3.1.10) and (3.1.11), we compute the 17×2 matrix $B(V^I)$. This is our solution matrix. The typical element shows the elasticity at V^I of the ith endogenous variable with respect to the jth exogenous variable.

In Table E3.6.1 we have given two solution matrices. The first was computed with the exogenous variables being x_3 and x_4 (employment of labor and capital). In this computation, the columns of $A_\alpha(V^I)$ are rows 1-13 and 16-19 of the transpose of $A(V^I)$ as displayed in Table E3.4.2 and $A_\beta(V^I)$'s columns are rows 14 and 15 of the same table. In the second computation the exogenous variables are p_3 and x_4 (the price of labor and the employment of capital). In going from the first to the second computation we switched column 14 out of the $A_\beta(V^I)$ matrix into the $A_\alpha(V^I)$ matrix and column 18 out of the $A_\alpha(V^I)$ matrix and into the $A_\beta(V^I)$ matrix. You might like to use the software and data on the companion diskettes described in Chapter 1 to carry out these two simulations for yourself and to check the results in Table E3.6.1.

In using a model, it is important to be able to explain the solution matrices in some detail. Convincing applications are possible only if we can isolate the particular aspects of the model which are responsible for particular results. In this exercise, your task is to explain various aspects of our two solution matrices for the Stylized Johansen model. Specifically, where $\eta_r(R,S)$ denotes the elasticity of endogenous variable R with respect to exogenous variable S in computation r (for example, $\eta_1(Y,X_3)$ is 0.6, $\eta_2(X_{10},P_3)$ is -1.5, etc.), account for the following relationships which are apparent in Table E3.6.1:

(a)
$$\eta_r(P_1,V) = 0 \qquad (E3.6.2)$$
where V is any exogenous variable and r = 1,2.

(b)
$$\eta_r(Y,V) = \eta_r(X_{10},V), \qquad (E3.6.3)$$
and
$$\eta_r(Y,V) = \eta_r(X_{20},V) + \eta_r(P_2,V) \qquad (E3.6.4)$$
where V is any exogenous variable and r = 1,2.

(c)
$$\eta_1(P_2,X_3) < 0. \qquad (E3.6.5)$$

(d)
$$\eta_1(V,X_3) + \eta_1(V,X_4) = 1 \qquad (E3.6.6)$$
where V is any endogenous quantity or income variable, and
$$\eta_1(V,X_3) + \eta_1(V,X_4) = 0 \qquad (E3.6.7)$$
where V is any endogenous price variable.

(e)
$$\eta_2(V,X_4) = 1 \qquad (E3.6.8)$$
where V is any endogenous quantity or income variable, and
$$\eta_2(V,X_4) = 0 \qquad (E3.6.9)$$
where V is any endogenous price variable.

(f)
$$\eta_2(V,P_3) = \eta_1(V,X_3)/\eta_1(P_3,X_3) , \qquad (E3.6.10)$$
$$\eta_2(V,X_4) = \eta_1(V,X_4) - \eta_1(V,X_3) \, \eta_1(P_3,X_4)/\eta_1(P_3,X_3) , \qquad (E3.6.11)$$
$$\eta_2(X_3,P_3) = 1/\eta_1(P_3,X_3) , \qquad (E3.6.12)$$
and
$$\eta_2(X_3,X_4) = - \eta_1(P_3,X_4)/\eta_1(P_3,X_3) , \qquad (E3.6.13)$$
where V is any variable which is endogenous in both computations 1 and 2. Can you see any practical application for relationships such as (E3.6.10) – (E3.6.13)?

(g)
$$\eta_1(X_{31},X_3) = \eta_1(X_{32},X_3) = 1 , \qquad (E3.6.14)$$
$$\eta_1(X_{41},X_3) = \eta_1(X_{42},X_3) = 0 , \qquad (E3.6.15)$$
$$\eta_1(X_{31},X_4) = \eta_1(X_{32},X_4) = 0 , \qquad (E3.6.16)$$
$$\eta_1(X_{41},X_4) = \eta_1(X_{42},X_4) = 1 , \qquad (E3.6.17)$$
$$-\eta_1(P_3,X_3) + \eta_1(P_4,X_3) = 1 , \qquad (E3.6.18)$$
and
$$\eta_1(P_3,X_4) - \eta_1(P_4, X_4) = 1 . \qquad (E3.6.19)$$

Table E3.6.1

Solutions for the Stylized Johansen Model under Alternative Closures

			(1) Exogenous factor employment		(2) Exogenous wages and capital employment	
Variable Number			14	15	18	15
Elasticity of ↓	with respect to →		X_3 employment of labor	X_4 employment of capital	P_3 price of labor	X_4 employment of capital
1	Y	Household expenditure	0.6	0.4	−1.5	1
2	X_{10}	Household	0.6	0.4	−1.5	1
3	X_{20}	demands	0.7	0.3	−1.75	1
4	X_{11}	Intermediate	0.6	0.4	−1.5	1
5	X_{21}	and primary	0.7	0.3	−1.75	1
6	X_{31}	factor inputs to	1	0	−2.5	1
7	X_{41}	industry 1	0	1	0	1
8	X_{12}	Intermediate	0.6	0.4	−1.5	1
9	X_{22}	and primary	0.7	0.3	−1.75	1
10	X_{32}	factor inputs to	1	0	−2.5	1
11	X_{42}	industry 2	0	1	0	1
12	X_1	Commodity	0.6	0.4	−1.5	1
13	X_2	supplies	0.7	0.3	−1.75	1
14	X_3	Employment	N.A.	N.A.	−2.5	1
15	X_4	levels	N.A.	N.A.	N.A.	N.A.
16	P_1	Commodity	0	0	0	0
17	P_2	and factor	−0.1	0.1	0.25	0
18	P_3	prices	−0.4	0.4	N.A.	N.A.
19	P_4		0.6	−0.6	−1.5	0

N.A. (not applicable). The variable indicated in the row is exogenous.

Answer to Exercise 3.6

(a) Recall from (E3.2.6) that the price of good 1 is fixed in all computations.

(b) Equations (E3.6.3) and (E3.6.4) follow from the household demand equations (E3.2.1). For interpreting (E3.6.3), it is again necessary to recall that the price of good 1 is fixed.

(c)   What we must explain is why an increase in the employment of labor, with the employment of capital held constant, reduces the price of good 2.

There are two avenues in the Stylized Johansen model for absorbing extra labor without changing the economy-wide employment of capital. First, there could be an increase in the labor/capital ratios of both[10] industries. This would require a reduction in the price of labor relative to that of capital leading to a reduction in the price of the labor intensive commodity relative to that of the capital intensive commodity. A glance at Table E3.3.1 is sufficient to convince us that good 2 is relatively labor intensive.

The second avenue is to increase the output of the labor intensive good (good 2) relative to that of the capital intensive good (good 1). Again this would require a reduction in P_2 relative to P_1. Otherwise, the change in the commodity composition of demands would not match the change in the composition of supply. Thus, with P_1 fixed, P_2 must fall if extra labor is to be absorbed through either avenue.

(d)   Equations (E3.6.6) – (E3.6.7) imply that a one per cent increase in the employment of both scarce factors causes all real quantities and income to increase by one per cent with no changes in any prices. This reflects an absence of scale effects. In the Stylized Johansen model there are constant returns to scale in production and unitary income elasticities in consumption. Therefore, if we increase the employment of both labor and capital by one per cent, we can arrive at the new equilibrium without any changes in prices by

   (i)   increasing household income by one per cent causing

   (ii)   increases of one per cent in all household commodity demands which can be satisfied by

   (iii)   one per cent expansions in all commodity outputs which are made possible by

   (iv)   one per cent increases in all inputs (primary and intermediate).

(e)   With the closure used in computation 2, capital is the only scarce factor. Equations (E3.6.8) and (E3.6.9) imply that if the wage rate is held constant, then a one per cent increase in the employment

---

10   From (E3.2.2) we find that: $x_{31} - x_{41} = P_4 - P_3 = x_{32} - x_{42}$. Hence, the labor/capital ratios in the two industries cannot move in opposite directions.

of the scarce factor leads to a uniform one per cent expansion in the real side of the economy with no price changes. This result again reflects an absence of scale effects. Again we can arrive at the new equilibrium by a simple sequence. First we increase the employment of capital by one per cent in each industry without any changes in prices. Then we must increase all other inputs in both industries by one per cent – otherwise we would violate the cost minimizing input demand equations (E3.2.2). This means that we have increases of one per cent in the outputs of both commodities. Since the use of both commodities as intermediate inputs has increased by one per cent, we can be sure that there are one per cent increases in the quantities left over for household consumption. Finally, we note that the increase in factor employment has expanded household income by one per cent. Thus we have an equilibrium because the increase in the availability of commodities for household consumption is matched by the increase in household demand.

(f) $\eta_2(V,P_3)$ is the percentage change in variable V arising from a one per cent increase in the wage rate holding constant the employment of capital. Obviously we can compute $\eta_2(V,P_3)$ by adopting closure 2 and by setting $p_3 = 1$ and $x_4 = 0$. Alternatively we could adopt closure 1. Then the percentage change in variable V is given by

$$v = \eta_1(V,X_3)x_3 + \eta_1(V,X_4)x_4 \ . \tag{E3.6.20}$$

Also we have

$$p_3 = \eta_1(P_3,X_3)x_3 + \eta_1(P_3,X_4)x_4 \ . \tag{E3.6.21}$$

If we now want to compute the effect on V of a one per cent increase in wages with zero effect on the employment of capital, we can evaluate v in (E3.6.20) – (E3.6.21) with $p_3 = 1$ and $x_4 = 0$. This gives (E3.6.10).

To obtain (E3.6.11) we first note that $\eta_2(V,X_4)$ is the percentage change in variable V arising from a one per cent increase in the employment of capital, holding constant the wage rate. Thus, $\eta_2(V,X_4)$ may be found by computing v in (E3.6.20) – (E3.6.21) with $x_4 = 1$ and $p_3 = 0$. This gives

$$v = \eta_1(V,X_4) - \eta_1(V,X_3)\eta_1(P_3,X_4) / \eta_1(P_3,X_3),$$

establishing (E3.6.11).

Equation (E3.6.12) is derived by using (E3.6.21) to evaluate x_3 when $p_3 = 1$ and $x_4 = 0$. Finally (E3.6.13) follows if we evaluate x_3 in (E3.6.21) with $x_4 = 1$ and $p_3 = 0$.

Relationships such as (E3.6.10) – (E3.6.13) enable us to go from one closure to another without having to repeat the partitioning and solving steps described in (3.1.9) – (3.1.11). By applying these relationships to the results in Table E3.6.1 for closure 1, we can deduce any of the results for closure 2.

Computations similar to this are often useful in analysing simulation results. For example, imagine that we are trying to interpret a set of results on the effects of increases in tariffs computed under the assumption that the real wage rate adjusts to ensure that there is no change in aggregate employment. We may wish to see how the results are affected if we adopt the alternative assumption that it is employment which adjusts rather than the real wage rate. This requires a change of closure with aggregate employment becoming endogenous and the real wage rate becoming exogenous. By using relationships such as (E3.6.10) — (E3.6.13), results for key variables under the new closure can be computed conveniently with a pocket calculator.

(g) The first step in understanding (E3.6.14) – (E3.6.19) is to recognize that in the Stylized Johansen model the ratio of the value of output in industry 1 (Z_1) to that in industry 2 (Z_2) will never change. This would be obvious if there were no intermediate inputs. Then the values of outputs from industries 1 and 2 would equal the values of household demands for commodities 1 and 2. Under the Cobb-Douglas utility function, (E3.1.1), value shares in household expenditure are constant which would imply that value shares in total production would be constant also.

With intermediate inputs in the story, the constancy of Z_1/Z_2 depends on the Cobb-Douglas specification of the production functions as well as that of the utility function. The Cobb-Douglas production functions mean that in each industry the share of each input in the total value of output is constant. Thus, in the Stylized Johansen model implemented with the data in Table E3.3.1, we know that the value of commodity 1 used in the production of commodity 1 will always be $\frac{1}{2}Z_1$ and that value of commodity 1 used in the production of commodity 2 will always be $\frac{1}{6}Z_2$. Since the value of household consumption of commodity 1 will always be one third of total expenditure (Y), we can write:

$$Z_1 = \tfrac{1}{2}Z_1 + \tfrac{1}{6}Z_2 + \tfrac{1}{3}Y \quad . \tag{E3.6.22}$$

Similarly

$$Z_2 = \tfrac{1}{4}Z_1 + \tfrac{1}{2}Z_2 + \tfrac{2}{3}Y \quad , \tag{E3.6.23}$$

implying that

$$Z_1 = \tfrac{4}{3}Y \quad \text{and} \quad Z_2 = 2Y \quad , \tag{E3.6.24}$$

giving

$$Z_1/Z_2 = 2/3 \quad . \tag{E3.6.25}$$

Now that we have shown that Z_1/Z_2 is constant, it is also clear that X_{i1}/X_{i2} is constant for i = 1, ...,4. Remember that input value shares in Z_1 and Z_2 are constant and that input prices do not vary across industries. In particular, the employment of labor will always be allocated between the two industries in the base period proportions, i.e., 25 per cent to industry 1 and 75 per cent to industry 2. Similarly, the employment of capital will always be allocated 50 per cent to industry 1 and 50 per cent to industry 2. Therefore, if there is an x per cent increase in the aggregate employment of labor, there must be an x per cent increase in the employment of labor in each industry. If we put x equal to one, we have explained (E3.6.14) and, if we put it equal to zero we have explained (E3.6.16). Equations (E3.6.15) and (E3.6.17) follow in a similar way when we consider x per cent increases in the aggregate capital stock with x = 0 and x = 1. Finally, if there is an increase in the employment of labor of one per cent in each industry with no change in the employment of capital, then P_4/P_3 must increase by one per cent – otherwise there would be changes in the labor and capital shares in the values of industry output. Consequently we observe (E3.6.18). Similarly, if the employment of capital increases by one per cent in each industry with no change in the employment of labor, then P_3/P_4 must increase by one per cent. This leads to (E3.6.19).

B. ELIMINATING JOHANSEN'S LINEARIZATION ERRORS

Given a vector V which satisfies the structural equations (3.1.1), the Johansen method allows us to evaluate the derivatives or elasticities of the endogenous variables with respect to the exogenous variables. By totally differentiating the system (3.1.1) and applying the matrix operations described in (3.1.9) – (3.1.11) we obtain a matrix B(V) of either derivatives or elasticities at the point V. Johansen (1960) evaluated his B matrix at V^I, the vector of prices and quantities revealed by his base-period input-output data. He then calculated the effects on the endogenous variables (v_α) of changes in the exogenous variables (v_β) according to (3.1.11). The well-known weakness of this calculation is that it fails to allow for changes in the derivative or elasticity matrix, B(V), as V moves away from V^I.

The first step in overcoming this weakness is to recognize that we are dealing with a problem treated in detail in texts on numerical analysis. We have a system of the form

$$F(V_\beta, V_\alpha) = 0 \quad .$$

We assume that the system has a solution of the form

$$V_\alpha = G(V_\beta)$$

where $$F(V_\beta, G(V_\beta)) = 0$$

for all V_β in a neighborhood of an initial point, V_β^I. While we do not know the form of the G functions, we do know how to evaluate a matrix B(V) which has the property that

$$\nabla G(V_\beta) = B(V)$$

for all V satisfying the structural equations, where $\nabla G(V_\beta)$ is the matrix of partial derivatives of G and V_β is the exogenous subvector of V. Thus our problem is the standard one of numerical integration, i.e., given a starting point V^I and a formula for $\nabla G(V_\beta)$ evaluate

$$\Delta V_\alpha = G(V_\beta^F) - G(V_\beta^I)$$

where V_β^F and V_β^I are the final and initial values of the exogenous variables.

Having recognized the nature of our problem, we are free to solve it by using one of the numerous methods described in texts on numerical analysis.[11] These methods can be applied in our situation by multi-step Johansen procedures. In Exercises 3.7 and 3.8 we ask you to apply the Euler method where the shifts, $(V_\beta^F - V_\beta^I)$, in the exogenous variables are broken into n equal parts or possibly n equal percentage parts. Conceptually this is the simplest approach and it has, as was mentioned in Section 3.1, proved adequate in applications to the solution of general equilibrium models. Nevertheless, it would be possible in multi-step Johansen computations to adopt strategies which normally generate faster convergence to the true solution as we increase the number of steps, e.g. the strategy of Runge and Kutta, (see Cohen, 1973, Chapter 11).

Exercise 3.7   An introductory example of a multi-step Johansen computation

In this exercise we return to the system (3.1.2). Assume, as we did in Section 3.1, that V_3 is the exogenous variable and that initial values for the variables are given by (3.1.4).

(a)   Use a two-step Johansen procedure to compute the effects on V_1 and V_2 of a 100 per cent increase in V_3. Base the calculations on (3.1.7), i.e., do the calculations using percentage changes in the variables. In the first step, calculate the effects on V_1 and V_2 of moving V_3 from 1 to 1.5. Then reevaluate the

---

11   See for example, Cohen (1973), Dahlquist, Bjorck and Anderson (1974) and Conte and de Boor (1980).

elasticities of V_1 and V_2 with respect to V_3. In the second step, use the reevaluated elasticities in calculating the effects on V_1 and V_2 of moving V_3 from 1.5 to 2.

(b)   Use a 4-step Johansen procedure to compute the effects on V_1 and V_2 of a 100 per cent increase in V_3. In the first step, increase V_3 from 1 to 1.25. In the second, increase V_3 from 1.25 to 1.50, etc. Continue to work with percentage changes rather than log changes.

(c)   At this stage we have three Johansen-style estimates based on (3.1.7) of the values of V_1 and V_2 after a 100 per cent increase in V_3: the one-step estimate (0.5, 1.5) derived in Section 3.1 via equation (3.1.16) and the 2- and 4-step estimates obtained in parts (a) and (b) of this exercise. In Table E3.7.1, we have done some more arithmetic and added the 8-step estimate. Can you see a relationship between these four estimates? How could we extrapolate from the one- and two-step results to obtain improved estimates of the effects on V_1 and V_2 of a 100 per cent increase in V_3? Can you provide an extrapolation using all four sets of results?

Answer to Exercise 3.7

(a)   In this example we have

$$\begin{bmatrix} v_1 \\ v_2 \end{bmatrix} = B(V) \, v_3 \quad , \tag{E3.7.1}$$

where

$$B(V) = - \begin{bmatrix} 2 & 0 \\ V_1/2 & V_2/2 \end{bmatrix}^{-1} \begin{bmatrix} 1 \\ 0 \end{bmatrix} = \begin{bmatrix} -0.5 \\ 0.5V_1/V_2 \end{bmatrix}. \tag{E3.7.2}$$

We interpret the v_is as percentage changes.

In the first step of the two-step procedure we use

$$\begin{bmatrix} v_1 \\ v_2 \end{bmatrix}_{1,2} = B(V^I)50 = \begin{bmatrix} -25 \\ 25 \end{bmatrix}$$

as our estimate of the percentage effects on V_1 and V_2 of moving V_3 from 1 to 1.5. Thus, at the end of the first step, V has moved from (1,1,1) to

$$(V)_{1,2} = (0.75, \ 1.25, \ 1.5)$$

where we use the notation $(V)_{r,s}$ to denote the value of V at the end of the rth step of an s-step procedure.

In the second step of the two-step procedure we use

$$\begin{bmatrix} v_1 \\ v_2 \end{bmatrix}_{2,2} = B\big((V)_{1,2}\big)\; 33\tfrac{1}{3} = \begin{bmatrix} -16.\underline{6} \\ 10 \end{bmatrix}$$

as our estimate of the percentage effects on V_1 and V_2 of moving V_3 from 1.5 to 2. Hence, our final estimate of V in the two-step procedure is

$$(V)_{2,2} = (0.625,\ 1.375,\ 2)\ . \tag{E3.7.3}$$

On comparing (3.1.4) and (E3.7.3) we conclude that a 100 per cent increase in V_3 induces a 37.5 per cent reduction in V_1 and a 37.5 per cent increase in V_2.

(b)   Our calculations give

$$\begin{bmatrix} v_1 \\ v_2 \end{bmatrix}_{1,4} = \begin{bmatrix} -12.5 \\ 12.5 \end{bmatrix} \qquad \text{leading to } (V)_{1,4}\ =\ (0.875,\ 1.125,\ 1.25),$$

$$\begin{bmatrix} v_1 \\ v_2 \end{bmatrix}_{2,4} = \begin{bmatrix} -10 \\ 7.\underline{7} \end{bmatrix} \qquad \text{leading to } (V)_{2,4} = (0.7875,\ 1.2125,\ 1.5),$$

$$\begin{bmatrix} v_1 \\ v_2 \end{bmatrix}_{3,4} = \begin{bmatrix} -8.\underline{3} \\ 5.4124 \end{bmatrix} \text{leading to } (V)_{3,4} = (0.7219,\ 1.2781,\ 1.75)\ ,$$

and finally

$$\begin{bmatrix} v_1 \\ v_2 \end{bmatrix}_{4,4} = \begin{bmatrix} -7.1429 \\ 4.0342 \end{bmatrix} \qquad \text{leading to } (V)_{4,4} = (0.6703,\ 1.3297,\ 2).$$

We conclude from the four-step procedure that a 100 per cent increase in V_3 induces a 32.97 per cent reduction in V_1 and a 32.97 per cent increase in V_2.

(c)   Let us denote the result for variable i from a procedure with step size h by $V_i(h)$. (For example, in Table E3.7.1, $V_2(\tfrac{1}{8}) = 1.3103$). We make two assumptions. First that

$$\lim_{h \to 0} V_i(h) = V_i^T \tag{E3.7.4}$$

where V_i^T, i = 1,2, is the true value for variable i after we increase V_3 to 2. V_1^T and V_2^T can be derived from (3.1.3) and are shown in the last row of Table E3.7.1 as 0.7071 and 1.2929. Our second assumption is that $V_i(h)$ can be expressed as

$$V_i(h)\ =\ \sum_{r=0}^{\infty} a_{ir} h^r\ ,\ i = 1,2, \tag{E3.7.5}$$

over the relevant range for h (in our example [0,1]).

Table E3.7.1

Solutions for V_1 and V_2 in the System (3.1.2) when V_3 is moved from 1 to 2: Calculations based on (3.1.7) [a]

Endogenous Variables	V_1	V_2
Initial Values	1	1
Estimated values after an increase in V_3 from 1 to 2		
1 - step computation	0.5	1.5
2 - step computation	0.625	1.375
4 - step computation	0.6703	1.3297
8 - step computation	0.6897	1.3103
1,2 step extrapolation [b]	0.75	1.25
1,2,4 step extrapolation [c]	0.7041	1.2959
1,2,4,8 step extrapolation [d]	0.7073	1.2927
Truth [e]	0.7071	1.2929

(a)   The calculations were done in percentage changes with the change in V_3 divided into equal parts. For example, in the first step of the 2-step calculation, we set $100(dV_3)/V_3 = 50$ thus moving V_3 from 1 to 1.5. In the second step we set $100(dV_3)/V_3 = 33.\underline{3}$, moving V_3 from 1.5 to 2.

(b)   Computed according to (E3.7.9).

(c)   Computed according to (E3.7.14).

(d)   Computed according to (E3.7.16).

(e)   Computed using (3.1.3).

Assumption (E3.7.4) says that by making the step size sufficiently small, i.e., by taking a sufficient number of steps, we can get arbitrarily close to the true answer. In other words, our n-step procedure converges to the true solution as n becomes large. If you want to read about convergence conditions, look under Euler's method in an intermediate text on numerical analysis, e.g., Young and Gregory (1972, pp. 441-449) and Conte and de Boor (1980, pp. 359-362). Convergence conditions are studied in detail in the specific context of a Johansen model in Dixon *et al.* (1982, section 35).

Assumption (E3.7.5) relies on the idea that continuous functions can be approximated arbitrarily closely by polynomials of sufficiently

high degree – see Young and Gregory (1972, p. 308).[12]   Notice that
(E3.7.4) and (E3.7.5) together imply that

$$V_i^T = a_{i0} \ , i = 1,2 \ . \tag{E3.7.6}$$

Now suppose that $V_i(h)$ can be approximated by

$$V_i(h) = a_{i0} + a_{i1}h \ , \ i = 1,2 \ . \tag{E3.7.7}$$

In (E3.7.7) we are assuming that the higher order terms in (E3.7.5) can
be ignored in the relevant range for h.   If (E3.7.7) were valid, then we
would have

$$V_i(h/2) - V_i(h) = -(a_{i1}/2)h \ , \ i = 1,2 \ . \tag{E3.7.8}$$

In particular, we would have

$$V_i(1/2) - V_i(1) = -(a_{i1}/2) \ ,$$

$$V_i(1/4) - V_i(1/2) = -(a_{i1}/2) \ (1/2)$$

and

$$V_i(1/8) - V_i(1/4) = -(a_{i1}/2) \ (1/4) \ , \ i = 1,2 \ .$$

Hence we would find that the gaps between the answers from the one-
and two-step procedures would be twice the gaps between the answers
from the two- and four-step procedures.   Similarly, the two/four gaps
would be twice the size of the four/eight gaps.   On looking at Table
E3.7.1 we see that these relationships are approximately satisfied.   For
example, the results for V_1 give

$$V_1(1/2) - V_2(1) = 0.125 \approx 0.0906 = 2(V_1(1/4) - V_1(1/2)) \ ,$$

and

$$V_1(1/4) - V_1(1/2) = 0.0453 \approx 0.0388 = 2(V_1(1/8) - V_1(1/4)) \ .$$

The importance of approximations such as (E3.7.7) is that they
often allow us to achieve adequate accuracy with multiple-step Johansen
computations even though our computer budget may be sufficient for
only a small number of steps.   Assume, for example, that we are able to
make only a one-step computation and a two-step computation.   In
terms of our example, we are able to evaluate $V_i(1)$ and $V_i(1/2)$ for i =
1,2.   Then (E3.7.7) suggests that we should estimate V_i^T by solving for
a_{i0} in the equations

$$V_i(1) = a_{i0} + a_{i1},$$

$$V_i(1/2) = a_{i0} + a_{i1}/2 \ .$$

---

12   It might be objected that h takes only the values 1, $\frac{1}{2}$, $\frac{1}{4}$, etc. and is not a
continuous variable. To overcome this problem, we can imagine that if h is
0.4, for example, then our procedure is to increase V_3 from 1 to 1.4, then
from 1.4 to 1.8 and finally from 1.8 to 2. If h = 0.7, we move V_3 from 1 to 1.7
and then from 1.7 to 2, etc.

That is, we should estimate V_i^T by extrapolation from our one- and two-step solutions according to

$$V_i^T = 2V_i(1/2) - V_i(1), \quad i = 1,2. \tag{E3.7.9}$$

The results of applying (E3.7.9) are shown in Table E3.7.1 in the row labelled *1,2 step extrapolation*.

If our computer budget is a little less limited so that we can afford to make one-, two- and four-step computations, then we can replace (E3.7.9) by a more sophisticated extrapolation equation. First, we replace (E3.7.7) by the improved approximation

$$V_i(h) = a_{i0} + a_{i1}h + a_{i2}h^2 . \tag{E3.7.10}$$

Then, assuming that we have computed $V_i(h)$, $V_i(h/2)$ and $V_i(h/4)$, we solve for a_{i0} in the system of equations

$$V_i(h) = a_{i0} + a_{i1}h + a_{i2}h^2 , \tag{E3.7.11}$$

$$V_i(h/2) = a_{i0} + (a_{i1}/2)h + (a_{i2}/4)h^2 , \tag{E3.7.12}$$

$$V_i(h/4) = a_{i0} + (a_{i1}/4)h + (a_{i2}/16)h^2 , \tag{E3.7.13}$$

The solution for a_{i0} can be obtained by first multiplying (E3.7.11) by -1, (E3.7.12) by 6, (E3.7.13) by -8 and then adding the resulting equations. This gives

$$-V_i(h) + 6V_i(h/2) - 8V_i(h/4) = -3a_{i0} ,$$

leading to the extrapolation equation

$$V_i^T = (8/3) V_i(h/4) - 2V_i(h/2) + (1/3)V_i(h) . \tag{E3.7.14}$$

Application of (E3.7.14) in our example with $h = 1$ gives the results shown in Table E3.7.1 in the row labelled *1,2,4 step extrapolation*.

When $V_i(h)$, $V_i(h/2)$, $V_i(h/4)$ and $V_i(h/8)$ are available, we can improve the approximation (E3.7.7) to

$$V_i(h) = a_{i0} + (a_{i1})h + a_{i2}h^2 + a_{i3}h^3 . \tag{E3.7.15}$$

Then following a strategy similar to that which lead to (E3.7.9) and (E3.7.14) we can derive the extrapolation equation

$$V_i^T = (64/21)V_i(h/8) - (56/21)V_i(h/4) + (14/21)V_i(h/2) - (1/21)V_i(h). \tag{E3.7.16}$$

Application of (E3.7.16) in Table E3.7.1 gives the results in the row labelled *1,2,4,8 step extrapolation*.

Readers who are familiar with the numerical-methods literature will recognize equations (E3.7.9), (E3.7.14) and (E3.7.16) as examples of Richardson's extrapolation.[13] Extrapolation techniques can usefully supplement any computational procedure where the aim is to evaluate F(h) in the limit as h approaches zero by computing a sequence $F(h_1)$, $F(h_2)$,.... for $h_1 > h_2 > ... > 0$. Dahlquist, Bjorck and Anderson (1974, p. 270), in referring to an extrapolation procedure, comment that: "This process is, in many numerical problems — especially the treatment of integral and differential equations — the simplest way to get results which have negligible truncation error".

Exercise 3.8   *A multi-step computation for the Stylized Johansen model*

Figure E3.8.1 is a flow diagram for a multi-step solution of a Johansen model. To start the computations (box 1), we must read in the input-output data (Table E3.3.1 for our Stylized model). Normally, we would also read in various substitution parameters. In the Stylized model, this is not necessary. Under the Cobb-Douglas specifications in this model, all the substitution elasticities are unity, and need not appear explicitly in our computations. Other data which can be supplied at the initial stage of the computations are the closure (i.e., the choice of exogenous variables), the shocks (i.e., the changes in the exogenous variables) and the number of steps to be used (denoted by s). Finally, we set a counter, r, which will keep track of how many steps have been completed.

The arithmetic starts in box 2 with an evaluation of either an A matrix or a condensed version of one. Condensing is not necessary in the Stylized model. We will work with the system (E3.2.1) – (E3.2.6). With our counter, r, at zero, the A matrix is evaluated using the initial input-output data. We denote this initial A matrix by $A((V)_{0,s})$ where $(V)_{r,s}$ is the vector of values attained by the variables at the end of r steps of an s-step procedure. $(V)_{0,s}$, which has previously been denoted as V^I, reflects the prices and quantities implied by the initial input-output data. For our Stylized model, $A((V)_{0,s})$ was derived in Exercise 3.4 and is displayed in Table E3.4.2.

On reaching box 3 with r = 0, we compute the shocks to be made to the exogenous variables in the first step of the computation, i.e., we evaluate the vector $(v_\beta)_{1,s}$. Many sensible schemes are available for dividing the total change in each exogenous variable into s parts. For example, in Exercise 3.7(a) where s was 2, we broke the total change (from 1 to 2) in the exogenous variable (which was V_3) into a

---

13   See especially Dahlquist, Bjorck and Anderson (1974, pp. 269-273).

pair of equal parts. Our first step was to compute the effects of moving V_3 from 1 to 1.5. In the second step we moved V_3 from 1.5 to 2. Because we interpreted the v_is as percentage changes, the total change in the V_3 was implemented as $(v_3)_{1,2} = 50$ followed by $(v_3)_{2,2} = 33.\underline{3}$.

Alternatively we could have broken the changes in the exogenous variable into equal percentage parts i.e.,

$$(v_3)_{r,2} = (\sqrt{2} - 1)100 = 41.4213 \qquad \text{for } r = 1,2. \qquad (E3.8.1)$$

Another possibility was to interpret the v_is as log changes. and to break the change in V_3 into equal logarithmic parts, i.e.,

$$(v_3)_{r,2} = \tfrac{1}{2} [ln(2) - ln(1)] = 0.34657 \qquad \text{for } r = 1,2 . \qquad (E3.8.2)$$

We suspect that the choice between schemes such as equal changes and equal percentage or log changes is not often an important one.

Box 4 of Figure E3.8.1 is where the shifts in the endogenous variables at each step are computed. First, the A matrix is partitioned into A_α consisting of the columns corresponding to the endogenous variables, and A_β consisting of the columns corresponding to the exogenous variables. Then the system of equations

$$A_\alpha((V)_{r,s})(v_\alpha)_{r+1,s} + A_\beta((V)_{r,s})(v_\beta)_{r+1,s} = 0 \qquad (E3.8.3)$$

is solved for $(v_\alpha)_{r+1,s}$. This can be done by computing $B((V)_{r,s})$ which is given by

$$B((V)_{r,s}) = - \left[A_\alpha((V)_{r,s}) \right]^{-1} A_\beta((V)_{r,s}) \ ,$$

and then post multiplying by $(v_\beta)_{r+1,s}$. In evaluating B matrices, computational costs can be kept low by avoiding the inversion of A_α. If B is a matrix of elasticities, the jth column, $(B._j)$, can be computed by considering the effects on the endogenous variables of a one per cent increase in the jth exogenous variable holding constant all other exogenous variables. If B is a matrix of derivatives, then we can consider the effects of a unit increase in the jth exogenous variable. Thus, in either case, we can compute $B._j$ by applying efficient methods[14] to the solution of the system

$$A_\alpha B._j = -(A_\beta)._j \ , \qquad (E3.8.4)$$

---

[14] In the context of Johansen models, these include Jacobi, Gauss-Seidel and other sparse matrix methods (see, for example, Tewarson, 1973) which take advantage of the fact that usually only a small fraction (less than 10 per cent) of the components of A_α are non-zero.

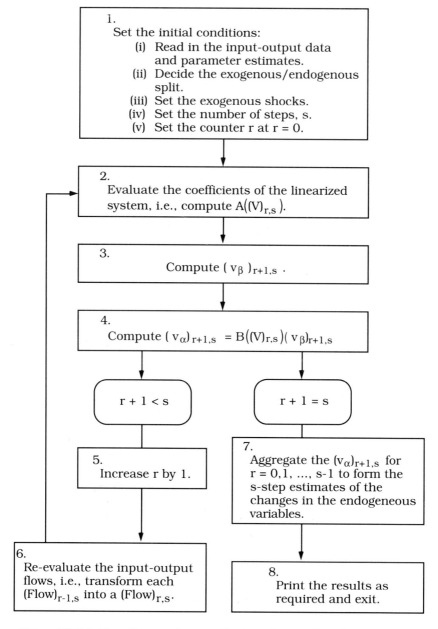

Figure E3.8.1 Flow diagram for a multi-step solution of a Johansen model

where $(A_\beta)._j$ is the jth column of A_β. In our Stylized model where there are only 2 exogenous variables, B matrices can be evaluated by solving just two systems of linear equations of the form (E3.8.4).[15] $B((V)_{0,s})$ matrices for two alternative closures of the Stylized model are displayed in Table E3.6.1.

With the completion of the work in box 4, we have come to the end of the $(r+1)^{th}$ step of our computation. Assuming that r+1 is less than s, we move to box 5. There we increase r by 1 and we commence the next step.

Our first task (box 6) in the new step is to update the input-output data taking account of changes in prices and quantities occurring in the previous step. For example, if we are just commencing the second step (r=1), then we will be concerned with how each input-output flow has been changed from its initial value, $(Flow)_{0,s}$, by the changes in prices and quantities in the first step. If our computations are being done in percentage changes, then when we reach box 6 with $r = \rho$, we can compute the updated flows according to

$$(Flow)_{\rho,s} = (Flow)_{\rho-1,s}(1 + 0.01p_{\rho,r})(1 + 0.01x_{\rho,s}) \quad , \quad (E3.8.5)$$

where $p_{\rho,s}$ and $x_{\rho,s}$ are the percentage changes in the ρth step in the relevant price and quantity. We can also use this formula when the computations are done in changes in the variables. However, we need an extra set of computations to get from results for changes in prices and quantities to the percentage changes required in (E3.8.5). If the computations are done in log changes, then a convenient updating formula is

$$(Flow)_{\rho,s} = exp[ln(Flow)_{\rho-1,s} + p_{\rho,s} + x_{\rho,s}] \quad (E3.8.6)$$

where $p_{\rho,s}$ and $x_{\rho,s}$ are log changes computed in step ρ.

Once the input-output data have been updated, we return to box 2. There, the A matrix is reevaluated using cost and sales shares computed from the updated input-output flows. Thus, at each step, the coefficients in the A matrix incorporate the effects on cost and sales shares of changes in prices and quantities taking place at previous steps.

The computations continue until eventually we pass through box 4 with r+1 = s. At this stage we have completed s steps. We can now

---

15 In large models we never evaluate the whole of B. By working with condensed systems we can limit our computations to selected rows. By applying (E3.8.4) for a subset of js we can limit our computations to selected columns.

compute the s-step estimates of the values reached by the endogenous variables given the total shocks in the exogenous variables. The relevant formulae for endogenous variable k are

$$(V_k)_{s,s} = (V_k)_{0,s} + \sum_{\rho=1}^{s} (v_k)_{\rho,s} \qquad \text{(E.3.8.7)}$$

when the v_ks are changes,

$$(V_k)_{s,s} = (V_k)_{0,s} \prod_{\rho=1}^{s} \left(1 + 0.01(v_k)_{\rho,s}\right) \qquad \text{(E.3.8.8)}$$

when the v_ks are percentage changes, and

$$(V_k)_{s,s} = exp\left[ln(V_k)_{0,s} + \sum_{\rho=1}^{s} (v_k)_{\rho,s} \right] \qquad \text{(E.3.8.9)}$$

when the v_ks are log changes. Rather than reporting the levels $(V_k)_{s,s}$, it is normally of more interest to report the percentage effects on the endogenous variables of the changes in the exogenous variables. The s-step estimates of these percentage effects can be computed as

$$100\big((V_k)_{s,s} - (V_k)_{0,s}\big) / (V_k)_{0,s} \ .$$

(a)   Use a sequence of calculations of the type outlined in Figure E3.8.1 to provide a two-step solution for the Stylized Johansen model. Assume that the initial situation is that depicted in Table E3.3.1. Assume that the exogenous variables are P_3 and X_4. Compute the effects of a 50 per cent increase (from 1 to 1.5) in the wage rate, P_3, holding constant the capital stock, X_4.

Hint: You will need only a pocket calculator if you work with log changes and use the information in Table E3.6.1. So that you can compare each stage of your calculations with ours, we suggest that you implement the 50 per cent increase in P_3 as two increases of $\frac{1}{2}ln(1.5)$ in $ln(P_3)$, i.e, put $(p_3)_{1,2} = (p_3)_{2,2} = \frac{1}{2}ln(1.5)$.

(b)   What is the true solution for the effects on the endogenous variables of a 50 per cent increase in P_3? Can you write down the solution functions? That is, can you express Y, X_{10}, X_{20}, etc. as functions of P_3 and X_4?

Answer to Exercise 3.8

(a) Following the procedure outlined in Figure E3.8.1, we start by setting r at zero. The first arithmetic operation (box 2) is the evaluation of $A((V)_{0,s})$. This has been done in Exercise 3.4 and the answer is displayed in Table E3.4.2. Moving on to box 3, we accept the hint and set

$$(v_\beta)_{1,2} = \begin{bmatrix} p_3 \\ x_4 \end{bmatrix}_{1,2} = \begin{bmatrix} \frac{1}{2}ln(1.5) \\ 0 \end{bmatrix} = \begin{bmatrix} 0.20273 \\ 0 \end{bmatrix}. \qquad (E.3.8.10)$$

Most of the computation in box 4 was completed in Exercise 3.6 where $B((V)_{0,2})$ was computed for the relevant closure (P_3, X_4 exogenous) and displayed in the right panel of Table E3.6.1. The vector $(v_\alpha)_{1,2}$ can be evaluated simply by multiplying the P_3-column of Table E3.6.1 by 0.20273. This gives

$$(v_\alpha)_{1,2} = (y, x_{10}, x_{20}, x_{11}, x_{21}, x_{31},$$

$$x_{41}, x_{12}, x_{22}, x_{32}, x_{42}, x_1,$$

$$x_2, x_3, p_1, p_2, p_4)_{1,2}$$

$$= \quad (-0.30410, -0.30410, -0.35478, -0.30410, -0.35478, -0.50683,$$

$$0, -0.30410, -0.35478, -0.50683, 0, -0.30410,$$

$$-0.35478, -0.50683, 0, 0.05068, -0.30410).$$

Since s = 2 and r+1 is currently at 1, we move to box 5. There, r is increased to 2 taking us through to box 6. In box 6 we reevaluate the initial input-output flows from Table E3.3.1 according to formula (E3.8.6). Thus, for example, we have

$$(\text{Flow 1 to 1})_{1,2} = exp[ln(\text{Flow 1 to 1})_{0,2} + (p_1)_{1,2} + (x_{11})_{1,2}]$$
$$= exp[ln(4) + 0 - 0.30410] = 2.9511.$$

The complete set of updated flows is in Table E3.8.1.

It is apparent that in generating Table E3.8.1, we have deflated each flow in Table E3.3.1 by the same percentage. Thus, in this particular example, when we return to box 2, we find that $A((V)_{1,2})$ is the same as the initial A matrix displayed in Table E3.4.2. This is because the elements of A are either ratios of flows (cost and sales shares) or constants. In box 3, we set p_3 and x_4 at the same values as they had in previous step, i.e., 0.20273 and 0. Since we arrive at box 4 with the same A matrix and v_β vector as in previous step, we emerge with the same v_α, that is

$$(v_\alpha)_{2,2} = (v_\alpha)_{1,2}.$$

Table E3.8.1

Input-Output Data after 1 Update; (Flow i to j)$_{1,2}$ in Dollars

		Industry		Households	Total Sales
		1	2		
Commodity	1	2.9511	1.4756	1.4756	5.9022
	2	1.4756	4.4267	2.9511	8.8534
Primary Factors	3	0.7378	2.2134		2.9511
	4	0.7378	0.7378		1.4756
Production		5.9022	8.8534	4.4267	

With r+1 at 2, we move to box 7. The two-step estimates of the values of the endogenous variables after a 50 per cent increase in P_3 can now be computed using (E3.8.9). For the first variable, household expenditure, we obtain

$$(Y)_{2,2} = exp[ln(Y_{0,2}) + y_{1,2} + y_{2,2}]$$
$$= exp[ln(6) - 0.30410 - 0.30410] = 3.2660.$$

Thus, our two-step estimate is that a 50 per cent increase in p_3 will reduce household expenditure by 45.57 per cent. Similarly we find that there are reductions of 45.57 per cent in X_{10}, X_{11}, X_{12}, X_1, and P_4. There are reductions of 50.81 per cent in X_{20}, X_{21}, X_{22}, and X_2. For X_{31}, X_{32} and X_3 the reductions are 63.71 per cent. P_2 increases by 10.67 per cent and there are no changes in X_{41}, X_{42} and P_1.

(b)   Apart from rounding errors, the two-step solution obtained in part (a) is the true solution. One way of checking this is by substitution back into the structural form (E3.1.9), (E3.1.10), (E3.1.12), (E3.1.6), (E3.1.7) and (E3.1.23). For example, consider the household demand equations (E3.1.9). With i = 1, we have

LHS = $(X_{10})_{2,2} = (0.5443)(X_{10})_{0,2} = (0.5443)(2) = 1.0886$

and

RHS = $\alpha_{10}(Y)_{2,2}/(P_1)_{2,2} = (0.\underline{3})(0.5443)(6)/1 = 1.0886$.

In this particular example, substitution back into the structural equations may not be the cleverest way of establishing that the two-step solution is free from linearization error. Nevertheless, it is illustrative of the method that is available in most models for checking the validity

Table E3.8.2

Input-Output Data after 2 Updates; (Flow i to j)$_{2,2}$ in Dollars †

		Industry		Households	Total Sales
		1	2		
Commodity	1	2.1773	1.0887	1.0887	4.3546
	2	1.0887	3.2660	2.1773	6.5320
Primary Factors	3	0.5443	1.6330		2.1773
	4	0.5443	0.5443		1.0887
Production		4.3546	6.5320	3.2660	

†These flows can be computed using (E3.8.6) with ρ = s = 2.

of a suggested solution. In a few very large models, it may be too cumbersome to substitute into the left and right hand sides of every structural equation. In such cases, a useful minimum check is provided by the post-solution input-output table, i.e., the table of flows implied by the suggested solution. To obtain this table, we can make an extra update of the input-output flows by carrying out the computations in box 6 of Figure E3.8.1 with r = s. (The post-solution input-output flows for the computations in part (a) are given in Table E3.8.2.) Violations of the row and column sum balancing conditions in the post-solution input-output table would imply that the suggested solution is inconsistent with the structural equations requiring that for each industry the value of inputs equals the value of output and for each commodity the value of output equals the value of sales.

Normally, substitution of an s-step solution into the structural equations would produce discrepancies between left and right hand sides beyond what could be explained by rounding errors. We would also expect there to be differences between the ith row and i^{th} column sums of the post-solution input-output table. We would be satisfied with the s-step solution if we judged the various discrepancies to be sufficiently small. In our Stylized model, however, we find that multi-step solutions computed with log changes produce no non-rounding discrepancies. This indicates that the solution equations are log linear. They are, in fact,

$$Y = C_1 X_4 P_3^{-1.5}, \ X_{10} = C_2 X_4 P_3^{-1.5}, \ ..., P_4 = C_{17} P_3^{-1.5},$$

where the exponents on the right hand sides have been taken from the right panel of Table E3.6.1 and the C_is are constants whose values can be determined from the initial data in Table E3.3.1. For example, C_1 is 6/2.

C.   ON DERIVING PERCENTAGE-CHANGE FORMS

The problems in this section provide practice in deriving percentage- or log-change[16] forms for demand and supply systems associated with a variety of production and utility functions and production possibilities frontiers. By the time you finish these problems, we hope that you will feel confident about deriving percentage-change forms for any of the specifications you are likely to want to use in practice.

Exercise 3.9   *Linearizing the input demand functions from a CES production function*[17]

Assume that a firm facing given input prices, $P_1, ..., P_n$, chooses input levels, $X_1, ..., X_n$, so they minimize the cost, $\Sigma_i P_i X_i$, of producing a given output, Y, subject to the CES (constant elasticity of substitution) production function

$$Y = A \left[\sum_{i=1}^{n} \delta_i X_i^{-\rho} \right]^{-1/\rho} \tag{E3.9.1}$$

where A and the δ_is are positive parameters with $\Sigma_i \delta_i = 1$ and ρ is a parameter whose value is greater than or equal to -1 but not equal to zero.[18]

Derive the percentage-change form for the input demand functions. Avoid corner solutions by assuming that $\rho > -1$.

---

16   Percentage-change and log-change forms are identical. For expositional simplicity we refer in the remainder of this section to percentage changes only.

17   The CES production function was first applied by Arrow, Chenery, Minhas and Solow (1961). For an exercise which develops the properties of the CES production function in detail, see Dixon, Bowles and Kendrick (1980, Exercise 4.20).

18   As ρ approaches zero, (E3.9.1) approaches a Cobb-Douglas form, see Dixon, Bowles and Kendrick (1980, E4.20).

Answer to Exercise 3.9

The first-order conditions for cost minimization are that there exists Λ such that Λ and the X_ks jointly satisfy

$$P_k = \Lambda A \left[\sum_{i=1}^{n} \delta_i X_i^{-\rho} \right]^{-(1+\rho)/\rho} \delta_k X_k^{-(1+\rho)} , \quad k = 1, ..., n \quad \text{(E3.9.2)}$$

and

$$Y = A \left[\sum_{i=1}^{n} \delta_i X_i^{-\rho} \right]^{-1/\rho} . \quad \text{(E3.9.3)}$$

By using (E3.9.3), we can replace (E3.9.2) with the more convenient equations

$$P_k = \Lambda A^{-\rho} Y^{(1+\rho)} \delta_k X_k^{-(1+\rho)} , \quad k = 1, ..., n. \quad \text{(E3.9.4)}$$

In percentage change form (E3.9.4) and (E3.9.3) can be written as

$$p_k = \lambda + (1+\rho)y - (1+\rho)x_k \quad \text{(E3.9.5)}$$

and

$$y = \sum_k S_k x_k \quad \text{(E3.9.6)}$$

where p_k, λ, y and x_k are percentage changes in P_k, Λ, Y and X_k, and

$$S_k = \delta_k X_k^{-\rho} / \left(\sum_i \delta_i X_i^{-\rho} \right) \quad \text{for all } k. \quad \text{(E3.9.7)}$$

Equation (E3.9.4) implies that

$$P_k X_k / \sum_i P_i X_i = \delta_k X_k^{-\rho} / \sum_i \delta_i X_i^{-\rho} . \quad \text{(E3.9.8)}$$

Thus, S_k is the share of input k in total costs.

From (E3.9.5) we find that

$$x_k = -\sigma p_k + \sigma \lambda + y \quad \text{(E3.9.9)}$$

where σ is the positive parameter defined by

$$\sigma = 1 / (1+\rho) . \quad \text{(E3.9.10)}$$

Substitution from (E3.9.9) into (E3.9.6) gives

$$y = -\sigma \sum_k S_k p_k + \sigma \lambda + y$$

leading to

$$\lambda = \sum_k S_k p_k . \quad \text{(E3.9.11)}$$

Now we substitute from (E3.9.11) into (E3.9.9) to obtain the percentage change form for the input demand functions:

$$x_k = y - \sigma \left(p_k - \sum_{i=1}^{n} S_i p_i \right) \quad \text{for } k = 1, ..., n. \quad \text{(E3.9.12)}$$

Equation (E3.9.12) says that in the absence of price changes, all input volumes move by the same percentage as output. This reflects the constancy of the returns to scale exhibited by the production function (E3.9.1). If the price of input k rises relative to a cost-share weighted index of all input prices, then the use of input k will fall relative to output (i.e., X_k/Y will decline). There will be substitution away from input k. The strength of this substitution effect depends on the size of the parameter σ, which is the elasticity of substitution between any pair of inputs.

It is worth noting that in our derivation of the percentage change form, (E3.9.12), we worked with a percentage change version of the first-order conditions (E3.9.2) and (E3.9.3). This approach is usually easier than the alternative where the input demand functions are first derived and then linearized.

Exercise 3.10 Linearizing the input demand functions from a CRESH production function[19]

Assume that the production function has the CRESH (constant ratios of elasticities of substitution, homothetic) form, i.e.,

$$\sum_{i=1}^{n} \left[\frac{X_i}{Y}\right]^{h_i} \frac{Q_i}{h_i} = \alpha \qquad (E3.10.1)$$

where Y is output, the X_is are inputs and the Q_is, h_is and α are parameters. Each h_i is less than 1 but not equal to zero. Each Q_i is positive and the Q_is and α are normalized so that $\sum_i Q_i = 1$. In general, α can have either sign but if each of the Q_i/h_i has the same sign, then α must have their common sign. As in Exercise 3.9, derive a percentage-change form for the input demand functions assuming that the firm treats input prices, P_k, k = 1, ..., n, as beyond its control and chooses its input levels to minimize the cost of producing any given level of output.

Answer to Exercise 3.10

The first-order conditions for cost minimization are that there exists Λ such that Λ and the X_ks jointly satisfy

$$P_k = \Lambda \left[\frac{X_k^{h_k-1}}{Y^{h_k}}\right] Q_k \ , \qquad k = 1, ..., n \quad (E3.10.2)$$

---

19   CRESH functions were introduced by Hanoch (1971). For an exercise which develops the properties of the CRESH production function in detail, see Dixon, Bowles and Kendrick (1980, Exercise 4.21).

and

$$\sum_{i=1}^{n} \left[\frac{X_i}{Y}\right]^{h_i} \frac{Q_i}{h_i} = \alpha .$$ (E3.10.3)

In percentage change form (E3.10.2) and (E3.10.3) can be written as

$$p_k = \lambda + (h_k-1)x_k - h_k y, \qquad k = 1, ..., n$$ (E3.10.4)

and

$$\sum_{i=1}^{n} h_i(x_i-y)W_i = 0$$ (E3.10.5)

where p_k, λ, y and x_k are percentage changes in P_k, Λ, Y and X_k, and

$$W_i = \left[\frac{X_i}{Y_i}\right]^{h_i} \frac{Q_i}{h_i}, \qquad i = 1, ..., n.$$ (E3.10.6)

By multiplying (E3.10.2) through by X_k, we can show that

$$h_k W_k \Big/ \sum_{i=1}^{n} h_i W_i = S_k, \qquad k = 1, ..., n,$$

where S_k is the share of input k in total costs. Hence, (E3.10.5) may be rewritten as

$$\sum_{k=1}^{n} S_k x_k = y.$$ (E3.10.7)

Next, we rearrange (E3.10.4) as

$$x_k = \left[\frac{1}{h_k-1}\right] (p_k - \lambda + h_k y).$$ (E3.10.8)

Then by substitution into (E3.10.7) we find that

$$y = \sum_k \frac{S_k}{(h_k-1)} (p_k - \lambda + h_k y) .$$ (E3.10.9)

Hence,

$$\lambda = y + \sum_k S_k^* p_k$$ (E3.10.10)

where S_k^* is the modified cost share defined by

$$S_k^* = \frac{S_k/(1-h_k)}{\sum_i S_i/(1-h_i)} .$$ (E3.10.11)

Now we substitute from (E3.10.10) into (E3.10.8) to obtain the percentage-change form for the input demand functions as

$$x_k = y - \sigma_k(p_k - \Sigma_i S_i^* p_i) , \qquad k = 1, ..., n, \qquad (E3.10.12)$$

where σ_k is the positive parameter defined by

$$\sigma_k = 1/(1-h_k). \qquad (E3.10.13)$$

Equation (E3.10.12) differs from (E3.9.12), which we derived for the CES case, in two respects. First, the weights used in computing the average movement in the input prices are 'modified' cost shares rather than cost shares. Second, (E3.10.12) generalizes (E3.9.12) by allowing the coefficient, σ_k, on the relative price term to vary across inputs.

Exercise 3.11 Supply response functions with CET and CRETH transformation frontiers[20]

Assume that a firm facing given prices, $P_1, ..., P_m$, for its m products chooses its output levels, $Y_1, ..., Y_m$, to maximize total revenue, $\Sigma_i P_i Y_i$, subject to the CET (constant elasticity of transformation) production possibilities frontier

$$Z = B \left[\sum_{i=1}^{m} \gamma_i Y_i^{-\rho} \right]^{-1/\rho} \qquad (E3.11.1)$$

where B and the γ's are positive parameters with $\Sigma_i \gamma_i = 1$ and ρ is a parameter whose value is less than or equal to -1.[21] Z is a measure of the firm's overall capacity to produce or activity level. The value of Z depends on the quantities of inputs. In the present problem, where we are determining the composition of the firm's output, we will treat Z as an exogenous variable.

---

20   CET functions were first applied by Powell and Gruen (1967 and 1968). CRETH functions were first applied by Vincent, Dixon and Powell (1980). CRETH functions are used in modeling the agricultural sector in the *ORANI* model of the Australian economy, see Dixon, Parmenter, Sutton and Vincent (1982, pp. 68-94 and 191-194).

21   The CET form is identical to the CES form apart from the restriction on ρ. With CES, ρ is greater than or equal to -1; with CET, ρ is less than or equal to -1. In the CES case, the contours are concave from above. In the CET case, the contours are concave from below.

(a)   Sketch the production possibilities frontier assuming that m = 2, $\gamma_1 = \gamma_2 = 1/2$, B = 1, Z = 1 and $\rho = -2$.

(b)   What happens to the production possibilities frontier as Z changes?

(c)   Assume that m = 2, $\gamma_1 = \gamma_2 = 1/2$, B = 1 and Z = 1. Describe how the shape of the production possibilities frontier changes as ρ moves from −1 towards negative infinity.

(d)   In this problem we are assuming that the product composition of the firm's output can be determined independently of the composition of the firm's inputs. Describe the circumstances under which such an assumption would be appropriate.

(e)   Derive percentage-change forms for the firm's supply response functions; i.e., relate the percentage changes, y_k, k = 1, ..., m, in output levels to the percentage change, z, in total capacity or activity and the percentage changes, p_k, k = 1, ..., m, in the product prices. To avoid corner solutions, assume that $\rho < -1$.

(f)   Replace the CET function (E3.11.1) by the more general CRETH (constant ratios of elasticities of transformation, homothetic) function,

$$\sum_{i=1}^{m} \left[\frac{Y_i}{Z}\right]^{h_i} \frac{V_i}{h_i} = \beta, \qquad (E3.11.2)$$

where the V_is, h_is and β are parameters. Each h_i is greater than 1, while β and each of the V_is is positive with $\Sigma_i V_i = 1$.[22] Derive a percentage-change form for the supply response functions.

Answer to Exercise 3.11

(a)   With the parameters set at the given values, we have

$$2 = Y_1^2 + Y_2^2. \qquad (E3.11.3)$$

Assuming that only nonnegative values are allowed for the Y_is, the production possibilities frontier is the quarter circle, ATB, shown in Figure E3.11.1.

(b)   Changes in Z produce radial expansions and contractions of the production possibilities frontier. If we increase input levels sufficiently

---

22   The CRETH form is identical to the CRESH form (see Exercise 3.10) apart from the restrictions on the h_is.

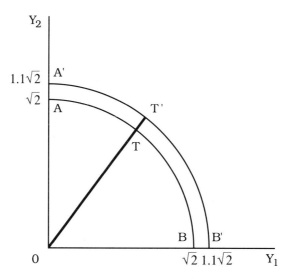

Figure E3.11.1 The quarter circle production possibilities frontier

ATB is the production possibilities frontier for the special case of (E3.11.1) where m = 2, $\gamma_1 = \gamma_2 = 0.5$, B = 1, Z = 1 and ρ = -2. A'T'B' is the production possibilities frontier after Z has been increased by 10 per cent.

to increase Z by, for example, 10 per cent, then we can increase the output of each commodity by 10 per cent.   All points on the new production possibilities frontier can be obtained by drawing rays (e.g., OT in Figure E3.11.1) from the origin to the initial production possibilities frontier and then extending their lengths by 10 per cent (to T').

(c)   With the given parameter values, the production possibilities frontier, (E3.11.1), is

$$Z = \left[\tfrac{1}{2}Y_1^{-\rho} + \tfrac{1}{2}Y_2^{-\rho}\right]^{-1/\rho} . \qquad (E3.11.4)$$

Its slope is given by[23]

$$Slope = -\frac{\partial Z/\partial Y_1}{\partial Z/\partial Y_2} = -\left(Y_1/Y_2\right)^{-\rho-1} . \qquad (E3.11.5)$$

---

[23]   When the axes are labeled as in Figure E3.11.1, the slope of the production possibilities frontier is (apart from sign) the marginal rate of transformation of good 1 into good 2, i.e., the rate of increase in the output of good 2 made possible per unit reduction in the output of good 1.

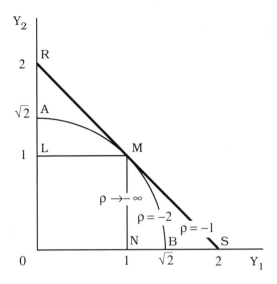

Figure E3.11.2 Production possibilities frontiers given by (E3.11.4) when
ρ = −1, −2 and − ∞

RMS is the production possibilities frontier given by (E3.11.4) when ρ = −1.
As ρ approaches negative infinity, the production possibilities frontier
approaches LMN. The quarter circle AMB is reproduced from Figure
E3.11.1 for the case ρ = −2.

If ρ = −1, then (E3.11.4) reduces to

$$Z = \frac{1}{2}Y_1 + \frac{1}{2}Y_2$$

and the production possibilities frontier is a straight line. In this case,
goods 1 and 2 are perfectly transformable. If ρ approaches negative
infinity, then at points where Y_1/Y_2 is less than one, (E3.11.5) implies
that the slope of the production possibilities frontier approaches zero.
At points where Y_1/Y_2 is greater than one, the slope approaches
negative infinity. Thus, with Z = 1, the production possibility frontier
moves closer and closer to LMN in Figure E3.11.2 as ρ approaches
negative infinity. In the extreme case, goods 1 and 2 will be produced
in fixed proportions and revenue maximizing production will be at point
M irrespective of commodity prices.

(d)   The assumption is appropriate only if the inputs are of a
general-purpose nature. For example, in modeling the agricultural production of a particular region, we could assume that the use of labor,

farm machinery, fertilizer and land gives the region a capacity (measured by Z) to produce. We might describe the creation of this capacity by

$$Z = f(L, K, F, N)$$

where f is a concave function[24] (perhaps of the CES or CRESH variety studied in Exercises 3.9 and 3.10) and L, K, F and N are inputs of labor, capital, fertilizer and land. Because these inputs are of a general-purpose nature, we might assume that the capacity to produce can be used to generate a variety of combinations of, say, wheat and wool, with the possible combinations being described by (E3.11.1) or some other convex function.[25] On the other hand, if silo space (wheat-specific) and shearing (wool-specific) were included among our inputs, then we could not separate the determination of the input-mix from that of the output-mix. The input and output mixes would need to be considered simultaneously.

(e) The first-order conditions for revenue maximization are that there exists Λ such that Λ and the Y_ks jointly satisfy

$$P_k = \Lambda B \left[\sum_{i=1}^{m} \gamma_i Y_i^{-\rho} \right]^{-(1+\rho)/\rho} \gamma_k Y_k^{-(1+\rho)}, \qquad k = 1, ..., m \quad (E3.11.6)$$

and

$$Z = B \left[\sum_{i=1}^{m} \gamma_i Y_i^{-\rho} \right]^{-1/\rho}. \qquad (E3.11.7)$$

---

24   f is a concave function on the convex set $S \subset \mathbf{R}^n$ if and only if

$$f[\alpha x + (1-\alpha)y] \geq \alpha f(x) + (1-\alpha)f(y) \text{ for all } \alpha \in [0,1] \text{ and } x,y \in S$$

(see Katzner (1970, p. 183)). The usual single-output production functions exhibiting constant or diminishing returns to scale and having isoquants of the familiar shape are concave on the positive orthant.

25   f is a convex function on the convex set $S \subset \mathbf{R}^n$ if and only if

$$f[\alpha x + (1-\alpha)y] \leq \alpha f(x) + (1-\alpha)f(y) \text{ for all } \alpha \in [0,1] \text{ and } x,y \in S$$

(see Katzner (1970, p.183)). Production possibilities functions exhibiting constant or diminishing returns to scale with production possibilities frontiers of the usual shape are convex on the positive orthant. Note that a production possibilities function exhibits diminishing returns to scale if a 1 per cent (say) increase in the output of all commodities requires a greater than one per cent increase in capacity (Z in this exercise). By contrast, a production function exhibits diminishing returns to scale if a 1 per cent increase in all inputs produces less than a one per cent increase in capacity.

By repeating the steps that took us from (E3.9.2) and (E3.9.3) to (E3.9.12), we can go from (E3.11.6) and (E3.11.7) to the percentage-change form

$$y_k = z - \theta(p_k - \Sigma_i R_i p_i) , \qquad k = 1, ..., m, \qquad (E3.11.8)$$

where θ is the negative[26] parameter defined by $\theta = 1/(1+\rho)$ and the Rs are revenue shares defined by $R_k = P_k Y_k / \Sigma_i P_i Y_i$, for all k.

The interpretation of (E3.11.8) is similar to that of (E3.9.12). In the absence of price changes, all output volumes move by the same percentage as overall capacity. This reflects the constancy of the returns to scale exhibited by the production possibilities function (E3.11.1). If the price of product k rises relative to a revenue-share weighted index of all product prices, then the output of k will rise relative to productive capacity (i.e., Y_k/Z will increase). There will be be transformation towards product k. The strength of this transformation effect depends on the size of the parameter θ which is the elasticity of transformation between any pair of outputs.

(f) By following the method used in Exercise 3.10, we find that

$$y_k = z - \theta_k(p_k - \Sigma_i R_i^* p_i) , \quad k = 1, ..., m, \qquad (E3.11.9)$$

where θ_k is the negative parameter defined by $\theta_k = 1/(1-h_k)$ and the R*s are modified revenue shares defined by

$$R_k^* = \frac{R_k/(1-h_k)}{\Sigma_i R_i/(1-h_i)} ,$$

with the Rs being revenue shares.

Equation (E3.11.9) differs from the corresponding equation, (E3.11.8), for the CET case in the same ways as (E3.10.12) differs from (E3.9.12). First, the weights used in computing the average movement in output prices are 'modified' revenue shares rather than revenue shares. Second, (E3.11.9) generalizes (E3.11.8) by allowing the coefficient, θ_k, on the relative price term to vary across outputs.

Exercise 3.12 *The translog unit cost function*

The transcendental logarithmic or translog function is a convenient specification for unit cost functions and indirect utility functions. It underlies much of the econometric work by Dale

---

26   Remember that $\rho < -1$.

Jorgenson and others[27] on systems of sectoral input demand equations and household consumption equations. Of particular importance to the further development of applied general equilibrium economics as an empirical field is Jorgenson's (1984) paper "Econometric methods for applied general equilibrium modeling" in which nested translog unit cost and indirect utility functions are estimated at a disaggregated level with U.S. data. In this exercise, we ask you to review the properties of the translog unit cost function.[28]

The translog unit cost function has the form

$$ln Q(P) \;=\; A + \sum_i B_i ln P_i + \frac{1}{2} \sum_i \sum_j C_{ij}(ln P_i)(ln P_j) \quad , \quad \text{(E3.12.1)}$$

where $Q(P)$ is the cost per unit of output[29] when the input prices are $P' = (P_1, P_2, ..., P_n)$[30] and A, B_i and C_{ij} are parameters with $C_{ij} = C_{ji}$ for all $i \neq j$.[31]

(a)   What restrictions should the B_is and C_{ij}s satisfy to ensure that Q is homogeneous of degree one with respect to input prices?

(b)   Assuming that (E3.12.1) is a legitimate description of the relationship between unit costs and input prices, derive a percentage-change form for the input demand functions convenient for use in a Johansen model.

---

27   Early applications of translog functions include Berndt and Jorgenson (1973), and Berndt and Wood (1975). See also Hudson and Jorgenson (1974) where translog unit cost functions form part of a general equilibrium model of U.S. energy usage. Recent work is reported in Jorgenson (1984).

28   For an exercise on the properties of cost functions in general, see Dixon, Bowles and Kendrick (1980, Exercise 4.17).

29   We assume that the underlying production function exhibits constant returns to scale. Otherwise, unit costs would not be independent of the output level. See Exercise 3.1(e).

30   We assume that all prices are greater than zero. The RHS of (E3.12.1) is not defined unless P > 0.

31   Let C be the $n \times n$ matrix of C_{ij}s. If C were not symmetric, then we could simply rewrite (E3.12.1) with our initial C matrix replaced by the symmetric matrix $\frac{1}{2}(C+C')$. Therefore, no loss of generality is incurred by assuming that we have chosen a symmetric C matrix.

(c)   In estimating the parameters of (E3.12.1) we can use the fact that cost functions are concave with respect to input prices.[32] What parameter restrictions are suggested by concavity?

Hint: Part (c) is rather difficult. We have provided a detailed answer which we hope will help you in reading Jorgenson (1984).

Answer to Exercise 3.12

(a)   We require that

$$Q(\lambda P) = \lambda Q(P) \quad \text{for all } P > 0 \text{ and } \lambda > 0. \tag{E3.12.2}$$

Equivalently, we require that

$$lnQ(\lambda P) = lnQ(P) + ln\lambda \quad \text{for all } P > 0 \text{ and } \lambda > 0. \tag{E3.12.3}$$

From (E3.12.1) we have

$$lnQ(\lambda P) = A + \sum_i B_i ln(\lambda P_i) + \frac{1}{2}\sum_i\sum_j C_{ij}\left(\left[ln(\lambda P_i)\right]\left[ln(\lambda P_j)\right]\right). \tag{E3.12.4}$$

Since $ln(\lambda P_k) = ln\lambda + lnP_k$ for all k and $C_{ij} = C_{ji}$ for all $i \neq j$, (E3.12.4) may be expanded as

$$lnQ(\lambda P) = lnQ(P) + (ln\lambda)\sum_i B_i + ln\lambda\sum_i(lnP_i)\sum_j C_{ij} + \frac{1}{2}(ln\lambda)^2\sum_i\sum_j C_{ij} .$$

$$\tag{E3.12.5}$$

Hence, necessary and sufficient conditions for (E3.12.3) are

$$\sum_i B_i = 1 \tag{E3.12.6}$$

and

$$\sum_j C_{ij} = 0 \quad \text{for all i.} \tag{E3.12.7}$$

(b)   We rewrite (E3.12.1) as

$$Q(P) = exp\left(A + \sum_i B_i lnP_i + \frac{1}{2}\sum_i\sum_j C_{ij}(lnP_i)(lnP_j)\right) . \tag{E3.12.8}$$

From Shepard's lemma (see for example, Dixon, Bowles and Kendrick (1980, Exercise 4.17)), we know that the input demands are the derivatives

$$X_k = Y\frac{\partial Q(P)}{\partial P_k} \quad \text{for all k,} \tag{E3.12.9}$$

where Y is the level of output and X_k is the demand for input k. Thus, from (E3.12.8), we have

$$X_k = YQ(P)\left(B_k + \sum_j C_{kj}(lnP_j)\right)/ P_k \quad \text{for all k.} \tag{E3.12.10}$$

---

[32]   If you have forgotten why cost functions are concave with respect to input prices, then you should look at Dixon, Bowles and Kendrick (1980, Exercise 4.17).

In percentage-change form (E3.12.10) becomes

$$x_k = y + q + \sum_j \left[\frac{C_{kj}}{B_k + \sum_t C_{kt}(lnP_t)} \right] P_j - P_k \quad \text{for all k, (E3.12.11)}$$

where, as usual, the lower case symbols, x, y, q and p represent percentage changes in the variables denoted by the corresponding upper case symbols. To turn (E3.12.11) into the required input demand functions we must eliminate q. We start by noting that

$$q = \sum_k \left[\frac{\partial Q(P)}{\partial P_k} \frac{P_k}{Q(P)} \right] P_k \; . \qquad (E3.12.12)$$

It follows easily from Shepard's lemma, (E3.12.9), that the elasticities of the unit cost function are the input shares in total costs, i.e.,

$$\frac{\partial Q(P)}{\partial P_k} \frac{P_k}{Q(P)} = S_k \quad \text{for all k,} \qquad (E3.12.13)$$

where $S_k = P_k X_k / (YQ(P))$. Hence (E3.12.12) may be rewritten as

$$q = \sum_k S_k P_k \; . \qquad (E3.12.14)$$

We also note from (E3.12.10) that in the case of translog unit cost functions, the cost shares are given by

$$S_k = B_k + \sum_j C_{kj}(lnP_j) \quad \text{for all k.} \qquad (E3.12.15)$$

On substituting from (E3.12.14) and (E3.12.15) into (E3.12.11) we obtain

$$x_k = y - \left(p_k - \sum_j S_{kj} p_j \right) \quad \text{for all k,} \qquad (E3.12.16)$$

where the S_{kj}s are modified cost shares[33] defined by

$$S_{kj} = S_j + (C_{kj} / S_k) \quad \text{for all k and j.}$$

Equation (E3.12.16) sets out the system of input demand equations in a form convenient for use in a Johansen model. It expresses percentage changes in the input demands as linear functions of percentage changes in the input prices and output. The coefficients are easily calculated modified cost shares. As in (E3.9.12) and (E3.10.12), the percentage change in the demand for input k is the difference between an activity term and a substitution term. In the

---

[33]   Note that $\sum_j S_{kj} = \sum_j S_j + \sum_j (C_{kj} / S_k) = 1$ for all k.

absence of changes in relative prices, the volume of each input increases by the same percentage as output reflecting constant returns to scale in the underlying production function.   There will be substitution away from input k if the price of input k rises relative to a weighted average of the percentage changes in all input prices. Unlike the weights appearing in   (E3.9.12) and (E3.10.12), the weights in (E3.12.16) need not all be positive.   The translog unit cost function allows for complementarity between inputs.   If C_{kj} is sufficiently negative, then S_{kj} will be negative and an increase in P_j (with all other prices and output held constant) will reduce the demand for input k.

(c)   There are two ways to interpret the translog unit cost function, (E3.12.1).   One is to think of it as a second-order Taylor's-series approximation to the true unit cost function.   On this interpretation, $Q(P)$ need exhibit concavity only in the neighborhood of a central price vector, $\bar{P}$, possibly a vector of sample means. The second interpretation is that $Q(P)$ is, itself, the true unit cost function. On this interpretation, the parameters of (E3.12.1) should be restricted to ensure concavity, if not globally, then at least over a large subset of the price space.

Consider, first, the Taylor's-series interpretation. Where $\Gamma(P)$ is the true unit cost function, it may be written as

$$ln\big(\Gamma(P)\big) = ln\Big[\Gamma\big(exp(lnP_1), ..., exp(lnP_n)\big)\Big] \qquad \text{(E3.12.17)}$$

or

$$ln\big(\Gamma(P)\big) = g(lnP_1, lnP_2, ..., lnP_n) , \qquad \text{(E3.12.18)}$$

with g being defined by (E3.12.17) and (E3.12.18). It is convenient to choose quantity units so that the central prices are all unity, giving[34]

$$ln\bar{P} = 0.$$

Then, (E3.12.18) can be expanded as

$$ln\big(\Gamma(P)\big) = g(0) + \sum_i \left[\frac{\partial g(0)}{\partial lnP_i}\right]lnP_i + \frac{1}{2}\sum_i\sum_j\left[\frac{\partial^2 g(0)}{\partial lnP_i\,\partial lnP_j}\right]lnP_i\, lnP_j$$

+ higher order terms.

Hence, under the Taylor's-series interpretation of (E3.12.1), we have

$$B_i = \frac{\partial g(0)}{\partial lnP_i}, \qquad i = 1, ..., n \qquad \text{(E3.12.19)}$$

---

34   We use the short-hand notation lnP to denote the vector $(lnP_1, lnP_2, ..., lnP_n)$.

and
$$C_{ij} = \frac{\partial^2 g(0)}{\partial lnP_i \, \partial lnP_j} , \quad i,j = 1, \, ..., \, n. \qquad \text{(E3.12.20)}$$

That is, the B_is and C_{ij}s in (E3.12.1) are first- and second-order partial derivatives of the g function evaluated at a central point, $ln\bar{P} = 0$. Notice also that

$$\frac{\partial g(lnP)}{\partial lnP_i} = \frac{\partial ln(\Gamma(P))}{\partial lnP_i} = \frac{\partial \Gamma(P)}{\partial P_i} \frac{P_i}{\Gamma(P)} \qquad \text{(E3.12.21)}$$

and that by Shepard's lemma

$$\partial \Gamma(P)/\partial P_i = X_i/Y \quad , \qquad \text{(E3.12.22)}$$

where X_i is the demand for input i and Y is the level of output. Thus, we see from (E3.12.19) that B_i is the share of input i in total costs when $P = \bar{P}$, i.e.,

$$B_i = \bar{P}_i \bar{X}_i \, / \left(\Gamma(\bar{P})Y \right) . \qquad \text{(E3.12.23)}$$

Since $\Gamma(P)$ is concave, we know that its Hessian, $H(P)$, (the matrix of second-order partial derivatives), must be negative semidefinite (see, for example, Katzner (1970, pp. 200-201).[35] In particular, $H(\bar{P})$ is negative semidefinite. Our task is to translate this condition on $H(\bar{P})$ into a condition on the parameters of (E3.12.1). First, we must express $H(P)$ in terms of partial derivatives of $g(lnP)$. Then we will be able to use (E3.12.19) and (E3.12.20) in translating the restriction on $H(\bar{P})$ into restrictions on C_{ij} and B_i.

Starting from (E3.12.21) we have

$$\frac{\partial \Gamma(P)}{\partial P_i} = \frac{\Gamma(P)}{P_i} \frac{\partial g(lnP)}{\partial lnP_i} . \qquad \text{(E3.12.24)}$$

Thus the ij^{th} entry in the Hessian matrix, $H(P)$, is given by

$$\frac{\partial^2 \Gamma(P)}{\partial P_i \partial P_j} = \frac{\partial \Gamma(P)}{\partial P_j} \frac{1}{P_i} \frac{\partial g}{\partial lnP_i} - \delta_{ij} \frac{\Gamma(P)}{P_i^2} \frac{\partial g}{\partial lnP_i} + \frac{\Gamma(P)}{P_i P_j} \left[\frac{\partial^2 g}{\partial lnP_i \, \partial lnP_j} \right]$$

$$\text{for } i,j = 1, \, ..., \, n, \qquad \text{(E3.12.25)}$$

where $\delta_{ij} = 0$ for $i \neq j$ and $\delta_{ii} = 1$. On substituting from (E3.12.19), (E3.12.20) and (E3.12.21) into (E3.12.25) and recalling that $\bar{P}_i = 1$ for all i, we obtain

$$H(\bar{P}) = \Gamma(\bar{P})(C + BB' - \hat{B}), \qquad \text{(E3.12.26)}$$

where C is the $n \times n$ matrix of C_{ij}s, B is the $n \times 1$ vector of B_is and $\hat{B}$ is the diagonal matrix formed from B.

---

35   Nothing more follows from concavity. Negative semidefiniteness of $H(P)$ is sufficient for concavity as well as necessary.

We assume that $\Gamma(\bar{P})$ is strictly positive. Hence, (E3.12.26) implies that $H(\bar{P})$ will be negative semidefinite if and only if $C + BB' - \hat{B}$ is negative semidefinite. Thus, in summary, the Taylor's-series interpretation of (E3.12.1) suggests that the B_is can be set equal to cost shares observed at a central point where all prices are unity and that C should be estimated as a symmetric matrix subject to the restrictions that

$$C\underline{1} = 0 \qquad\qquad (E3.12.27)^{36}$$

and

$$C + BB' - \hat{B} \quad \text{is negative semidefinite.} \qquad (E3.12.28)$$

Now consider the second interpretation of (E3.12.1). Under this interpretation, the true unit cost function is

$$Q(P) = exp[A + \sum_i B_i lnP_i + \frac{1}{2}\sum_i\sum_j C_{ij}(lnP_i)(lnP_j)] . \qquad (E3.12.29)$$

Thus we have, as we did in part (b),

$$\frac{\partial Q(P)}{\partial P_i} = \frac{Q(P)}{P_i} (B_i + \sum_j C_{ij} lnP_j) . \qquad (E3.12.30)$$

Notice that $\partial Q(P)/\partial P_i$ cannot be nonnegative for all $P > 0$ unless $C_{ij} = 0$ for all i and j. Obviously we would not wish to restrict the C_{ij}s to zero. If we did so, we would be back to the Cobb-Douglas situation of fixed cost shares. If we had been happy with a Cobb-Douglas specification, we would not be worrying about translog functions. Thus, in using the translog function, we cannot insist on global monotonicity, i.e., we cannot insist that

$$\frac{\partial Q(P)}{\partial P_i} \geq 0 \qquad \text{for all } P > 0, \qquad i = 1, ..., n.$$

---

36 In (E3.12.27) we have simply repeated restriction (E3.12.7) derived in part (a). However, the derivation in part (a) was based on the assumption that $Q(P)$ is the true unit cost function, not just a second-order approximation. In the present context, we know that $\Gamma(P)$ is homogeneous of degree 1 with respect to prices. Therefore $\Gamma_i(P)$ is homogeneous of degree zero where we use the subscript i to denote partial differentiation with respect to P_i. Hence, from Euler's theorem, we have $\quad \sum_j \Gamma_{ij}(P)P_j = 0$ for all i,

where $\Gamma_{ij}(P)$ is the second-order partial derivative of $\Gamma(P)$ with respect to P_i and P_j. By substituting from (E3.12.25) and by recalling that the linear homogeneity of $\Gamma(P)$ implies that $\quad \sum_j \Gamma_j(P) P_j = \Gamma(P)$,

we find that

$$\sum_j \frac{\partial^2 g(lnP)}{\partial lnP_i \partial lnP_j} = 0 \text{ for all i.}$$

In particular, this condition holds at $P = \bar{P}$, justifying (E3.12.27).

Consequently, we cannot interpret (E3.12.29) as a globally valid description of unit costs.

In his econometric estimation of the parameters of translog unit cost functions, Jorgenson (1984) interpreted (E3.12.29) as the true unit cost function for all P > 0 such that monotonicity is satisfied. In addition to the usual symmetry and homogeneity restrictions,

$$C' = C \ , \tag{E3.12.31}$$

$$\Sigma_i B_i = 1 \ , \tag{E3.12.32}$$

and

$$C\underline{1} = 0 \ , \tag{E3.12.33}$$

he imposed the restriction

$$C \text{ is negative semidefinite.} \tag{E3.12.34}$$

This ensures that the Hessian matrix of $Q(P)$, $H_Q(P)$, is negative semidefinite for all P in the set

$$L = \left\{ P \,|\, P > 0, \ \frac{\partial Q(P)}{\partial P_i} \geq 0, i = 1, ..., n \right\} \ . \tag{E3.12.35}$$

This, in turn, ensures that $Q(P)$ is concave over any convex set in L.[37]

To demonstrate the negative semidefiniteness of $H_Q(P)$ under (E3.12.31) - (E3.12.34), we start by differentiating in (E3.12.30) with respect to P_j to obtain the components of $H_Q(P)$ as

$$\frac{\partial^2 Q}{\partial P_i \partial P_j} = \frac{Q(P)}{P_i P_j} \ [S_i(P)S_j(P) - \delta_{ij}S_i(P) + C_{ij}] \qquad \text{for all i, j} \tag{E3.12.36}$$

where $\delta_{ij} = 1$ if $i = j$ and $\delta_{ij} = 0$ if $i \neq j$, and

$$S_i(P) = \frac{\partial Q(P)}{\partial P_i} \frac{P_i}{Q(P)}, \quad i = 1, ..., n. \tag{E3.12.37}$$

(E3.12.36) can be rewritten as

$$H_Q(P) = Q(P) \ \hat{P}^{-1} \left(C + S(P)S(P)' - \hat{S}(P) \right) \hat{P}^{-1}, \tag{E3.12.38}$$

where $\hat{P}$ is the diagonal matrix of P_is, $S(P)$ is the column vector of $S_i(P)$s and $\hat{S}(P)$ is the diagonal matrix formed by $S(P)$. In view of (E3.12.30) – (E3.12.33), we know that

---

[37]   Apart from the case in which n = 2, (E3.12.31) - (E3.12.34) are not sufficient to ensure that L is convex.

$$\sum_i S_i(P) = \sum_i B_i + \sum_i \sum_j C_{ij} ln P_j = 1.$$

Thus, for all $P \in L$, $0 \le S_i(P) \le 1$, $i = 1, ..., n$. It follows that for all $P \in L$, $S(P)S(P)' - \hat{S}(P)$ is negative semidefinite.[38] Hence, if C is negative semidefinite, then $H_Q(P)$ is negative semidefinite for all $P \in L$.

At this stage it may be objected that (E3.12.34) is overly restrictive. Perhaps the negative semidefiniteness of $H_Q(P)$ for all $P \in L$ could be guaranteed under a weaker prior restriction. However, this is not the case. Assume, for example, that we are able to find $P^* \in L$ so that

$$S_i(P^*) = B_i + \sum_j C_{ij} ln P_j^* = 1 \qquad \text{for i = i*}$$

$$= 0 \qquad \text{for i} \ne \text{i*}.$$

Then, we would have

$$S(P^*)S(P^*)' - \hat{S}(P^*) = 0$$

and $H_Q(P^*)$ would not be negative semidefinite if C were not negative semidefinite.

Nevertheless, it is clear that Jorgenson's concavity condition (E3.12.34) is more restricting on the parameter estimates than the corresponding condition, (E3.12.28), derived under the Taylor's-series interpretation of (E3.12.1). Jorgenson emphasizes the importance of his concavity condition in influencing his parameter estimates. It would be of interest, therefore, to repeat his work using condition (E3.12.28) in place of (E3.12.34).

---

38   Let $Z(x) = x'(SS' - \hat{S}) x$ where $S \ge 0$ and $\underline{1}'S=1$. We can write $Z(x)$ as

$$
\begin{aligned}
Z(x) &= \sum_i \sum_j x_i x_j S_i S_j - \sum_i x_i^2 S_i \\
&= \sum_i \sum_{j \ne i} x_i x_j S_i S_j + \sum_i x_i^2 S_i^2 - \sum_i x_i^2 S_i \\
&= \sum_i \sum_{j \ne i} x_i x_j S_i S_j + \sum_i S_i (S_i - 1) x_i^2 \\
&= \sum_i \sum_{j \ne i} x_i x_j S_i S_j - \sum_i \sum_{j \ne i} S_i S_j x_i^2 \\
&= \sum_i \sum_{j \ne i} S_i S_j (x_i x_j - x_i^2) \\
&= \sum_i \sum_j S_i S_j (x_i x_j - x_i^2) \\
&= \frac{1}{2} \sum_i \sum_j S_i S_j (2 x_i x_j - x_i^2 - x_j^2) \\
&= -\frac{1}{2} \sum_i \sum_j S_i S_j (x_i - x_j)^2 \le 0.
\end{aligned}
$$

Exercise 3.13   *Linearizing the demand functions for separable production and utility functions*

Nearly all applied general equilibrium models use separable production functions and utility functions. Separability assumptions reduce the number of parameters requiring explicit evaluation. They also lead to simplifications in the representation of systems of demand equations. In this exercise, we give you various separable specifications for production and utility functions and ask you to derive demand equations in forms suitable for use in Johansen-style models.

We start with a definition of separability. A function $f(X_\alpha, X_\beta, ...)$ is separable[39] with respect to the partition $N_1, ..., N_k$ if it can be written in the form

$$f(X_\alpha, X_\beta, ...) = V\big(g_1(X^{(1)}), g_2(X^{(2)}), ..., g_k(X^{(k)})\big), \qquad (E3.13.1)$$

where $N_1, ..., N_k$ are a non-overlapping coverage of the set $\{\alpha, \beta, ... \}$, and $X^{(j)}$ is the subvector of $(X_\alpha, X_\beta, ...)$ formed by the components X_η for which $\eta \in N_j$.

An example of a separable production function is the widely used specification

$$Y = \min \{CES(X_{(11)}, X_{(12)}), ..., CES(X_{(n+1,1)}, X_{(n+1,2)})\}, \qquad (E3.13.2)$$

where Y is output; $X_{(is)}$ for $i = 1, ..., n$, $s = 1, 2$, is the input of good i from source s with $s = 1$ referring to domestic products and $s = 2$ referring to imports; $X_{(n+1,s)}$ for $s = 1,2$ is the input of primary factor of type s with $s = 1$ indicating labor and $s = 2$ indicating capital; and the notation $CES(X_{(i1)}, X_{(i2)})$ means that $X_{(i1)}$ and $X_{(i2)}$ are to be combined according to a CES function (see (E3.9.1)). In this example, the V of (E3.13.1) is a Leontief function and the g_is are each CES functions of two inputs. Under (E3.13.2), output is viewed as a Leontief combination of effective inputs where effective inputs are CES combinations of domestic and imported materials[40] and of labor and capital. The underlying assumptions are that there is no substitution between different materials and between materials and primary factors. However, substitution can take place between domestic and imported materials of the same commodity classification and between labor and capital.

---

39   The definition given here is for what is often called "weak separability" (see, for example, Katzner (1970, p. 28)).

40   This treatment of imports in general equilibrium modeling was pioneered by Armington (1969 and 1970).

(a)   Assume that the production function has the form (E3.13.2). Assuming cost minimizing behavior, derive the percentage-change form for the input demand functions.

(b)   Assume that the production function has the form

$$Y = CD\{CES(X_{(11)},X_{(12)}), ..., CES(X_{(n+1,1)},X_{(n+1,2)})\},$$

where CD denotes Cobb-Douglas function. Again derive the percentage-change form for the input demand functions.

(c)   Letting Q be the number of households, assume that the consumption bundle, X_k/Q, $k = 1,..., n$, of effective inputs for the average household is chosen to maximize the strictly quasiconcave utility function

$$U(X_1/Q, X_2/Q, ..., X_n/Q) \qquad (E3.13.3)$$

subject to

$$X_k = CES(X_{(k1)},X_{(k2)}) , \; k = 1, ..., n \qquad (E3.13.4)$$

and

$$\sum_{k=1}^{n} \sum_{s=1}^{2} P_{(ks)}X_{(ks)} = M, \qquad (E3.13.5)$$

where M is the aggregate household budget, and $X_{(is)}$ and $P_{(is)}$ are the quantity consumed and price of good i from source s, with s = 1 referring to domestic sources and s = 2 referring to imports. Show that the percentage-change form of the system of household demand equations may be written as

$$x_{(ks)} = x_k - \sigma_k\left(p_{(ks)} - \sum_{t=1}^{2} S_{(kt)}p_{(kt)}\right) \quad k = 1, ..., n, \; s = 1,2,$$

$$(E3.13.6)$$

with

$$x_k - q = \varepsilon_k(m - q) + \sum_{i=1}^{n} \eta_{ki}p_i, \; k = 1, ..., n, \qquad (E3.13.7)$$

and

$$p_k = \sum_{s=1}^{2} S_{(ks)}p_{(ks)}, \quad k = 1, ..., n, \qquad (E3.13.8)$$

where $S_{(ks)}$ is the share of the household sector's expenditure on good k which is devoted to good k from source s, σ_k is the elasticity of substitution between the alternative types of good k, and the ε_ks and the η_{ki}s are expenditure and own- and cross-price elasticities satisfying the restrictions flowing from utility maximization, namely[41]

$$\sum_{k=1}^{n} \varepsilon_k \alpha_k = 1, \qquad (Engel's\ aggregation) \quad (E3.13.9)$$

$$\sum_{i=1}^{n} \eta_{ki} = -\varepsilon_k, \ k = 1, ..., n, \qquad (homogeneity) \quad (E3.13.10)$$

and

$$\alpha_i(\eta_{ik} + \varepsilon_i \alpha_k) = \alpha_k (\eta_{ki} + \varepsilon_k \alpha_i), \quad i \neq k, \quad (symmetry) \quad (E3.13.11)$$

where α_k is the share of the household sector's budget devoted to good k from both sources.

Answer to Exercise 3.13

(a)   Total costs, C, are given by

$$C = \sum_{i=1}^{n+1} \sum_{s=1}^{2} P_{(is)} X_{(is)}, \qquad (E3.13.12)$$

where $P_{(is)}$ is the cost of input i of type s. With the production function (E3.13.2), cost minimization requires that we put[42]

$$Y = CES\big(X_{(k1)}, X_{(k2)}\big) \quad \text{for all } k = 1, ..., n+1. \qquad (E3.13.13)$$

Thus, to minimize (E3.13.12) subject to (E3.13.2), we must for each k choose $X_{(k1)}$ and $X_{(k2)}$ to minimize

$$\sum_{s=1}^{2} P_{(ks)} X_{(ks)} \qquad (E3.13.14)$$

subject to (E3.13.13). This later problem was studied in Exercise 3.9. By adapting (E3.9.12) to the notation of the present problem, we find that the percentage change form for the input demand system is

---

41   For exercises on (E3.13.9) – (E3.13.11), see Dixon, Bowles and Kendrick (1980, Exercises 2.1, 2.2, 2.6 and 2.7).

42   If (E3.13.13) were not satisfied, we could cut costs while holding output constant by reducing the use of inputs k for which
$$Y < CES(X_{(k1)}, X_{(k2)}).$$

$$x_{(ks)} = y - \sigma_k \Big(p_{(ks)} - \sum_{t=1}^{2} S_{(kt)} p_{(kt)} \Big), \quad k = 1, ..., n+1, \; s = 1,2,$$

$$(E3.13.15)$$

where the lower case symbols, $x_{(ks)}$, y and $p_{(ks)}$, are percentage changes in variables denoted by the corresponding upper case symbols, σ_k is the elasticity of substitution between the alternative types of input k and $S_{(ks)}$ is the share of input k of type s in the total cost of input k, i.e,

$$S_{(ks)} = P_{(ks)} X_{(ks)} / \sum_t P_{(kt)} X_{(kt)} .$$

(b) Let $\qquad X_k = CES(X_{(k1)}, X_{(k2)}) \qquad$ (E3.13.16)

i.e., let X_k denote the effective level of input k. If we are to minimize costs, then we must spend as little as possible on $X_{(k1)}$ and $X_{(k2)}$ subject to achieving the optimal level for X_k. Thus, $X_{(k1)}$ and $X_{(k2)}$ will minimize

$$\sum_{s=1}^{2} P_{(ks)} X_{(ks)} \qquad (E3.13.17)$$

subject to (E3.13.16) with X_k set at its optimal level. It follows that movements in $X_{(ks)}$, $P_{(ks)}$, $s = 1,2$ and X_k will be related by

$$x_{(ks)} = x_k - \sigma_k \Big(p_{(ks)} - \sum_{t=1}^{2} S_{(kt)} \, p_{(kt)} \Big), \quad k = 1, ..., n+1, \; s = 1,2,$$

$$(E3.13.18)$$

where the notation is familiar from part (a).

To determine the x_ks we can consider the problem of choosing $X_1, X_2, ..., X_{n+1}$ to minimize

$$\sum_{k=1}^{n+1} P_k X_k \qquad (E3.13.19)$$

subject to

$$Y = CD(X_1, ..., X_{n+1}) , \qquad (E3.13.20)$$

where P_k is the minimum cost per unit of effective input k. From (E3.13.19) – (E3.13.20), we find that

$$x_k = y - \Big(p_k - \sum_{i=1}^{n+1} \alpha_i p_i \Big), \quad k = 1, ..., n+1, \qquad (E3.13.21)$$

where α_i is the share of input i of both types in total costs. Next we note that P_k is given by

$$P_k = \left(\sum_{s=1}^{2} P_{(ks)} X_{(ks)} \right) / X_k \; , \qquad (E3.13.22)$$

where $X_{(k1)}$ and $X_{(k2)}$ minimize (E3.13.17) subject to (E3.13.16). From (E3.13.22) we obtain

$$P_k = \sum_{s=1}^{2} S_{(ks)} \left(P_{(ks)} + x_{(ks)} \right) - x_k \; . \qquad (E3.13.23)$$

On applying (E3.13.18) we find that

$$P_k = \sum_{s=1}^{2} S_{(ks)} P_{(ks)} \; . \qquad (E3.13.24)$$

Finally, we combine (E3.13.18), (E3.13.21) and (E3.13.24) to generate the percentage-change form for the input demand system as

$$x_{(ks)} = y - \sigma_k \left(P_{(ks)} - \sum_{t=1}^{2} S_{(kt)} P_{(kt)} \right)$$

$$- \left(\sum_{t=1}^{2} S_{(kt)} P_{(kt)} - \sum_{i=1}^{n+1} \sum_{t=1}^{2} \alpha_{(it)} P_{(it)} \right),$$

$$k = 1, \dots, n+1, \; s = 1,2, \qquad (E3.13.25)$$

where $\alpha_{(is)}$ is the share of input i from source s in total costs, i.e. $\alpha_{(is)} = \alpha_i S_{(is)}$.

On the right hand side of (E3.13.25) we have two substitution terms, a within-group term and a between-group term. The first substitution term implies that if the price of input k of type s rises relative to the general price of input k, then the demand for input k of type s will fall relative to the overall demand for input k. The percentage change in the general price of input k is a cost-share weighted average of the percentage changes in $P_{(k1)}$ and $P_{(k2)}$. The second substitution term shows that if the general price of input k rises relative to a cost-share weighted index of all input prices, then there will be substitution away from both types of input k towards effective inputs of other materials or primary factors.

(c) If we are to maximize utility subject to budget constraint, then we must spend as little as possible in achieving whatever are the optimal levels for effective inputs. Hence, $X_{(k1)}$ and $X_{(k2)}$ will minimize

$$\sum_{s=1}^{2} P_{(ks)}X_{(ks)} \qquad\qquad \text{(E3.13.26)}$$

subject to

$$X_k = CES\big(X_{(k1)}, X_{(k2)}\big) \qquad\qquad \text{(E3.13.27)}$$

As we have noted earlier in this exercise, problem (E3.13.26) – (E3.13.27) leads to percentage-change equations of the form (E3.13.6).

To determine the effective input levels, we consider the problem of choosing X_1, X_2, ..., X_n to maximize

$$U(X_1/Q, X_2/Q, ..., X_n/Q) \qquad\qquad \text{(E3.13.28)}$$

subject to

$$\sum_{k=1}^{n} P_kX_k = M, \qquad\qquad \text{(E3.13.29)}$$

where P_k is the minimum cost per unit of effective input k. We know from (E3.13.24) in part (b) that percentage movements in P_k are described by (E3.13.8). Thus, all that remains is to establish (E3.13.7).

We can rewrite problem (E3.13.28) – (E3.13.29) as follows: choose X_1^*, ..., X_n^* to maximize

$$U(X_1^*, ..., X_n^*) \qquad\qquad \text{(E3.13.30)}$$

subject to

$$\sum_{k=1}^{n} P_k^*X_k^* = M, \qquad\qquad \text{(E3.13.31)}$$

where $X_k^* = X_k/Q$ and $P_k^* = P_kQ$. From (E3.13.30) – (E3.13.31) we have

$$x_k^* = \varepsilon_k m + \sum_{i=1}^{n} \eta_{ki}p_i^*, \quad k = 1, ..., n, \qquad \text{(E3.13.32)}$$

where the η_{ki}s and ε_ks satisfy the restrictions, (E3.13.9) – (E3.13.11), flowing from the utility maximizing model with α_k interpreted as

$$\alpha_k = P_k^*X_k^*/M = P_kX_k/M \quad \text{for all k.}$$

Since $x_k^* = x_k - q$ and $p_k^* = p_k + q$, (E3.13.32) implies that

$$x_k - q = \varepsilon_k m + \sum_{i=1}^{n} \eta_{ki}(p_i + q) . \qquad \text{(E3.13.33)}$$

In view of (E3.13.10), (E3.13.33) can be rearranged as (E3.13.7).

The interpretation of the system (E3.13.6) – (E3.13.8) is straightforward. In (E3.13.6) we see that the demand for good k of type s moves with the demand for effective units of good k. However, if the price of good k of type s increases relative to the overall price of good k, then there will be substitution away from good k of type s towards the alternative source of good k. Movements in the overall price of good k are defined by (E3.13.8). Equation (E3.13.7) explains the movements in the demand per household for effective units of good k in terms of the movement in the budget per household and movements in the overall prices of all goods. The ε_k appearing in this equation is the expenditure elasticity for effective units of good k while the η_{ki}s are own- and cross- price elasticities for effective units of good k with respect to the overall prices, $P_1, \dots, P_n$. Since the ε_ks and η_{ki}s satisfy the conditions flowing from utility maximization, in assigning values for them we are free to draw from the extensive literature on the systems approach to applied demand theory (see Powell (1974), Phlips (1974) and Deaton and Muellbauer (1980)).

Chapter 4

The Construction of A Model for Practical Policy Analysis

4.1 Introduction

This chapter is concerned with the same class of models as were studied in Chapter 3. Again, an equilibrium will be a vector, V, of length n, satisfying a system of equations

$$F(V) = 0, \qquad (4.1.1)$$

where F is a differentiable vector function of length m, with n > m. Here, however, we will leave behind the heuristic models of the last chapter. We will make a detailed examination of the model developed at the World Bank by Kemal Dervis, Jaime de Melo and Sherman Robinson (1982) (hereafter, DMR) for analyzing problems of developing countries.

We have chosen the DMR model for several reasons. First, it is an advanced contribution of practical importance. Variants exist for about a dozen countries and have been used in the regular reporting and advising functions of the World Bank. If you understand the DMR model in detail, then you are ready to participate actively in applied general equilibrium modeling. Second, it provides a convenient framework for extending the discussion of the previous chapter to include international trade, taxes and investment. Third, it has been directed towards macro issues of general interest. For example, special attention has been given to analyzing the effects of different approaches to coping with exchange shortages. Finally, members of the DMR model team, particularly Sherman Robinson and Jeffrey Lewis, have generously made themselves available for answering questions. Even with the best documented models, it is difficult to conduct the sort of examination attempted in this chapter without some inside help.

The plan of the chapter is as follows. In Section 4.2 we provide goals, reading guide and references. Then in Section 4.3 we list the equations of our version of the DMR model and discuss the notation. It is important to realize that we are not attempting to explain the model. We want you to work out all the details by completing the problem set. What we have done in Section 4.3 is to provide tables of equations, variables, coefficients and parameters. In the problem set, we make frequent reference to these tables. At a first reading of Section 4.3, you should try to get an overview of the model by becoming familiar with the structure of the tables, not their detailed contents.

Section 4.4 describes the input-output data requirements of the DMR model. Again, frequent reference is made in the problem set to this section. In reading it, you may find it useful to check your understanding by considering various national accounting and input-output identities in the context of Table 4.1.1. This is a schematic version of DMR's input-output data requirements.

The heart of the chapter is the problem set. Exercises 4.1 to 4.12 are concerned with the equations of the DMR model and the parameter and coefficient values. In this chapter we use the term 'coefficients' to refer to a set of quantities in our differential, linearized version of the DMR model. Coefficients are quantities which at any step in a Johansen-style computation are held constant while we compute the effects on endogenous variables of shifts in exogenous variables. As we move from step to step, the coefficients are re-evaluated. Examples of coefficients include cost shares and sales shares. We use the term 'parameter' in the usual way to refer to quantities which are treated as constants throughout the computation of any solution. Examples of parameters in the DMR model include substitution elasticities between capital and labor and substitution elasticities between imported and domestic products.

The derivation of the linearized, differential version of the DMR model and the calculation of the values of its coefficients from input-output data and elasticity estimates is illustrated by reference to a database listed in Appendix 4.1. This data, which was provided by Sherman Robinson, is for South Korea in 1963. In Exercises 4.13 and 4.15 we ask you to interpret various solutions of the DMR model implemented with these South Korean data. By using the companion set of computer diskettes described in Chapter 1, you will be able to compute for yourself these and other solutions.

4.2   *Goals, Reading Guide and References*

By the time you have finished with this chapter, we hope that you will be able both to build practical general equilibrium models of your own and to use and assess the modeling efforts of others. To attain these objectives, it will be necessary to add to the skills you acquired in Chapter 3. The material in this chapter will help you to deepen and broaden your knowledge of:

(1)   the treatment of investment in general equilibrium models. How do model builders handle the allocation of investment funds between industries? How do they handle the demands for inputs to be used in the construction of capital goods? What do they usually mean by: rate of return on capital, rental per unit of capital and cost per unit of capital?

(2)   the treatment of imports. What is the Armington assumption and why is it popular with model builders?

(3)   the treatment of exports. How are export demand elasticities usually measured? What difficulty sometimes arises in general equilibrium models in which high values are adopted for export demand elasticities? What difficulty arises when low values are adopted? What are some of the ways that have been used to model export supply?

(4)   the treatment of taxes. How are taxes and subsidies on imports, exports and production handled in general equilibrium models? How do DMR model import quotas? What are the alternatives to their fix-price rationing approach?

(5)   computing strategies and algorithms. What is the distinction that DMR make between computing strategies and algorithms? What are the advantages and disadvantages of the Johansen strategy of solving linearized versions of models compared with strategies involving the applications of special purpose algorithms to the nonlinear form of models?   What are some of the common algorithms employed in solving general equilibrium models?

(6)   the calibration step. This is the evaluation of the parameters and coefficients of the model's equations from base-period input-output data and estimates of elasticity parameters.   Under Johansen's strategy, calibration consists mainly of using input-output data to compute cost and sales shares. When nonlinear computing strategies are adopted, calibration involves some rather tedious algebra. Make sure that you can evaluate the parameters of a CES function from input-output data and a given value for the substitution elasticity under the assumption that cost minimizing behavior prevailed in the base period. Can you do the evaluations under the DMR assumption that the base-period input-output

data reflect fix-price rationing? Can you evaluate the parameters of a CET function from input-output data and a given value for the transformation elasticity under the assumption of revenue maximization?

(7)   procedures for detecting errors in general equilibrium computations. Can you suggest some test simulations for the DMR model?

and, finally

(8)   the interpretation and analysis of results from general equilibrium models. Are you able to formulate interesting policy questions requiring different closures of the DMR model? Are you aware of the potential trap of looking to plausible real world phenomena to explain model results in situations where these phenomena are not imbedded in the model?

Problem Set 4 uses the DMR model in illustrating all of these features of general equilibrium modeling. Other illustrations can be found by following Reading guide 4. However, the main point of the readings is to introduce you to the literature describing applications of general equilibrium modeling. The associated reference list contains full citations for material referred to in the reading guide and also includes other references appearing in the chapter.

Reading Guide to Chapter 4

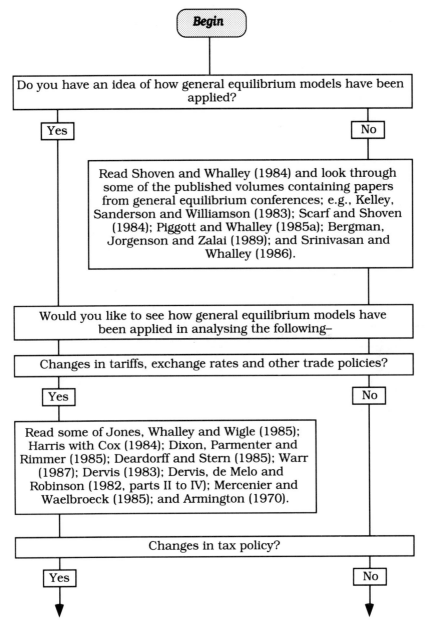

Reading guide to Chapter 4 (continued)

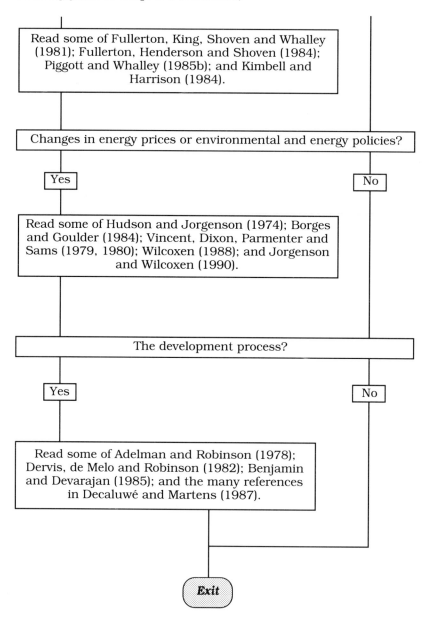

References for Chapter 4

Adams, P.D. and P.J. Higgs "Calibration of Computable General Equilibrium Models from Synthetic Benchmark Equilibrium Data Sets", *Economic Record*, Vol. 66, pp.110-126

Adelman, I., and S. Robinson (1978) *Income Distribution Policy in Developing Countries*, Oxford University Press for the World Bank, New York.

Alaouze, C. (1977) "Estimates of the Elasticity of Substitution between Imported and Domestically Produced Goods Classified at the Input-Output Level of Aggregation", *Impact Project Working Paper* No. 0–13, mimeo, 33 pp. Available from Impact Information Officer, Industry Commission, P.O. Box 80, Belconnen ACT 2616, Australia.

Alaouze C., J.S. Marsden and J. Zeitsch (1977) "Estimates of the Elasticity of Substitution between Imported and Domestically Produced Commodities at the Four-Digit ASIC Level", *Impact Project Working Paper* No. 0–11, mimeo, 66 pp. Available from Impact Information Officer, Industry Commission, P.O. Box 80, Belconnen ACT 2616, Australia.

Allen, R.G.D. (1967) *Macroeconomic Theory: A Mathematical Treatment*, St Martins, New York.

Armington, P.S. (1969) "The Geographic Pattern of Trade and the Effects of Price Changes", *IMF Staff papers*, Vol. 16, pp. 179-199.

Armington, P.S. (1970) "Adjustment of Trade Balances: Some Experiments with a Model of Trade Among Many Countries", *IMF Staff Papers*, Vol. 17, pp. 488-523.

Benjamin, N.C. and S. Devarajan (1985) "Oil Revenue and Economic Policy in Cameroon: Results from a Computable General Equilibrium Model", World Bank *Staff Working Paper* No. 714, Washington, D.C.

Boadway R. and J. Treddenick (1978) "A General Equilibrium Computation of the Effects of the Canadian Tariff Structure", *Canadian Journal of Economics*, Vol. 11, pp. 424-446.

Bergman L., D.W. Jorgenson and E. Zalai (eds) (1989) *General Equilibrium Modeling and Economic Policy Analysis*, Blackwell, Oxford and New York.

Borges, A.M. and L.H. Goulder (1984) "Decomposing the Impact of Higher Energy Prices on Long-term Growth", pp. 319-362 in H.E. Scarf and J.B. Shoven (eds), *Applied General Equilibrium Analysis*, Cambridge University Press, Cambridge.

Bowles, S. (1970) "Aggregation of Labour Inputs in the Economics of Growth and Planning: Experiments with a two level CES Function, *Journal of Political Economy*, Vol. 78, pp. 68-81.

Brown, F. and J. Whalley (1980) "General Equilibrium Evaluation of Tariff-Cutting Proposals in the Tokyo Round and Comparisons with More Extensive Liberalization of World Trade", *Economic Journal*, Vol. 90, pp. 838-866.

Caddy, V. (1976) "Empirical Estimation of the Elasticity of Substitution: A Review", *Impact Project Preliminary Working Paper* No. OP–09, mimeo, 43 pp. Available from Impact Information Officer, Industry Commission, P.O. Box 80, Belconnen ACT 2616, Australia.

Cox, D. and R. Harris (1983) "Trade Liberalization and Industrial Organisation: Some Estimates for Canada, *Discussion Paper* No. 523, Department of Economics, Queen's University, Canada, April, 34 pp.

Cronin, M.R. (1979) "Export Demand Elasticities with Less than Perfect Markets", *Australian Journal of Agricultural Economics*, Vol. 23 (1) (April), pp. 69-72.

Deardorff, A.V., and R.M. Stern (1979) *An Economic Analysis of the Effects of the Tokyo Round of Multilateral Trade Negotiations on the United States and Other Major Industrialized Countries.* A report prepared at the request of the Subcommittee on International Trade of the Committee on Finance of the United States Senate, US Government Printing Office, Washington, D.C.

Deardorff, A.V. and R.M. Stern (1985) "The Effects of Exchange-Rate Changes on Domestic Prices, Trade and Employment in the US, European Community and Japan", pp. 282-306 in K. Jungenfelt and D. Hague (eds), *Structural Adjustment in Developed Open Economies*, Macmillan, London.

Decaluwé, B. and A. Martens (1987) "Developing Countries and General Equilibrium Models — A Review of the Empirical Literature", University of Montreal, International Development Research Centre, *Manuscript Report*, June, 104 pp.

Dervis K. (1980) "Analysing the Resource Pull Effect of a Devaluation Under Exchange Control", *Journal of Development Economics*, Vol. 7, pp. 233-47.

Dervis, K., J. de Melo and S. Robinson (1982) *General Equilibrium Models for Development Policy*, Cambridge University Press, New York.

Dervis, K. (1983) "Foreign Protectionism and Resource Allocation in a Developing Economy: A General Equilibrium Analysis", pp. 44-56 in A. Kelley *et al.* (eds), *Modeling Growing Economies in Equilibrium and Disequilibrium*, Duke Press Policy Studies, Durham, N.C.

Dixon, P.B. (1978) "Economies of Scale, Commodity Disaggregation and the Costs of Protection, *Australian Economic Papers*, Vol. 17, pp. 63-80.

Dixon, P.B., A.A. Powell and B.R. Parmenter (1979) *Structural Adaptation in an Ailing Macroeconomy*, Melbourne University Press, Melbourne.

Dixon, P.B., B.R. Parmenter, J. Sutton and D.P. Vincent (1982) *ORANI: A Multisectoral Model of the Australian Economy*, North-Holland, Amsterdam.

Dixon P.B., B.R., Parmenter, A.A. Powell and D.P. Vincent (1983) "The Agricultural Sector of ORANI 78: Theory, Data and Application", pp. 237-276 in A.C. Kelley, W.G. Sanderson and J.G. Williamson (eds), *Modeling Growing Economies in Equilibrium and Disequilibrium*, Duke Policy Studies, Durham.

Dixon, P.B., B.R. Parmenter and R.J. Rimmer (1985) "The Sensitivity of ORANI Projections of the Short-Run Effects of Increases in Protection to Variations in the Values Adopted for Export Demand Elasticities", pp. 317-346 in K. Jungenfelt and D. Hague (eds), *Structural Adjustment in Developed Open Economies*, Macmillan, London.

Fullerton, D., A. King, J.B. Shoven and J. Whalley (1981) "Corporate Tax Integration in the United States: A General Equilibrium Approach", *American Economic Review*, Vol. 71, pp. 677-691.

Fullerton D., Y.K. Henderson and J.B. Shoven (1984) "A Comparison of Methodologies in Empirical General Equilibrium Models of Taxation", pp. 367-410 in H.E. Scarf and J.B. Shoven (eds), *Applied General Equilibrium Analysis*, Cambridge University Press, Cambridge.

Hudson, E. and D. Jorgenson (1974) "U.S. Energy Policy and Economic Growth, 1975-2000", *Bell Journal of Economics and Management Science*, Vol. 5, pp. 461-514.

Harris, R., with D. Cox (1984) *Trade, Industrial Policy and Canadian Manufacturing*, Ontario Economic Council, Toronto.

Higgs, P.J. (1986) *Adaptation and Survival in Australian Agriculture, A Computable General Equilibrium Analysis of Shocks Originating Outside the Domestic Agricultural Sector*, Oxford University Press, Melbourne.

Jones, R., J. Whalley and R. Wigle (1985) "Regional Impacts of Tariffs in Canada: Preliminary Results from a Small Dimensional Numerical General Equilibrium Model", pp. 175-188 in J. Piggott and J. Whalley (eds), *New Developments in Applied General Equilibrium Analysis*, Cambridge University Press, Cambridge.

Jorgenson, D.W. (1984) "Econometric Methods for Applied General Equilibrium Analysis", pp. 139-207 in H.E. Scarf and J.B. Shoven (eds), *Applied General Equilibrium Analysis*, Cambridge University Press, New York.

Jorgenson, D.W. and P.J. Wilcoxen (1990) "Environmental Regulation and U.S. Economic Growth", *Rand Journal of Economics*, Vol.21, No.2 (Summer), pp. 314-340.

Kelley, A.C., W.C. Sanderson and J.G. Williamson (eds) (1983) *Modeling Growing Economies in Equilibrium and Disequilibrium*, Duke Press Policy Studies, Durham, N.C.

Kimbell, L.J. and G.W. Harrison (1984) "General Equilibrium Analysis of Regional Fiscal Incidence", pp. 275-313 in H.E. Scarf and J.B. Shoven (eds), *Applied General Equilibrium Analysis*, Cambridge University Press, Cambridge.

Lluch, C., A.A. Powell and R.A. Williams (1977) *Patterns in Household Demand and Saving*, Oxford University Press for the World Bank, New York.

McKay, L., D. Lawrence and C. Vlastuin (1983) "Profit, Output Supply, and Input Demand Functions for Multiproduct Firms: The Case of Australian Agriculture", *International Economic Review*, Vol. 24, pp. 323-339.

Mercenier, J. and J. Waelbroeck (1985) "The Impact of Protection on Developing Countries: A General Equilibrium Analysis", pp. 219 - 239 in K. Jungenfelt and D. Hague (eds), *Structural Adjustment in Developed Open Economies*, Macmillan, London.

Murphy, C.W., I.A. Bright, R.J. Brooker, W.D. Geeves and B.K. Taplin (1986) *A Macroeconomic Model of the Australian Economy for Medium Term Policy Analysis*, Office of the Economic Planning Advisory Council, Canberra.

Parmenter B.R. (1983) "The Impact Macro Package and Export Demand Elasticities", *Australian Economic Papers*, Vol. 22, pp. 411-417.

Piggott, J. and J. Whalley (eds) (1985a) *New Developments in Applied General Equilibrium Analysis*, Cambridge University Press, Cambridge.

Piggott, J. and J. Whalley (1985b) *U.K. Tax Policy and Applied General Equilibrium Analysis*, Cambridge University Press, New York.

Powell, A.A. and F.H. Gruen (1967) "The Estimation of Production Frontiers: The Australian Livestock/Cereals Complex", *Australian Journal of Agricultural Economics*, Vol. 11, pp. 315-328.

Powell, A.A and F.H. Gruen (1968) "The Constant Elasticity of Transformation Production Frontier and Linear Supply System", *International Economic Review*, Vol. 9, pp. 315-328.

Ryland G.J. and D.J. Parham (1978) "Estimation of Occupational Demands in Australian Industry", *Impact Project Preliminary Working Paper* No. OP–21, mimeo, pp. 15. Available from Impact Information Officer, Industry Commission, P.O. Box 80, Belconnen ACT 2616, Australia.

Scarf, H.E. and J.B. Shoven (eds) (1984) *Applied General Equilibrium Analysis*, Cambridge University Press, Cambridge.

Scobie, G.M. and P.R. Johnson (1979) "The Price Elasticity of Demand for Exports: A Comment on Throsby and Rutledge", *Australian Journal of Agricultural Economics*, Vol. 23 (1) (April), pp. 62-66.

Sevaldson, P. (1976) "Price Changes as Causes of Variations in Input-Output Coefficients", in K.R. Polenske and F. Skolka (eds), *Advances in Input-Output Analysis*, Ballinger, Cambridge, Massachusetts.

Shoven J.B. and J. Whalley (1984) "Applied General-Equilibrium Models of Taxation and International Trade: An Introduction and Survey", *Journal of Economic Literature*, Vol. 22, pp. 1007-1051.

Shumway, C.R. and A.A. Powell (1984) "A Critique of the Constant Elasticity of Transformation (CET) Linear Supply System" *Western Journal of Agricultural Economics*, Vol. 9, pp. 314-321.

Staelin, C.P. (1976) "A General Equilibrium Model of Tariffs in a Non-Competitive Economy", *Journal of International Economics*, Vol. 6, pp. 39-63.

Stern R.M., J. Francis and B. Schumacher (1976) *Price Elasticities in International Trade: An Annotated Bibliography*, Macmillan, London.

Srinivasan, T.N. and J. Whalley (eds) (1986) *General Equilibrium Trade Policy Modeling*, MIT Press, Cambridge, Massachusetts.

Taylor L. and S.L. Black (1974) "Practical General Equilibrium Estimation of Resource Pulls under Trade Liberalization", *Journal of International Economics*, Vol. 4, pp. 35-58.

Tinbergen, J. (1975) "Substitution of Academically Trained by Other Manpower", *Weltwirtschaftliches Archiv*, 111, pp. 466-475.

Vincent D., P. Dixon, B. Parmenter and D. Sams (1979) "The Short Term Effects of Oil Price Increases on the Australian Economy with Special Reference to the Agricultural Sector", *Australian Journal of Agricultural Economics*, Vol.23, pp. 79-101.

Vincent D., P. Dixon, B. Parmenter and D. Sams (1980) "Implications of World Energy Price Increases in the Rural and Other Sectors of the Australian Economy", in K. M. W. Howes and R. A. Rummery (eds), *Energy and Agriculture*, Commonwealth Scientific and Industrial Research Organization (Australia), pp. 29-39.

Vincent, D.P., P.B. Dixon and A.A. Powell (1980) "The Estimation of the Supply Response in Australian Agriculture: the CRESH/ CRETH Production System", *International Economic Review*, Vol. 21, pp. 221-242.

Warr, P.G. (1987) "Structural Effects of Increasing Australia's Imports from Less Developed Countries", pp. 189-211 in L. Pasinetti and P.J. Lloyd (eds), *Structural Adjustment in Developed Open Economies*, Macmillan, London.

Weiss, R.D. (1977) "Elasticities of Substitution among Capital and Occupations in U.S. Manufacturing", *Journal of the American Statistical Association*, Vol. 72, pp. 764-771.

Wilcoxen, P.J. (1988) "The Effects of Environmental Regulation and Energy Prices on U.S. Economic Performance", Ph.D thesis, Department of Economics, Harvard University.

4.3 Equations, Variables and Notation for the DMR Model: An Overview

This section contains seven tables. Table 4.3.1 sets out the equations of the DMR model both in their levels form and in a percentage-change form suitable for use in Johansen-style computations. Table 4.3.2 lists the variables of the two systems of equations appearing Table 4.3.1. Other notation used in the two representations of the model are presented in Tables 4.3.3 and 4.3.4. For the percentage change version, Table 4.3.4 refers to the input-output, the parameter and the supplementary data files used to supply values for coefficients and parameters. The input-output data is discussed in detail in Section 4.4. The contents of the other two files are listed in Tables 4.3.6 and 4.3.7. Table 4.3.5 shows some alternative sets of exogenous variables corresponding to two different closures of the model.

At a first reading, you should merely glance through the tables. The problem set is designed to take you through them in detail. Initially, you should note that the equations are set out under five headings: final demands, industry decisions (including input demands and output composition), zero pure profits, market clearing and miscellaneous. All of these categories were present in the stylized Johansen model (Chapter 3) except the last. These miscellaneous equations are mainly definitions of useful aggregates, e.g., price indexes, aggregate trade flows, aggregate employment, household income and net government revenue.

From the "description" column of Table 4.3.1, it is clear that the DMR model is much more detailed than the stylized Johansen model. In the latter, households were the only source of final demands. In the DMR model there are three additional sources: investment expenditures, government consumption and exports.

There is also an added dimension in the second category of equations, those describing industry decisions. In the stylized Johansen model we treated each industry as producing a single product. Here, each industry can vary the commodity composition of its output between an exportable product and a product designed for the local market. Consequently, DMR's industries have output-composition decisions to make in addition to input-composition decisions. On the input side, the DMR industries use labor drawn from different skill groups, industry-specific capital, and intermediate inputs of composite commodities. These composite commodities are combinations of domestic and imported commodities.

Tables 4.3.1 — 4.3.7 follow. Text resumes on page 182.

Table 4.3.1[a]

The DMR Equations: Levels and Percentage-Change Representations*

Identifier		Equation[†]	Subscript Range	No.
		Final Demands		
(4.3.1)		*Household demands for composite commodities*		
	(a)	$X^{(3)}_{(ic)} = \alpha^{(3)}_{(ic)} C^{(3)} / P_{(ic)}$	$i=1,\dots,n$	n
	(b)	$x^{(3)}_{(ic)} = c^{(3)} - p_{(ic)}$		
(4.3.2)		*Government demands for composite commodities*		
	(a)	$X^{(4)}_{(ic)} = \left(\alpha^{(4)}_{(ic)} C^{(4)} / P_{(ic)} \right) F^{(4)}_{(ic)}$	$i=1,\dots,n$	n
	(b)	$x^{(4)}_{(ic)} = c^{(4)} - p_{(ic)} + f^{(4)}_{(ic)}$		
(4.3.3)		*Demands for composite commodities to be used in capital creation*		
	(a)	$X^{(2j)}_{(ic)} = A^{(2j)}_{(ic)} I_j$	$i,j=1,\dots,n$	n^2
	(b)	$x^{(2j)}_{(ic)} = i_j$		
(4.3.4)		*Export demand functions*		
	(a)	$P^{(w)}_{(i3)} = F^{(w)}_{(i3)} \left(X^{(w)}_{(i3)} \right)^{-\gamma_i}$	$i=1,\dots,n$	n
	(b)	$p^{(w)}_{(i3)} = -\gamma_i x^{(w)}_{(i3)} + f^{(w)}_{(i3)}$		
		Industry Decisions (input demands and output composition)		
(4.3.5)		*Commodity composition of output*		
	(a)	$X_{(j3)} = \left(Z_j \psi_{(j3)}(P_{(j1)}, P_{(j3)}) \right) F_{(j3)}$	$j=1,\dots,n$	n
	(b)	$x_{(j3)} = z_j - \sigma^{(0)}_j \left(p_{(j3)} - \sum_{s=1\&3} R_{(js)} p_{(js)} \right) + f_{(j3)}$		
(4.3.6)				
	(a)	$Z_j = CET\left(X_{(j1)}, X_{(j3)} \right)$	$j=1,\dots,n$	n
	(b)	$z_j = \eta^{(Zj)}_{(j1)} x_{(j1)} + \eta^{(Zj)}_{(j3)} x_{(j3)}$		
(4.3.7)		*Intermediate input demands*		
	(a)	$X^{(1j)}_{(ic)} = A^{(1j)}_{(ic)} Z_j$	$i,j=1,\dots,n$	n^2
	(b)	$x^{(1j)}_{(ic)} = z_j$		
(4.3.8)		*Industry demands for primary factors*	$s=1\&2$ $j=1,\dots,n$	2n
	(a)	$X^{(1j)}_{(n+1,s)} = A^{(1j)}_{n+1} Z_j \psi^{(1j)}_{(n+1,s)} \left(P^{(1j)}_{(n+1,1)}, P^{(1j)}_{(n+1,2)} \right)$		
	(b)	$x^{(1j)}_{(n+1,s)} = a^{(1j)}_{n+1} + z_j - \sigma^{(1j)}_{n+1} \left(p^{(1j)}_{(n+1,s)} - \sum_{t=1\&2} S^{(1j)}_{(n+1,t)} p^{(1j)}_{(n+1,t)} \right)$		

---

[a] Footnotes appear on page 168.

Table 4.3.1 (continued)

Identifier	Equation†	Subscript Range	No.
(4.3.9)	*Demands for labor classified by industry & occupational group*		

(a) $$X_{(n+1,1,k)}^{(1j)} = X_{(n+1,1)}^{(1j)} \, \Psi_{(n+1,1,k)}^{(1j)} \left(P_{(n+1,1,1)}^{(1j)} \, ..., \, P_{(n+1,1,m)}^{(1j)} \right)$$

(b) $$X_{(n+1,1,k)}^{(1j)} =$$

$$X_{(n+1,1)}^{(1j)} - \sigma_{(n+1,1)}^{(1j)} \left(P_{(n+1,1,k)}^{(1j)} - \sum_{v \in \langle 1,m \rangle} S_{(n+1,1,v)}^{(1j)} \, P_{(n+1,1,v)}^{(1j)} \right)$$

$j=1,...,n$
$k=1,...,m$ nm

(4.3.10) *Defining equation for the price of labor to industry j*

(a) $$P_{(n+1,1)}^{(1j)} \, X_{(n+1,1)}^{(1j)} = \sum_{k \in \langle 1,m \rangle} P_{(n+1,1,k)}^{(1j)} \, X_{(n+1,1,k)}^{(1j)}$$

(b) $$P_{(n+1,1)}^{(1j)} = \sum_{v \in \langle 1,m \rangle} S_{(n+1,1,v)}^{(1j)} \, P_{(n+1,1,v)}^{(1j)}$$

$j=1,...,n$ n

(4.3.11) *Desired demands for domestic and imported inputs in the creation of composite commodities*

(a) $$X_{(is)}^{(c)*} = X_{(ic)}^{(c)} \, \Psi_{(is)}^{(c)} \left(P_{(i1)}, \, P_{(i2)} \right)$$

(b) $$X_{(is)}^{(c)*} = X_{(ic)}^{(c)} - \sigma_i^{(c)} \left(P_{(is)} - \sum_{t=1\&2} S_{(it)}^{(c)*} \, P_{(it)} \right)$$

$s=1\&2$
$i=1,...,n$ 2n

Equations relating actual demands to desired input levels in the creation of composite commodities

(4.3.12)(a) $$X_{(i2)}^{(c)} = X_{(i2)}^{(c)*} \, F_{(i2)}^{(c)} \, F_2^{(c)}$$

(b) $$X_{(i2)}^{(c)} = X_{(i2)}^{(c)*} + f_{(i2)}^{(c)} + f_2^{(c)}$$

$i=1,...,n$ n

(4.3.13)(a) $$X_{(i1)}^{(c)} = X_{(i1)}^{(c)*} \, F_{(i1)}^{(c)} \, F_{(i2)}^{(c)}$$

(b) $$X_{(i1)}^{(c)} = X_{(i1)}^{(c)*} + f_{(i1)}^{(c)} + f_{(i2)}^{(c)}$$

$i=1,...,n$ n

(4.3.14)(a) $$X_{(ic)} = CES \left(X_{(i1)}^{(c)}, \, X_{(i2)}^{(c)} \right)$$

(b) $$x_{(ic)} = \eta_{(i1)}^{(ic)} \, x_{(i1)}^{(c)} + \eta_{(i2)}^{(ic)} \, x_{(i2)}^{(c)}$$

$i=1,...,n$ n

Zero Pure Profits

(4.3.15)(a) *Zero pure profits in production*

$$\left[\sum_{s=1\&3} P_{(is)} \, X_{(is)} \right] T_i^{(0)} =$$

$$\sum_{j \in \langle 1,n \rangle} P_{(jc)} \, X_{(jc)}^{(1i)} + \sum_{t=1\&2} P_{(n+1,t)}^{(1i)} \, X_{(n+1,t)}^{(1i)}$$

$i=1,...,n$ n

... *(continued)*

Table 4.3.1 (continued)

Identifier	Equation[†]	Subscript Range	No.

(4.3.15)(continued)

(b)
$$\sum_{s=1\&3} R_{(is)} \left(p_{(is)} + x_{(is)} \right) + t_i^{(0)} =$$

$$\sum_{j\in\langle 1,n\rangle} H_{(jc)}^{(1i)} \left(p_{(jc)} + x_{(jc)}^{(1i)} \right) + \sum_{t=1\&2} H_{(n+1,t)}^{(1i)} \left(p_{(n+1,t)}^{(1i)} + x_{(n+1,t)}^{(1i)} \right)$$

(4.3.16)   *Zero pure profits in the creation of composite commodities*

(a)
$$P_{(ic)} X_{(ic)} = \sum_{t=1\&2} P_{(it)} X_{(it)}^{(c)}$$
$i=1,...,n$ n

(b)
$$P_{(ic)} + x_{(ic)} = \sum_{t=1\&2} S_{(it)}^{(c)} \left(p_{(it)} + x_{(it)}^{(c)} \right)$$

(4.3.17)   *Zero pure profits in exporting*

(a)
$$P_{(i3)} = P_{(i3)}^{(w)} \Phi \left(T_{(i3)} + T_{(3)} - 1 \right)$$
$i=1,...,n$ n

(b)
$$P_{(i3)} = p_{(i3)}^{(w)} + \phi + \left(T_{(i3)} / (T_{(i3)} + T_{(3)} - 1) \right) t_{(i3)}$$
$$+ \left(T_{(3)} / (T_{(i3)} + T_{(3)} - 1) \right) t_{(3)}$$

(4.3.18)   *Zero pure profits in importing*

(a)
$$P_{(i2)} = P_{(i2)}^{(w)} \Phi \left(T_{(i2)} + T_{(2)} - 1 \right)$$
$i=1,...,n$ n

(b)
$$P_{(i2)} = p_{(i2)}^{(w)} + \phi + \left(T_{(i2)} / (T_{(i2)} + T_{(2)} - 1) \right) t_{(i2)}$$
$$+ \left(T_{(2)} / (T_{(i2)} + T_{(2)} - 1) \right) t_{(2)}$$

(4.3.19)   *Zero pure profits in capital creation*

(a)
$$P_K^{(j)} = \sum_{i\in\langle 1,n\rangle} A_{(ic)}^{(2j)} P_{(ic)}$$
$j=1,...,n$ n

(b)
$$p_K^{(j)} = \sum_{i\in\langle 1,n\rangle} H_{(ic)}^{(2j)} P_{(ic)}$$

Market Clearing

(4.3.20)   *Supply equals demand for domestically produced,*
domestically oriented commodities

(a)
$$X_{(i1)} = X_{(i1)}^{(c)}$$
$i=1,...,n$ n

(b)
$$x_{(i1)} = x_{(i1)}^{(c)}$$

Table 4.3.1 (continued)

Identifier	Equation†	Subscript Range	No.
(4.3.21)	Supply equals demand for imported commodities		
(a)	$X_{(i2)} = X^{(c)}_{(i2)}$		
		$i=1,...,n$	n
(b)	$x_{(i2)} = x^{(c)}_{(i2)}$		
(4.3.22)	Supply equals demand for exports		
(a)	$X_{(i3)} = X^{(w)}_{(i3)}$		
		$i=1,...,n$	n
(b)	$x_{(i3)} = x^{(w)}_{(i3)}$		
(4.3.23)	Supply equals demand for composite commodities		
(a)	$X_{(ic)} = X^{(3)}_{(ic)} + X^{(4)}_{(ic)} + \sum_{j\in\langle 1,n\rangle} \sum_{g=1\&2} X^{(gj)}_{(ic)}$		
		$i=1,...,n$	n
(b)	$x_{(ic)} = B^{(3)}_{(ic)} x^{(3)}_{(ic)} + B^{(4)}_{(ic)} x^{(4)}_{(ic)}$ $+ \sum_{j\in\langle 1,n\rangle} \sum_{g=1\&2} B^{(gj)}_{(ic)} x^{(gj)}_{(ic)}$		
(4.3.24)	Employment of labor classified by occupational group		
(a)	$L_k = \sum_{j\in\langle 1,n\rangle} X^{(1j)}_{(n+1,1,k)}$		
		$k=1,...,m$	m
(b)	$l_k = \sum_{j\in\langle 1,n\rangle} B^{(1j)}_{(n+1,1,k)} x^{(1j)}_{(n+1,1,k)}$		
(4.3.25)	Demand equals supply for capital in each industry		
(a)	$X^{(1j)}_{(n+1,2)} = K_j$		
		$j=1,...,n$	n
(b)	$x^{(1j)}_{(n+1,2)} = k_j$		

Miscellaneous Equations

Identifier	Equation†	Subscript Range	No.
(4.3.26)	Allocation of the investment budget across industries		
(a)	$I_j = F^{(2j)} \alpha^{(2j)} C^{(2)} / P^{(j)}_K$		
		$j=1,...,n$	n
(b)	$i_j = c^{(2)} - p^{(j)}_K + f^{(2j)}$		
(4.3.27)	Rates of return		
(a)	$R_j = \left(P^{(1j)}_{(n+1,2)} / P^{(j)}_K\right) - D_j$		
		$j=1,...,n$	n
(b)	$r_j = Q_j \left(p^{(1j)}_{(n+1,2)} - p^{(j)}_K\right)$		
(4.3.28)	Four price indexes. The first has weights equal to industry shares in value of total output. The others use investment weights, household consumption weights and government expenditure weights respectively.		
(a)	$\Xi^{(v)} = \prod_{i\in\langle 1,n\rangle} \left(P_{(ic)}\right)^{W^{(v)}_i}$		

... (continued)

Table 4.3.1 (continued)

Identifier	Equation†	Subscript Range	No.

(4.3.28) *(continued)*

(b) $\quad \xi^{(v)} = \sum_{i \in \langle 1,n \rangle} w_i^{(v)} \, P_{(ic)}$ $\qquad v=1,...,4 \qquad$ 4

(4.3.29) *Foreign currency value of imports*

(a) $\quad M = \sum_{i \in \langle 1,n \rangle} P_{(i2)}^{(w)} \, X_{(i2)}$

$\qquad$ 1

(b) $\quad m = \sum_{i \in \langle 1,n \rangle} M_{(i2)} \left(x_{(i2)} + p_{(i2)}^{(w)} \right)$

(4.3.30) *Foreign currency value of exports*

(a) $\quad E = \sum_{i \in \langle 1,n \rangle} P_{(i3)}^{(w)} \, X_{(i3)}$

$\qquad$ 1

(b) $\quad e = \sum_{i \in \langle 1,n \rangle} E_{(i3)} \left(x_{(i3)} + p_{(i3)}^{(w)} \right)$

(4.3.31) *Balance of Trade*

(a) $\quad B = E - M$

(b) $\quad 100 \Delta B = Ee - Mm$ $\qquad$ 1

(4.3.32) *Wage indexing equations*

(a) $\quad P_{(n+1,1,k)}^{(1j)} = \left[\Xi^{(3)} \right]^{h_1} \bar{F}_{(n+1,1,k)}^{(1j)} F_{(n+1,1,k)} F_{(n+1,1)}$

(b) $\quad P_{(n+1,1,k)}^{(1j)} = h_1 \xi^{(3)} + f_{(n+1,1,k)} + f_{(n+1,1)}$ $\qquad \begin{array}{l} j=1,...,n \\ k=1,...,m \end{array} \qquad$ mn

(4.3.33) *Capital rental indexing equations*

(a) $\quad P_{(n+1,2)}^{(1j)} = \left[\Xi^{(3)} \right]^{h_2} F_{(n+1,2)}^{(1j)}$

(b) $\quad P_{(n+1,2)}^{(1j)} = h_2 \xi^{(3)} + f_{(n+1,2)}^{(1j)}$ $\qquad j=1,...,n \qquad$ n

(4.3.34) *Aggregate capital stock*

(a) $\quad K = \sum_{j \in \langle 1,n \rangle} K_j \, \bar{P}_K^{(j)}$

$\qquad$ 1

(b) $\quad k = \sum_{j \in \langle 1,n \rangle} B_j^K \, k_j$

Table 4.3.1 (continued)

Identifier	Equation†	Subscript Range	No.

(4.3.35) *Aggregate employment*

(a)
$$L = \sum_{v \in \langle 1,m \rangle} L_v$$

(b)
$$l = \sum_{v \in \langle 1,m \rangle} B_v^L \, l_v$$

1

(4.3.36) *Household income*

(a)
$$Y^{(3)} = \sum_{j \in \langle 1,n \rangle} \sum_{t=1\&2} P_{(n+1,t)}^{(1j)} \; X_{(n+1,t)}^{(1j)}$$

(b)
$$y^{(3)} = \sum_{j \in \langle 1,n \rangle} \sum_{t=1\&2} G_{(n+1,t)}^{(1j)3} \left(p_{(n+1,t)}^{(1j)} + x_{(n+1,t)}^{(1j)} \right)$$

1

(4.3.37) *Government revenue net of subsidies*

(a)
$$Y^{(4)} = \sum_{i \in \langle 1,n \rangle} \left(1 - T_i^{(0)} \right) \left[\sum_{s=1\&3} P_{(is)} \, X_{(is)} \right]$$
$$+ \sum_{i \in \langle 1,n \rangle} \left(T_{(i2)} + T_{(2)} - 2 \right) P_{(i2)}^{(w)} \, \Phi \, X_{(i2)}$$
$$- \sum_{i \in \langle 1,n \rangle} \left(T_{(i3)} + T_{(3)} - 2 \right) P_{(i3)}^{(w)} \, \Phi \, X_{(i3)} + T^H Y^{(3)}$$

1

(b)
$$y^{(4)} = - \sum_{i \in \langle 1,n \rangle} t_i^{(0)} \, G_i^{(0)4} + \sum_{i \in \langle 1,n \rangle} \sum_{s=1\&3} \left(p_{(is)} + x_{(is)} \right) R_{(is)} \, J_i^{(0)4}$$
$$+ \sum_{i \in \langle 1,n \rangle} t_{(i2)} \, G_{(i2)}^4 + t_{(2)} \, G_2^4 + \sum_{i \in \langle 1,n \rangle} \left(p_{(i2)}^{(w)} + \phi + x_{(i2)} \right) J_{(i2)}^4$$
$$- \sum_{i \in \langle 1,n \rangle} t_{(i3)} \, G_{(i3)}^4 - t_{(3)} \, G_3^4 - \sum_{i \in \langle 1,n \rangle} \left(p_{(i3)}^{(w)} + \phi + x_{(i3)} \right) J_{(i3)}^4$$
$$+ \left(t^H + y^{(3)} \right) J_H^4$$

... (continued)

Table 4.3.1 (continued)

Identifier	Equation[†]	Subscript Range	No.
(4.3.38)	*Household aggregate expenditure function*		
(a)	$C^{(3)} = Q^{(3)} \, Y^{(3)} \left(1 - T^H\right)$		1
(b)	$c^{(3)} = q^{(3)} + y^{(3)} - \left(T^H /(1 - T^H)\right) t^H$		
(4.3.39)	*Government aggregate expenditure function*		
(a)	$C^{(4)} = Q^{(4)} \, Y^{(4)}$		1
(b)	$c^{(4)} = q^{(4)} + y^{(4)}$		

Equations for fixing the macro allocation of aggregate expenditure

(4.3.40)(a)	$C^{(4)} = C^{(3)} \, V_{43}$		
(b)	$c^{(4)} = c^{(3)} + v_{43}$		1
(4.3.41)(a)	$C^{(4)} = C^{(2)} \, V_{42}$		
(b)	$c^{(4)} = c^{(2)} + v_{42}$		1
(4.3.42)(a)	$C^{(2)} = C^{(3)} \, V_{23}$		
(b)	$c^{(2)} = c^{(3)} + v_{23}$		1
(4.3.43)	*These equations define real expenditure by investors, households and government*		
(a)	$C^{(v)} = C_R^{(v)} \, \Xi^{(v)}$	$v \in \{2,3,4\}$	3
(b)	$c^{(v)} = c_R^{(v)} + \xi^{(v)}$		

$$\text{Total} = 26n + 2mn + 2n^2 + m + 19$$

[*] To save space in this table, we have denoted ranges of summation by expressions like $j \in \langle 1,n \rangle$ written under the operator Σ instead of the more usual expressions like that displayed at right.

$$\sum_{j=1}^{n}$$

[†] The equations making up the levels representation are marked (a); those in the percentage-change representation are marked (b).

Table 4.3.2[a]

Variables in the DMR Model

Variables[†]	Subscript Range	Number	Description
$A_{n+1}^{(1j)}$, $a_{n+1}^{(1j)}$	j=1,...,n.	n	The number of effective units of primary factor input required per unit of activity in industry j. Changes in this variable allow for primary-factor-augmenting technological change.
B, ΔB		1	Balance of trade in foreign currency.
$C^{(v)}$, $c^{(v)}$	v=2,3,4.	3	Aggregate investment (v=2), household expenditure (v=3) and government expenditure (v=4).
$C_R^{(v)}$, $c_R^{(v)}$	v=2,3,4.	3	Real investment, household expenditure and government expenditure
E, e		1	Foreign currency value of exports.
$F^{(2j)}$, $f^{(2j)}$	j=1,...,n.	n	Variables allowing exogenous shifts in the allocation of investment across industries.
$F_{(ic)}^{(4)}$, $f_{(ic)}^{(4)}$	i=1,...,n.	n	Variables allowing exogenous treatment of government expenditure by commodity.
$F_{(i3)}^{(w)}$, $f_{(i3)}^{(w)}$	i=1,...,n.	n	Shifts in export demand curves.
$F_{(i3)}$, $f_{(i3)}$	i=1,...,n.	n	Variables allowing exogenous treatment of export supplies.
$F_{(i2)}^{(c)}$, $f_{(i2)}^{(c)}$	i=1,...,n.	n	Variables relating desired demands for imports and domestic goods to actual usage levels.
$F_2^{(c)}$, $f_2^{(c)}$		1	
$F_{(i1)}^{(c)}$, $f_{(i1)}^{(c)}$	i=1,...,n.	n	
$F_{(n+1,1,k)}$, $f_{(n+1,1,k)}$	k=1,...,m.	m	Variables allowing different treatments of wages.
$F_{(n+1,1)}$, $f_{(n+1,1)}$		1	
$F_{(n+1,2)}^{(1j)}$, $f_{(n+1,2)}^{(1j)}$	j=1,...,n.	n	Variables allowing different treatments of rentals on capital.
I_j, i_j	j=1,...,n.	n	Number of units of capital created for industry j.
K, k		1	Aggregate capital stock.
K_j, k_j	j=1,...,n.	n	Number of units of capital available to industry j.

[a] Footnote appears on page 171.

... (continued)

Table 4.3.2 continued

Variables[†]	Subscript Range	Number	Description
L, l		1	Aggregate employment.
L_k, l_k	$k=1,\ldots,m.$	m	Employment in occupation k.
M, m		1	Foreign currency value of imports.
$P^{(w)}_{(i2)}$, $p^{(w)}_{(i2)}$	$i=1,\ldots,n.$	n	Foreign currency price of imported commodity i.
$P_{(ic)}$, $P_{(ic)}$	$i=1,\ldots,n.$	n	Price of composite commodity i.
$P^{(w)}_{(i3)}$, $P^{(w)}_{(i3)}$	$i=1,\ldots,n.$	n	Foreign currency price of exports.
$P^{(1j)}_{(n+1,s)}$, $P^{(1j)}_{(n+1,s)}$	$j=1,\ldots,n,$ $s=1,2.$	2n	Unit cost of labor (s=1) and rental price of capital (s=2) to industry j.
$P^{(1j)}_{(n+1,1,k)}$, $P^{(1j)}_{(n+1,1,k)}$	$k=1,\ldots,m,$ $j=1,\ldots,n.$	nm	Cost of unit of labor of occupation k to industry j.
$P_{(is)}$, $P_{(is)}$	$i=1,\ldots,n,$ $s=1,2,3.$	3n	Domestic price of domestic good i (s=1), imported good i (s=2) and exportable good i (s=3).
$P^{(j)}_K$, $p^{(j)}_K$	$j=1,\ldots,n.$	n	Cost of unit of capital for industry j.
$Q^{(v)}$, $q^{(v)}$	$v=3,4.$	2	Average propensity to spend by households (v=3) and government (v=4).
R_i, r_i	$i=1,\ldots,n.$	n	Rate of return in industry i.
$T^{(o)}_i$, $t^{(o)}_i$	$i=1,\ldots,n.$	n	One minus the tax rate on the revenue of industry i.
$T_{(i3)}$, $t_{(i3)}$	$i=1,\ldots,n.$	n	One plus the particular rate of export subsidy applicable to commodity i.
$T_{(3)}$, $t_{(3)}$		1	One plus the general rate of export subsidy.
$T_{(i2)}$, $t_{(i2)}$	$i=1,\ldots,n.$	n	One plus the particular rate of tariff applicable to imports of commodity i.
$T_{(2)}$, $t_{(2)}$		1	One plus the general rate of tariff.
T^H, t^H		1	Rate of household income tax.
V_{42}, v_{42}		1 ⎫	Variables allowing exogenous treatment of the macro allocation of aggregate expenditure.
V_{43}, v_{43}		1 ⎬	
V_{23}, v_{23}		1 ⎭	

Table 4.3.2 continued

Variables[†]	Subscript Range	Number	Description
$X_{(ic)}^{(g)}$, $x_{(ic)}^{(g)}$	$g=3,4,$ $i=1,\dots,n.$	$2n$	Demand for composite commodity i by households ($g=3$) and the government ($g=4$).
$X_{(ic)}^{(gj)}$, $x_{(ic)}^{(gj)}$	$g=1,2,$ $i, j=1,\dots,n.$	$2n^2$	Demand for composite commodity i to be used as an input to production ($g=1$) or capital creation ($g=2$) by industry j.
$X_{(ic)}$, $x_{(ic)}$	$i=1,\dots,n.$	n	Supply or output of composite commodity i.
$X_{(i3)}^{(w)}$, $x_{(i3)}^{(w)}$	$i=1,\dots,n.$	n	Foreign demand for exportable good i.
$X_{(is)}$, $x_{(is)}$	$i=1,\dots,n,$ $s=1,2,3.$	$3n$	Supply of domestic good i ($s=1$), imported good i ($s=2$) and exportable good i ($s=3$).
$X_{(is)}^{(c)}$, $x_{(is)}^{(c)}$	$i=1,\dots,n,$ $s=1,2.$	$2n$	Usage of domestic good i ($s=1$) and imported good i ($s=2$) in making composite good i.
$X_{(is)}^{(c)*}$, $x_{(is)}^{(c)*}$	$i=1,\dots,n,$ $s=1,2.$	$2n$	Desired usage of domestic good i ($s=1$) and imported good i ($s=2$) in making composite good i.
$X_{(n+1,s)}^{(1j)}$, $x_{(n+1,s)}^{(1j)}$	$j=1,\dots,n,$ $s=1,2.$	$2n$	Demand for labor ($s=1$) and capital ($s=2$) by industry j.
$X_{(n+1,1,k)}^{(1j)}$, $x_{(n+1,1,k)}^{(1j)}$	$j=1,\dots,n,$ $k=1,\dots,m.$	nm	Demand for labor of occupation k by industry j.
$Y^{(v)}$, $y^{(v)}$	$v=3,4.$	2	Household income ($v=3$) and government revenue net of subsidies ($v=4$).
Z_i, z_i	$i=1,\dots,n.$	n	Activity level in industry i.
Φ, ϕ		1	Exchange rate.
$\Xi^{(v)}$, $\xi^{(v)}$	$v=1,2,3,4.$	4	Four price indexes. The first ($v=1$) has weights equal to industry shares in the gross value of output. The others have investment weights ($v=2$), household consumption weights ($v=3$) and government expenditure weights ($v=4$).

Total = $37n + 2n^2 + 2nm + 2m + 28$

[†] Variables represented by lower-case symbols are percentage changes in those represented by the corresponding uppercase symbols. The lower-case variables appear in the system (4.3.1)(b) - (4.3.43)(b), whereas the uppercase variables are in the system (4.3.1)(a) - (4.3.43)(a). For the balance of trade (B), it is the change (ΔB) rather than the percentage change which appears in the system (4.3.1)(b) - (4.3.43)(b).

Table 4.3.3

Other Notation Appearing in the Levels Representation (Equations
(4.3.1)(a) - (4.3.43)(a) in Table 4.3.1) of the DMR Model

Symbol	Appearing in equation(s)	Description
$\alpha_{(ic)}^{(g)}$	(4.3.1)(a) and (4.3.2)(a)	Parameters whose values are fixed at the shares of household expenditure (g=3) and government expenditure (g=4) devoted to composite commodity i in the input-output tables reflecting the initial situation.
$A_{(ic)}^{(2j)}$, $A_{(ic)}^{(1j)}$	(4.3.3)(a), (4.3.7)(a) & (4.3.19)(a)	Parameters whose values are the numbers of units of composite commodity i required per unit of capital creation and per unit of output activity in industry j.
γ_i	(4.3.4)(a)	Parameter giving the reciprocal of the export elasticity of demand for exportable good i.
$\psi(...)$	(4.3.5)(a) (4.3.8)(a) (4.3.9)(a)& (4.3.11)(a)	The ψs are functions of prices. In (4.3.5)(a), $\Psi_{(j3)}(P_{(j1)}, P_{(j3)})$ is the revenue maximizing output of good (j3) per unit of activity in industry j. In (4.3.8)(a), (4.3.9)(a) and (4.3.11)(a), the ψs are each cost minimizing input levels per unit of an appropriately defined activity level. The specific form of the ψ functions follows from CET revenue maximizing and CES cost minimizing problems; see Exercises 4.3(a), 4.5(a) and (4.8)
$CET(...)$	(4.3.6)(a)	This denotes the CET function; see (E3.11.1).
$CES(...)$	(4.3.14)(a)	This denotes the CES function; see (E3.9.1).
$\alpha^{(2j)}$	(4.3.26)(a)	Parameter whose value is fixed at the share of industry j in total investment in the input-output tables reflecting the initial situation.
D_i	(4.3.27)(a)	Rate of depreciation of capital in industry i.
$w_i^{(v)}$	(4.3.28)(a)	Weight of composite commodity i in price index v.
$\bar{F}_{(n+1,1,k)}^{(1j)}$	(4.3.32)(a)	Parameter whose value is fixed at the wage rate of occupation k in industry j in the initial situation.
h_1, h_2	(4.3.32)(a)& (4.3.33)(a)	User-specified parameters for handling indexation of wage and rental rates.
$\bar{P}_K^{(j)}$	(4.3.34)(a)	Parameter whose value is fixed at the price of a unit of capital for industry j in the initial situation.

Table 4.3.4[a]

Other Notation Appearing in the Percentage-Change Representation of the DMR Model: The Coefficients and Parameters of the System (4.3.1)(b) – (4.3.43)(b) in Table 4.3.1

Equation	Coefficient or Parameter[†]	Description and Evaluation[#]
(4.3.4)(b)	γ_i	Reciprocal of the foreign elasticity of demand for exportable good i, i=1,...,n — parameter.
(4.3.5)(b)	$\sigma_j^{(0)}$	Elasticity of transformation between goods (j1) and (j3), j=1,...,n — parameter.
	$R_{(js)}$	Share of revenue in industry j accounted for by sales of good (js), s=1,3, j=1,...,n — calculated from input-output data files: $$R_{(j3)} = (\widetilde{F1})_j / \widetilde{T}_j, \quad R_{(j1)} = \left(1 - R_{(j3)}\right) .$$
(4.3.6)(b)	$\eta_{(js)}^{(Zj)}$	Elasticity of the CET activity function with respect to $X_{(js)}$, s=1,3, j=1,...,n If revenue maximizing is not assumed to underlie the base period data, then values for the ηs must be supplied from a supplementary data file (see Exercise 4.3). Under revenue-maximizing, the ηs may be found from input-output data as: $$(\eta_{(js)}^{(Zj)})^I = (R_{(js)})^I .$$ For updating in a multistep solution we can use (E4.4.7).
(4.3.8)(b)	$\sigma_{n+1}^{(1j)}$	Elasticity of substitution between capital and labor in industry j, j=1,...,n — parameter.
	$S_{(n+1,t)}^{(1j)}$	Share of primary factor t in total primary factor cost of industry j, j=1,...,n, t=1,2 — calculated from input-output data file: $$S_{(n+1,1)}^{(1j)} = (\underline{1}'\widetilde{G})_j / [(\underline{1}'\widetilde{G})_j + \widetilde{H}_j];$$ $$S_{(n+1,2)}^{(1j)} = 1 - S_{(n+1,1)}^{(1j)} .$$
(4.3.9)(b)	$\sigma_{(n+1,1)}^{(1j)}$	Elasticity of substitution between different types of labor in industry j, j=1,...,n — parameter.
	$S_{(n+1,1,v)}^{(1j)}$	Share of labor of type v in the total labor costs of industry j, j=1,...,n, v=1,...,m — calculated from input-output data files: $$S_{(n+1,1,v)}^{(1j)} = (\widetilde{G})_{vj} / (\underline{1}'\widetilde{G})_j .$$
(4.3.10)(b)	$S_{(n+1,1,v)}^{(1j)}$	Covered under (4.3.9)(b).
(4.3.11)(b)	$\sigma_i^{(c)}$	Elasticity of substitution between domestic and imported good i, i=1,...,n — parameter.

[a] Footnotes appear on page 178.

... *(continued)*

Table 4.3.4 (continued)

Equation	Coefficient or Parameter[†]	Description and Evaluation[#]
(4.3.11)(b) *(continued)*	$S_{(it)}^{(c)*}$	Desired share of good (it) in the total cost of composite commodity i, i=1,...,n, t=1,2 — $$S_{(i2)}^{(c)*} = S_{(i2)}^{(c)} / \left(\Omega_i\, S_{(i1)}^{(c)} + S_{(i2)}^{(c)} \right), \quad \text{and}$$ $$S_{(i1)}^{(c)*} = 1 - S_{(i2)}^{(c)*}.$$ The $S_{(it)}^{(c)}$s are the actual cost shares available in the input-output tables (see discussion of (4.3.16)(b) below). $$\Omega_i = F_{(2)}^{(c)}/F_{(i1)}^{(c)}.$$ The initial value of Ω_i must be included in the supplementary data file. Ω_i can be updated in multistep solutions according to: $$\%\Delta\Omega_i = f_{(2)}^{(c)} - f_{(i1)}^{(c)}.$$
(4.3.14)(b)	$\eta_{(it)}^{(ic)}$	Elasticity of the output of the composite commodity (ic) with respect to inputs of commodity (it), i=1,...,n, t=1,2 — the initial value of $\eta_{(i1)}^{(ic)}$ is given by: $$\left[\eta_{(i1)}^{(ic)}\right]^{-1} = \left(1 + \Omega_i^{-1/\sigma_i^{(c)}}\, S_{(i2)}^{(c)} /S_{i1}^{(c)}\right)^{-1}$$ where Ω_i and $S_{(it)}^{(c)}$ are set at their initial values. (Ω_i and $S_{(it)}^{(c)}$ are defined under (4.3.11)(b) and (4.3.16) (b)). Updating in multistep solutions can be performed according to: $$\%\Delta\eta_{(i1)}^{(ic)} = \left((\sigma_i^{(c)}-1)/\sigma_i^{(c)}\right)\left(x_{(i1)}^{(c)} - x_{(ic)}\right).$$ $\eta_{(i2)}^{(ic)}$ is evaluated as $1 - \eta_{(i1)}^{(ic)}$.
(4.3.15)(b)	$R_{(is)}$	Covered under (4.3.5)(b).
	$H_{(jc)}^{(1i)}$	Share of composite good j in the total before tax costs of industry i, i,j=1,...,n — calculated from the input-output data files: $$H_{(jc)}^{(1i)} = (\tilde{A})_{ji} /(\tilde{T}_i - \tilde{J}_i).$$
	$H_{(n+1,t)}^{(1i)}$	Shares of labor (t=1) and capital (t=2) in the total before tax costs of industry i, i=1,...,n, t=1,2 — calculated from the input-output data files: $$H_{(n+1,1)}^{(1i)} = (\underline{1}'\tilde{G})_i/(\tilde{T}_i - \tilde{J}_i),$$ $$H_{(n+1,2)}^{(1i)} = \tilde{H}_i/(\tilde{T}_i - \tilde{J}_i).$$
(4.3.16)(b)	$S_{(it)}^{(c)}$	Share of good (it) in the total cost of composite good i, i=1,...,n, t=1,2, — calculated from the input–output data files: $$S_{(i2)}^{(c)} = (-\tilde{E}\underline{1})_i/ \left(\tilde{T}_i +(-\tilde{E}\underline{1})_i - (\tilde{F}\underline{1})_i\right),$$ $$S_{(i1)}^{(c)} = 1 - S_{(i2)}^{(c)}.$$

Table 4.3.4 (continued)

Equation	Coefficient or Parameter[†]	Description and Evaluation[#]
(4.3.17)(b) $\dfrac{T_{(i3)}}{T_{(i3)} + T_{(3)} - 1}$		The power of the special subsidy applying to exports of good (i3) divided by the power of the total subsidy applying to export of (i3), i=1,...,n — calculated from the input-output data files: $\dfrac{T_{(i3)}}{T_{(i3)} + T_{(3)} - 1} = (\tilde{F})_{i1}/(\tilde{F\underline{1}})_i$.
$\dfrac{T_{(3)}}{T_{(i3)} + T_{(3)} - 1}$		The power of the general subsidy applying to all exports divided by the power of the total subsidy applying to export of (i3), i=1,...,n: $\dfrac{T_{(3)}}{T_{(i3)} + T_{(3)} - 1} = (\tilde{F})_{i2}/(\tilde{F\underline{1}})_i$.
(4.3.18)(b) $\dfrac{T_{(i2)}}{T_{(i2)} + T_{(2)} - 1}$		The power of the special tariff applying to imports of good (i2) divided by the power of the total tariff applying to imports of (i2), i=1,...,n — calculated from the input-output data files: $\dfrac{T_{(i2)}}{T_{(i2)} + T_{(2)} - 1} = (-\tilde{E})_{i1}/(-\tilde{E\underline{1}})_i$,
$\dfrac{T_{(2)}}{T_{(i2)} + T_{(2)} - 1}$		The power of the general tariff applying to all imports divided by the power of the total tariff applying to imports of (i2), i=1,...,n — $\dfrac{T_{(2)}}{T_{(i2)} + T_{(2)} - 1} = (-\tilde{E})_{i2}/(-\tilde{E\underline{1}})_i$.
(4.3.19)(b)	$H_{(ic)}^{(2j)}$	Share of composite good i in the total costs of capital creation for industry j, i,j=1,...,n — calculated from the input-output data files: $H_{(ic)}^{(2j)} = (\tilde{B})_{ij}/(\underline{1}'\tilde{B})_j$.
(4.3.23)(b)	$B_{(ic)}^{(k)}$	Share of the total demand for composite good i accounted for by households (k=3) and the government (k=4), i=1,...,n — calculated from the input-output data files: $B_{(ic)}^{(3)} = \tilde{C}_i/\left(\tilde{T}_i + (-\tilde{E\underline{1}})_i - (\tilde{F\underline{1}})_i\right)$, $B_{(ic)}^{(4)} = \tilde{D}_i/\left(\tilde{T}_i + (-\tilde{E\underline{1}})_i - (\tilde{F\underline{1}})_i\right)$.
	$B_{(ic)}^{(gj)}$	Share of the total demand for composite good i accounted for by the intermediate usage (g=1) and the capital creation (g=2) of industry j, i,j=1,...,n — $B_{(ic)}^{(1j)} = (\tilde{A})_{ij}/\left(\tilde{T}_i + (-\tilde{E\underline{1}})_i - (\tilde{F\underline{1}})_i\right)$, $B_{(ic)}^{(2j)} = (\tilde{B})_{ij}/\left(\tilde{T}_i + (-\tilde{E\underline{1}})_i - (\tilde{F\underline{1}})_i\right)$.
(4.3.24)(b)	$B_{(n+1,1,k)}^{(1j)}$	Share of the total demand for man years of labor of occupation k accounted for by employment in industry j, k=1,...,m, j=1,...,n — calculated from the input-output data files together with industry/occupation wage rates: *(continued next page)*

... (continued)

Table 4.3.4 (continued)

Equation	Coefficient or Parameter[†]	Description and Evaluation[#]
(4.3.24)(b) *(continued)*		$$B^{(1j)}_{(n+1,1,k)} = \frac{(\tilde{G})_{kj}/P^{(1j)}_{(n+1,1,k)}}{\displaystyle\sum_{j=1}^{n} (\tilde{G})_{kj}/P^{(1j)}_{(n+1,1,k)}}.$$ Initial values for the industry/occupation wage rates, $P^{(1j)}_{(n+1,1,k)}$, must be included in the supplementary data files.
(4.3.27)(b)	Q_j	Ratio of gross (before depreciation) to net (after depreciation) rate of return in industry j, j=1,...,n — $$Q_j = \frac{P^{(1j)}_{(n+1,2)}/P^{(j)}_K}{\left(P^{(1j)}_{(n+1,2)}/P^{(j)}_K\right) - D_j}.$$ Initial values for gross rates of return, $\left(P^{(1j)}_{(n+1,2)}/P^{(j)}_K\right)^I$, are included in the supplementary data files. The depreciation rates, D_j, are parameters. For updating in a multistep solution we can use: $$\%\Delta Q_j = \left(1-Q_j\right)\left(p^{(1j)}_{(n+1,2)} - p^{(j)}_K\right).$$
(4.3.28)(b)	$w_i^{(v)}$	Base-period shares of output of industry i in total output (v=1), of composite good i in total investment expenditure (v=2), of composite good i in household expenditure (v=3), and of composite good i in government expenditure (v=4), i=1,...,n — parameters whose values are calculated from the initial input-output data: $$w_i^{(1)} = \tilde{T}_i/\sum_{i=1}^{n}\tilde{T}_i, \quad w_i^{(2)} = (\tilde{B}\underline{1})_i/\sum_{i=1}^{n}(\tilde{B}\underline{1})_i,$$ $$w_i^{(3)} = \tilde{C}_i/\sum_{i=1}^{n}\tilde{C}_i \quad \text{and} \quad w_i^{(4)} = \tilde{D}_i/\sum_{i=1}^{n}\tilde{D}_i.$$
(4.3.29)(b)	$M_{(i2)}$	Share of good (i2) in the total foreign currency value of imports, i=1,...,n — calculated from input-output data files: $$M_{(i2)} = (\tilde{E})_{i3}/(\underline{1}'\tilde{E})_3.$$
(4.3.30)(b)	$E_{(i3)}$	Share of good (i3) in the total foreign currency value of exports, i=1,...,n — calculated from input-output data files: $$E_{(i3)} = (-\tilde{F})_{i3}/(-\underline{1}'\tilde{F})_3.$$

Table 4.3.4 (continued)

Equation	Coefficient or Parameter[†]	Description and Evaluation[#]
(4.3.31)(b)	E	Total foreign currency value of exports.
	M	Total foreign currency value of imports — calculated from input-output data files:

$$E = (-\underline{1}'\tilde{F})_3 \quad \text{and} \quad M = (\underline{1}'\tilde{E})_3 \, .$$

(4.3.32)(b)	h_1	Wage indexing parameter — usually set at 1.
(4.3.33)(b)	h_2	Parameter for linking the rentals on capital to the consumer price index — usually set at 1.
(4.3.34)(b)	B_j^K	Share of the economy's total capital stock accounted for by industry j, j=1,...,n —

$$B_j^K = K_j / \sum_{i=1}^{n} K_i \, .$$

The initial value for the capital stock, K_j, is calculated by dividing the rental, $(H)_j$, in the initial input-output table by the initial gross rate of return. Initial values for the gross rates of return are in the supplementary data file. The B_j^K can be updated in a multistep solution according to:

$$\%\Delta B_j^K = k_j - k \, .$$

(4.3.35)(b)	B_v^L	Share of total employment accounted for by occupation v, v=1,...,m — calculated from the input-output data files together with industry/occupation wage rates:

$$B_v^L = \frac{\sum_j \tilde{G}_{vj} / P_{(n+1,1,v)}^{(1j)}}{\sum_v \sum_j \tilde{G}_{vj} / P_{(n+1,1,v)}^{(1j)}} \, .$$

Initial values for the industry/occupation wage rates must be included in the supplementary data files.

(4.3.36)(b)	$G_{(n+1,t)}^{(1j)3}$	Shares of gross (before tax and depreciation) household income accounted for by wages (t=1) and rentals on capital (t=2) in industry j, j=1,...,n, t=1,2, — calculated from input-output data files:

$$G_{(n+1,1)}^{(1j)3} = (\underline{1}'\tilde{G})_j / \sum_j ((\underline{1}'\tilde{G})_j + \tilde{H}_j)$$

and

$$G_{(n+1,2)}^{(1j)3} = \tilde{H}_j / \sum_j ((\underline{1}'\tilde{G})_j + \tilde{H}_j) \, .$$

... *(continued)*

Table 4.3.4 (continued)

Equation	Coefficient or Parameter[†]	Description and Evaluation[#]
(4.3.37)(b)	$G_i^{(0)4}$	Value of output net of production taxes in industry i divided by government income, i=1,...,n — calculated from input-output data file: $$G_i^{(0)4} = (\tilde{T}_i - \tilde{J}_i)/\tilde{V}.$$
	$R_{(is)}$	Covered under (4.3.5)(b).
	$J_i^{(0)4}$	Production taxes on industry i as a share of government income, i=1,...,n: $$J_i^{(0)4} = \tilde{J}_i/\tilde{V}.$$
	$G_{(i2)}^4$	Value of imports of commodity i including the special tariff but excluding the general tariff divided by government income, i=1,...,n: $$G_{(i2)}^4 = (-\tilde{E})_{i1}/\tilde{V}.$$
	G_2^4	Total value of imports including the general tariff but excluding the special tariffs divided by government income: $$G_2^4 = (-\underline{1}'\tilde{E})_2/\tilde{V}.$$
	$J_{(i2)}^4$	Revenue from tariffs on good (i2) as a share of government income, i=1,...,n: $$J_{(i2)}^4 = \left((-\tilde{E})_{i1} + (-\tilde{E})_{i2} - 2(\tilde{E})_{i3}\right)/\tilde{V}.$$
	$G_{(i3)}^4$	Value of exports of commodity i including the special subsidy but excluding the general subsidy divided by government income, i=1,...,n: $$G_{(i3)}^{(4)} = (\tilde{F})_{i1}/\tilde{V}.$$
	G_3^4	Total value of exports including the general subsidy but excluding the special subsidies divided by government income: $$G_3^4 = (\underline{1}'\tilde{F})_2/\tilde{V}.$$
	$J_{(i3)}^4$	Subsidies on exports of (i3) as a share of government income: $$J_{(i3)}^4 = \left((\tilde{F})_{i1} + (\tilde{F})_{i2} + 2(\tilde{F})_{i3}\right)/\tilde{V}.$$
	J_H^4	Taxes on household income as a share of government income: $$J_H^4 = \tilde{K}/\tilde{V}.$$
(4.3.38)(b)	$\dfrac{T^H}{(1-T^H)}$	Taxes on household income as a fraction of net (after tax) household income — calculated from the input-output data files: $$\frac{T^H}{1-T^H} = \frac{\tilde{K}}{\tilde{U} - \tilde{K}}.$$

† The distinction between parameters and coefficients is explained in Section 4.1.

For tilde (˜) notation, see Table 4.4.1; the database is in Appendix 4.1.

Table 4.3.5[a]

Two Selections of Exogenous Variables†

Selection 1: Standard ORANI Closure[#]	Selection 2: Standard DMR Closure[¶]	Sub-script range	Num-ber	Description and comments*
$a_{n+1}^{(1j)}$	$a_{n+1}^{(1j)}$	$j=1,...,n$	n	Technical change is exogenous in both selections.
$c_R^{(2)}$	ΔB		1	In selection 1, the balance of trade, the household tax rate and the government's average propensity to spend adjust to accommodate exogenously given real absorption levels. In selection 2, the real absorption levels adjust to accommodate the exogenously given balance of trade, household tax rate and government average propensity to spend.
$c_R^{(3)}$	t^H		1	
$c_R^{(4)}$	$q^{(4)}$		1	
$f^{(2j)}$	$f^{(2j)}$	$j=1,...,n$	n	The treatment of the f variables is the same in both selections with one exception. In selection 1, $f_{(n+1,\ 1)}$ which can normally be interpreted as the percentage change in the real wage rate, is exogenous. In selection 2, it is replaced by l, the percentage change in the aggregate level of employment. In selection 1, the level of employment adjusts to exogenously given real wages. In selection 2, real wages adjust to allow the achievement of an exogenously given level of total employment.
$f_{(ic)}^{(4)}$	$f_{(ic)}^{(4)}$	$i=1,...,n$	n	
$f_{(i3)}^{(w)}$	$f_{(i3)}^{(w)}$	$i=1,...,n$	n	
$f_{(i3)}$	$f_{(i3)}$	$i=1,...,n$	n	
$f_2^{(c)}$	$f_2^{(c)}$		1	
$f_{(i1)}^{(c)}$	$f_{(i1)}^{(c)}$	$i=1,...,n$	n	
$f_{(n+1,1,k)}$	$f_{(n+1,1,k)}$	$k=1,...,m$	m	
$f_{(n+1,1)}$	l		1	
$p_{(i2)}^{(w)}$	$p_{(i2)}^{(w)}$	$i=1,...,n$	n	World prices of imports are exogenous in both selections.
$q^{(3)}$	$q^{(3)}$		1	Both selections exogenize the average propensity to consume of households.
$t_i^{(0)}$	$t_i^{(0)}$	$i=1,...,n$	n	Rates of production taxes, export subsidies and tariffs, are exogenous under both selections.
$t_{(i3)}$	$t_{(i3)}$	$i=1,...,n$	n	
$t_{(3)}$	$t_{(3)}$		1	
$t_{(i2)}$	$t_{(i2)}$	$i=1,...,n$	n	
$t_{(2)}$	$t_{(2)}$		1	
$x_{(n+1,2)}^{(1j)}$	$x_{(n+1,2)}^{(1j)}$	$j=1,...,n$	n	In both selections the availability of capital in each industry is set exogenously.
ϕ	$\xi^{(1)}$		1	The two selections differ with regard to the choice of numeraire.

Total = $11n + m + 9$

(a)   Footnotes to this table appear at the bottom of the next page.

Table 4.3.6

*Required Parameters for the Percentage-
Change Version of the DMR Model*

Parameter	Appearing in equation(s)	Description
γ_i	(4.3.4)(b)	Reciprocal of the foreign elasticity of demand for exportable good i.
$\sigma_j^{(o)}$	(4.3.5)(b)	Elasticity of transformation between goods (j1) and (j3).
$\sigma_{n+1}^{(1j)}$	(4.3.8)(b)	Elasticity of substitution between capital and labor in industry j.
$\sigma_{(n+1,1)}^{(1j)}$	(4.3.9)(b)	Elasticity of substitution between different types of labor in industry j.
$\sigma_i^{(c)}$	(4.3.11)(b)	Elasticity of substitution between domestic and imported good i (the Armington elasticities).
D_i	(4.3.27)(b) (implicit)	Depreciation rate for industry i (needed for calculating the coefficient Q_j — see Table 4.3.4).
$w_i^{(v)}$ [see note below]	(4.3.28)(b)	Price index number weights representing: the contribution of industry i to total output (v=1); of composite good i to total investment (v=2); of composite good i to household expenditure (v=3); of composite good i to government expenditure (v=4).
h_1	(4.3.32)(b)	Wage indexing parameter.
h_2	(4.3.33)(b)	Parameter for linking the rentals on capital to the consumer price index.

Note: In the implementation described in this book, these weights are taken as base-period shares — see entry for equation (4.3.28)(b) in Table 4.3.4.

Footnotes to Table 4.3.5 :

† For convenience of presentation we list the variables in the percentage change forms only.

\# This selection of exogenous variables is similar to that often used in simulations with the *ORANI* model of the Australian economy (see Dixon, Parmenter, Sutton and Vincent (1982, section 23)).

¶ This selection of exogenous variables is close to that often adopted by DMR. The only significant deviation concerns employment. In our selection 2 we set aggregate employment exogenously. DMR usually exogenize employment in each occupation.

* For definitions of the variables see Table 4.3.2.

Table 4.3.7
*Supplementary Data File for the DMR Model: Variables whose Initial Values
are not Implied by the Initial Input-Output Table*

Variable,	the initial value of which is required for setting the initial value of the coefficient(s),	appearing in equation(s)
$F^{(c)}_{(2)}/F^{(c)}_{(i1)}(\equiv\Omega_i)$ (Actual import/ domestic ratio divided by the desired ratio)	$\begin{cases} S^{(c)*}_{(it)} \\ \text{and} \\ \eta^{(ic)}_{(it)} \end{cases}$	(4.3.11)(b) (4.3.14)(b)
$P^{(1j)}_{(n+1,1,k)}$ (Wage rates by occupation and industry)	$\begin{cases} B^{(1j)}_{(n+1,1,k)} \\ \text{and} \\ B^{L}_{v} \end{cases}$	(4.3.24)(b) (4.3.35)(b)
$P^{(1j)}_{(n+1,2)}/P^{(j)}_{K}$ $[=(R_j+D_j)]$ (Gross, i.e., before depreciation, rates of return)	$\begin{cases} \mathcal{Q}_j \\ \text{and} \\ B^{K}_{j} \end{cases}$	(4.3.27)(b) (4.3.34)(b)
$\eta^{(Zj)}_{(j1)}$ *[see note below]* (Elasticity of overall activity level in industry j with respect to the output of domestically oriented (s=1) or ex-portable (s=3) product j)	$\eta^{(Zj)}_{(js)}$, s = 1, 3	(4.3.6)(b)

Note: If revenue maximization is assumed, the values of $\eta^{(Zj)}_{(js)}$ are revenue shares obtainable from the input-output database (see entry for equation (4.3.6)(b) in Table 4.3.4). Otherwise, values of $\eta^{(Zj)}_{(j1)}$ must be supplied as supplementary data ($\eta^{(Zj)}_{(j3)} = 1 - \eta^{(Zj)}_{(j1)}$).

In the third category of equations, the stylized Johansen model contained zero-pure-profit conditions only for current production. In the DMR model we require additional zero-pure-profits conditions to relate the prices of composite commodities to the cost of creating them, the prices of exportables to the revenue received per unit of export (including export subsidies), the prices of imports to the costs of importing (including tariffs), and the prices of units of capital to the costs of creating them.

Finally, in the market-clearing section of the DMR model we find, as in the stylized Johansen model, equalities between demands and supplies for both commodities and primary factors. In the DMR model, however, we have a greater variety in both categories: commodities include domestically-oriented goods, imports, exportables, and composites; primary factors include labor classified by occupation, and capital classified by industry.

At the foot of Table 4.3.1, the total number of equations is shown as $26n + 2mn + 2n^2 + m + 19$, where n is the number of industries and m is the number of occupations. In our implementation of the DMR model we used a database containing 8 industries and 4 occupations (see Appendix 4.1), generating a system of 423 equations. The number of variables is shown at the foot of Table 4.3.2 as $37n + 2n^2 + 2nm + 2m + 28$, which equals 524 in our implementation. Therefore, in each of our simulations with the DMR model, there will be 101 exogenous variables $(11n + m + 9)$. Two possible selections of exogenous variables are shown in Table 4.3.5.

On looking more closely at the "equation" column in Table 4.3.1 and the "variables" column of Table 4.3.2, you will see that we have made extensive use of subscripts and superscripts. The only alternative in a detailed model is to use multiple-letter symbols. The latter option was taken by DMR. Their style of notation is apparent from the equation

$$PWE_i = PD_i/[(1 + te_i) ER] \ ,$$

given in DMR (1982, p. 250). In this equation, PWE_i is the world price of exports of good i in foreign currency, PD_i is the domestic price, ER is the exchange rate and te_i is the rate of export subsidy on commodity i. An advantage of multiple-letter notation is that we can sometimes choose easily remembered acronyms. On the other hand, multiple-letter notation is awkward in algebraic manipulations. It reduces the scope for using operators such as Σ and Π. While multiple-letter notation may be suitable for a final presentation of a small model, it is not usually suitable as a working notation, nor as a language for the definitive description of a large model. Since this is a work-book, we prefer to avoid multiple-letter symbols by adopting a notation which is heavily subscripted and superscripted. The remainder of this section is an overview of the main ideas underlying this notation.

In explaining the notation, we use the opportunity to review various important theoretical features of the DMR model, some of which have been alluded to already. We start by noting that the model identifies 4n commodities consisting of 4 types of commodities within each of n commodity categories.

Commodity category i contains:

> domestic commodity i, which we indicate by subscript (i1);
> imported commodity i, which we indicate by subscript (i2);
> exportable commodity i, which we indicate by subscript (i3);

and

> composite commodity i, which we indicate by subscript (ic).

There are n industries in our representation of the DMR model. Industry i produces types 1 and 3 in commodity category i, i.e., the output of industry i is a combination of commodities (i1) and (i3). Commodity (i3) is exported while units of (i1) are combined with imported commodity i, commodity (i2), to form units of composite commodity i, commodity (ic).

Commodity (ic) is used by industries as an input to both current production and the creation of capital. It is also consumed by households and the government. We indicate the various uses of commodity (ic) by superscripts:

> superscript (1j) denotes use in current production by industry j;
> superscript (2j) denotes use in capital creation for industry j;
> superscript (3) denotes consumption by households;

and

> superscript (4) denotes consumption by the government.

With Xs denoting quantities, we see in Table 4.3.2, that $X_{(ic)}^{(1j)}$ is the demand for commodity (ic) to be used as an intermediate input by industry j. $X_{(ic)}^{(2j)}, X_{(ic)}^{(3)}$ and $X_{(ic)}^{(4)}$ are the demands for (ic) for capital creation in industry j, for household consumption and for government consumption. The quantities of (i1) and (i2) which are combined to form composite commodities are denoted by $X_{(i1)}^{(c)}$ and $X_{(i2)}^{(c)}$.

As well as inputs of composite commodities, industrial production in the DMR model requires inputs of primary factors. We indicate primary factors by subscript n + 1. Subscript (n + 1, 1) refers to labor (primary factor of type 1) while subscript (n + 1, 2) refers to capital (primary factor of type 2). Labor is disaggregated into occupations with subscript $(n + 1, 1, k)$ denoting labor of occupation k. Thus in Table 4.3.2, $X^{(1j)}_{(n+1,s)}$ is defined for $s = 1$ as the input of labor to current production in industry j, and for $s = 2$ as the input of capital. $X^{(1j)}_{(n+1,1,k)}$ is defined as the input of labor of occupation k and is a component of the composite labor input index $X^{(1j)}_{(n+1,1)}$.

Xs without superscripts denote commodity supplies. $X_{(is)}$ for $s = 1, 2, 3$ and c, is the supply of commodity (is). Although it would be possible to use subscripted Xs without superscripts for factor supplies, instead, we let L_k denote the total employment of labor of occupation k and K_j denote the quantity of capital available for industry j.

The subscripting/superscripting scheme adopted for the Xs has also been used for the Ps, which denote prices. $P_{(is)}$ for $s = 1, 2, 3$ and c, is the local market price of commodity (is). No superscripts are necessary because DMR assume that domestic users and suppliers face a single price for each commodity. No allowance is made for differences in transport or other costs which separate prices received by suppliers (producers and importers) from those paid by users, and no allowance is made for differences in commodity tax rates applying to different categories of commodity users.

For primary factor prices, superscripts are required. $P^{(1j)}_{(n+1,1)}$ is the cost per unit of labor used by industry j in current production. (Labor in the DMR model is used only in current production. It could be argued, therefore, that a superscript 1 is superfluous when used in conjunction with a subscript n+1.) Unit labor costs vary across industries because of differences in the occupational compositions of their labor forces. DMR also allow for differences across industries in the wage rates paid per unit of labor of each occupational type. Consequently, we need an industry superscript on the price of labor of type k. We let $P^{(1j)}_{(n+1,1,k)}$ denote the wage rate of occupation k in industry j. For capital, there are two prices for each industry: a rental price and a construction price. The rental price for units or capital used in current production by industry j is denoted by $P^{(1j)}_{(n+1,2)}$. The construction price is $P^{(j)}_{k.}$. Rental prices differ across industries reflecting the demands and supplies for different types of industrial capacity. Construction prices differ across industries reflecting differences in the commodity composition of units of capital used in different industries.

The remaining price variables listed in Table 4.3.2 are $P_{(i2)}^{(w)}$ and $P_{(i3)}^{(w)}$. The superscript "w" stands for world. $P_{(i2)}^{(w)}$ is the world price in foreign currency which must be paid per unit of import of commodity (i2). $P_{(i3)}^{(w)}$ is the foreign currency receipt per unit of export of commodity (i3).

Taxes and subsidies are denoted by T. With two exceptions these variables are "powers" in our version of the DMR model, i.e., they are one plus *ad valorem* rates. In Exercises 4.13 and 4.15 we will be doing some Johansen-style percentage-change calculations and by using powers rather than rates we minimize the risk of trying to compute the nonsense of a percentage-change in a variable whose initial value is zero. The two exceptions are $T_i^{(0)}$, which is one minus the rate of tax on the value of output of industry i; and T^H, which is the rate of tax on household income. We can safely assume that both these variables will always be strictly positive.

The final sets of heavily subscripted and superscripted variables in Table 4.3.2 are the As and Fs. These variables allow for shifts in various functions. Movements in $A_{(n+1)}^{(1j)}$, for example, shift industry j's production function by introducing primary-factor-augmenting technical change, while the $F_{(ic)}^{(4)}$s allow for shifts in the functions describing the commodity composition of government consumption. $F_{(i3)}^{(w)}$ allows for shifts in the foreign demand curve for commodity (i3) while $F_{(i3)}$ allows for shifts in the function describing industry i's supply of commodity (i3). The $F_{(i1)}^{(c)}$s, $F_{(i2)}^{(c)}$s and $F_{(2)}^{(c)}$ are concerned with shifts in the mix of domestic and imported commodities used in the formation of composite commodities. Shifts in primary factor pricing functions are accommodated by F-variables carrying n+1 subscripts.

The system of superscripts and subscripts adopted for the variables of the DMR model has been carried over to the coefficients and parameters. When we see $\alpha_{(ic)}^{(3)}$ in (4.3.1)(a), we should associate the subscript (ic) with composite commodity i and the superscript 3 with household consumption. We see from the "description" column of Table 4.3.3 that $\alpha_{(ic)}^{(g)}$ for g = 3 is the share of household expenditure devoted to composite commodity i. To take a more elaborate example, when we see $S_{(n+1,1,v)}^{(1j)}$ in (4.3.9)(b), we should associate the subscript (n+1,1,v) with primary factor, source 1, type v; i.e., labor of occupation v. We should associate the superscript (1j) with current production in industry j. On referring to Table 4.3.4, we see that $S_{(n+1,1,v)}^{(1j)}$ is the share of labor of type v in the total labor costs of industry j.

Figure 4.3.1 illustrates some of our notation and indicates the directions of commodity and factor flows.

4.4   *The Input-Output Database*

The main data requirements for the implementation of a general equilibrium model can be met by a suitable set of input-output accounts. As we saw in Exercise 3.3, input-output accounts are used in the evaluation of "share" parameters and coefficients. A suitable set of accounts must identify all the commodity, factor and tax flows included in the model. The accounts should also depict a situation which is model-compatible.

Many of the equations of the DMR model are derived from constrained optimization problems. In solving these problems, we will often do the mathematics as though the solution values for the choice variables are strictly positive. However, on glancing at the input-output data in Appendix 4.1, we see many zero flows. Since we will be assuming that these flows are consistent with the DMR equations, we are faced with an inconsistency.

One approach to resolving the inconsistency is to do the mathematics more carefully; i.e., to make explicit provisions for zero flows in the theory. However, this makes for tedious algebra. Another approach is to assume that where we have 0.00 in the input-output tables, the real values is 10^{-6} , say. The replacement in the input-output data of zero flows with negligible non-zero flows has a negligible impact on our eventual simulation results. At the same time, it allows us to restrict our mathematics to interior solutions and means that percentage change forms of variables exist and can be used in a Johansen solution.

The problem of zero flows aside, it is often necessary to make further adjustments to published accounts before using them with particular models. For example, published accounts sometimes contain a few industries with negative gross operating surpluses. In many models, this is incompatible with the assumption of non-negative returns to fixed factors. Even where published accounts are model-compatible, adjustments might still be desirable to eliminate atypical features, e.g., an excessive inventory accumulation of wheat arising from an unusually large harvest. For a discussion of the 'typicalization' of a database prior to its use, see Higgs (1986) or Adams and Higgs (1990).

A schematic version of the input-output data for the DMR model is given in Table 4.4.1. The matrices and vectors in this table are marked with tildes so as to avoid confusion with other uses in this chapter of the symbols A, B, etc. Matrix $\tilde{A}$ shows the flows of commodities to be used by

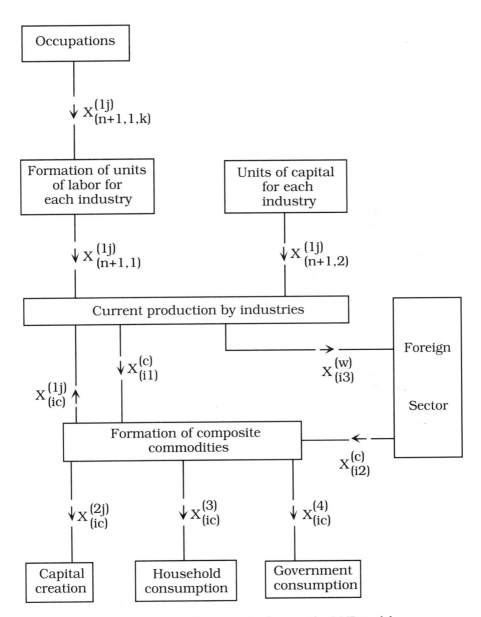

Figure 4.3.1: Commodity and factor flows in the DMR model

The arrows indicate the direction of the commodity or factor flows.
The X's indicate the demands which are being satisfied by each flow

Table 4.4.1

Schematic Representation of the Input-Output Data Files for the DMR Model

	Industries (current production) ← n →	Industries (capital formation) ← n →	Household Consumption ← 1 →	Government and other ← 1 →	Imports* c.i.f. values multiplied by $-T_{(i2)}, -T_{(2)}, 1$ ← 3 →			Exports# f.o.b. values multiplied by $T_{(i3)}, T_{(3)}, -1$ ← 3 →			Row totals
Commodities n	$\tilde{A}$	$\tilde{B}$	$\tilde{C}$	$\tilde{D}$	$\tilde{E}$			$\tilde{F}$			$\tilde{T}$
Labor m	$\tilde{G}$										$\tilde{S}$
Capital 1	$\tilde{H}$										$\tilde{X}$
Taxes 1	$\tilde{J}$		$\tilde{K}$								$\tilde{Z}$
Savings 1			$\tilde{L}$	$\tilde{M}$							$\tilde{I}$
Column Totals	$\tilde{T}'$	$\tilde{P}$	$\tilde{U}$	$\tilde{V}$	$\tilde{W}$			$\tilde{Y}$			

* The first column of $\tilde{E}$ shows the negative of imports valued at c.i.f. prices plus the commodity-specific tariffs. In the notation of Table 4.3.2, $(\tilde{E})_{i1} = -T_{(i2)} P^{(w)}_{(i2)} Φ X_{(i2)}$. The second column shows the negative of imports valued at c.i.f. prices plus the general tariffs, i.e., $(\tilde{E})_{(i2)} = -T_{(2)} P^{(w)}_{(i2)} Φ X_{(i2)}$. The third column shows the imports at c.i.f. prices, i.e., $(\tilde{E})_{(i3)} = P^{(w)}_{(i2)} Φ X_{(i2)}$.

\# The first column of F shows exports valued at f.o.b. prices plus the commodity-specific export subsidies, i.e., $(F)_{i1} = T_{(i3)} P^{(w)}_{(i3)} Φ X_{(i3)}$. The second column shows exports valued at f.o.b. prices plus the general export subsidies, i.e., $(F)_{(i2)} = T_{(3)} P^{(w)}_{(i3)} Φ X_{(i3)}$. The third column shows the negative of exports valued at f.o.b. prices, i.e., $(F)_{(i3)} = -P^{(w)}_{(i3)} Φ X_{(i3)}$.

industries as intermediate inputs. $\tilde{B}$ shows commodity flows to capital formation. The typical component of $\tilde{B}$ is the use of commodity i in the creation of capital capacity (buildings, plant and equipment) for industry j. The vector $\tilde{C}$ shows the commodity composition of household consumption. Government consumption and possibly some miscellaneous demands (e.g., inventory accumulation) are shown in the vector $\tilde{D}$. All of the flows in $\tilde{A}$, $\tilde{B}$, $\tilde{C}$ and $\tilde{D}$ include purchases of both domestic and imported commodities valued at basic prices, i.e., they are flows of the type appearing in input-output tables at basic prices with indirect allocation of imports (see Exercise 2.2). In applying the data to the DMR model, we interpret the ith rows of $\tilde{A}$, $\tilde{B}$, $\tilde{C}$ and $\tilde{D}$ as being sales of composite commodity i, i.e., commodity (ic).

Matrix $\tilde{E}$ records total imports for each commodity (sales of commodity (i2) for i = 1,...., n) valued in three different ways whilst $\tilde{F}$ records three different valuations of export sales (sales of commodity (i3) for i = 1,...., n). In the first column of $\tilde{E}$, commodity-specific tariffs are included in the values of the imports. Similarly, in the first column of $\tilde{F}$, commodity-specific export subsidies are included in the values of the exports. In the second column of $\tilde{E}$, commodity-specific tariffs are excluded but the general tariff applying to all imports is included. The second column of $\tilde{F}$ excludes commodity-specific subsidies but includes the general export subsidy. The third columns of $\tilde{E}$ and $\tilde{F}$ exclude all tariffs and subsidies.

From the point of view of having a neatly balanced table, it is convenient to record the first two columns in $\tilde{E}$ and the third column of $\tilde{F}$ as negative numbers. If the foreign currency cost (converted into domestic currency) of imports of commodity 1 were 100, and if there were a general tariff of 10 per cent applying to all imports and an additional tariff of 50 per cent applying to imports of commodity 1, then the entries in the first row of $\tilde{E}$ would be –150, –110, and 100. Similarly if the foreign currency value of exports of commodity 1 were 100 while exports of this commodity were subject to commodity-specific and general subsidies of 50 and 10 per cent respectively, then the first row of $\tilde{F}$ would be (150, 110, –100). By including the negative signs, we ensure that the row sums of $\tilde{E}$ are the negative of the import vector valued at basic prices (i.e., including tariffs) and that the row sums of $\tilde{F}$ are the export vector values at basic prices (i.e., including export subsidies). Then recalling that $\tilde{A}$, $\tilde{B}$, $\tilde{C}$, and $\tilde{D}$ include imports valued at basic prices, we see that the sums, $\tilde{T}$, across the rows of $\tilde{A}$, $\tilde{B}$, $\tilde{C}$, $\tilde{D}$, $\tilde{E}$ and $\tilde{F}$ are the basic values of the industry outputs.

The matrix $\tilde{G}$ shows labor costs for each industry disaggregated into m occupations. The vector $\tilde{H}$ shows the gross operating surplus (or return to capital) for each industry. In the version of the DMR model that we are considering, there are no taxes payable by industries on capital income or on the use of inputs, all imposts on income appearing as levies on households' receipts of income from capital and labor. Production taxes are the only taxes payable by industries. Taxes paid by industries on their production levels are recorded in the row vector $\tilde{J}$. By adding down the columns of $\tilde{A}$, $\tilde{G}$, $\tilde{H}$ and $\tilde{J}$ we again obtain the values of industry outputs, $\tilde{T}$.

The scalars $\tilde{K}$, $\tilde{L}$ and $\tilde{M}$ show, respectively, taxes paid by households, saving by households, and saving by the government. The total income of households (apportioned over expenditure, taxes and saving) is the sum, $\tilde{U}$, of the entries in $\tilde{C}$, $\tilde{K}$ and $\tilde{L}$. Household income is also the sum of labor income $\underline{1}'\tilde{S}$ (where $\underline{1}$ is a vector of units of appropriate length — in this case m), and of capital income $\tilde{X}$. Government income is the sum, $\tilde{V}$, of the entries in $\tilde{D}$ and $\tilde{M}$. Alternatively, it can be calculated as taxes plus tariffs minus subsidies, i.e., as

$$\tilde{Z} + [-(\tilde{W})\,\underline{1} - (\tilde{W}_3)] - [\tilde{Y}\,\underline{1} - (-\tilde{Y})_3],$$

where the subscripts 3 refer to the third elements in the vectors $\tilde{W}$ and $\tilde{Y}$.

The matrices $\tilde{A}$, $\tilde{B}$, etc., used in our version of the DMR model are set out in Appendix 4.1. This data, which refers to South Korea in 1963, has often been used by Sherman Robinson and his co-workers in illustrative applications of their model. To reinforce your understanding of Table 4.4.1, it might be useful to use the data in the appendix to check the following:

(a)   *Value of output in industry 1*

   = sum across first row of $\tilde{A}$, $\tilde{B}$, $\tilde{C}$, $\tilde{D}$, $\tilde{E}$, $\tilde{F}$ *(total sales)*

   = sum down first column of $\tilde{A}$, $\tilde{G}$, $\tilde{H}$, $\tilde{J}$ *(total costs)*

   = 657.36.

(b)   *Tariff revenue*

   $= (-\tilde{W})\underline{1} - (\tilde{W})_3 = 193.47 - 164.83 = 28.64$.

(c)   *Export subsidies*

   $= \tilde{Y}\,\underline{1} - (-\tilde{Y})_3 = 66.89 - 66.89 = 0$.

(d)   *Revenue from general tariff*

   $= (-\tilde{W})_2 - (\tilde{W})_3 = 0$.

(e)   *Revenue from commodity-specific tariffs*

   $= (-\tilde{W})_1 - (\tilde{W})_3 = 28.64$.

(f)   *Household income (before taxes)*

$$= \underline{1}' \ \tilde{C} + \tilde{K} + \tilde{L} \qquad\qquad\qquad \textit{(expenditure + saving + taxes)}$$

$$= \underline{1}' \ \tilde{\underline{S}} + \tilde{X} \qquad\qquad\qquad\qquad \textit{(labor + capital income)}$$

$$= 1070.52 \ .$$

(g)   *Government income*

$$= \underline{1}' \ \tilde{D} + \tilde{M} \qquad\qquad\qquad\qquad \textit{(expenditure + saving)}$$

$$= \tilde{Z} + [(-\tilde{W})\underline{1} - (\tilde{W})_3] - [\tilde{\underline{Y}}\underline{1} - (-\tilde{Y})_3] \qquad \textit{(taxes + tariffs - subsidies)}$$

$$= 194.03.$$

(h)   *GDP*

$$= \underline{1}' \ \tilde{\underline{S}} + \tilde{X} + \tilde{J}'\underline{1} + [(-\tilde{W})\underline{1} - (\tilde{W})_3] - [\tilde{\underline{Y}}\underline{1} + (\tilde{Y})_3] \qquad \textit{(factor income +}$$
$$\textit{production taxes + tariffs - subsidies)}$$

$$= \underline{1}' \ \tilde{C} + \tilde{P}\underline{1} + \underline{1}' \ \tilde{D} - [(\tilde{W})_3 - (-\tilde{Y})_3] \qquad \textit{(final demands - balance}$$
$$\textit{of trade deficit)}$$

$$= 1164.42.$$

(i)   *Investment*

$$= \tilde{P}\underline{1} \qquad\qquad\qquad\qquad\qquad \textit{(capital expenditure)}$$

$$= \tilde{L} + \tilde{M} + [(\tilde{W})_3 - (-\tilde{Y})_3] \qquad \textit{(domestic saving + the balance of trade}$$
$$\textit{deficit, i.e., foreign saving)}$$

$$= 159.14.$$

PROBLEM SET 4

Exercise 4.1   ***Final demands in the DMR model: equations (4.3.1) – (4.3.4)***

Equations (4.3.1) (a) – (4.3.4)(a) describe four categories of final demands. They show household, government and investment demands for composite goods and foreign demands for exportable goods.

(a)   Assume that households maximize utility subject to budget constraint. What is the form of the utility function underlying the household demand equations (4.3.1)(a)? Are you surprised that DMR choose this particular form? Compute the values of the parameter $\alpha_{(1c)}^{(3)}$ implied by the input-output data in Appendix 4.1.

(b)   Assuming that the $F_{(ic)}^{(4)}$s in (4.3.2)(a) are fixed at unity, what utility maximizing behavior underlies the government's demand equations? The $F_{(ic)}^{(4)}$s are not part of the original DMR model. Can you see any advantage from including them? Compute the values of some of the $\alpha_{(ic)}^{(4)}$ parameters, e.g., $\alpha_{(1c)}^{(4)}$, implied by the input-output data in Appendix 4.1.

(c)   What cost minimizing model is consistent with (4.3.3)(a) as a description of the demands for inputs to make units of industrial capital? Are you surprised that no primary factors are required to make capital?   Compute the values of some of the $A_{(ic)}^{(2j)}$ parameters, e.g., $A_{(5c)}^{(23)}$, from the data in Appendix 4.1. To do this, you will need to introduce definitions of quantity units. Can you see anything in the data matrix $\tilde{B}$ in Appendix 4.1 that seems implausible?

(d)   Show that γ_i is the reciprocal of the foreign elasticity of demand for good (i3). What role do you see for the variable $F_{(i3)}^{(w)}$ in (4.3.4)(a)?

(e)   Derive the percentage change forms, (4.3.1)(b) — (4.3.4)(b), from (4.3.1)(a) — (4.3.4)(a).

Answer to Exercise 4.1

(a)   The household demand equations (4.3.1)(a) can be derived from utility maximizing problems of the form:

$$\text{choose} \quad X_{(ic)}^{(3)}, \quad i = 1,..., n,$$

to maximize

$$f\left(\prod_{i=1}^{n} [X_{(ic)}^{(3)}]^{\alpha_{(ic)}^{(3)}} \right) \tag{E4.1.1}$$

subject to

$$\sum_{i=1}^{n} P_{(ic)} X_{(ic)}^{(3)} = C^{(3)} \quad , \tag{E4.1.2}$$

where f is any monotonic, increasing function.

Model builders occasionally assume utility maximizing behavior of the form (E4.1.1) – (E4.1.2) for reasons of empirical expediency. The only parameters required for implementing the resulting demand systems are budget shares, the $\alpha_{(ic)}^{(3)}$s in (4.3.1)(a).   Budget shares are readily obtainable from input-output tables. For example, in the input-output data in Appendix 4.1, we find from the matrix $\tilde{C}$ that $\alpha_{(1c)}^{(3)} = 452.16/962.08 = 0.47$. Nevertheless, for most countries, it would be difficult to justify the specification (E4.1.1) – (E4.1.2) as a description of household behavior. The resulting demand system (4.3.1)(a) implies that all expenditure elasticities are unity. As we pointed out in Exercise 3.2, this is inconsistent with the results of many empirical studies. Normally, in policy-oriented models, more advanced specifications of household behavior are adopted. For example, DMR (1982, pp. 482-485) have generalized their basic model described in this chapter by using Klein-Rubin utility specifications with parameters based on estimates by Lluch, Powell and Williams (1977) of the linear expenditure system.

(b)   With the $F_{(ic)}^{(4)}$s fixed at 1, the government demand equations (4.3.2)(a) can be derived from utility maximizing problems of the form (E4.1.1) – (E4.1.2) with the superscript (3)s replaced by superscript (4)s.

In most general equilibrium models, government purchases (the $X_{(ic)}^{(4)}$s) are treated as exogenous variables. DMR, whose model does not include our $F_{(ic)}^{(4)}$s, choose instead to fix the share of total government consumption $(C^{(4)})$ devoted to each commodity i at its base-period value, $\alpha_{(ic)}^{(4)}$. ('Base period' refers to the year of the input-output data.) The $\alpha_{(ic)}^{(4)}$s can be evaluated from input-output data. For example, matrix $\tilde{D}$ in Appendix 4.1 implies that $\alpha_{(1c)}^{(4)} = 2.82/141.14 = 0.020$. By including the $F_{(ic)}^{(4)}$s, we allow for both the DMR treatment of government expenditure and for the more usual approach. We obtain the DMR specification by solving the model with the $F_{(ic)}^{(4)}$s as exogenous variables whose values are fixed at 1. We could also simulate the effects of changes in the commodity shares of government expenditure by introducing exogenous shifts in the $F_{(ic)}^{(4)}$s. Alternatively, we can solve the model with the $X_{(ic)}^{(4)}$s treated as exogenous variables in place of the $F_{(ic)}^{(4)}$s.

(c)   Equation (4.3.3)(a) can be derived from the cost minimizing problem,

$$\text{choose} \qquad X_{(ic)}^{(2j)}, \qquad\qquad i = 1,..., n,$$

$$\text{to minimize} \qquad\qquad \sum_{i=1}^{n} P_{(ic)} X_{(ic)}^{(2j)} \qquad\qquad\qquad \text{(E4.1.3)}$$

subject to

$$I_j = \min \left\{ \frac{X_{(1c)}^{(2j)}}{A_{(1c)}^{(2j)}}, \dots, \frac{X_{(nc)}^{(2j)}}{A_{(nc)}^{(2j)}} \right\} \qquad (E4.1.4)$$

In (E4.1.4), the quantity of capital, I_j, created for industry j, is assumed to be a Leontief function of inputs of composite commodities. The minimum number of units of composite commodity i required to make a unit of capital for industry j is given by the parameter $A_{(ic)}^{(2j)}$. To measure this parameter we need first to choose units for both composite commodities and capital. The most convenient approach is to define a unit of composite commodity (ic) as the quantity which had a basic value of (say) one million dollars in the base period, and a unit of capital for industry j as the quantity of capital which had an equal base-period construction cost. In other words, we choose our quantity units so that base-period prices are unity (where a unit of money is one million dollars). This allows us to read flows of composite commodity values in our data matrices as quantities. Similarly, we can read investment expenditures by industry (vector $\tilde{P}$) as numbers of units of capital created. The $A_{(ic)}^{(2j)}$s can then be evaluated as column shares in the investment matrix. On applying this approach with the input-output data in Appendix 4.1, we find, for example, that $A_{(5c)}^{(23)} = 15.68/23.63 = 0.66$.

No inputs of primary factors are included in the capital-creation function (E4.1.4). DMR follow the usual practice of accounting for the use of labor and capital in capital creation via inputs of "construction". The construction industry is modeled as using capital and labor in current production while capital creation is modeled as requiring substantial inputs supplied by the construction industry. Nevertheless, it would be surprising to find industries whose investment expenditures were as construction-intensive as those of industries 6 and 8 (construction and services) in the database in Appendix 4.1. For both these industries, the $\tilde{B}$ matrix implies that construction accounted for 92.6 per cent of investment expenditure while expenditures on machines were zero. Before accepting such an implausibility, it would be wise to check for a data handling error. Sherman Robinson checked out this possibility for us. He confirmed that the lack of machinery expenditures by industries 6 and 8 reflects a data misclassification rather than an actual feature of the economy of South Korea. Because our work here is purely illustrative and because we suspect that any correction would have very little effect on the simulation results reported later in this chapter, we did not think it worthwhile to re-compute using a more plausible $\tilde{B}$ matrix.

(d)   From (4.3.4)(a) we have

$$X_{(i3)}^{(w)} = \left(P_{(i3)}^{(w)}\right)^{-1/\gamma_i} \left(1/F_{(i3)}^{(w)}\right)^{-1/\gamma_i} \quad .$$

The elasticity of demand for commodity (i3) is

$$- [\partial X_{(i3)}^{(w)}/\partial P_{(i3)}^{(w)}] \ [P_{(i3)}^{(w)}/X_{(i3)}^{(w)}] = 1/\gamma_i \quad .$$

The variable $F_{(i3)}^{(w)}$ can be used in simulations of the effects of shifts in the foreign demand curve for commodity (i3). For example, we can move the foreign demand curve upwards by increasing $F_{(i3)}^{(w)}$.

(e)   The percentage change forms can be derived by applying the three rules set out in Exercise 3.2, treating $\alpha_{(ic)}^{(3)}$, $\alpha_{(ic)}^{(4)}$, $A_{(ic)}^{(2j)}$ and γ_i as parameters.

Exercise 4.2   Assigning values for the export demand elasticities

In Appendix 4.1, the γ_is are set at zero, i.e., it is assumed that the export demand elasticities are infinite. This is the conventional small-country assumption, justified by the idea that variations in South Korea's export volumes do not have sufficient influence on world commodity supplies to produce noticeable effects on world commodity prices.

Despite the excellent survey of trade elasticity estimates by Stern, Francis and Schumacher (1976), from the available econometric evidence on export demand elasticities it is difficult to know whether the small-country assumption is really appropriate. Most econometric studies find improbably low elasticity values. Values less than 1 often have been reported, implying that the country involved could increase its export revenue simply by reducing the quantities of some of its exports. Some of the long-standing econometric problems which bias estimates of export demand elasticities downwards are reviewed briefly by Scobie and Johnson (1979), who argue in favour of the small-country assumption. Parmenter (1983) illustrates some of the bizarre implications of using very low export demand elasticities in a general equilibrium model.

In the absence of any clearly superior procedure, many model builders rely on judgement to set values for export demand elasticities, supplemented in some cases by sensitivity analysis. DMR (1982, chapters 8 and 9) checked the sensitivity of various results from their model of Turkey to variations in the export demand elasticities in the range 2.0 to 6.0. Boadway and Treddenick (1978) in their model of Canada considered a range of values from 1 to 25 while Dixon, Parmenter and Rimmer (1985) explored values all the way from zero to infinity in their work on Australia. Taylor and Black (1974) fixed the export demand elasticities for different

Chilean products at values between 4.5 and 10 and Staelin (1976) used 10 for all export products from the Ivory Coast. Much lower values (1 to 2) were chosen by Dervis (1980) for his model of Turkey. Low values were also used in multicountry modeling by Deardorff and Stern (1979) and Brown and Whalley (1980). Both these latter studies relied mainly on the survey of econometric results in Stern *et al.* (1976).

While we would expect differences across countries and products in export demand elasticities, we suspect that it is not actual differences which explain the range of values used in general equilibrium models. The differences across models seem to be a reflection of the high degree of uncertainty regarding the appropriate values and how they should be estimated.

Among the possible methods, a popular choice has been the derived demand technique. The underlying algebra starts with the equation

$$E_{iA} = \sum_{j \neq A} C_{ij} - \sum_{j \neq A} S_{ij} \quad , \tag{E4.2.1}$$

where E_{iA} is the volume of exports of commodity i by country A, C_{ij} is the absorption of commodity i by country j and S_{ij} is country j's production of commodity i. By differentiating (E4.2.1) with respect to the export price of good i from country A, we can arrive at the following formula:

$$\alpha_{iA} = - \sum_{j \neq A} \eta_{ij} U_{ijA}(C_{ij}/E_{iA}) + \sum_{j \neq A} \varepsilon_{ij} V_{ijA}(S_{ij}/E_{iA}) \quad , \tag{E4.2.2}$$

where α_{iA} is the export demand elasticity for i from country A, η_{ij} and ε_{ij} are the own-price elasticities of demand and supply for commodity i in country j, and U_{ijA} and V_{ijA} are price transmission elasticities. Price transmission elasticities measure the impact of changes in country A's export price (P_{iA}^e) on consumer and supplier prices (P_{ij}^c and P_{ij}^s) in country j. More specifically,

$$U_{ijA} = [\partial P_{ij}^c/\partial P_{iA}^e] \, [P_{iA}^e/P_{ij}^c] \quad , \tag{E4.2.3}$$

and

$$V_{ijA} = [\partial P_{ij}^s/\partial P_{iA}^e] \, [P_{iA}^e/P_{ij}^s] \quad . \tag{E4.2.4}$$

(a)   Derive formula (E4.2.2) from (E4.2.1).

(b)   Table E4.2.1 was prepared by Cronin (1979) to illustrate the application of formula (E4.2.2) in the estimation of the export demand elasticity for Australian beef. Column I shows the total consumption of beef outside Australia as 100 units distributed across four composite countries. Column II shows beef production

Table E4.2.1
*Cronin's Notional Database for Calculating the Export
Demand Elasticity for Australian Beef*

		I Consumption outside Australia C_{ij}	II Supply S_{ij}	III Demand elasticity η_{ij}	IV Supply elasticity ε_{ij}
Country					
1.	Subsistence economies	10	10	-1	1
2.	Communist countries	28	27	-1	1
3.	USA, W. Europe, Japan	60	55	-1	1
4.	Open markets	2	5	-1	2
[Australian exports]			3		
Totals		100	100		

in these composite countries and Australian exports. Columns III and IV are Cronin's best guesses of demand and supply elasticities. Use the information in Table E4.2.1 to calculate the export demand elasticity for Australian beef assuming that all price transmission elasticities are unity. Now assume that consumer and supplier prices in countries 1, 2 and 3 are not influenced by the Australian beef export price, perhaps because of quotas. Continued to assume that $U_{i4A} = V_{i4A} = 1$ and recalculate the export demand elasticity for Australian beef.

(c)   Describe circumstances under which it would be appropriate to set all the price transmission elasticities at unity.

Answer to Exercise 4.2

(a)   On differentiating (E4.2.1) with respect to P_{iA}^e we obtain

$$\frac{\partial E_{iA}}{\partial P_{iA}^e} = \sum_{j \neq A} \frac{\partial C_{ij}}{\partial P_{iA}^e} - \sum_{j \neq A} \frac{\partial S_{ij}}{\partial P_{iA}^e} . \qquad (E4.2.5)$$

Equation (E4.2.5) can be written as

$$
-\frac{\partial E_{iA}}{\partial P_{iA}^e} \frac{P_{iA}^e}{E_{iA}} = -\sum_{j \neq A} \begin{bmatrix} \dfrac{\partial C_{ij}}{\partial P_{ij}^c} & \dfrac{P_{ij}^c}{C_{ij}} \end{bmatrix} \begin{bmatrix} \dfrac{\partial P_{ij}^c}{\partial P_{iA}^e} & \dfrac{P_{iA}^e}{P_{ij}^c} \end{bmatrix} \frac{C_{ij}}{E_{iA}}
$$

$$
+ \sum_{j \neq A} \begin{bmatrix} \dfrac{\partial S_{ij}}{\partial P_{ij}^s} & \dfrac{P_{ij}^s}{S_{ij}} \end{bmatrix} \begin{bmatrix} \dfrac{\partial P_{ij}^s}{\partial P_{iA}^e} & \dfrac{P_{iA}^e}{P_{ij}^s} \end{bmatrix} \frac{S_{ij}}{E_{iA}} \quad . \tag{E4.2.6}
$$

This establishes (E4.2.2) where we interpret export demand elasticities as positive numbers, i.e.,

$$
\alpha_{iA} = - \ [\partial E_{iA}/\partial P_{iA}^e] \ [P_{iA}^e/E_{iA}] \quad ,
$$

and own-price elasticities of demand as negative numbers, i.e.,

$$
\eta_{ij} = [\partial C_{ij}/\partial P_{ij}^c] \ [P_{ij}^c/C_{ij}] \quad .
$$

Own-price elasticities of supply are the positive numbers,

$$
\varepsilon_{ij} = [\partial S_{ij}/\partial P_{ij}^s] \ [P_{ij}^s/S_{ij}] \quad .
$$

(b)   With all the price transmission elasticities at unity, we find that

$$
\alpha_{beef,Australia} = 67\tfrac{1}{3} \quad .
$$

When we assume that prices in composite countries 1, 2 and 3 are not affected by Australian export prices, then we obtain

$$
\alpha_{beef,Australia} = 4 \quad .
$$

(c)   In contributions to the pure theory of international trade it is often assumed that there is world price (P_i^w) (measured in US dollars, say) for each commodity i and that each country's export price equals the world price, i.e.,

$$
P_{iA}^e = P_i^w \quad \text{for all A} \quad . \tag{E4.2.7}
$$

No distinction is made between consumer and supplier prices and it is assumed that domestic prices in each country j are given by

$$
P_{ij}^c = P_{ij}^s = P_i^w \ \Phi_j \ T_{ij} \quad , \tag{E4.2.8}
$$

where Φ_j is the exchange rate translating US dollars into the currency of country j and T_{ij} is the power (i.e., one plus the *ad valorem* rate) of either the export subsidy or of the tariff, depending on whether country j is an exporter or importer of good i. Assuming that the Φ_js and T_{ij}s are constant, we see that the model {(E4.2.7), (E4.2.8)} implies that all price transmission elasticities for commodity i are unity.

With the U_{ijA}s and V_{ijA}s equal to 1, (E4.2.2) reduces to

$$\alpha_{iA} = - \sum_{j \neq A} \eta_{ij} (C_{ij}/E_{iA}) + \sum_{j \neq A} \epsilon_{ij}(S_{ij}/E_{iA}) \quad . \qquad (E4.2.9)$$

Application of (E4.2.9) almost always generates high values (greater than 10 for example) for export demand elasticities. Even where quite small values are adopted for the demand and supply elasticities, (E4.2.9) will give a high value for α_{iA} except in the rare cases where E_{iA} is a large fraction of world production and consumption of good i.

Sensitivity analyses usually indicate that variations in export demand elasticities in the range 5 to infinity have little influence on the results from general equilibrium models. Thus, provided that we can believe (E4.2.9), we can simply assign high values, e.g. 5, to the export demand elasticities without doing detailed work on the demand and supply elasticities. However, for many products the assumptions which allowed us to eliminate the price transmission elasticities are unrealistic. They imply that good i produced in one country is perfectly substitutable with good i produced in every other country, i.e., that good i is homogenous. They rule out interferences with international trade apart from *ad valorem* export subsidies and import tariffs. In particular, they fail to allow for import quotas, home-price support schemes and many other protective devices. Even transport costs are left out of consideration. We must conclude that (E4.2.9) provides no more than upper bounds for export demand elasticities. Equation (E4.2.2) is also of limited value. Although we might be prepared to make some guesses about the demand and supply elasticities, we know of no practical method of estimating price transmission elasticities.

Exercise 4.3   *The commodity composition of an industry's output: the derivation of (4.3.5) and (4.3.6)*

In most CGE models the output of each industry is viewed as consisting of a single commodity. An exception is the *ORANI* model of Australia which contains multi-product agricultural industries able to vary the commodity composition of their outputs between wheat, wool, beef, oats, etc., (see Dixon *et al.*, 1982 and 1983). This approach reflects elements of jointness which apply to the production technology of much of Australian agriculture. In the DMR model each industry produces two commodities; however this reflects DMR's response to an aggregation difficulty rather than an attempt to model the actual production technology. Under the broad industry classifications which are often used in general equilibrium models, it is possible (even likely) that an industry's export products in a given commodity class are of a different nature from those it supplies to the domestic market. DMR's distinction between (j1) and (j3), both of which can be produced by industry j, allows for this.

Commodity (j1) is absorbed domestically while commodity (j3) is exported. DMR do not adopt an explicit optimizing framework for explaining the proportions in which these commodities appear in industry j's output. Instead, they specify the export share in total production as a logistic function of the price ratio, $P_{(j3)}/P_{(j1)}$ (see DMR, 1982, p. 228). This gives very similar results to those obtained with the revenue-maximizing specification which we now describe. The advantage of our specification is the greater visibility of its theoretical underpinnings. Thus, in implementing the DMR two-commodity approach, our standard assumption will be that for any given activity level (Z_j) and commodity prices $(P_{(j1)}$ and $P_{(j3)})$, industry j chooses its outputs of (j1) and (j3) to maximize

$$P_{(j1)} X_{(j1)} + P_{(j3)} X_{(j3)} \qquad \text{(revenue) (E4.3.1)}$$

subject to

$$Z_j = \text{CET} (X_{(j1)}, X_{(j3)}) . \quad \text{(production possibilities frontier) (E4.3.2)}$$

The CET function was described in Exercise 3.11. By adopting the notation in (E3.11.1) we can rewrite (E4.3.2) more explicitly as

$$Z_j = B_j \left[\sum_{s=1\&3} \gamma_{(js)} X_{(js)}^{-\rho_j^{(o)}} \right]^{-1/\rho_j^{(o)}} , \qquad \text{(E4.3.3)}$$

where B_j and the $\gamma_{(js)}$s are positive parameters with $\gamma_{(j1)} + \gamma_{(j3)} = 1$, and $\rho_j^{(o)}$ is a parameter whose value is less than or equal to -1.

(a)   Avoid corner solutions by assuming that $\rho_j^{(o)} < -1$. Then show that (E4.3.1) – (E4.3.3) imply that

$$X_{(jt)} = Z_j \left(\frac{1}{B_j} \right) \left[\sum_{s=1\&3} \gamma_{(js)} \left[\frac{P_{(js)} \; \gamma_{(jt)}}{P_{(jt)} \; \gamma_{(js)}} \right]^{\rho_j^{(o)}/(1+\rho_j^{(o)})} \right]^{1/\rho_j^{(o)}}$$

for t = 1 and 3 .   (E4.3.4)

Note that $\psi_{(j3)}(P_{(j1)}, P_{(j3)})$ appearing in (4.3.5) (a) is defined as the revenue maximizing output of good (j3) per unit of activity in industry j (see Table 4.3.3). From (E4.3.4) we see that

$$\psi_{(jt)}\left(P_{(j1)}, P_{(j3)}\right) = \left(\frac{1}{B_j}\right)\left[\sum_{s=1\&3}\gamma_{(js)}\left[\frac{P_{(js)}\ \gamma_{(jt)}}{P_{(jt)}\ \gamma_{(js)}}\right]^{\rho_j^{(0)}/(1+\rho_j^{(0)})}\right]^{1/\rho_j^{(0)}}$$

for t = 1 and 3 . (E4.3.5)

(b)   In (4.3.5) (a) we will normally fix $F_{(j3)}$ exogenously at 1. Show that if $F_{(j3)} = 1$, then the system of supply response equations,

$$X_{(jt)} = Z_j\ \psi_{(jt)}\left(P_{(j1)}, P_{(j3)}\right)\ ,\quad \text{for } j = 1,...., n;\quad t = 1 \text{ and } 3 \text{ (E4.3.6)}$$

is equivalent to (4.3.5)(a) – (4.3.6)(a). (Our reason for excluding one of the supply response functions (that for (j1)) from Table 4.3.1 and replacing it with the constraint (4.3.6)(a) is the subject of part (c).)

(c)   Can you see any role for the variable $F_{(j3)}$ in (4.3.5)(a)? Can you see any reason for representing industry j's output-composition equations in the form (4.3.5)(a) – (4.3.6)(a) rather than in the form (E4.3.6)?

(d)   In the maximization problem (E4.3.1) – (E4.3.2) we assume that the commodity composition of industry output is determined independently of the composition of inputs. Describe the circumstances under which such an assumption would be appropriate.

(e)   Assume that $F_{(j3)}$ is fixed at 1. Show that a percentage change form for (4.3.5)(a) is

$$X_{(j3)} = z_j - \sigma_j^{(0)}\left(P_{(j3)} - \sum_{s=1\&3}R_{(js)}\ P_{(js)}\right)\ ,\qquad (E4.3.7)$$

where $R_{(js)}$ is the share of commodity (js) in industry j's total revenue and $\sigma_j^{(0)}$ is the elasticity of transformation between commodities (j1) and (j3) defined by

$$\sigma_j^{(0)} = 1/(1 + \rho_j^{(0)})\ .\qquad (E4.3.8)$$

(Notice that $\sigma_j^{(0)}$ lies in the interval $(-\infty, 0)$.)

(f)   In Table 4.3.1 we have simply appended an $f_{(j3)}$ to (E4.3.7) to obtain our percentage change form for (4.3.5). This is not strictly correct. Why? However, no damage is done. Why?

(g)   In obtaining the percentage change form for (4.3.6)(a), we have to be more careful. Show that the elasticity of the CET activity function with respect to $X_{(js)}$ is given by

$$\eta_{(js)}^{(Zj)} = \gamma_{(js)}\ B_j^{-\rho_j^{(0)}}\left[\frac{X_{(js)}}{Z_j}\right]^{-\rho_j^{(0)}}\ .\qquad (E4.3.9)$$

Show that if industry j is revenue maximizing, (i.e., if $F_{(j3)} = 1$) then

$$\eta_{(js)}^{(Zj)} = R_{(js)} \ . \tag{E4.3.10}$$

Could we legitimately use

$$z_j = \sum_{s=1\&3} R_{(js)} \, x_{(js)} \tag{E4.3.11}$$

in place of (4.3.6)(b)?

Answer to Exercise 4.3

(a)   The first-order conditions for revenue maximization are that there exists Λ such that Λ, $X_{(j1)}$ and $X_{(j3)}$ jointly satisfy

$$P_{(jt)} = \Lambda \, B_j \left[\sum_{s=1\&3} \gamma_{(js)} \, X_{(js)}^{-\rho_j^{(o)}} \right]^{-[(1+\rho_j^{(o)})/\rho_j^{(o)}]} \gamma_{(jt)} \, X_{(jt)}^{-(1+\rho_j^{(o)})} \ ,$$

$$\text{for } t = 1 \text{ and } 3, \tag{E4.3.12}$$

and the constraint (E4.3.3).

From (E4.3.12) we find that

$$X_{(js)} = \left[\frac{P_{(js)} \, \gamma_{(jt)}}{P_{(jt)} \, \gamma_{(js)}} \right]^{-[1/(1+\rho_j^{(o)})]} X_{(jt)} \quad \text{for all s, t=1 or 3.} \tag{E4.3.13}$$

Substitution of this last expression into the constraint, (E4.3.3), yields

$$Z_j = B_j \left[\sum_{s=1\&3} \gamma_{(js)} \left[\frac{P_{(js)} \, \gamma_{(jt)}}{P_{(jt)} \, \gamma_{(js)}} \right]^{\rho_j^{(o)}/(1+\rho_j^{(o)})} \right]^{-1/\rho_j^{(o)}} X_{(jt)} \ ,$$

$$\text{for } t = 1 \text{ and } 3. \tag{E4.3.14}$$

On rearranging (E4.3.14) we obtain (E4.3.4).

(b)   To establish the equivalence of the two systems, we must show (i) that we can deduce (4.3.6)(a) from (E4.3.6); and (ii) that we can deduce (E4.3.6) from (4.3.5)(a) and (4.3.6)(a).

To demonstrate (i), we start by noting that (E4.3.6) implies

$$\left[\sum_{t=1\&3} \gamma_{(jt)} \, X_{(jt)}^{-\rho_j^{(o)}} \right]^{-1/\rho_j^{(o)}} = Z_j \left[\sum_{t=1\&3} \gamma_{(jt)} \, \psi_{(jt)}^{-\rho_j^{(o)}} \right]^{-1/\rho_j^{(o)}} \ . \tag{E4.3.15}$$

Then, by substituting from the definitions of $\psi_{(j1)}$ and $\psi_{(j3)}$ given in (E4.3.5), we find that

$$\text{RHS (E4.3.15)} =$$

$$\left(\frac{Z_j}{B_j}\right)\left[\sum_{t=1\&3}\gamma_{(jt)}\left[\sum_{s=1\&3}\gamma_{(js)}\left[\frac{P_{(js)}\ \gamma_{(jt)}}{P_{(jt)}\ \gamma_{(js)}}\right]^{\rho_j^{(o)}/(1+\rho_j^{(o)})}\right]^{-1}\right]^{-1/\rho_j^{(o)}}.$$

Hence

$$\text{RHS (E4.3.15)} =$$

$$\left(\frac{Z_j}{B_j}\right)\left[\sum_{t=1\&3}\gamma_{(jt)}\left[\frac{P_{(jt)}}{\gamma_{(jt)}}\right]^{\rho_j^{(o)}/(1+\rho_j^{(o)})}\left[\sum_{s=1\&3}\gamma_{(js)}\left[\frac{P_{(js)}}{\gamma_{(js)}}\right]^{\rho_j^{(o)}/(1+\rho_j^{(o)})}\right]^{-1}\right]^{-1/\rho_j^{(o)}},$$

i.e.,

$$\text{RHS (E4.3.15)} = Z_j/B_j. \tag{E4.3.16}$$

(E4.3.16) and (E4.3.15) imply that

$$Z_j = B_j\left[\sum_{t=1\&3}\gamma_{(jt)}\ X_{(jt)}^{-\rho_j^{(o)}}\right]^{-1/\rho_j^{(o)}} = \text{CET}\,(X_{j1},\,X_{j3}).$$

To demonstrate (ii), we start by rewriting (4.3.6)(a) as

$$X_{(j1)} = \left[\frac{1}{\gamma_{(j1)}}\left[\frac{Z_j}{B_j}\right]^{-\rho_j^{(o)}} - \frac{X_{(j3)}^{-\rho_j^{(o)}}\ \gamma_{(j3)}}{\gamma_{(j1)}}\right]^{-1/\rho_j^{(o)}}. \tag{E4.3.17}$$

Then, using the definition of $\psi_{(j3)}$ given in (E4.3.5), we substitute from (4.3.5)(a) into (E4.3.17) to obtain

$$X_{(j1)} = \frac{Z_j}{B_j}\left[\frac{1}{\gamma_{(j1)}}\left[1 - \frac{\gamma_{(j3)}\big(P_{(j3)}/\gamma_{(j3)}\big)^{\rho_j^{(o)}/(1+\rho_j^{(o)})}}{\displaystyle\sum_{s=1\&3}\gamma_{(js)}\big(P_{(js)}/\gamma_{(js)}\big)^{\rho_j^{(o)}/(1+\rho_j^{(o)})}}\right]\right]^{-1/\rho_j^{(o)}}. \tag{E4.3.18}$$

By rearranging (E4.3.18), we find that

$$X_{(j1)} = Z_j \, \psi_{(j1)} \, (P_{(j1)}, P_{(j2)})$$.

(c)   The inclusion of the $F_{(j3)}$s in (4.3.5)(a) adds flexibility to our specification of export supply. On the one hand, we can treat $F_{(j3)}$ as an exogenous variable set at 1. Then the allocation of industry j's output between domestic and foreign markets is determined in the revenue maximizing problem (E4.3.1) – (E4.3.2). On the other hand, it is common in general equilibrium models to treat exports from at least some industries as exogenously determined. For example, in dealing with a non-traded commodity, it is often convenient to fix export supply exogenously at a level close to zero. The inclusion of $F_{(j3)}$ in (4.3.5)(a) allows us to set $X_{(j3)}$ exogenously in place of $F_{(j3)}$. While the endogenously determined value of $F_{(j3)}$ may have no interesting interpretation, its presence in the model causes no problems. This is because $F_{(j3)}$ appears in no equation apart from (4.3.5)(a).

One problem that does arise is in the determination of $X_{(j1)}$. If $X_{(j3)}$ is fixed exogenously, then neither of the revenue maximizing equations (E4.3.6) has any clear justification. Once we reject the solution for $X_{(j3)}$ from the revenue maximizing problem (E4.3.1) – (E4.3.2), then we cannot accept the revenue maximizing solution for $X_{(j1)}$ without rejecting the constraint (E4.3.2). We have chosen to retain the constraint by including (4.3.6)(a) in the model in preference to (E4.3.6) for j = 1. Consequently, we force each industry to remain on its production possibilities frontier but we keep the option of running simulations in which the point chosen on the frontier is not revenue maximizing.

(d)   This question has already been discussed in general terms in Exercise 3.11(d). There we argue that if the commodity composition of output is modeled as being independent of the input mix, then the implied assumption is that inputs are of a multipurpose nature.

DMR do not explicitly justify this assumption in describing their export/domestic supply equations. Instead, they refer to an aggregation problem (DMR, 1982, p. 228). They describe a situation in which the mining industry produces two products: coal which is mainly for domestic use and copper which is mainly for export. Ideally, in these circumstances, coal and copper production should be modeled as separate industries. However, we may wish to avoid this, especially if the available input-output data aggregates production into a single "mining" industry. As a second-best approach, DMR suggest that mining should be treated as a single industry producing two products, one for export and one for domestic use.

This avoids the problem, sometimes found in general equilibrium simulations, of exaggerated export and output responses to increases in export prices. For example, if we use a single-product mining industry in the situation described by DMR, then in simulations of the effects of an increase in the mining export price (which is really an increase in the price of copper), we are likely to obtain supply responses compatible with the stimulation of the whole of the mining industry, not just the part producing copper. Provided that we have data on the base-period value of mining exports, then with the multi-product approach we can be sure that the stimulatory impact of an increase in the export price will be confined in our model to the appropriate fraction of the industry. Nevertheless, we cannot avoid potentially spurious results on the input side. By having a single mining industry whose input mix is independent of its copper/coal output mix, we are assuming that the input requirements of the two products are identical.

An alternative to DMR's multi-product solution to the aggregation problem is to disaggregate in spite of data inadequacies. If we are prepared to make the assumption, implied by the DMR approach, that coal and copper have identical input structures, then we can split the mining column in the input-output tables on the basis of coal and copper output levels. Usually we would expect to be able to do better than this. Although it may not be possible to obtain separate information on all coal and copper inputs, we would expect separate employment figures to be available. Consequently, unless there are strong reasons for wishing to limit the number of industries in a model, we believe that industry disaggregation, even crudely implemented, will normally provide a better solution to the problem described by DMR than their single industry, multi-product approach.

(e)   To derive (E4.3.7) we could start by putting the first-order conditions, (E4.3.12) and (E4.3.3), into percentage change form. This was the approach adopted in Exercise 3.11(e) and 3.9. It has the advantage of allowing us to avoid the derivation of supply response functions in their levels forms. However, the levels forms have already been derived in this exercise — see (E4.3.4). We can obtain (E4.3.7) by first noting that (E4.3.4) implies

$$X_{(j3)} = z_j + \frac{1}{\rho_j^{(o)}} \left[\sum_{s=1\&3} \frac{\rho_j^{(o)}}{(1+\rho_j^{(o)})} (P_{(js)} - P_{(j3)}) R_{(js)}^* \right] , \quad (E4.3.19)$$

where

$$R^*_{(js)} = \gamma_{(js)} \left[\frac{P_{(js)}}{\gamma_{(js)}}\right]^{\rho_j^{(o)}/(1+\rho_j^{(o)})} \Bigg/ \sum_{s=1\&3} \gamma_{(js)} \left[\frac{P_{(js)}}{\gamma_{(js)}}\right]^{\rho_j^{(o)}/(1+\rho_j^{(o)})}$$

(E4.3.20)

Then since $\displaystyle\sum_{s=1\&3} R^*_{(js)} = 1$, we can rearrange (E4.3.19) as

$$x_{(j3)} = z_j - \sigma_j^{(o)} \left[P_{(j3)} - \sum_{s=1\&3} R^*_{(js)} P_{(js)}\right] .$$

(E4.3.21)

Now to complete the derivation of (E4.3.7), we need to show that

$$R^*_{(js)} = R_{(js)} \qquad \text{for s = 1 and 3.} \qquad \text{(E4.3.22)}$$

This can be done by again using (E4.3.4): we find that

$$P_{(js)} X_{(js)} \Bigg/ \sum_{r=1\&3} P_{(jr)} X_{(jr)} =$$

$$\gamma_{(js)} \left[\frac{P_{(js)}}{\gamma_{(js)}}\right]^{\rho_j^{(o)}/(1+\rho_j^{(o)})} \Bigg/ \sum_{r=1\&3} \gamma_{(jr)} \left[\frac{P_{(jr)}}{\gamma_{(jr)}}\right]^{\rho_j^{(o)}/(1+\rho_j^{(o)})} \qquad \text{for s = 1 and 3.}$$

(E4.3.23)

The LHS of this equation is the revenue share, $R_{(js)}$. From (E4.3.20), we see that the RHS is $R^*_{(js)}$. We have, therefore, established (E4.3.22), thereby completing the derivation of (E4.3.7).

(f)   From (4.3.5) (a) we have

$$x_{(j3)} = z_j + \%\Delta\psi_{(j3)} + f_{(j3)} ,$$

(E4.3.24)

where "$\%\Delta(\bullet)$" means "percentage change in $(\bullet)$". It follows from (E4.3.5) that

$$\%\Delta\psi_{(j3)} = -\sigma_j^{(o)} \left[P_{(j3)} - \sum_{s=1\&3} R^*_{(js)} P_{(js)}\right] ,$$

(E4.3.25)

where $R^*_{(js)}$ is defined by (E4.3.20). On combining (E4.3.24) and (E4.3.25) we obtain an equation very similar to (4.3.5)(b):

$$X_{(j3)} = Z_j - \sigma_j^{(o)} \left[P_{(j3)} - \sum_{s=1\&3} R^*_{(js)} P_{(js)} \right] + f_{(j3)} . \qquad (E4.3.26)$$

But unless $F_{(j3)} = 1$ we do not have $R^*_{(js)} = R_{(js)}$. With $F_{(j3)} \neq 1$, the $X_{(jt)}s$ are not at their revenue maximizing levels. Consequently, we cannot equate the actual revenue shares (the $R_{(js)}s$) with the revenue maximizing shares (the $R^*_{(js)}s$). Nevertheless, no damage is done by using the more convenient equation (4.3.5)(b) in place of the correct equation (E4.3.26). The situations in which we allow $F_{(j3)}$ to deviate from unity are those in which $X_{(j3)}$ is exogenous and $F_{(j3)}$ is endogenous. In these situations, the use of (4.3.5)(b) in place of (E4.3.26) affects only the endogenously determined value of $f_{(j3)}$, a variable of no interest.

(g)   From (E4.3.3) we have

$$\eta_{(js)}^{(Zj)} \equiv \frac{\partial Z_j}{\partial X_{(js)}} \frac{X_{(js)}}{Z_j} = \gamma_{(js)} X_{(js)}^{-\rho_j^{(o)}} / \sum_{s=1\&3} \gamma_{(js)} X_{(js)}^{-\rho_j^{(o)}} , \qquad (E4.3.27)$$

and

$$\left[\frac{Z_j}{B_j} \right]^{-\rho_j^{(o)}} = \sum_{s=1\&3} \gamma_{(js)} X_{(js)}^{-\rho_j^{(o)}} . \qquad (E4.3.28)$$

These last two equations give (E4.3.9).

When industry j is a revenue maximizer, (E4.3.12) applies. On multiplying (E4.3.12) through by $X_{(jt)}$ and then adding over all t, we find that

$$R_{(jt)} \equiv \frac{P_{(jt)} X_{(jt)}}{\sum_{t=1\&3} P_{(jt)} X_{(jt)}} = \frac{\gamma_{(jt)} X_{(jt)}^{-\rho_j^{(o)}}}{\sum_{t=1\&3} \gamma_{(jt)} X_{(jt)}^{-\rho_j^{(o)}}} \quad \text{for } t = 1 \text{ and } 3. \quad (E4.3.29)$$

(E4.3.27) and (E4.3.29) imply (E4.3.10).

Because (E4.3.10) relies on the assumption of revenue maximization, we should evaluate $\eta_{(js)}^{(Zj)}$ according to (E4.3.9) rather than (E4.3.10). If we were to replace (4.3.6)(b) by (E4.3.11), then we would need to restrict the model to the case in which $F_{(j3)} = 1$.

Exercise 4.4.   Evaluating the parameters and coefficients in the output composition equations

On reviewing the definitions of CET and $\psi_{(j3)}$ given in (E4.3.3) and (E4.3.5), we see that the parameters in (4.3.5)(a) and (4.3.6)(a) are B_j, $\gamma_{(j1)}$, $\gamma_{(j3)}$ and $\rho_j^{(o)}$ for $j = 1,..., n$.

The aim of this exercise is to show that these parameters can be evaluated from the base-period input-output data and given values for the transformation elasticities, $\sigma_j^{(o)}$, $j = 1,...,n$.

Following the early studies by Powell and Gruen (1967 and 1968), considerable work has been done on the estimation of transformation elasticities between agricultural products: see, for example, Vincent, Dixon and Powell (1980), and McKay, Lawrence and Vlastuin (1983) and Shumway and Powell (1984).   DMR's modeling of export supply has not, to our knowledge, attracted any concentrated body of econometric work.   We know of only one estimate of an export/domestic transformation elasticity; namely, an estimate of –0.85 (std error 0.40) of the elasticity of transformation between domestic good and export goods produced by the Australian non-farm business sector (Murphy *et al.* 1986).   DMR have simply taken unity as the base-period value of all export supply elasticities.   In terms of our notation, the export supply elasticity for industry j refers to the percentage effect on $X_{(j3)}$ for a one per cent increase in $P_{(j3)}$ holding constant Z_j, $P_{(j1)}$ and $F_{(j3)}$.   Assuming that $F_{(j3)}$ has a base-period value of 1 (and thus avoiding the complications described in Exercise 4.3(f)), we see from (4.3.5)(b) that the DMR assumption is that

$$1 = -\sigma_j^{(o)} \left(1 - (R_{(j3)})^I\right) \qquad \text{for all } j, \quad (E4.4.1)$$

where $[R_{(j3)}]^I$ is the initial or base-period share of industry j's total revenue accounted for by exports.   On rearrangement, (E4.4.1) gives

$$\sigma_j^{(o)} = -1/(R_{(j1)})^I, \qquad j = 1,..., n. \quad (E4.4.2)$$

The values shown in Appendix 4.1 for the transformation elasticities were computed according to (E4.4.2).   We should emphasize that there is no convincing justification for these values.   In the absence of the necessary econometric work, sensitivity analysis can be useful.   It would be interesting to check the sensitivity of DMR results for the effects of tariff changes, for example, to variations in the values assigned to the $\sigma_j^{(o)}$s.

(a)   Check that the input-output data in Appendix 4.1 applied to (E4.4.2) gives $\sigma_1^{(o)} = -1.0244$.   What is the implied value for $\rho_1^{(o)}$?

(b)   Now use the input-output data to evaluate B_1, $\gamma_{(11)}$ and $\gamma_{(13)}$.

Hint: The evaluation of B_js and $\gamma_{(js)}$s requires some decisions about quantity units. We suggest that you follow the approach of Exercise 4.1(c). Define a unit of commodity (js) for s = 1 and 3 as the quantity which had a basic value of one million dollars in the base period and define a unit of activity in industry j as a level which would have produced revenue of one million dollars. Base period values of the $F_{(j3)}$s are also required. Assume that

$$\left(F_{(j3)}\right)^I = 1 \text{ for all } j \; . \tag{E4.4.3}$$

(c)   Continue to adopt (E4.4.3). Compute the initial value of the coefficients in (4.3.5)(b) and (4.3.6)(b) for j = 1. How would you reevaluate these coefficients in a multi-step Johansen computation?

Answer to Exercise 4.4

(a)   The share of industry 1's revenue accounted for by commodity (1,1) can be calculated from the input-output data as

$$\left(R_{(11)}\right)^I = 1 - \left(R_{(13)}\right)^I = 1 - \left[\sum_{r=1}^{3} \tilde{F}_{1r}\right]/\tilde{T}_1 = 1 - (15.66/657.37) = 0.976.$$

By substituting into (E4.4.2) and (E4.3.8) we obtain

$$\sigma_1^{(o)} = -1.024 \text{ and } \rho_1^{(o)} = -1.976.$$

(b)   Under the suggested definitions for quantity units, the basic prices of commodities (1,1) and (1,3) in the base-period are both 1. Therefore we can read the value flows of these commodities in the input-output data as quantity flows. Thus we have

$$\left(X_{(13)}\right)^I = 15.66 \text{ and } \left(X_{(11)}\right)^I = 657.36 - 15.66 = 641.70.$$

Under our definition of quantity units for activity levels, we have

$$\left(Z_1\right)^I = \left[\tilde{T}_1\right]^I = 657.36.$$

We assume that our base-period input-output data and our model are compatible. In particular, we assume that the input-output data satisfy (4.3.5)(a) and (4.3.6)(a) for j=1. Remembering that the base period prices and $(F_{(13)})^I$ each have the value 1, and using (E4.3.4) we see that

$$15.66 = (657.36) \left[\frac{1}{B_1}\right] \left[\gamma_{(11)} \left[\frac{\gamma_{(13)}}{\gamma_{(11)}}\right]^{1.976/.976} + \gamma_{(13)}\right]^{-1/(1.976)} \quad ; \text{(E4.4.4)}$$

while from (E4.3.3) we know that

$$657.36 = B_1 \left[\gamma_{(11)} (641.70)^{1.976} + \gamma_{(13)} (15.66)^{1.976}\right]^{1/1.976} . \quad \text{(E4.4.5)}$$

We also recall that $\gamma_{(11)} + \gamma_{(13)} = 1.$ (E4.4.6)

(E4.4.4) – (E4.4.6) gives us three equations with which to evaluate the three unknown parameters B_1, $\gamma_{(11)}$ and $\gamma_{(13)}$. After some arithmetic we find that

$$B_1 = 6.420, \quad \gamma_{(11)} = 0.026, \quad \text{and} \quad \gamma_{(13)} = 0.974.$$

(c)   The coefficients in (4.3.5)(b) are $R_{(11)}$ and $R_{(13)}$. $\left(R_{(11)}\right)^I$ has already been computed as 0.976. Since $R_{(13)} = 1 - R_{(11)}$, the initial value for $R_{(13)}$ is 0.024. With $\left(F_{(j3)}\right)^I = 1$ for all j, the initial values for the ηs in (4.3.6)(b) are the same as those for the revenue shares (see Exercise 4.3(g)).

Multi-step Johansen computations were described in part B of Problem Set 3. In these computations changes in prices and quantities are calculated at each step and then used in a re-evaluation of the input-output flows. The re-evaluated flows are used to calculate the share coefficients for the next step. Since the $R_{(js)}$s are among the share coefficients computed from the input-output flows, their re-evaluation presents no special problems in a multi-step Johansen solution of the DMR model.

We have already seen that under assumption (E4.4.3), the initial values of the ηs in (4.3.6)(b) can be calculated as revenue shares from the base-period input-output data. However, if we want to allow for the possibility of non-revenue maximizing behavior, then we cannot assume that the ηs will continue to be revenue shares as we leave the base-period or initial situation (see Exercise 4.3(g)). Consequently we cannot use the re-evaluated input-output flows as the basis for re-evaluating the ηs during a multi-step Johansen computation. Instead, we can use (E4.3.9). This equation implies that the percentage changes in the ηs are given by

$$\%\Delta\eta_{(js)}^{(Zj)} = -\rho_j^{(o)} (x_{(js)} - z_j) . \quad \text{(E4.4.7)}$$

After the calculation of percentage changes in outputs and activity levels in the rth step of a multi-step Johansen computation, (E4.4.7) can be applied in resetting the ηs in preparation for the (r+1)th step.

Exercise 4.5   *Demands for inputs for use in current production: the derivation of equations (4.3.7) – (4.3.10)*

Each industry j in the DMR model uses inputs of composite commodities, $X_{(ic)}^{(1j)}$, i = 1,....,n, inputs of effective units of labor, $X_{(n+1,1)}^{(1j)}$, and inputs of capital, $X_{(n+1,2)}^{(1j)}$. Effective units of labor for industry j are formed by combining labor hours, $X_{(n+1,1,k)}^{(1j)}$, k = 1,...., m, provided by workers of different occupational groups. Equations (4.3.7), (4.3.8) and (4.3.9) are DMR's industry demand equations for intermediate inputs, primary factors and labor disaggregated by occupation. Equation (4.3.10) defines the price to industry j, $P_{(n+1,1)}^{(1j)}$, of effective units of labor.

Before deriving these equations, you may find it useful to interpret them. We will concentrate on the percentage-change forms because we find their interpretation easier than that of the levels forms.

Equation (4.3.7)(b) says industry j's input of each composite commodity moves by the same percentage as the industry's level of activity. No prices are involved, indicating that there is no allowance for substitution of units of (ic) for units of any other input. Equation (4.3.8)(b) allows industry j's inputs of labor and capital to be affected by changes in technology, changes in the activity level and changes in relative prices. The price term indicates that labor and capital are being treated as substitutes. At fixed values for $A_{n+1}^{(1j)}$ and Z_j (i.e., with $a_{n+1}^{(1j)} = z_j = 0$), (4.3.8)(b) implies that increases in the price of factor s relative to a weighted average of both factor prices will induce a reduction in the demand for s in favor of the other factor. Equation (4.3.9)(b) explains percentage changes in the demand for each type of labor in terms of percentage changes in the demand for effective units of labor and percentage changes in the prices of different types of labor. It is clear that different types of labor are being modeled as substitutes in satisfying industry j's labor requirements. Equation (4.3.10)(b) defines the percentage change in the overall price of labor to industry j (the price of an effective unit) as a weighted average of the percentage changes in the prices to industry j of each type of labor.

DMR make the usual assumption that industries choose their inputs to minimize the costs of achieving their activity levels.

(a)   Show that (4.3.7)(a) – (4.3.10)(a) follow from the following cost minimizing problem:

choose $X_{(ic)}^{(1j)}$, $i = 1,..., n$, (inputs of composite commodities);
$X_{(n+1,s)}^{(1j)}$, $s = 1, 2$ (inputs of labor and capital) and $X_{(n+1,1,k)}^{(1j)}$,
$k = 1,..., m$, (inputs of labor classified by occupation)

to minimize

$$\sum_{i=1}^{n} P_{(ic)} X_{(ic)}^{(1j)} + \sum_{k=1}^{m} P_{(n+1,1,k)}^{(1j)} X_{(n+1,1,k)}^{(1j)} + P_{(n+1,2)}^{(1j)} X_{(n+1,2)}^{(1j)} \quad \text{(E4.5.1)}$$

subject to

$$Z_j = \min \left[\frac{X_{(1c)}^{(1j)}}{A_{(1c)}^{(1j)}}, \dots, \frac{X_{(nc)}^{(1j)}}{A_{(nc)}^{(1j)}} ; \frac{CES\left(X_{(n+1,1)}^{(1j)}, X_{(n+1,2)}^{(1j)}; \rho_{n+1}^{(1j)}\right)}{A_{n+1}^{(1j)}} \right]$$

$$\text{(E4.5.2)}$$

and

$$X_{(n+1,1)}^{(1j)} = \underset{k=1,\dots,m}{CES} \left[X_{(n+1,1,k)}^{(1j)}; \rho_{(n+1,1)}^{(1j)} \right] . \quad \text{(E4.5.3)}$$

The notation CES(...) is used, as it was in Exercise 3.13, to indicate a CES combination of inputs. Because DMR often adopt Cobb-Douglas specifications, we extend our earlier definition of the CES function (see Exercise 3.9) to include the Cobb-Douglas case. More explicitly,

$$CES \left[X_{(n+1,1)}^{(1j)}, X_{(n+1,2)}^{(1j)}; \rho_{n+1}^{(1j)} \right]$$

$$= D_{(n+1)}^{(1j)} \left[\sum_{s=1\&2} \delta_{(n+1,s)}^{(1j)} \left[X_{(n+1,s)}^{(1j)} \right]^{-\rho_{n+1}^{(1j)}} \right]^{-1/\rho_{n+1}^{(1j)}} \quad \text{for } \rho_{n+1}^{(1j)} \neq 0$$

$$\text{(E4.5.4)}$$

$$= D_{(n+1)}^{(1j)} \prod_{s=1}^{2} \left[X_{(n+1,s)}^{(1j)} \right]^{\delta_{(n+1,s)}^{(1j)}} \quad \text{for } \rho_{n+1}^{(1j)} = 0, \quad \text{(E4.5.5)}$$

and

$$\underset{k=1,\dots,m}{CES} \left[X_{(n+1,1,k)}^{(1j)}; \rho_{(n+1,1)}^{(1j)} \right]$$

$$= D_{(n+1,1)}^{(1j)} \left[\sum_{k=1}^{m} \delta_{(n+1,1,k)}^{(1j)} [X_{(n+1,1,k)}^{(1j)}]^{-\rho_{(n+1,1)}^{(1j)}} \right]^{-1/\rho_{(n+1,1)}^{(1j)}}$$

$$\text{for } \rho_{(n+1,1)}^{(1j)} \neq 0 \qquad (E4.5.6)$$

$$= D_{(n+1,1)}^{(1j)} \prod_{k=1}^{m} [X_{(n+1,1,k)}^{(1j)}]^{\delta_{(n+1,1,k)}^{(1j)}}$$

$$\text{for } \rho_{(n+1,1)}^{(1j)} = 0. \qquad (E4.5.7)$$

The Ds and δs are positive parameters with

$$\sum_{s=1}^{2} \delta_{(n+1,s)}^{(1j)} = \sum_{k=1}^{m} \delta_{(n+1,1,k)}^{(1j)} = 1 ,$$

and the ρs are parameters whose values are greater than −1. By insisting that ρ is strictly greater than −1 we rule out the possibility of corner solutions to cost minimization problems.

What are the explicit forms of $\psi_{(n+1,s)}^{(1j)}$ (...) and $\psi_{(n+1,1,k)}^{(1j)}$ (...) appearing in (4.3.8)(a) and (4.3.9)(a)?

(b)   Discuss the assumptions built into the input-activity specification (E4.5.2) – (E4.5.3). Give examples of situations in which these assumptions would be inappropriate.

(c)   Derive the percentage change forms, (4.3.7)(b) – (4.3.10)(b), of (4.3.7)(a) – (4.3.10)(a).

Answer to Exercise 4.5

(a)   Equation (E4.5.2) implies that the activity level is a Leontief combination of inputs of composite goods and the effective input of primary factors. The effective input of primary factors is a CES combination of the effective input of labor and the input of capital. The effective input of labor is defined in (E4.5.3) as a CES combination of occupational inputs. In Exercise 3.13, we studied nested or separable production specifications of forms similar to (E4.5.2) – (E4.5.3). It may be useful to review Exercise 3.13 if you are having difficulty with the current exercise.

As in Exercise 3.13(a), we note that for cost minimization, we must equate all the arguments of the Leontief function. That is, we must choose our input levels so that

$$Z_j = X_{(ic)}^{(1j)}/A_{(ic)}^{(1j)}, \qquad i = 1,...., n, \qquad (E4.5.8)$$

and

$$Z_j = CES\left[X_{(n+1,1)}^{(1j)}, X_{(n+1,2)}^{(1j)}; \rho_{n+1}^{(1j)}\right] / A_{n+1}^{(1j)}. \qquad (E4.5.9)$$

Equation (4.3.7)(a) follows immediately from (E4.5.8). Equation (4.3.9)(a) is also easy to derive once we recognize that whatever the optimal level for the effective labor input, $X_{(n+1,1)}^{(1j)}$, cost minimization requires that the occupational inputs are chosen to minimize

$$\sum_{k=1}^{m} P_{(n+1,1,k)}^{(1j)} X_{(n+1,1,k)}^{(1j)} \qquad (E4.5.10)$$

subject to (E4.5.3). To solve this problem we proceed along lines similar to the derivation of (E4.3.4) – (E4.3.5) in Exercise 4.3(a). We obtain (4.3.9)(a), in which

$$\psi_{(n+1,1,k)}^{(1j)} (P_{(n+1,1,1)}^{(1j)} ,...., P_{(n+1,1,m)}^{(1j)}) =$$

$$\frac{1}{D_{(n+1,1)}^{(1j)}} \left[\sum_{v=1}^{m} \delta_{(n+1,1,v)}^{(1j)} \left[\frac{P_{(n+1,1,v)}^{(1j)}\delta_{(n+1,1,k)}^{(1j)}}{P_{(n+1,1,k)}^{(1j)}\delta_{(n+1,1,v)}^{(1j)}} \right]^{\rho_{(n+1,1)}^{(1j)}/(1+\rho_{(n+1,1)}^{(1j)})} \right]^{1/\rho_{(n+1,1)}^{(1j)}}$$

$$\text{for } \rho_{(n+1,1)}^{(1j)} \neq 0. \qquad (E4.5.11)$$

When the relevant ρ does equal zero, we proceed as in Exercise 3.1(c), obtaining

$$\psi_{(n+1,1,k)}^{(1j)} (P_{(n+1,1,1)}^{(1j)} ,...., P_{(n+1,1,m)}^{(1j)}) =$$

$$\frac{\delta^{(1j)}_{(n+1,1,k)}}{D^{(1j)}_{(n+1,1)}} \left[\prod_{v=1}^{m} \left(\delta^{(1j)}_{(n+1,1,v)} \right)^{-\delta^{(1j)}_{(n+1,1,v)}} \right] \frac{\prod_{v=1}^{m} \left(P^{(1j)}_{(n+1,1,v)} \right)^{\delta^{(1j)}_{(n+1,1,v)}}}{P^{(1j)}_{(n+1,1,k)}}$$

$$\text{for } \rho^{(1j)}_{(n+1,1,k)} = 0 . \qquad \text{(E4.5.12)}$$

To obtain (4.3.10)(a), we define the price of an effective unit of labor to industry j by

$$P^{(1j)}_{(n+1,1)} = \left[\sum_{k=1}^{m} P^{(1j)}_{(n+1,1,k)} X^{(1j)}_{(n+1,1,k)} \right] / X^{(1j)}_{(n+1,1)} , \qquad \text{(E4.5.13)}$$

where $X^{(1j)}_{(n+1,1)}$ is the number of effective units used and the $X^{(1j)}_{(n+1,1,k)}$s are the cost minimizing occupational inputs given by (4.3.9)(a). Under this definition, $P^{(1j)}_{(n+1,1)}$ is the minimum cost to industry j of an effective unit of labor. It is, therefore, the appropriate price to attach to effective units of labor in considering the choice of labor and capital inputs to be used in forming effective units of primary factors. Hence $X^{(1j)}_{(n+1,1)}$ and $X^{(1j)}_{(n+1,2)}$ must be chosen to minimize

$$\sum_{s=1}^{2} P^{(1j)}_{(n+1,s)} X^{(1j)}_{(n+1,s)} \qquad \text{(E4.5.14)}$$

subject to (E4.5.9). The solution to this problem is (4.3.8)(a) with

$$\psi^{(1j)}_{(n+1,s)} \left(P^{(1j)}_{(n+1,1)}, P^{(1j)}_{(n+1,2)} \right) =$$

$$\frac{1}{D^{(1j)}_{(n+1)}} \left[\sum_{t=1}^{2} \delta^{(1j)}_{(n+1,t)} \left[\frac{P^{(1j)}_{(n+1,t)} \delta^{(1j)}_{(n+1,s)}}{P^{(1j)}_{(n+1,s)} \delta^{(1j)}_{(n+1,t)}} \right]^{\rho^{(1j)}_{n+1}/(1+\rho^{(1j)}_{n+1})} \right]^{1/\rho^{(1j)}_{n+1}}$$

$$\text{for } \rho^{(1j)}_{n+1} \neq 0, \qquad \text{(E4.5.15)}$$

$$= \frac{\delta_{(n+1,s)}^{(1j)}}{D_{(n+1)}^{(1j)}} \left[\prod_{t=1}^{2} \left(\delta_{(n+1,t)}^{(1j)} \right)^{-\delta_{(n+1,t)}^{(1j)}} \right] \frac{\prod_{t=1}^{2} \left(P_{(n+1,t)}^{(1j)} \right)^{\delta_{(n+1,t)}^{(1j)}}}{P_{(n+1,s)}^{(1j)}}$$

$$\text{for } \rho_{n+1}^{(1j)} = 0 . \qquad \text{(E4.5.16)}$$

(b) The input-activity specification, (E4.5.2) – (E4.5.3), exhibits constant returns to scale and is of a three level form (see Figure E4.5.1). At the top level, the Leontief assumption has been adopted. There is no substitution between different materials (chemicals, steel, etc.) or between materials and primary factors in the creation of units of industry activity. This assumption, which is very common in applied general equilibrium modeling, has been inherited from input-output analysis. It has been justified by appeal to numerous studies that have failed in attempts to establish changes in relative input prices as major determinants of changes in relative input quantities (see, for example, Sevaldson (1976), who examines a long time-series of Norwegian input-output tables). Recent work by Jorgenson and others has, however, demonstrated the feasibility of estimating material/material and material/primary factor substitution elasticities at a detailed level for the United States (see particularly Jorgenson (1984) and the references cited in Exercise 3.12). Consequently, it is likely that in future generations of applied general equilibrium models, the Leontief specification will be phased out. This will be important in improving general equilibrium analyses of issues involving sharp changes in the relative prices of competitive inputs, e.g., oil and coal.

At the second and third levels, DMR have adopted CES functions to describe substitution possibilities between units of labor and capital in the creation of a unit of primary factor, and between labor of different occupational types in the creation of a unit of labor. The CES function implies equality between all pair-wise substitution elasticities (see Exercise 3.9). For example, under the DMR specification, the elasticity of substitution between labor inputs from occupations 1 and 2 is assumed to be the same as that between labor inputs from occupations 2 and 3. The only justification for such an assumption is that not enough is known about labor/labor substitution to support the use of any other assumption. Similarly, very little is known about the relationship between the occupational composition of labor inputs and capital intensity. Under

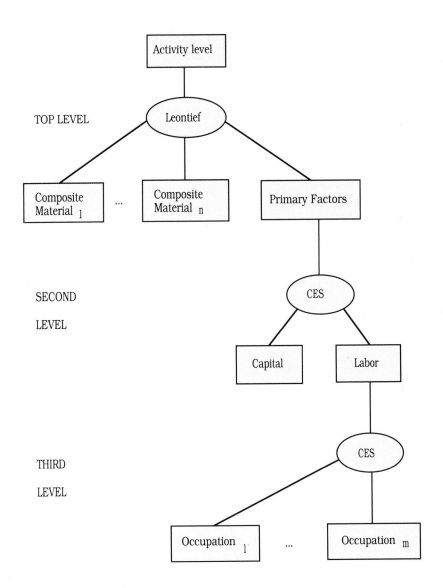

Figure E4.5.1   The input-activity specification in the DMR model: schematic representation of equations (E4.5.2) - (E4.5.3)

the particular nesting (or separability) assumptions used by DMR, the occupational composition of the labor input is determined independently of the level of capital inputs. Modifications of this specification would be required if it were found, for example, that professionals were complementary with capital while unskilled workers were competitive.

Finally, it is worth commenting on the assumption of constant returns to scale. This assumption is inappropriate if the production function leaves out some inflexible inputs. In the DMR model there is no agricultural land. If we were to make 50 per cent increases in the inputs to agriculture of materials, labor and capital (the inputs recognized by DMR) we would expect agricultural output to increase by less than 50 per cent because of shortages of land. Hence, if land is omitted, we would expect the agricultural production function to exhibit diminishing returns to scale. For some other industries it may be appropriate to allow for increasing returns to scale. For example, in small inward-looking economies, we often find that vehicle manufacturers are limited to production volumes well below minimum efficient scale. In designing models for analyzing the long-run effects of reductions in protection in these economies, it is important to allow for the possibility of exploitation of economies of scale based on increased export sales (a point emphasized by Dixon (1978), Cox and Harris (1983) and Harris and Cox (1984)).

(c)   Equation (4.3.7)(b) follows from (4.3.7)(a), assuming that $A_{(ic)}^{(1j)}$, is a parameter.

In part (a) we saw that (4.3.8)(a) is derived by minimizing (E4.5.14) subject to the CES constraint (E4.5.9). The derivation of percentage change forms for input demand functions arising from cost minimization problems of this type was studied in Exercise 3.9 ($\rho \neq 0$) and Exercises 3.1 – 3.2 ($\rho = 0$). By adapting results (E3.9.12) and (E3.2.2) to the present situation, we quickly arrive at (4.3.8)(b). The parameter $\sigma_{n+1}^{(1j)}$, which equals $1/(1 + \rho_{n+1}^{(1j)})$, has the value 1 in the Cobb-Douglas case.

Perhaps the only feature of (4.3.8)(b) which requires further comment is the technological change term, $a_{n+1}^{(1j)}$, appearing on the right hand side. Notice that the LHS of the CES constraint in (E3.9.1) was denoted by Y and the LHS of the Cobb-Douglas constraint in (E3.1.4) was denoted by X_j. Here the LHS of the constraint is $A_{n+1}^{(1j)} Z_j$ obtained by rearranging (E4.5.9) so that the CES function is on the right and $A_{n+1}^{(1j)} Z_j$ is on the left. Where the percentage change in Y appears in (E3.9.12) and the percentage change in X_j appears in (E3.2.2), in (4.3.8)(b) we find the percentage change in $A_{n+1}^{(1j)}Z_j$, i.e., we find $a_{n+1}^{(1j)} + z_j$.

By treating $A_{n+1}^{(1j)}$ as a variable, DMR are allowing the possibility of simulating the effects of primary-factor-augmenting technical change (see Allen, 1967, pp. 236-258). A reduction in $A_{n+1}^{(1j)}$ is a reduction in the number of effective units of primary factor input required per unit of activity in industry j. From the point of view of generating activity in industry j, a reduction in $A_{n+1}^{(1j)}$ is equivalent to an augmentation of the input of primary factors. It would be possible in the DMR model to simulate the effects of other input-augmenting technical change if the $A_{(ic)}^{(1j)}$s in (4.3.7)(a) were treated as variables rather than as parameters.

Equation (4.3.9)(a) is derived by minimizing (E4.5.10) subject to the CES constraint (E4.5.3). Again, we can adapt (E3.9.12) and (E3.2.2) to obtain the percentage form (4.3.9)(b).

To derive (4.3.10)(b), we first apply the Product and Sum Rules of Exercise 3.2 to (4.3.10)(a). This gives

$$P_{(n+1,1)}^{(1j)} + x_{(n+1,1)}^{(1j)} = \sum_{v=1}^{m} (P_{(n+1,1,v)}^{(1j)} + x_{(n+1,1,v)}^{(1j)}) S_{(n+1,1,v)}^{(1j)} . \qquad (E4.5.17)$$

From (4.3.9)(b) we see that

$$\sum_{k=1}^{m} S_{(n+1,1,k)}^{(1j)} x_{(n+1,1,k)}^{(1j)} = x_{(n+1,1)}^{(1j)} . \qquad (E4.5.18)$$

On using (E4.5.18) in (E4.5.17) we obtain (4.3.10)(b).

Exercise 4.6   *Evaluating the parameters and coefficients in the input demand equations*

The parameters in equation (4.3.7)(a) are $A_{(ic)}^{(1j)}$, i, j = 1,..., n. By referring to (E4.5.15) – (E4.5.16) and (E4.5.11) – (E4.5.12) we see that the parameters in (4.3.8)(a) and (4.3.9)(a) are

$$D_{(n+1)}^{(1j)}, \quad P_{n+1}^{(1j)}, \quad \delta_{(n+1,s)}^{(1j)}, \quad D_{(n+1,1)}^{(1j)}, \quad P_{(n+1,1)}^{(1j)} \quad \text{and} \quad \delta_{(n+1,1,v)}^{(1j)}$$

for j = 1,..., n, s=1, 2 and v=1,...,m.

Equation (4.3.10)(a) contains no parameters requiring evaluation.

The main difficulty in evaluating the parameters of the input demand equations is to decide on values for the capital/labor substitution elasticities ($\sigma_{n+1}^{(1j)}$, j = 1,..., n) and the labor/labor substitution elasticities ($\sigma_{(n+1,1)}^{(1j)}$, j = 1,..., n). Once these σs are evaluated, the ρs can be computed via the relationship $\rho = (1 - \sigma)/\sigma$. The remaining parameters can then be evaluated from the base-period input-output data.

Numerous econometric studies have been made of capital labor substitution elasticities. (An often-quoted survey and review of the empirical literature is Caddy (1976). For more recent work, see Jorgenson (1984).) Although the results of these studies do not allow us to distinguish between substitution elasticities indifferent industries with any confidence, they do indicate that the most likely range is 0.5 to 1. DMR usually use 1. In their parameter file (reported in Appendix 4.1), only the construction industry has a labor/capital substitution elasticity different from 1. For this industry, DMR use the surprisingly high value of 2. Sherman Robinson has explained to us that all the capital/labor substitution elasticities were originally set at 1. However, in simulations of the effects of investment booms, the construction industry exhibited too little flexibility in its output response and too much flexibility in its price response. More plausible results were obtained with the higher substitution elasticity.

There have also been econometric studies of substitution elasticities between different types of labor. Estimates have ranged from very large (Bowles (1970)) to very small (Weiss (1977) and Ryland and Parham (1978)). Tinbergen (1975) selected 1 as the most reasonable value. This is the choice of DMR (see Appendix 4.1).

(a)   Use the input-output data in Appendix 4.1 to evaluate $A_{(7c)}^{(13)}$

(b)   DMR set $\sigma_{(n+1,1)}^{(1j)} = 1$ for all j. Evaluate $\rho_{(n+1,1)}^{(12)}$, $D_{(n+1,1)}^{(12)}$ and $\delta_{(n+1,1,v)}^{(12)}$ for v = 1,...,4.

Hint: To make these evaluations, you will need units for effective labor inputs in each industry and for labor inputs by occupation. For the effective labor inputs, define the units as the quantities which cost $1 million in the base period. For occupational labor inputs, define a unit as 1 million manyears. The reason for breaking our usual convention of defining units as quantities which cost $1 million is that we will want to add across industries to find the total demands for labor of each occupation — see (4.3.24)(a). The DMR database shows that there are differences across industries in occupational wage rates. For example, the wage rate per manyear for "organized labor" in industry 1 is $193.39. In industry 2 it is $109.75. Hence, $1 million bought a different number of manyears of organized labor in industry 1 from the number it bought in industry 2.

(c)   In the DMR database, $\sigma_{n+1}^{(11)} = 1$ and $\sigma_{n+1}^{(16)} = 2$. Evaluate

$P_{n+1}^{(1j)}$, $D_{(n+1)}^{(1j)}$, and $\delta_{(n+1,s)}^{(1j)}$ for s = 1, 2 and j = 1 and 6.

What are the base period values for $A_{n+1}^{(11)}$ and $A_{n+1}^{(16)}$?

Hint: Here we need units for effective labor inputs, capital inputs, effective inputs of primary factors and industry activity levels. In part (b) we defined units for effective labor inputs. In Exercise 4.1(c) we defined a unit of capital for each industry as the quantity which had a base-period construction cost of $1 million. The database in Appendix 4.1 lists base-period rates of return. These can be combined with vector $\tilde{H}$ in the input-output data to calculate the values of capital inputs. For example, returns to capital of $266.46 million in industry 1 represented a gross rate of return of 40.52 per cent. This implies that the value of the capital input was $657.60 million (= 226.46/0.4052). We assume that units of capital are valued at their cost of construction. Since the value of capital in use in the base period was $657.60 million, the number of units in use was 657.60. That is,

$$[X_{(n+1,2)}^{(11)}]^I = 657.60 .$$

Units of effective primary factor inputs for each industry also can be defined as the quantities which had base period costs of $1 million. Units for industry activity levels have already been defined in Exercise 4.4(b) as producing base-period revenues of $1 million.

(d)   What is the initial value of coefficient $S_{(n+1,1)}^{(17)}$ appearing in (4.3.8)(b)? What is the initial value of $S_{(n+1,1,3)}^{(14)}$ in (4.3.9)(b) and (4.3.10)(b)?

Answer to Exercise 4.6

(a)   The parameter $A_{(ic)}^{(1j)}$ is the number of units of composite commodity i required per unit of activity in industry j. In Exercise 4.1(c) we defined quantity units for composite commodities and in Exercise 4.4(b) we defined units for industry activity levels. With these definitions in mind, we note that in the base-period, industry 3 achieved an activity level of 321.45 with an input of (7c) of 7.03, implying that

$$A_{(7c)}^{(13)} = 7.03/321.45 = 0.022 \ .$$

(b)   Since $\sigma_{(n+1,1)}^{(1j)} = 1$ for all j, $\rho_{(n+1,1)}^{(1j)} = 0$ for all j.

In the Cobb-Douglas case, the $\delta_{(n+1,1,v)}^{(1j)}$s are cost shares. From $\tilde{G}$ in the input-output database, we have

$$[\delta_{(n+1,1,v)}^{(12)}, \ v=1,...,4] = (0, \ 7.65/11.77, \ 4.12/11.77, \ 0)$$

$$= (0, 0.650, \ 0.350, \ 0).$$

To evaluate $D_{(n+1,1)}^{(12)}$, we start by noting from the database that

$$\left\{ \left[P_{(n+1,1,v)}^{(12)} \right]^{I}, v = 1,..., \ 4 \right\} = \left\{ 73.67, 86.78, \ 109.75, \ 152.44 \right\} \ .$$

Next we calculate occupational inputs by dividing labor costs (matrix $\tilde{G}$) by the base-period wage rates. For industry 2, this gives

$$\left\{ \left[X_{(n+1,1,v)}^{(12)} \right]^{I}, v = 1,..., \ 4 \right\} = \left\{ 0, 0.0882, 0.0375, \ 0 \right\} \ .$$

On using (E4.5.12) with k=2 (other choices for k could also be made), we find that in the base-period

$$\psi_{(n+1,1,2)}^{(12)} = \frac{0.650}{D_{(n+1,1)}^{(12)}} \left[(.650)^{-.650} (.350)^{-.350} \right] \frac{(86.78)^{.650} (109.75)^{.350}}{86.78}$$

$$= 1.348/D_{(n+1,1)}^{(12)} \ .$$

Now we substitute into (4.3.9)(a), obtaining

$$0.0882 = 11.77 \left[1.348/D_{(n+1,1)}^{(12)} \right] \ .$$

This gives

$$D_{(n+1,1)}^{(12)} = 179.9 \ .$$

(c)   For industry 1, we have the Cobb-Douglas case. Hence $\rho_{n+1}^{(11)} = 0$ and the $\delta_{(n+1,s)}^{(11)}$ s are labor and capital shares in total primary factor costs. These may be evaluated from $\tilde{G}$ and $\tilde{H}$ as

$$[\delta_{(n+1,s)}^{(11)}, s=1,2] = \left(\frac{218.00}{218.00 + 266.46}, \frac{266.46}{218.00 + 266.46}\right) = (0.45, 0.55) .$$

Next we compute the initial value of $A_{(n+1)}^{(11)}$. This is the number of units of primary factor input required per unit of activity in industry 1. Thus we have

$$\left[A_{n+1}^{(11)}\right]^{I} = (218.00 + 266.46)/657.36 = 0.737 .$$

In view of our units definitions for effective inputs of labor and inputs of capital, we have

$$\left[P_{(n+1,1)}^{(1j)}\right]^{I} = 1 \text{ and } \left[P_{(n+1,2)}^{(1j)}\right]^{I} = 0.4052 .$$

We can now evaluate $D_{(n+1)}^{(11)}$ by substituting base-period values of variables into (E4.5.16) and then into (4.3.8)(a). For s = 1, this gives

$$218.00 = (.737)(657.36)\frac{0.45}{D_{(n+1)}^{(11)}}\left[(.45)^{-.45}(.55)^{-.55}\right](.4052)^{.55},$$

implying that

$$D_{(n+1)}^{(11)} = 1.21 .$$

Alternatively, we can set s = 2. Check that this also gives 1.21 as the value for $D_{(n+1)}^{(11)}$.

For industry 6,

$$\rho_{n+1}^{(16)} = -0.5 ;$$

$$\left[A_{n+1}^{(16)}\right]^{I} = (30.52 + 6.68)/111.82 = 0.333 ;$$

$$(Z_{6})^{I} = 111.82 ;$$

$$\left[X_{(n+1,1)}^{(16)}\right]^{I} = 30.52 ;$$

$$\left[X_{(n+1,2)}^{(16)}\right]^{I} = 6.68/0.3339 = 20.00 ;$$

and

$$[P^{(16)}_{(n+1,1)}, P^{(16)}_{(n+1,2)}]^I = (1, 0.3339) \quad .$$

By using this information in (E4.5.15) and (4.3.8)(a) with j set at 6, and on recalling that

$$\delta^{(16)}_{(n+1,1)} + \delta^{(16)}_{(n+1,2)} = 1 \quad , \tag{E4.6.1}$$

we obtain a system of three equations in which the unknowns are $D^{(16)}_{(n+1)}$ and $\delta^{(16)}_{(n+1,s)}$ for s=1,2. On solving this system, we find that

$$D^{(16)}_{(n+1)} = 1.32 \quad \text{and that} \quad [\delta^{(16)}_{(n+1,s)}, s=1,2] = (0.787, 0.213).$$

(d)   By referring to data matrices $\tilde{G}$ and $\tilde{H}$ we find that

$$[S^{(17)}_{(n+1,1)}]^I = 29.97/(29.97 + 18.41) = 0.62$$

and

$$[S^{(14)}_{(n+1,1,3)}]^I = 17.47/24.97 = 0.70 \quad .$$

Exercise 4.7   ***The creation of composite commodities: substitution between imported and domestic products: equations (4.3.11) – (4.3.14)***

DMR assume that users of domestic and imported commodity i regard them as imperfect substitutes. This assumption has become common in general equilibrium modeling since it was first introduced by Armington (1969, 1970). By handling imported and domestic commodities as imperfect substitutes, the unsatisfactory consequences of either of the two extremes frequently found in earlier modeling exercises are avoided. At one extreme, imported and domestic footwear, for example, were treated as a single product implying perfect substitutability. This assumption is inconsistent with the observation that the relative prices of imported and domestic commodities can change without causing the exclusion of either product from the market. At the other extreme, imported and domestic products were treated as non-substitutable. This is inconsistent with the observation that the quantity share of imported footwear in the domestic market responds to changes in the import/domestic price ratio.

Imperfect substitutability between domestic and imported products is modeled by DMR through composite commodities. They assume that domestic users of good i purchase only the composite commodity, (ic). This composite commodity can be viewed as the product of a mixing industry. In creating units of (ic), the mixing industry treats units of the domestic commodity (i1) and the imported commodity (i2) as imperfectly substitutable inputs.   More specifically, the supply of composite commodity (ic) is assumed to be a CES combination of domestic and imported inputs, $X^{(c)}_{(i1)}$ and $X^{(c)}_{(i2)}$, to the mixing industry.

In most models employing the Armington specification, it is assumed that the mixing industry chooses the cost-minimizing combination of domestic and imported inputs compatible with its output level, $X_{(ic)}$. Where the CES technology is assumed, we obtain demand equations for domestic and imported goods of the form

$$X^{(c)}_{(is)} = X_{(ic)} \, \psi^{(c)}_{(is)} \left(P_{(i1)}, P_{(i2)} \right), \quad s = 1, 2 . \quad \text{(E4.7.1)}$$

DMR depart from usual practice by assuming that cost-minimization determines only the desired inputs, $X^{(c)*}_{(is)}$, $s = 1$, 2, of domestic and imported commodities. They emphasize the possibility that imported commodities may be rationed by nonprice mechanisms, e.g., import quotas, so that desired inputs to the mixing industry can differ from actual inputs.

(a)   Look at equations (4.3.11)(a) – (4.3.14)(a) in Table 4.3.1. Show that the usual Armington specification (where the actual inputs, $X^{(c)}_{(is)}$, $s = 1$, 2, to the mixing industry are cost-minimizing) can be obtained as a special case in the DMR model by setting $F^{(c)}_{(i2)} = F^{(c)}_2 = 1$. Should we also set $F^{(c)}_{(i1)}$ equal to 1?

(b)   How should we set $F^{(c)}_{(i2)}$, $F^{(c)}_2$ and $F^{(c)}_{(i1)}$ if we want to conduct simulations with the DMR model under the assumption that the actual imports of commodity i are restricted to 90 per cent of the desired level? How should we set the Fs to incorporate the restriction that the ratio of imported to domestic products is 90 per cent of the desired ratio?

(c)   Assume that the technology equation (4.3.14)(a) for the mixing industry has the specific form:

$$X_{(ic)} = \left\{ \frac{1}{2} \left(X^{(c)}_{(i1)} \right)^{\frac{1}{2}} + \frac{1}{2} \left(X^{(c)}_{(i2)} \right)^{\frac{1}{2}} \right\}^2 . \quad \text{(E4.7.2)}$$

Assume that $X_{(ic)} = P_{(i1)} = P_{(i2)} = 1$ and that actual imports are restricted to 90 per cent of desired imports. Compute $X^{(c)*}_{(i1)}$, $X^{(c)*}_{(i2)}$, $X^{(c)}_{(i1)}$ and $X^{(c)}_{(i2)}$. Compare the cost of the actual input bundle, $X^{(c)}_{(i1)}, X^{(c)}_{(i2)}$, with that of the desired bundle, $X^{(c)*}_{(i1)}, X^{(c)*}_{(i2)}$.

(d)   Under what circumstances would it be inappropriate to assume that all domestic demands for good i are satisfied by units of a single composite commodity?

(e)   When DMR force actual imports to be less than desired imports, they refer to the situation as one of

" 'fixprice' rationing to underline the fact that the user price [$P_{(i2)}$ in our notation] remains fixed in spite of an overall shortage"
(DMR (1982, p. 293)).

They argue that the fixprice specification

"is appropriate for countries where imports of producer goods are tied to user specific quotas and licenses, where resale is prohibited, and where consumer goods imports are insignificant. In such countries there is some justification for adopting a stylized model that specifies that realized sectoral imports are proportional to desired sectoral imports and that desired sectoral imports are based on the customs clearance price with the rents due to the restrictive import regime accruing directly to the users of the imported producer goods. What is crucial here is the assumption that users of imports do not have to pay more than the tariff-inclusive c.i.f. price ..." (DMR (1982, p. 293)).

Why is the DMR fixprice rationing specification inappropriate for modeling quota-restricted imports of consumer goods or other goods where resale is possible? Are shortages (i.e., gaps between desired and actual imports) a necessary ingredient of a model in which resale of quota-restricted imports is not possible? What do DMR mean by "the rents due to the restrictive import regime"?

Answer to Exercise 4.7

(a)   With $F_{(i2)}^{(c)} = F_2^{(c)} = 1$,   (E4.7.3)

(4.3.12)(a) implies that
$$X_{(i2)}^{(c)} = X_{(i2)}^{(c)*} .$$

It then follows from (4.3.11)(a) that

$$X_{(i2)}^{(c)} = X_{(ic)} \, \psi_{(i2)}^{(c)} \, (P_{(i1)}, P_{(i2)}) \; ; \qquad (E4.7.4)$$

i.e., the input to the mixing industry of (i2) is consistent with $X_{(i1)}^{(c)}$ and $X_{(i2)}^{(c)}$ being chosen to minimize

$$\sum_{s=1}^{2} P_{(is)} X_{(is)}^{(c)} \tag{E4.7.5}$$

subject to

$$X_{(ic)} = CES\left[X_{(i1)}^{(c)}, X_{(i2)}^{(c)}\right] . \tag{E4.7.6}$$

Since the constraint, (E4.7.6), is imposed in the DMR model by (4.3.14)(a), we can conclude that the input of (i1) to the mixing industry must also be consistent with the cost minimization problem (E4.7.5) – (E4.7.6). Hence, under condition (E4.7.3), the DMR model will imply

$$X_{(i1)}^{(c)} = X_{(ic)} \; \psi_{(i1)}^{(c)} \left(P_{(i1)}, P_{(i2)}\right) . \tag{E4.7.7}$$

(E4.7.4) and (E4.7.7) are the usual Armington specification.

With $F_{(i2)}^{(c)}$ and $F_2^{(c)}$ treated as exogenous variables, $F_{(i1)}^{(c)}$, appearing in equation (4.3.13)(a), should be treated as an endogenous variable. Otherwise, we may introduce an inconsistency. For example, under condition (E4.7.3), we have shown that $X_{(i1)}^{(c)} = X_{(i1)}^{(c)*}$, implying that $F_{(i1)}^{(c)} = 1$. Attempts to introduce exogenous variations in $F_{(i1)}^{(c)}$ away from 1 would lead to contradictions.

(b)   Actual imports of commodity i in the DMR model will be restricted to 90 per cent of the desired level if we set $F_2^{(c)} = 1$ and $F_{(i2)}^{(c)} = 0.9$. With $F_2^{(c)}$ and $F_{(i2)}^{(c)}$ set exogenously, it follows from the argument in part (a) that $F_{(i1)}^{(c)}$ should be treated as an endogenous variable. On the other hand, if we want to restrict the ratio of imported to domestic products to 90 per cent of the desired ratio, i.e., if we require

$$X_{(i2)}^{(c)}/X_{(i1)}^{(c)} = 0.9 \; \left(X_{(i2)}^{(c)*}/X_{(i1)}^{(c)*}\right) ,$$

then we should set $F_{(i1)}^{(c)}$ exogenously at $(1/0.9)$. $F_2^{(c)}$ should be set at 1 and $F_{(i2)}^{(c)}$ should be endogenous.

(c)   The desired input levels, $X_{(i1)}^{(c)*}$ and $X_{(i2)}^{(c)*}$, will minimize

$$\sum_{s=1}^{2} P_{(is)} X_{(is)}^{(c)*}$$

subject to

$$X_{(ic)} = \left\{ \frac{1}{2} \left[X_{(i1)}^{(c)*} \right]^{\frac{1}{2}} + \frac{1}{2} \left[X_{(i2)}^{(c)*} \right]^{\frac{1}{2}} \right\}^2 .$$

With $P_{(i1)} = P_{(i2)} = 1$ and

We obtain

$$X_{(ic)} = 1 , \tag{E4.7.8}$$

$$X_{(is)}^{(c)*} = 1 , \qquad s = 1, 2 .$$

Given that actual imports are 90 per cent of the desired level, we have

$$X_{(i2)}^{(c)} = 0.9 \; X_{(i2)}^{(c)*} = 0.9 . \tag{E4.7.9}$$

$X_{(i1)}^{(c)}$ can now be computed by substitution from (E4.7.8) and (E4.7.9) into (E4.7.2), yielding

$$X_{(i1)}^{(c)} = 1.10527 .$$

Finally, we note that the desired input bundle, (1,1), has a cost of 2, whereas the bundle, (1.10527, 0.9), costs 2.00527. The restriction on imports increases the cost of units of composite good i by 0.26 per cent.

(d)   This assumption is inappropriate if we need to allow for differences across users in the ratios of imported to domestic goods in their purchases of good i. For example, in a multi-household model, it might be important to recognize that the import-domestic ratio in the food purchases of rich households is higher than that of poor households.

(e)   Under DMR's fixprice rationing assumption, it is possible for desired imports permanently to exceed actual imports. This contrasts with the normal assumption that resale by importers will eventually lead to a domestic price for imported products at which desired imports are equal to actual imports despite the presence of quotas. In terms of our notation for the DMR model, if $X_{(i2)}^{(c)*}$ were greater than $X_{(i2)}^{(c)}$, then there would be people with unsatisfied demands for units of (i2) who would be willing to pay more than the domestic market price, $P_{(i2)}$. Given this situation, the usual assumption is that $P_{(i2)}$ will increase as people with unsatisfied demands try to purchase units of (i2) from those who are fortunate enough to have import licenses. $P_{(i2)}$ will continue to increase, according to this story, until $X_{(i2)}^{(c)*}$ falls sufficiently so that

$$X_{(i2)}^{(c)*} = X_{(i2)}^{(c)} . \tag{E4.7.10}$$

At this stage, the domestic market price of units of (i2), $P_{(i2)}$, will be established at a higher level than the tariff inclusive c.i.f. price, which is the cost to importers. The difference is the quota rent per unit of imports or the rent "due to the restrictive import regime". The quota rent (or pure profit) accrues to people holding import licenses.

DMR's fixprice rationing specification can be interpreted as a device for ensuring that quota rents in their model accrue to import users. Consequently their specification is inappropriate if resale is possible. With resale, the import users can be different people from the license holders who receive the quota rents. Even when we wish to adopt the DMR assumption that quota rents accrue to import users, it is not essential to leave the market-clearing framework. Gaps between desired and actual import levels are not a fundamental part of the DMR story. Computations of DMR fixprice rationing solutions can be made in a market-clearing model in which quota rents are first generated as if there were a separation between license holders and import users and then allocated to import users as subsidies.

Exercise 4.8   *Evaluating the parameters and coefficients in the import/domestic substitution equations*

The only parameters requiring evaluation in equations (4.3.11)(a) – (4.3.14)(a) are those of the $\psi_{(is)}^{(c)}$ functions in (4.3.11)(a). These parameters also appear in the CES functions in (4.3.14)(a).

To save space, in the equations below we will not allow explicitly for the Cobb-Douglas case. In any event, none of the import/domestic substitution elasticities used by DMR has a value of precisely 1.

Equations (4.3.11)(a) and (4.3.14)(a) can be written explicitly as

$$X_{(is)}^{(c)*} = X_{(ic)} \frac{1}{D_i^{(c)}} \left[\sum_{t=1}^{2} \delta_{(it)}^{(c)} \left[\frac{P_{(it)}}{P_{(is)}} \frac{\delta_{(is)}^{(c)}}{\delta_{(it)}^{(c)}} \right]^{\rho_i^{(c)} / (1+\rho_i^{(c)})} \right]^{1/\rho_i^{(c)}}$$

$$s = 1, 2, i = 1,..., n, \qquad (E4.8.1)$$

and

$$X_{(ic)} = D_i^{(c)} \left[\sum_{t=1}^{2} \delta_{(it)}^{(c)} [X_{(it)}^{(c)}]^{-\rho_i^{(c)}} \right]^{-1/\rho_i^{(c)}}, \quad i = 1,..., n, \qquad (E4.8.2)$$

where the Ds and δs are positive parameters with

$$\sum_{t=1}^{2} \delta_{(it)}^{(c)} = 1 \text{ for all } i ,$$

(E4.8.3)

and the ρs are parameters whose values are greater than -1 but not equal to zero. The Ds, δs and ρs can be evaluated by combining three types of information: (i) estimates of substitution elasticities between imported and domestic products, (ii) base-period input-output data and (iii) information on the base-period relationships between the desired and actual import flows, i.e., information on the initial values of the Fs in (4.3.12)(a) and (4.3.13)(a).

The values used by DMR for import/domestic substitution elasticities are listed in Appendix 4.1. DMR have chosen higher values for agricultural goods, food and other consumer goods than for capital goods and equipment. This accords with various empirical studies. For example, in their work on Australia, Alaouze *et al.* (1977) and Alaouze (1977) found substitution elasticities of 6.8 for footwear, 5.0 for motor vehicles and 3.4 for clothing. For electrical machinery, chemical fertilizers, clay products and cement their estimates were respectively, 1.3, 1.4, 1.4 and 0.8. (A summary of the work of Alaouze and co-workers can be found in Dixon, *et al.* (1982, section 29.1).) Other studies of import elasticities (substitution elasticities and import demand elasticities) are surveyed in Stern *et al.* (1976).

(a)   DMR set the elasticity of substitution between imported and domestic commodity 1 at 2.0. What is the implied value of $\rho_1^{(c)}$?

(b)   Let

$$\Omega_i = F_2^{(c)}/F_{(i1)}^{(c)} , \quad i = 1,...., n.$$

(E4.8.4)

By looking at (4.3.12)(a) and (4.3.13)(a) we see that Ω_i is a ratio of ratios. It is the actual import/domestic ratio $[X_{(i2)}^{(c)}/X_{(i1)}^{(c)}]$ divided by the desired import/domestic ratio $[X_{(i2)}^{(c)*}/X_{(i1)}^{(c)*}]$. DMR do not give us any guidance as to what data could be applied in determining initial values for the Ω_is. However, our impression is that these initial values do not often have an important influence on simulation results. Assume that base-period imports of commodity 1 were restricted so that

$$(\Omega_1)^I = 0.9 .$$

(E4.8.5)

Using the value of $\rho_1^{(c)}$ found in part (a) and the input-output data in Appendix 4.1, evaluate $D_1^{(c)}$, $\delta_{(11)}^{(c)}$ and $\delta_{(12)}^{(c)}$. You will require quantity units for commodities (ic), (i1) and (i2). Those for (ic) and (i1) have been defined earlier as the quantities with basic values in the base period of one million dollars. A unit of (i2) can also be defined as the quantity which had a basic value (including the tariff) of one million dollars.

(c) Derive the percentage change forms, (4.3.11)(b) – (4.3.14)(b), from (4.3.11)(a) – (4.3.14)(a). Continue to adopt (E4.8.5). Then use the input-output data in Appendix 4.1 to find the initial values for the coefficients $S_{(11)}^{(c)*}$, $S_{(12)}^{(c)*}$, $\eta_{(11)}^{(1c)}$ and $\eta_{(12)}^{(1c)}$. Discuss how these coefficients could be re-evaluated during a multi–step Johansen computation.

Answer to Exercise 4.8

(a) With
$$\sigma_1^{(c)} = 2 ,$$
$$\rho_1^{(c)} = -0.5 . \tag{E4.8.6}$$

(b) From our definition of units we know that
$$[P_{(1t)}]^I = 1 \text{ for } t = 1, 2. \tag{E4.8.7}$$

Using (E4.8.6) and (E4.8.7) in (E4.8.1) we obtain

$$\frac{[X_{(12)}^{(c)*}]^I}{[X_{(11)}^{(c)*}]^I} = \left[\frac{\delta_{(11)}^{(c)} (\delta_{(12)}^{(c)}/\delta_{(11)}^{(c)})^{-1} + \delta_{(12)}^{(c)}}{\delta_{(11)}^{(c)} + \delta_{(12)}^{(c)} (\delta_{(11)}^{(c)}/\delta_{(12)}^{(c)})^{-1}} \right]^{-2} = \left[\frac{\delta_{(12)}^{(c)}}{\delta_{(11)}^{(c)}} \right]^2 . \tag{E4.8.8}$$

Now we use (E4.8.5) to rewrite (E4.8.8) as

$$[X_{(12)}^{(c)}]^I / [X_{(11)}^{(c)}]^I = 0.9 \left[\delta_{(12)}^{(c)}/\delta_{(11)}^{(c)} \right]^2 . \tag{E4.8.9}$$

Base-period values for $X_{(12)}^{(c)}$ and $X_{(11)}^{(c)}$ in Appendix 4.1 are

$$[X_{(12)}^{(c)}]^I = (-\tilde{E}1)_1 = 69.94 ,$$

and
$$[X_{(11)}^{(c)}]^I = \tilde{T}_1 - (\tilde{F}1)_1 = 657.36 - 15.66 = 641.70 .$$

By substituting these into (E4.8.9) and by using (E4.8.3) we find that

$$(\delta_{(11)}^{(c)} , \delta_{(12)}^{(c)}) = (0.742, 0.258) . \tag{E4.8.10}$$

To evaluate $D_1^{(c)}$ we can substitute the parameter values found in (E4.8.6) and (E4.8.10), and base-period values for $X_{(11)}^{(c)}$, $X_{(12)}^{(c)}$ and $X_{(1c)}$, into (E4.8.2).   Base-period values have already been noted for $X_{(11)}^{(c)}$ and $X_{(12)}^{(c)}$ and the basic value in the base period of the supply of commodity (1c) is \$711.64 million.   On making the substitution into (E4.8.2), we obtain

$$711.64 = D_1^{(c)} \, [0.742(641.70)^{0.5} + 0.258(69.94)^{0.5}]^2 \ ,$$

yielding

$$D_1^{(c)} = 1.621 \ . \tag{E4.8.11}$$

(c)   Equation (4.3.11)(b) can be derived by following the steps in Exercise 3.9 that lead to (E3.9.12). The only notable feature of (4.3.11)(b) is that the share coefficients on the RHS are desired cost shares rather than actual shares. They are given by

$$S_{(it)}^{(c)*} = P_{(it)} \, X_{(it)}^{(c)*} \, / \, \sum_{s=1}^{2} P_{(is)} \, X_{(is)}^{(c)*} \ , \quad t = 1, 2. \tag{E4.8.12}$$

On recalling that Ω_i is the actual import-domestic quantity ratio divided by the desired ratio, it is not difficult to show, via (E4.8.12), that these desired cost shares are related to actual costs shares $(S_{(it)}^{(c)})$ by

$$S_{(i2)}^{(c)*} = (S_{(i2)}^{(c)}/\Omega_i)/(S_{(i1)}^{(c)} + S_{(i2)}^{(c)}/\Omega_i) \tag{E4.8.13}$$

and

$$S_{(i1)}^{(c)*} = S_{(i1)}^{(c)}/(S_{(i1)}^{(c)} + S_{(i2)}^{(c)}/\Omega_i). \tag{E4.8.14}$$

The derivations of (4.3.12)(b) and (4.3.13)(b) involve simple applications of the Product Rule of Exercise 3.2 to (4.3.12)(a) and (4.3.13)(a). Finally, to derive (4.3.14)(b), we totally differentiate (4.3.14)(a) and make various divisions and off-setting multiplications to obtain

$$\frac{dX_{(ic)}}{X_{(ic)}} = \sum_{s=1}^{2} \left[\frac{\partial CES \, X_{(is)}^{(c)}}{\partial X_{(is)}^{(c)}} \frac{X_{(is)}^{(c)}}{X_{(ic)}} \right] \frac{dX_{(is)}^{(c)}}{X_{(is)}^{(c)}} \ ,$$

i.e.,

$$X_{(ic)} = \sum_{s=1}^{2} \eta_{(is)}^{(ic)} \, X_{(is)}^{(ic)} \ ,$$

where
$$\eta^{(ic)}_{(is)} = \frac{\partial CES}{\partial X^{(c)}_{(is)}} \frac{X^{(c)}_{(is)}}{X_{(ic)}} . \qquad (E4.8.15)$$

By referring to (E4.8.2), and following a route very similar to that used in the derivation of (E4.3.9) from (E4.3.3) in Exercise 4.3(g), we can rewrite (E4.8.15) more explicitly as

$$\eta^{(ic)}_{(is)} = \delta_{(is)} [D^{(c)}_i]^{-\rho^{(c)}_i} [X^{(c)}_{(is)}/X_{(ic)}]^{-\rho^{(c)}_i} \qquad \text{for } s = 1, 2. \qquad (E4.8.16)$$

To find initial values for the desired shares, $S^{(c)*}_{(11)}$ and $S^{(c)*}_{(12)}$, we first compute the initial values of the actual shares. From the input-output data, we have

$$[S^{(c)}_{(11)}]^I = 641.70/711.64 = 0.902 \quad \text{and} \quad [S^{(c)}_{(12)}]^I = 0.098. \qquad (E4.8.17)$$

By substituting from (E4.8.5) and (E4.8.17) into (E4.8.13) and (E4.8.14), we obtain

$$\left([S^{(c)*}_{(1t)}]^I, \quad t=1,2 \right) = (0.892, 0.108) .$$

Initial values for $\eta^{(1c)}_{(1s)}$, $s = 1, 2$ can be computed by substituting initial values for $X^{(c)}_{(1s)}$, $s = 1, 2$ and $X_{(1c)}$ into (E4.8.16) together with the parameter values already given in (E4.8.6), (E4.8.10) and (E4.8.11). We obtain

$$\eta^{(1c)}_{(11)} = (0.742)(1.621)^{.5} (641.70/711.64)^{.5} = 0.897$$

and
$$\eta^{(1c)}_{(12)} = 1 - \eta^{(1c)}_{(11)} = 0.103 .$$

At the end of each step of a multi-step Johansen computation, the coefficients $S^{(c)*}_{(is)}$ and $\eta^{(ic)}_{(is)}$ must be re-evaluated in preparation for the next step. For the $S^{(c)*}_{(is)}$s, re-evaluation can be based on (E4.8.13) and (E4.8.14). First we update the input-output flows to take account of the changes in prices and quantities computed in the current step. Then we use these updated flows in re-evaluating the actual shares, the $S^{(c)}_{(is)}$s. Next, we re-evaluate the Ω_i s. this could be done according to the formula

$$\Omega_i^{(new)} = \Omega_i^{(old)} \left[1 + f^{(c)}_2/100 - f^{(c)}_{(i1)}/100 \right] ,$$

where $f_2^{(c)}$ and $f_{(i1)}^{(c)}$ are the percentage changes in the current step in $F_2^{(c)}$ and $F_{(i1)}^{(c)}$. Finally, we use the updated $S_{(is)}^{(c)}$s and Ω_is in (E4.8.13) and (E4.8.14) to obtain the new values for the $S_{(is)}^{(c)*}$s.

For re-evaluating the $\eta_{(is)}^{(ic)}$s, we can follow a similar approach to that outlined in Exercise 4.4(c) for re-evaluating the $\eta_{(js)}^{(zj)}$s. From (E4.8.16) we find that a suitable rule for moving the $\eta_{(is)}^{(ic)}$s is

$$\%\Delta\, \eta_{(is)}^{(ic)} = -\, \rho_i^{(c)}\, \left[x_{(is)}^{(c)} - x_{(ic)} \right] \,. \tag{E4.8.18}$$

Exercise 4.9   The zero-pure-profits conditions in the DMR model: equations (4.3.15) – (4.3.19)

The DMR model recognizes five types of "production" activities: production of commodities by industries, the creation of composite goods, exporting, importing and the construction of units of capital. For each of these activities it is assumed that there are zero pure profits. That is, it is assumed that values of outputs are equal to the costs of inputs. Profits, if any, are interpreted as costs, e.g., profits in current production are interpreted as payments for the use of capital.

Write short notes on each of the zero-pure-profits conditions (4.3.15)(a) – (4.3.19)(a). Check your understanding of the various tax and tariff variables by computing initial values for $T_2^{(0)}$, $T_{(23)}$, $T_{(3)}$, $T_{(12)}$, $T_{(2)}$ from the input-output data in Appendix 4.1. Derive the percentage change forms (4.3.15)(b) – (4.3.19)(b) from (4.3.15)(a) – (4.3.19)(a). Use the input-output data in Appendix 4.1 in evaluating the coefficients $H_{(3c)}^{(12)}$, $H_{(n+1,1)}^{(12)}$, $S_{(51)}^{(c)}$, $T_{(23)}/(T_{(23)} + T_{(3)} - 1)$, $T_{(3)}/(T_{(23)} + T_{(3)} - 1)$, $T_{(12)}/(T_{(12)} + T_{(2)} - 1)$, $T_{(2)}/(T_{(12)} + T_{(2)} - 1)$ and $H_{(5c)}^{(21)}$.

Answer to Exercise 4.9

The first of the zero-pure-profits conditions, (4.3.15)(a), equates revenue in each industry, net of revenue taxes, to production costs. Net revenue in industry i is the sum of the values of the outputs of commodities (i1) and (i3) multiplied by one minus the rate of tax on revenue, $T_i^{(0)}$. The inclusion of the $T_i^{(0)}$s in the model is a convenient technique for allowing for sales taxes applied to domestically produced goods. It would not be adequate if the rates of sales tax were different for different categories of sales, e.g., if sales taxes were charged on sales to households but not on intermediate sales.   The base-period or initial values for the $T_i^{(0)}$s can be calculated from the input-output data in Appendix 4.1. For example, base-period revenue in industry 2 is 188.71. Revenue taxes are 26.42. Net revenue is therefore 162.29, implying an initial value for $T_2^{(0)}$ of 0.86.

Production costs for an industry are the value of its intermediate inputs of composite commodities plus the value of its primary factor inputs. Since the left hand side of (4.3.15)(a) is net of revenue taxes, these taxes are not included among the costs on the right hand side.

The percentage change form, (4.3.15)(b), can be derived from (4.3.15)(a) by applying the three rules given in Exercise 3.2. The Rs appearing on the left hand side of (4.3.15)(b) are, for industry i, the shares of its revenue accounted for by sales of commodities (i1) and (i3). These revenue shares have already been encountered in (4.3.5)(b) — see Exercise 4.4. The Hs, appearing on the right hand side of (4.3.15)(b), are cost shares. $H_{(jc)}^{(1i)}$ is the share of industry i's production costs made up of inputs of composite commodity j and $H_{(n+1,t)}^{(1i)}$ is the share accounted for by inputs of primary factor t (t = 1 for labor and 2 for capital). The base period values for these cost shares are easily calculated from the input-output data in Appendix 4.1. For example,

$$H_{(3c)}^{(12)} = 10.83/162.29 = 0.0667 \quad \text{and} \quad H_{(n+1,1)}^{(12)} = 11.77/162.29 = 0.0725.$$

The second set of zero-pure-profits conditions, (4.3.16)(a), equates the values of the supply of each composite commodity (ic) with the costs of its creation. These costs are the values of the inputs of commodities (i1) and (i2).

The derivation of the percentage change form, (4.3.16)(b) from (4.3.16)(a) involves straightforward applications of the "Sum" and "Product" rules given in Exercise 3.2. The coefficients, $S_{(it)}^{(c)}$, appearing (4.3.16)(b) are the domestic (t=1) and import (t=2) shares in the costs of creating commodity (ic). They can be evaluated from the input-output tables. For example, the base period value of $S_{(51)}^{(c)}$ is given by

$$S_{(51)}^{(c)} = (59.62 - 1.54)/\left((59.62 - 1.54) + 37.45\right) = 0.608 .$$

Equation (4.3.17)(a) imposes zero pure profits in exporting. On the left hand side is the cost of exporting a unit of good (i3). This is $P_{(i3)}$, the price which producers of (i3) receive from exporters. On the right hand side is the revenue per unit of export. This is the foreign currency price $P_{(i3)}^{(w)}$ converted to domestic currency via the exchange rate Φ and inflated by two export subsidy terms $T_{(i3)}$ and $T_{(3)}$. With a suitable choice of foreign currency units we may assume that the initial value of Φ is 1. The first of the export subsidies is specific to commodity (i3). The second applies to all exports. Simulations of the effects of uniform changes in export subsidies can be conducted by varying the value of $T_{(3)}$. Variations in the $T_{(i3)}$s can be used in simulations of the effects of changes in the subsidy rates applying to particular products. The variables $T_{(i3)}$ and $T_{(3)}$ are the "powers" of the subsidies, i.e., they are, respectively, one plus the commodity-specific subsidy rate and one plus the general subsidy rate. If the specific rate on commodity (i3) were 10 per cent and the general rate were 5 per cent, then the subsidy-inflating term, $T_{(i3)} + T_{(3)} - 1$, on the right hand side of (4.3.17)(a) would have the value 1.15, indicating a total subsidy of 15 per cent. In fact, as is revealed by inspection of matrix F in Appendix 4.1, the base-period export subsidy rates are all zero, i.e., $[T_{(i3)}]^I$ = 1 for all i and $[T_{(3)}]^I = 1$. This means that in the percentage-change form, (4.3.17)(b), all the coefficients $T_{(i3)}/(T_{(i3)} + T_{(3)} - 1)$ and $T_{(3)}/(T_{(i3)} + T_{(3)} - 1)$ have initial values of 1. The use of powers, $T_{(3)}$ and $T_{(i3)}$, rather than rates as the subsidy variables facilitates Johansen-style computations where it is awkward to handle percentage changes in variables whose initial values can be zero.

Equation (4.3.18)(a) imposes zero pure profits in importing. On the left hand side is the revenue per unit of import of commodity (i2), i.e, the domestic selling price. On the right hand side is the cost per unit of import. This is the foreign currency price converted to domestic currency and inflated by a general tariff and a commodity-specific tariff. Initial values for the powers of the tariffs ($T_{(i2)}$ and $T_{(2)}$) and for the coefficients in the percentage change equation, (4.3.18)(b), can be obtained from matrix E in the input-output data. For example,

$$[T_{(12)}]^I = 69.94/63.58 = 1.10 \qquad \text{and} \qquad [T_{(2)}]^I = 1 \ .$$

The initial values for the coefficients $T_{(12)}/(T_{(12)} + T_{(2)} - 1)$ and $T_{(2)}/(T_{(12)} + T_{(2)} - 1)$ are, respectively, 1.0 and 0.9091.

The final zero-pure-profit condition, (4.3.19)(a), equates the price of a unit of capital for industry j to the costs of its creation. The evaluation of the parameter $A_{(ic)}^{(2j)}$ (the number of units of (ic) required per unit of capital for industry j) has already been discussed in Exercise 4.1 in connection with equation (4.3.3)(a). The coefficient $H_{(ic)}^{(2j)}$ appearing in the percentage-change equation (4.3.19)(b) is the share of the costs of a unit of capital in industry j accounted for by inputs of (ic). It may be evaluated from matrix $\tilde{B}$ in the input-output data. For example $H_{(5c)}^{(21)} = 7.50/20.69 = 0.362$.

Exercise 4.10   The market-clearing equations: (4.3.20) – (4.3.25)

There are 4n commodities in the DMR model: (i1), (i2), (i3) and (ic) for i = 1, ..., n. There are m types of labor and n types of capital (one for each industry). Consequently, there are 4n + m + n market clearing conditions. They are (4.3.20)(a) – (4.3.25)(a).

Equations (4.3.20)(a) – (4.3.22)(a) have very simple forms because commodities (i1), (i2) and (i3) have only single sources of demand. All of the demand for (i1) and (i2) comes from the "industry" creating composite goods and commodity (i3) is demanded only by foreigners. For composite good (ic), the total demand given on the right hand side of (4.3.23)(a) is the sum of demands by households, the government, intermediate input users and capital creators. The total demand for labor type k given on the right hand side of (4.3.24)(a) is the sum over demands by industries. On the other hand, for capital of type j, there is only a single source of demand, namely industry j. Therefore, no summations are made in (4.3.25)(a).

(a)   Use the data in Appendix 4.1 in evaluating the coefficients $B_{(5c)}^{(3)}$, $B_{(5c)}^{(4)}$, $B_{(5c)}^{(17)}$, $B_{(5c)}^{(27)}$ and $B_{(n+1,1,3)}^{(15)}$ appearing in (4.3.23)(b) and (4.3.24)(b).

(b)   What are DMR assuming about the mobility of labor and capital?

(c)   Does (4.3.24)(a) rule out the possibility of involuntary unemployment? Does (4.3.25)(a) rule out the possibility of idle capacity?

Answer to Exercise 4.10

(a)   Total sales of commodity (5c) in the base-period are given by

Sales (5c) = 17.48 + 57.40 + 19.24 + 1.41 = 95.53   .

Sales of (5c) to households, to the government, to industry 7 as an intermediate input, and to industry 7 for capital creation were, respectively, 19.24, 1.41, 4.64 and 22.54. Thus, the initial values of the sales-share coefficients $B_{(5c)}^{(3)}$, $B_{(5c)}^{(4)}$, $B_{(5c)}^{(17)}$ and $B_{(5c)}^{(27)}$ are 0.201, 0.015, 0.049 and 0.236.

The coefficient $B_{(n+1,1,3)}^{(15)}$ is the share of the total demand for manyears of labor of occupation 3 accounted for by industry 5. (Calculations of employment in manyears have already been described in Exercise 4.6.) From the wage and labor cost data in Appendix 4.1, we calculate that base-period employment in occupation 3 was 0.4636 million manyears. Of this, the share accounted for by industry 5 is given by

$$B_{(n+1,1,3)}^{(15)} = \frac{10.92/199.8}{0.4636} = 0.1179 \ .$$

(b)   One possibility in the DMR model is to assume that there are fixed numbers of manyears available to the economy in each occupation. Under the assumption that each occupation is fully employed, the L_ks would be set exogenously at these availability levels. Then equation (4.3.24)(a) would restrict the total employment of labor of occupation k to the available supply. There are, however, no supply restrictions in the model on the allocation of employment in occupation k across industries. Thus it would be assumed that the economy behaves as if workers of occupation k are completely mobile between industries but cannot move to other occupations.

Another possibility is to allow the L_ks to be determined endogenously without reference to occupational full employment levels. Then it may not be necessary to assume that changes in the industrial composition of the employment of occupation k are accommodated by transfers of workers between industries — these changes could also be accommodated by movements of workers into and out of unemployment. Nor is it necessary to assume that there is no inter-occupational mobility.

The availability to industry j of capital is normally treated in the DMR model as an exogenous or predetermined variable. It is then assumed via (4.3.25)(a) that industry j's demand for capital adjusts (through variations in the rental rate, $P_{(n+1,2)}^{(1j)}$) to equal the given supply. Capital is, therefore, regarded as immobile between industries.

(c) L_k on the left hand side of (4.3.24)(a) should be interpreted as the employment of labor of type k. This may be set exogenously at the full employment level. Alternatively, it may be determined endogenously or set exogenously at less than the full employment level. Consequently, (4.3.24)(a) does not, by itself, rule out the possibility of involuntary unemployment.

Similarly, (4.3.25)(a) does not necessarily rule out idle capacity. Normally, however, K_j is interpreted as the available supply of capital for industry j. Equation (4.3.25)(a) then imposes full employment of capital in each industry. Nevertheless, the model can still be interpreted as being compatible with the existence of idle capacity. We can think of a situation of idle capacity as being one in which the labor/capital ratio is abnormally low. That is, idle capacity occurs when the capital stock, although fully used, is used only lightly.

Exercise 4.11   The allocation of the investment budget across industries: equations (4.3.26) - (4.3.27)

Equation (4.3.26)(a) allocates total investment expenditure across industries. Normally, the $F^{(2j)}$s are set exogenously at 1 and the $\alpha^{(2j)}$s are non-negative parameters summing to 1 showing the shares of each industry in the economy's total investment budget, $C^{(2)}$. The effects of changes in industry shares in total investment can be simulated via exogenous shifts in the $F^{(2j)}$s.

(a)   Assume that the $F^{(2j)}$s are fixed at 1. Use the data in Appendix 4.1 to evaluate $\alpha^{(27)}$.

(b)   Suggest a constrained optimization problem which would yield (4.3.26)(a). Does your constrained optimization problem seem a plausible description of investor behavior? If not, what key variable is missing?

Answer to Exercise 4.11

(a)   Total base-period investment is 159.14. Industry 7's share is given by

$$\alpha^{(27)} = 41.38/159.14 = 0.26 \quad .$$

(b)   Equation (4.3.26)(a) is consistent with Cobb-Douglas or log-linear constrained utility maximizing behavior by the agent (the government?) responsible for allocating investment. Assuming that $\sum_j F^{(2j)}\alpha^{(2j)}$ equals 1, equation (4.3.26)(a) can be derived from, for example, the problem of choosing I_j, $j = 1,..., n$, to maximize

$$\sum_{j=1}^{n} F^{(2j)}\, \alpha^{(2j)}\, ln(I_j) \qquad \text{(E4.11.1)}$$

subject to

$$\sum_{j=1}^{n} P_K^{(j)}(I_j) = C^{(2)} \quad . \qquad \text{(E4.11.2)}$$

We do not find (E4.11.1) – (E4.11.2) a convincing description of investment behavior: it gives no role to rates of return, which are usually considered key variables in determining the allocation of investment across industries.

Equation (4.3.27)(a) defines rates of returns. According to (4.3.27)(a), if units of capital in industry j earn rent or gross profit at the rate of $10 per annum (i.e., $P^{(1j)}_{(n+1,2)} = 10$), depreciate at the rate of 5 per cent per annum (i.e., $D_j = 0.05$) and cost $50 to construct (i.e., $P^{(j)}_k = 50$), then the current rate of return on capital of type j is 0.15 or 15 per cent. Rates of return in our version of the DMR model do not appear in any other equation. They have no influence on the share of total investment undertaken for each industry. In some models, including the *ORANI* model (Dixon *et al.*, 1982, pp.118-122) and other versions of the DMR model (e.g., DMR, 1982, pp. 175-178), these shares are assumed to be sensitive to variations in rates of return: industries with relatively increased rates of return are assumed to gain share at the expense of other industries.

Exercise 4.12   *The remaining miscellaneous equations: (4.3.28) – (4.3.43)*

Write short notes describing the interpreting each of the remaining equations, (4.3.28) – (4.3.43), in Table 4.3.1. Most of these are straightforward definitions of aggregate variables. However, be sure to consider the following questions:

(a)   In (4.3.31)(b) we use the change in the balance of trade (ΔB) rather than the percentage change. Why?

(b)   In equation (4.3.32)(a), how would you set the parameter h_1 and the variables $F_{(n+1,1,k)}$ and $F_{(n+1,1)}$ if you wanted to use the DMR model in simulating the effects of a policy change under the assumption of fixed real wages? How would you change these settings if you wished to assume 70 per cent wage indexation throughout the labor market rather than fixed real wages? How would you set h_1 and the Fs in simulating the effects of a 10 per cent increase in all real wages? What would the settings be if you were concerned with the effects of a 10 per cent increase in real wages paid only to people in occupation q?

(c)   If h_2 in (4.3.33)(a) were set at 1, how would you interpret the variable $F^{(1j)}_{(n+1,2)}$?

(d)   Why do the tariff rate on imported good i and the subsidy rate on exported good i appear in equation (4.3.37)(a) as the rather clumsy expressions $(T_{(i2)} + T_{(2)} - 2)$ and $(T_{(i3)} + T_{(3)} - 2)$? Can you derive (4.3.37)(b)?

Answer to Exercise 4.12

Equation (4.3.28)(a) defines four commodity price indices, of which the last three are of most interest. Different weighting schemes are used. Composite commodities are weighted by their shares in investment expenditure, household expenditure and government expenditure. The weights can be calculated from the base-period data in Appendix 4.1. For example,

$$w_5^{(2)} = 57.40/159.14 = 0.361.$$

Equations (4.3.29)(a) and (4.3.30)(a) sum across commodities to give foreign currency values of total imports and exports. The coefficients, $M_{(i2)}$ and $E_{(i3)}$, appearing in the percentage change equations are shares in these total foreign currency values of commodities (i2) and (i3). From the data in Appendix 4.1, we find, for example, that

$$M_{(5,2)} = 31.21/164.83 = 0.189 \quad \text{and} \quad E_{(5,2)} = 1.54/66.89 = 0.023 \quad.$$

Equation (4.3.31)(a) defines the balance of trade. This is a variable which can pass through zero. Therefore, its percentage changes may not always be defined. This difficulty is avoided in our differential version of the DMR model where we use the *change* in the balance of trade, not the percentage change. In the change equation, (4.3.31)(b), the coefficients E and M are the aggregate values of exports and imports. Initial values for these coefficients can be read from Appendix 4.1 as E=66.89 and M=164.83.

In equation (4.3.32)(a) we assume that the variables $F_{(n+1,1,k)}$ and $F_{(n+1,1)}$ have initial values of one. In Exercise 4.1(c) we defined a unit of composite commodity (ic) as the quantity which had a value of \$1 million in the base period. Our monetary unit is also \$1 million. Consequently, the initial prices of all composite goods are unity. Thus we can be sure from (4.3.28)(a) that the consumer price index, $\Xi^{(3)}$, also has an initial value of one. The parameters, $\tilde{F}^{(ij)}_{(n+1,1,k)}$, must, therefore, be set at the initial occupation/industry wage rates. Base-period occupation/industry wage rates for our application of the DMR model are given in Table A4.1.10 of Appendix 4.1.

Equation (4.3.32)(a) allows for various treatments of wage behavior. For example, if we want to use the DMR model in simulating the effects of a policy change under the assumption of fixed real wage rates, we can fix the variables $F_{(n+1,1)}$ and $F_{(n+1,1,k)}$ at their initial values and set the parameter h_1 at unity. Equation (4.3.32)(a) then implies that there are no changes in the ratios of wage rates to the consumer price index; i.e., there are no changes in real wage rates.

If we were to continue setting the variables $F_{(n+1,1)}$ and $F_{(n+1,1,k)}$ at their initial values, but set h_1 at 0.7 rather than unity, then wage rates would be 70 per cent indexed. That is, they would increase by 0.7 per cent in response to a one per cent increase in the consumer price index.

In simulations of a ten per cent increase in all real wage rates, we would compute the effects of an increase in $F_{(n+1,1)}$ from its initial value of 1 to a final value of 1.1. The parameter h_1 and the variables $F_{(n+1,1,k)}$, $k = 1,...,$ m, would be set at unity. If we were interested in the effects of a 10 per cent increase in the real wage rates of people in occupation q alone, then we would move $F_{(n+1,1,q)}$ from 1 to 1.1. The variables $F_{(n+1,1)}$, and $F_{(n+1,1,k)}$ for all $k \neq q$, would be held constant at 1. The parameter h_1 would continue to be set at unity.

Equation (4.3.33)(a) introduces the variable $F_{(n+1,2)}^{(1j)}$. With h_2 set at unity, (4.3.33)(a) implies that

$$F_{(n+1,2)}^{(1j)} = P_{(n+1,2)}^{(1j)}/\Xi^{(3)} \ .$$

$F_{(n+1,2)}^{(1j)}$ can then be interpreted as the real rental on units of capital for industry j. The inclusion of equation (4.3.33)(a) in our model is useful if we want to report results for real rental rates or if we want to exogenize these rates. Setting rental rates exogenously can be used to simulate a fixed mark-up pricing rule — see Dixon, Powell and Parmenter (1979, pp. 36-40.)

Equation (4.3.34)(a) gives a measure of the economy's capital stock. In this measure, units of capital in each industry are valued at their base-period prices, $\bar{P}_K^{(j)}$. As noted in Exercises 4.1(c) and 4.6(c), our choice of quantity units implies that each of these base-period prices has the value 1.

The coefficients B_j^K in (4.3.34)(b) are the shares of industry capital stocks in the total capital stock. Since the $\bar{P}_K^{(j)}$s all have the value 1,

$$B_j^K = K_j/ \sum_{j=1}^{n} K_j \quad \text{for all j .} \tag{E4.12.1}$$

In Exercise 4.6(c) we used data from Appendix 4.1 in calculating the initial value of the capital stock in industry 1 as

$$\left(X^{(11)}_{(n+1,2)}\right)^I = (K_1)^I = rental/(gross\ rate\ of\ return)$$

$$= 266.46/0.4052 = 657.60 \ .$$

Similar calculations can be performed to evaluate $(K_j)^I$, $j = 2,..., 8$. Equation (E4.12.1) can then be used in computing initial values for the B_j^K s. We find for example that

$$(B_1^K)^I = 657.60/2544.96 = 0.2584 \ .$$

Equation (4.3.35)(a) defines total employment in manyears as the sum of employment across occupations. The coefficients, B_v^L, in (4.3.35)(b) are occupational shares in aggregate employment. Evaluation of those shares from Appendix 4.1 involves the labor cost matrix and the wage rate matrix. We find, for example, that L_1 is 2.5159 million manyears (i.e., 185.35/73.67). Employment levels in millions of manyears in occupations 2, 3 and 4 are 1.1023, 0.4636 and 0.9481. Thus total employment is 5.0299 million manyears and the initial of values B_v^L for $v = 1,..., 4$ are 0.500, 0.219, 0.092 and 0.188.

Equation (4.3.36)(a) defines gross (i.e., before tax) household income as the sum of wage and capital income. In our version of the DMR model, there is only one household. Thus the problem of allocating income to different types of households does not arise. DMR (1982, Chapter 12) contains a discussion of issues in distribution-oriented multi-household modeling. For the pioneering example of such a model, see Adelman and Robinson (1978).

The coefficient $G^{(1j)3}_{(n+1,t)}$ in equation (4.3.36)(b) is the share in household income of primary factor t employed in industry j. Our database in Appendix 4.1 implies, for example, that

$$G^{(12)3}_{(n+1,1)} = 11.77/(548.76 + 521.76) = 0.011 \ .$$

Equation (4.3.37)(a) defines government tax revenue less subsidies. The first term on the RHS is the collection of taxes on industry sales. In interpreting this term, it should be recalled that $T_i^{(0)}$ is one minus the rate of the tax so that $(1 - T_i^{(0)})$ is the rate itself.

The second term is the collection of tariff revenue. Recall from Exercise 4.9 that our version of the DMR model distinguishes two types of tariffs: general and commodity-specific. $T_{(i2)}$ is one plus the commodity-specific rate applicable to imports of commodity i, while $T_{(2)}$ is one plus the general rate. The total tariff rate applicable to commodity (i2) is $(T_{(i2)} - 1)$

plus $(T_{(2)} - 1)$; i.e., $(T_{(i2)} + T_{(2)} - 2)$. Similarly, in the third term on the RHS of (4.3.37)(a), $(T_{(i3)} + T_{(3)} - 2)$, is the total rate of export subsidy applicable to commodity (i3).

In the final term on the RHS of (4.3.37)(a), T^H is the rate of tax on household income. We assume that T^H will always be greater than zero. Consequently, there is no difficulty in using the percentage change in T^H as a variable in our differential version of the DMR model. On the other hand, tariff and subsidy rates can be zero. We have, therefore, used powers (one plus rates) rather than the raw rates as our tariff and subsidy variables. This leads to the appearance of the rather clumsy expressions $(T_{(i2)} + T_{(2)} - 2)$ and $(T_{(i3)} + T_{(3)} - 2)$ in (4.3.37)(a).

To derive the percentage change form, (4.3.37)(b), we first rewrite (4.3.37)(a) as

$$
Y^{(4)} = - \sum_{t=1}^{n} T_i^{(0)} \left[\sum_{s=1\&3} P_{(is)} X_{(is)} \right] + \sum_{i=1}^{n} \sum_{s=1\&3} P_{(is)} X_{(is)}
$$

$$
+ \sum_{i=1}^{n} T_{(i2)} P_{(i2)}^{(w)} \Phi X_{(i2)} + T_{(2)} \sum_{i=1}^{n} P_{(i2)}^{(w)} \Phi X_{(i2)}
$$

$$
- 2 \sum_{i=1}^{n} P_{(i2)}^{(w)} \Phi X_{(i2)} - \sum_{i=1}^{n} T_{(i3)} P_{(i3)}^{(w)} \Phi X_{(i3)}
$$

$$
- T_{(3)} \sum_{i=1}^{n} P_{(i3)}^{(w)} \Phi X_{(i3)} + 2 \sum_{i=1}^{n} P_{(i3)}^{(w)} \Phi X_{(i3)} + T^H Y^{(3)} \ .
$$

Then

$$
y^{(4)} = - \sum_{i=1}^{n} t_i^{(0)} \left[T_i^{(0)} \sum_{s=1\&3} P_{(is)} X_{(is)} / Y^{(4)} \right]
$$

$$
+ \sum_{i=1}^{n} \left[\sum_{s=1\&3} (P_{(is)} + x_{(is)}) R_{(is)} \right] \left[(-T_i^{(0)} + 1) \sum_{s=1\&3} P_{(is)} X_{(is)} / Y^{(4)} \right]
$$

equation continues next page

$$+ \sum_{i=1}^{n} t_{(i2)} \left[T_{(i2)} \, P_{(i2)}^{(w)} \, \Phi \, X_{(i2)}/Y^{(4)} \right] + t_{(2)} \sum_{i=1}^{n} \left[T_{(2)} \, P_{(i2)}^{(w)} \, \Phi \, X_{(i2)}/Y^{(4)} \right]$$

$$+ \sum_{i=1}^{n} \left[P_{(i2)}^{(w)} + \phi + x_{(i2)} \right] \left[(T_{(i2)} + T_{(2)} - 2) \, P_{(i2)}^{(w)} \, \Phi \, X_{(i2)}/Y^{(4)} \right]$$

$$- \sum_{i=1}^{n} t_{(i3)} \left[T_{(i3)} \, P_{(i3)}^{(w)} \, \Phi \, X_{(i3)}/Y^{(4)} \right] - t_{(3)} \sum_{i=1}^{n} \left[T_{(3)} \, P_{(i3)}^{(w)} \, \Phi \, X_{(i3)}/Y^{(4)} \right]$$

$$- \sum_{i=1}^{n} \left[P_{(i3)}^{(w)} + \phi + x_{(i3)} \right] \left[(T_{(i3)} + T_{(3)} - 2) \, P_{(i3)}^{(w)} \, \Phi \, X_{(i3)}/Y^{(4)} \right]$$

$$+ (t^{H} + y^{(3)}) \, (T^{H} \, Y^{(3)}/Y^{(4)}) \,, \tag{E4.12.2}$$

where $R_{(is)}$ is as defined in Exercise 4.3; namely, the share of the sales revenue in industry i accounted for by product (is). We can reduce (E4.12.2) to (4.3.37)(b) when we recognize that the definitions (given in Table 4.3.4) of the coefficients in the latter equation imply that

$$G_{i}^{(0)4} = \left[T_{i}^{(0)} \sum_{s=1\&3} P_{(is)} \, X_{(is)} \right] / Y^{(4)} \,,$$

$$J_{i}^{(0)4} = \left[-T_{i}^{(0)} + 1 \right] \sum_{s=1\&3} P_{(is)} \, X_{(is)}/Y^{(4)} \,,$$

$$G_{(i2)}^{4} = T_{(i2)} \, P_{(i2)}^{(w)} \, \Phi \, X_{(i2)} \, /Y^{(4)} \,, \quad \text{etc.}$$

Evaluation of the coefficients in (4.3.37)(b) can be made from input-output data. For example, using the data in Appendix 4.1, we obtain

$$G_{2}^{(0)4} = (188.70 - 26.42)/194.03, \qquad\qquad J_{2}^{(0)4} = 26.42/194.03,$$

$$G_{(22)}^{4} = 11.63/194.03, \qquad G_{2}^{4} = 164.83/194.03, \qquad J_{(22)}^{4} = 1.51/194.03,$$

$$G_{(23)}^4 = 6.94/194.03, \qquad G_3^4 = 66.89/194.03, \qquad J_{(23)}^4 = 0/194.03.$$

and
$$J_H^4 = 100.11/194.03 \quad .$$

Equation (4.3.38)(a) is a consumption function. If the variable $Q^{(3)}$ is held constant, then household expenditure will change by the same percentage as household disposable income. Other assumptions could be imposed by shifting $Q^{(3)}$ exogenously or by treating it as an endogenous variable. In the percentage-change form (4.3.38)(b), the coefficient, $T^H/(1-T^H)$, can be evaluated from input-output data. In Appendix 4.1, we have $T^H/(1-T^H) = 100.11/(1070.52 - 100.11) = 0.103$.

Equation (4.3.39)(a) is an expenditure function for the government. $Q^{(4)}$ can be held constant so that government expenditure moves in proportion to government income. Alternatively, $Q^{(4)}$ can be treated as an endogenous variable. This allows different specifications of government expenditure with movements in $Q^{(4)}$ indicating the implications for the governments' average propensity to spend.

Equations (4.3.40)(a) – (4.3.42)(a) define three new variables, V_{43}, V_{42} and V_{23}. These are ratios of aggregate expenditure levels: government to household, government to investment, and investment to household. Equation (4.3.43)(a) defines three further variables $C_R^{(v)}$, $v = 2$, 3, 4. These are aggregate expenditure levels in real terms.

Exercise 4.13   *Five test simulations for the DMR model under the standard ORANI closure*

One way to check for computational errors is to run simulations for which the correct results are either known *a priori* from the theoretical structure of the model or can be obtained very easily using a pocket calculator. In this exercise we ask you to describe the expected results for some test simulations which we have used in checking our computing in the DMR model. You should assume that the model is being run with the database in Appendix 4.1 and that h_1 and h_2 in equations (4.3.32) and (4.3.33) are both set at 1. Assume that the exogenous variables are those listed under selection 1 in Table 4.3.5. After you have worked out the expected results for each of the test simulations below, you may like to verify that your answers agree with those obtained using the software and data on the companion diskettes described in Chapter 1.

(a)   What results should be obtained if we increase the exchange rate by 10 per cent holding all other exogenous variables constant?

That is, what should happen to the endogenous variables under the shock $\phi = 10$?

(b) What should happen to the endogenous variables if we increase the availability of each industrial capital stock by 10 per cent and also make 10 per cent increases in each component of real aggregate demand while holding constant all other exogenous variables? That is, what are the expected results when

$$X^{(1j)}_{(n+1,2)} = 10 \qquad \text{for } j = 1,...,\, n \qquad \text{(E4.13.1)}$$

and

$$c^{(v)}_R = 10 \qquad \text{for } v = 2,\, 3,\, 4. \qquad \text{(E4.13.2)}$$

Does the answer depend on the fact that the γ_i in (4.3.4) are set at zero? Why?

(c) Describe the expected results when we increase all foreign currency import prices by 10 per cent and simultaneously make 10 per cent vertical upward shifts in all export demand curves; i.e., we shock the model with

$$p^{(w)}_{(i2)} = 10 \qquad \text{for } i = 1,...,\, n \qquad \text{(E4.13.3)}$$

and

$$f^{(w)}_{(i3)} = 10 \qquad \text{for } i = 1,...,\, n \;\; . \qquad \text{(E4.13.4)}$$

(d) What should be the effects of a 10 per cent increase in the household average propensity to spend? That is, what should happen under the shock $q^{(3)} = 10$?

(e) What should be the effects of a 10 per cent primary-factor-augmenting technical change in each industry combined with 10 per cent increases in all real wages rates and 10 per cent reductions in the availabilities of capital in all industries? That is, describe the expected results when the exogenous shocks are as follows:

$$a^{(1j)}_{n+1} = -10 \;, \qquad j = 1,...,\, n \qquad \text{(E4.13.5)}$$

$$x^{(1j)}_{(n+1,2)} = -10 \;, \qquad j = 1,...,\, n \qquad \text{(E4.13.6)}$$

and

$$f_{(n+1,1)} = 10 \;. \qquad \text{(E4.13.7)}$$

Answer to Exercise 4.13

(a) Under the standard *ORANI* closure (see Table 4.3.5) with h_1 and h_2 set at 1, a 10 per cent increase in the exchange rate should increase all domestic dollar variables (of which all, except the exchange rate, are endogenous) by 10 per cent. It should have no effect on any other variable.

To demonstrate this, we can work through the system (4.3.1)(b) – (4.3.43)(b), showing that LHSs equal RHSs when the percentage changes in the exchange rate and all the endogenous domestic-dollar variables (listed in the panel below) are set at 10, while the percentage changes in all

> *Domestic-dollar variables:*
> all p s (except $p^{(w)}_{(i2)}$ and $p^{(w)}_{(i3)}$), $c^{(2)}$, $c^{(3)}$, $c^{(4)}$,
> $y^{(3)}$, $y^{(4)}$; ϕ; $\xi^{(v)}$ for $v = 1, 2, 3, 4$.

other variables are set at zero. We give a few examples:

$$\text{LHS (4.3.1)(b)} \;=\; x^{(3)}_{(ic)} \;=\; 0 \;,$$

and

$$\text{RHS (4.3.1)(b)} \;=\; c^{(3)} - p_{(ic)} = 10 - 10 \;=\; 0 \;.$$

$$\text{LHS (4.3.11)(b)} \;=\; x^{(c)*}_{(is)} \;=\; 0$$

and

$$\text{RHS (4.3.11)(b)} \;=\; x_{(ic)} - \sigma^{(c)}_i \left(p_{(is)} - \sum_{t=1}^{2} s^{(c)*}_{(it)} \, p_{(it)} \right) \;,$$

$$=\; 0 - \sigma^{(c)}_i \left(10 - 10 \sum_{t=1}^{2} s^{(c)*}_{(it)} \right) \;=\; 0 \;.$$

(The sum over t of the desired shares is 1.)

$$\text{LHS (4.3.15)(b)} \;=\; \sum_{s=1\&3} R_{(is)} (10 + 0) + 0 \;=\; 10,$$

and

$$\text{RHS (4.3.15)(b)} \;=\; \sum_{j=1}^{n} H^{(1i)}_{(jc)} (10 + 0) \;+\; \sum_{t=1}^{2} H^{(1i)}_{(n+1,t)} (10 + 0) = 10.$$

(The sum over all subscripts of the $H^{(1i)}$s, that is, the sum of the cost shares for industry i over all inputs is 1.)

(b)   In our version of the DMR model there are no scale effects. (This was also a property of the stylized Johansen model — see Exercise 3.6(d).) There are constant returns to scale in the production of commodities and capital goods; and there are unitary expenditure elasticities in household and government consumption. Moreover, foreign currency prices of both exports and imports are determined independently of changes in the scale of activity in the local economy : $p_{(i2)}^{(w)}$ is exogenous for all i and with $\gamma_i = 0$ for all i, movements in $p_{(i3)}^{(w)}$ are determined entirely by movements in the exogenous variable $F_{(i3)}^{(w)}$, see (4.3.4) .

Under these conditions, a 10 per cent increase in the three components of aggregate absorption combined with a 10 per cent expansion in all capital stocks produces a uniform 10 per cent increase in the size of the economy with no changes in prices. That is, with the shocks (E4.13.1) – (E4.13.2), the solution should exhibit the common value 10 for the percentage increases in all the endogenous quantity and value variables ($C^{(v)}$, E, Ij, K, K_j, L, L_k, M, B and the Xs, Ys and Zs), and zero changes in all the endogenous ratio and price variables ($F_{(i2)}^{(c)}$, $F_{(n+1,2)}^{(1j)}$, $Q^{(4)}$, R_j, T^H and the Vs, Ps and Ξs).

The balanced expansion of the economy implied by the set of shocks under discussion can be demonstrated by substitutions into the left and right hand sides of the system (4.3.1)(b) – (4.3.43)(b). For example, under the hypothesized solution we have

$$\text{LHS (4.3.4)(b)} \quad = \quad p_{(i3)}^{(w)} \quad = \quad 0$$

and

$$\text{RHS (4.3.4)(b)} \quad = \quad -\gamma_i \, x_{(i3)}^{(w)} + f_{(i3)}^{(w)} \quad = \quad 0 \times 10 + 0 = 0 \; .$$

$$\text{LHS (4.3.23)(b)} \quad = \quad x_{(ic)} \quad = \quad 10$$

and

$$\text{RHS (4.3.23)(b)} \quad = \quad \left(B_{(ic)}^{(3)} + B_{(ic)}^{(4)} + \sum_{j=1}^{n} \sum_{g=1}^{2} B_{(ic)}^{(gj)} \right) 10 = 10 \; .$$

$$\text{LHS (4.3.31)(b)} \quad = \quad 100\Delta B \quad = \quad -979.4$$

and

$$\text{RHS (4.3.31)(b)} = (E - M) \times 10 = (-97.94) \times 10 = -979.4 \; .$$

(In the database, the balance of trade is -$97.94m. Since we expect B to expand by 10 per cent, the expected value of ΔB is -9.794.)

(c)   Under the shock (E4.13.3) – (E4.13.4), all the endogenous domestic-dollar variables (listed in part (a) above) and the foreign-currency export prices $p_{(i3)}^{(w)}$ increase by 10 per cent. There should also be a 10 per cent expansion in the foreign currency values of imports, exports and the balance of trade. ΔB therefore should be –9.794.   All the remaining variables should be unaffected.

Again, we can establish the validity of our hypothesized solution by evaluating the left and right hand sides of the system (4.3.1)(b) – (4.3.43)(b). We have, for example,

$$\text{LHS (4.3.17)(b)} \;=\; p_{(i3)} \;=\; 10$$

and

$$\text{RHS (4.3.17)(b)} = p_{(i3)}^{(w)} + \phi + \left(T_{(i3)}/(T_{(i3)} + T_{(3)} - 1)\right)t_{(i3)} +$$

$$\left(T_{(3)}/(T_{(i3)} + T_{(3)} - 1)\right)t_3 = 10 + 0 + 0 + 0 = 10 \;.$$

$$\text{LHS (4.3.29)(b)} \;=\; m \;=\; 10$$

and

$$\text{RHS (4.3.29)(b)} = \sum_{i=1}^{m} M_{(i2)} \,(0 + 10) = 10 \;.$$

(d)   Since real household consumption is exogenous, it should not be affected by variations in the household average propensity to spend. Under the shock $q^{(3)} = 10$, the model should produce a compensating variation in the rate of income tax (T^H).   Similarly, real government consumption should be unaffected. Although there should be an increase in government income $(Y^{(4)})$, there should be a compensating reduction in the government's average propensity to consume $(Q^{(4)})$. Apart from the movements in T^H, $Y^{(4)}$ and $Q^{(4)}$, the increase in $Q^{(3)}$ should have no impact.

To deduce the numerical results for T^H, $Y^{(4)}$ and $Q^{(4)}$, we refer to the input-output data in Appendix 4.1. We see that the initial values for $C^{(3)}$ and $Y^{(3)}$ are given by

$$(C^{(3)})^I \;=\; \underline{1}' \, \tilde{C} \;=\; 962.08$$

and

$$(Y^{(3)})^I \;=\; \underline{1}' \; \tilde{S} + \tilde{X} \;=\; 548.76 + 521.76 \;=\; 1070.52 \;.$$

The initial income tax collection is 100.11 implying an initial tax rate of

$$(T^H)^I = 100.11/1070.52 = 0.0935$$

With $Q^{(3)}$ increasing by 10 per cent and with $Y^{(3)}$ and $C^{(3)}$ unchanged, it follows from (4.3.38)(a) that $(1-T^H)$ must be reduced by a factor of 1.1 from its initial value of 0.9065 to 0.8241. Hence, T^H must increase from 0.0935 to 0.1759, i.e., T^H should increase by 88.13 per cent. This should increase the government's revenue by 88.23 $(=100.11 \times 0.8813)$. Since

$$(Y^{(4)})^I = \tilde{V} = 194.03,$$

the percentage increase in government revenue should be given by:

$$y^{(4)} = (88.23/194.03) \times 100 = 45.5 \ .$$

The compensating reduction the government's average propensity to spend should also be 45.5 per cent. If the effects of a 10 per cent increase in $Q^{(3)}$ are computed by a one-step Johansen solution of the system (4.3.1)(b) – (4.3.43)(b), there is a small linearization error. The results are $t^H = 96.95$, $y^{(4)} = 50.02$ and $q^{(4)} = -50.02$.

(e) Under the shocks (E4.13.5) – (E4.13.7), the use of primary factors in each industry should fall. There are, however, compensating primary-factor-augmenting technical changes, so that there should be no effect on industry outputs or intermediate input levels. Factor incomes should also be unaffected because there should be compensating increases in primary factor prices.

More specifically, by making substitutions into the left and right hand sides of the system (4.3.1)(b) – (4.3.43)(b), it can be shown that all endogenous primary factor quantity variables $\{K, K_{(j)}, L, L_{(k)}, X_{(n+1,1)}^{(1j)}, X_{(n+1,1,k)}^{(1j)}\}$ should fall by 10 per cent and all primary-factor usage prices $\{P_{(n+1,s)}^{(1j)}, P_{(n+1,1,k)}^{(1j)}\}$ should increase by 10 per cent. The only other endogenous variables which should exhibit non-zero changes are the rates of return (R_j) and the shift variables $(F_{(n+1,2)}^{(1j)})$ appearing in (4.3.33). Since the cost of creating capital $(P_K^{(j)})$ should be unchanged and the costs of using capital $(P_{(n+1,2)}^{(1j)})$ should be increased by 10 per cent, equation (4.3.27)(b) implies that in a one-step Johansen computation, the percentage increase in R_j should be ten times the value of the coefficient Q_j. With h_2 set at 1, the increase in $F_{(n+1,2)}^{(1j)}$ should be 10 per cent.

Exercise 4.14   *Finishing the specification: adding GDP, real GDP and the GDP deflator*

The version of the DMR model set out Tables 4.3.1 and 4.3.2 contains $26n + 2mn + 2n^2 + m + 19$ equations connecting $37n + 2mn + 2n^2 + 2m + 28$ variables.

(a)   Do you consider the specification of the model finished?   Should we add some more equations or variables?

(b)   Add equations defining, for this model, GDP, real GDP and the GDP deflator from the expenditure-side of the national accounts. Now define GDP from the income-side of the national accounts. Show that the model implies that GDP calculated from the expenditure side of the accounts equals GDP calculated from the income side.

(c)   An additional concept that is often useful in discussing simulation results is aggregate absorption. Absorption is the part of GDP that ends up with domestic agents: consumption, investment and government spending.   Add equations to the model defining absorption, real absorption and the price deflator for absorption.

Answer to Exercise 4.14

(a)   There is no simple answer to the question of whether or not the specification is complete. In a trivial sense it never is.   We can always think of another variable which could be defined by an additional equation. For example, in part (b) you are asked to add equations defining GDP, real GDP and the GDP deflator.   Including these variables, and possibly others, will facilitate the interpretation of results from the model. Our experience has been that users of a model will add equations defining variables of interest in their particular applications. As a model matures, it is likely to grow gradually in size.

In a more fundamental sense, we can judge the completeness of a model by looking at typical selections of exogenous variables. We will feel that the model is incompletely specified for assessing the effects of a change in variable X, say a tariff, if the exogenous list includes variables which we think would be affected by variations in X.

In our version of the DMR model, $11n + m + 9$ variables must be treated exogenously.   In Table 4.3.5 we show two possible selections. Under either selection, the technological change variables are set exogenously. Because there are no equations explaining technological change, exogenous treatment will be required in almost all applications of the model. This would be a problem if we were using the model to assess the long-run implications of reductions in protection: we might expect such reductions to induce technological improvement. On the other hand, exogenous treatment of technological change might be satisfactory in a short-run assessment of the effects of tariff reductions.

(b)   We define GDP from the expenditure side of the national accounts as follows:

$$
\text{GDPE} = \sum_i P_{(ic)} \left(\sum_{k=3,4} X_{(ic)}^{(k)} + \sum_j X_{(ic)}^{(2j)} \right)
$$

$$
+ \sum_i \Phi P_{(i3)}^{(w)} X_{(i3)} - \sum_i \Phi P_{(i2)}^{(w)} X_{(i2)} , \qquad (E4.14.1)
$$

that is, GDPE equals consumption plus government expenditure plus investment plus exports minus imports. In percentage change form (E4.14.1) can be written as

$$
\text{gdpe} = \sum_i P_{(ic)} N_{(ic)} + \sum_i \left(\phi + p_{(i3)}^{(w)} \right) N_{(i3)} - \sum_i \left(\phi + p_{(i2)}^{(w)} \right) N_{(i2)}
$$

$$
+ \sum_i x_{(ic)}^F N_{(ic)} + \sum_i x_{(i3)} N_{(i3)} - \sum_i x_{(i2)} N_{(i2)} , \quad (E4.14.2)
$$

where $N_{(ic)}$, $N_{(i3)}$ and $N_{(i2)}$ are the shares in GDPE of final demands for commodity (ic), of exports of (i3) and imports of (i2), and $x_{(ic)}^F$ is the percentage change in final demand for commodity (ic):

$$
x_{(ic)}^F = \left(\sum_{k=3,4} B_{(ic)}^{(k)} x_{(ic)}^{(k)} + \sum_j B_{(ic)}^{(2j)} x_{(ic)}^{(2j)} \right) \Bigg/ \left(\sum_{k=3,4} B_{(ic)}^{(k)} + \sum_j B_{(ic)}^{(2j)} \right), \quad (E4.14.3)
$$

where the Bs are sales shares as defined in Table 4.3.4 for equation (4.3.23)(b).

We define the first three terms on the RHS of (E4.14.2) as the percentage change in the GDP deflator calculated from the expenditure side of the national accounts:

$$
\text{pgdpe} = \sum_i P_{(ic)} N_{(ic)} + \sum_i \left(\phi + p_{(i3)}^{(w)} \right) N_{(i3)} - \sum_i \left(\phi + p_{(i2)}^{(w)} \right) N_{(i2)} .
$$

$$
(E4.14.4)
$$

The final three terms are the percentage change in real GDP:

$$\text{gdpre} = \sum_i x_{(ic)}^F \, N_{(ic)} + \sum_i x_{(i3)} \, N_{(i3)} - \sum_i x_{(i2)} \, N_{(i2)} \quad . \qquad \text{(E4.14.5)}$$

Notice that with these definitions,

$$\text{gdpe} = \text{gdpre} + \text{pgdpe} \quad . \qquad \text{(E4.14.6)}$$

From the income side of the national accounts, we can define another measure of GDP, GDPY:

$$\text{GDPY} = \sum_i \sum_{t=1}^{2} P_{(n+1,t)}^{(1i)} \, X_{(n+1,t)}^{(1i)} + \sum_i \left(\sum_{s=1\&3} P_{(is)} \, X_{(is)} \right) \left(1 - T_i^{(0)} \right)$$

$$+ \sum_i \Phi \, P_{(i2)}^{(w)} \left(T_{(i2)} + T_{(2)} - 2 \right) X_{(i2)} - \sum_i \Phi \, P_{(i3)}^{(w)} \left(T_{(i3)} + T_{(3)} - 2 \right) X_{(i3)} \;\;,$$

$$\text{(E4.14.7)}$$

that is, gross domestic product from the income side of the accounts is labor and capital income plus production taxes plus tariffs minus subsidies on exports.

In our model GDPY, as defined in (E4.14.7), is the same as GDPE as defined in (E4.14.1). This can be demonstrated as follows. By adding over all i in equation (4.3.15)(a) and making some simple rearrangements, we obtain

$$\sum_i P_{(i1)} \, X_{(i1)} \quad + \sum_i P_{(i3)} \, X_{(i3)} - \sum_i \sum_j P_{(jc)} \, X_{(jc)}^{(1i)}$$

$$= \sum_i \sum_{t=1}^{2} P_{(n+1,t)}^{(1i)} \, X_{(n+1,t)}^{(1i)} + \sum_i \left(\sum_{s=1\&3} P_{(is)} \, X_{(is)} \right) \left(1 - T_i^{(0)} \right) . \qquad \text{(E4.14.8)}$$

The LHS of this equation can be rewritten as:

$$\text{LHS(E4.14.8)} = \left[\sum_i P_{(i1)} \, X_{(i1)} \quad + \sum_i P_{(i2)} \, X_{(i2)} \right] - \sum_i P_{(i2)} \, X_{(i2)}$$

$$+ \sum_i P_{(i3)} \, X_{(i3)} - \sum_i \sum_j P_{(jc)} \, X_{(jc)}^{(1i)} \quad . \qquad \text{(E4.14.9)}$$

Now we use (4.3.20)(a), (4.3.21)(a), (4.3.16)(a), (4.3.17)(a) and (4.3.18)(a), and we rewrite (E4.14.9) as:

$$\text{LHS(E4.14.8)} = \sum_i P_{(ic)} X_{(ic)} - \sum_i \sum_j P_{(ic)} X_{(ic)}^{(1j)} - \sum_i \Phi P_{(i2)}^{(w)} X_{(i2)}$$

$$+ \sum_i \Phi P_{(i3)}^{(w)} X_{(i3)} - \sum_i \Phi P_{(i2)}^{(w)} \left(T_{(i2)} + T_{(2)} - 2 \right) X_{(i2)}$$

$$+ \sum_i \Phi P_{(i3)}^{(w)} \left(T_{(i3)} + T_{(3)} - 2 \right) X_{(i3)} \quad . \tag{E4.14.10}$$

On using (4.3.23)(a) in (E4.14.10) and on returning to (E4.14.8) we obtain

$$\sum_i P_{(ic)} \left(\sum_{k=3,4} X_{(ic)}^{(k)} + \sum_j X_{(ic)}^{(2j)} \right) + \sum_i \Phi P_{(i3)}^{(w)} X_{(i3)} - \sum_i \Phi P_{(i2)}^{(w)} X_{(i2)} \quad =$$

$$\sum_i \sum_{t=1}^{2} P_{(n+1,t)}^{(1i)} X_{(n+1,t)}^{(1i)} + \sum_i \left(\sum_{s=1\&3} P_{(is)} X_{(is)} \right) \left(1 - T_i^{(o)} \right)$$

$$+ \sum_i \Phi P_{(i2)}^{(w)} (T_{(i2)} + T_{(2)} - 2) X_{(i2)} - \sum_i \Phi P_{(i3)}^{(w)} (T_{(i3)} - T_{(3)} - 2) X_{(i3)} \quad .$$

That is,

$$\text{GDPE} \quad = \quad \text{GDPY} \quad = \quad \text{GDP} \quad . \tag{E4.14.11}$$

(c)   Suitable equations are

$$C = C^{(2)} + C^{(3)} + C^{(4)} \quad , \qquad \text{(absorption)}$$

$$C_R = C_R^{(2)} + C_R^{(3)} + C_R^{(4)} \quad , \qquad \text{(real absorption)}$$

and

$$\underline{\Xi}^{(a)} = C/C_R \quad . \quad \text{(price deflator for absorption)}$$

The percentage change forms for these equations are

$$c = \sum_{i=2}^{4} S^i c^{(i)} \tag{E4.14.12}$$

$$c_R = \sum_{i=2}^{4} S^i c_R^{(i)} \tag{E4.14.13}$$

and

$$\xi^{(a)} = c - c_R \tag{E4.14.14}$$

where the $S^{(i)}$, for $i=2,3,4$, are the shares in base-period absorption represented by investment ($i=2$), consumption ($i=3$) and government spending ($i=3$). Underlying our use of the same shares in both equations (E4.14.12) and (E4.14.13) is the convention that nominal and real expenditure levels are the same in the base period.

Exercise 4.15   *Simulating a decline in the terms of trade*

One of the most difficult aspects of applied general equilibrium modeling is interpreting simulation results. Even a small model will produce a vast amount of output, usually hundreds or thousands of numbers, and sorting through them all can be a formidable task. Nevertheless, this is essential. Discovering and explaining the fundamental mechanisms behind a simulation is at least as important as the actual numbers obtained.

There are several reasons why the result-interpretation phase is crucial. The first is that someone reading the results might legitimately ask why they turned out the way they did. The naive answer is everything in the model is simultaneously determined, so the results depend on all the equations and exogenous variables together. In a limited sense this is true, but it doesn't provide much economic intuition. Many of the equations affect the solution very little, and only through indirect channels.

A better answer is to describe the principal mechanisms behind the simulation results. We have found that it is always possible to track down a handful of equations and exogenous variables which are primarily responsible for the outcome. Finding these makes it possible to explain exactly why the results were obtained. It also identifies which of the assumptions used in building the model ended up being important.

Another reason for working out detailed explanations is to verify that there are no critical errors in the model. The path from economic theory to a fully implemented computable general equilibrium model is long, and there are plenty of opportunities for mistakes. In Exercise 4.13, we showed how models can be tested using special simulations, but even a program that passes can still have many kinds of errors. A simple example, and one that might be hard to detect, is a misplaced decimal point in an elasticity. There's no mechanical way to find that particular problem because the erroneous program would be a perfectly legitimate model of some economy, just not the one intended. Fortunately, tracking down the primary mechanisms behind each simulation usually exposes mistakes like this, especially if they are important to the results.

Unfortunately, the process of finding an explanation is more art than science. Worse yet, it is not easy to say exactly what constitutes a good explanation. As a rough guide, an interpretation should be pithy and avoid circularity. The trick to producing a first class analysis is to pare away the unimportant mechanisms, which will be numerous, leaving a small core that does most of the work. How much to leave in and how much to discard is mostly a matter of experience. Generally, parsimonious explanations are better, as long as they have enough detail to show the relationship between the shock and the outcome.

One trap to avoid is circular reasoning. Since general equilibrium models are really just sets of simultaneous equations, it's easy to inadvertently end up explaining that A causes B, B causes C, and C causes A. Circularity almost always results from explaining endogenous variables purely in terms of other endogenous variables. As an example, suppose a simulation shows a reduction in the foreign currency price of a country's principal export, an expansion in the volume of the export and a devaluation. A circular explanation might go as follows:

> The foreign currency price has fallen because the export volume has risen; the export volume has risen because devaluation has improved the profitability of exporting; devaluation has occurred because of a reduction in the foreign currency export price, i.e. an adverse movement in the terms of trade.

While it is probably true that these effects are present in the model, it should be clear that the explanation is circular. What is missing is the link between the exogenous shock, whatever it was, and the results being explained.

The process of finding a convincing interpretation of a simulation can be difficult at first, but becomes easier with experience. Initially, it is hard to know where to begin. One approach is to work outward from the shock: how does it affect variables that depend on it, how do they affect other variables, and so on. On the other hand, it is sometimes possible to start at the top and work down: first explaining what happens to economy-wide variables such as GDP, and then showing how they affect others. Usually, the most effective approach is a combination of these two, but each simulation is different and it is impossible to apply the same rule in all cases.

In the remainder of this exercise, we present the results of a typical simulation using the DMR model and work through an analysis of it. We hope to illustrate both how the analysis should be done, and what a sound interpretation looks like. It turns out that in this case the tops-down approach works best.

Table E4.15.1 sets out some results from the DMR model on the effects of a 10 percent decline in the world price of exports of commodity 8 (services). These results were calculated with the exogenous variables

Table E4.15.1

Macroeconomic Impact of a 10 Per Cent Fall in the World Price of Exportable Commodity 8 under the Standard DMR Closure

Variable	Percentage change
Real GDP	−0.0768
GDP price deflator	−0.2298
Real absorption	−0.2002
Price deflator for absorption	0.0137
Nominal exchange rate (devaluation)	1.2411
Real investment, $c_R^{(2)}$	0.4822
Real consumption, $c_R^{(3)}$	−0.3185
Real government spending, $c_R^{(4)}$	−0.1639
Real wage rate	−0.2617

chosen as in the standard DMR closure (see Table 4.3.5). The only exogenous variable given a non-zero shock was $f_{(8,3)}^{(w)}$, the shift in the export demand function for commodity 8. We set

$$f_{(8,3)}^{(w)} = -10.$$

In making our calculations we used a 1-step Johansen procedure. The database and parameter settings are those set out in Appendix 4.1. The complete results of the simulation appear in Appendix 4.2, but you may want to calculate them yourself using the programs on the companion diskettes described in Chapter 1.

(a)   Is the shock equivalent to specifying a 10 percent decline in the world price of commodity 8?

(b)   In simulating the effects of a 10 percent reduction in the world price of exported commodity 8, should we also move the price of imported commodity 8 ($p_{(8,2)}^{(w)}$)?

(c)   If you think about its definition, you might be surprised that GDP declines. Why? Now explain why it does decline when the world price of commodity 8 falls. If you need them, the complete results for the simulation are in Appendix 4.2.

(d)   Real absorption declines much more than real GDP. What accounts for this?

(e)   The decline in absorption is not uniform across sectors. In particular, absorption shifts towards investment and away from consumption and government spending. Can you explain this? What role does the choice of exogenous variables play?

(f)   The shock has quite different effects on employment in different industries (see column (1) of Table E4.15.2 or Appendix 4.2). Briefly describe why this is so.

Answer to Exercise 4.15

(a)   Because γ_8 is zero in the parameter file (see Appendix 4.1), equation (4.3.4) implies that the shock is equivalent to a 10 per cent reduction in the world price of exported commodity 8.

(b)   Whether or not the price of imports should also be shocked is a matter of judgement. If exported commodity 8 is very similar to imported commodity 8, then it is probably best to shock both prices since the goods would be close substitutes in the world market. On the other hand, if the exported product and the corresponding import are fairly different, a shock applied to the export price alone gives a potentially interesting simulation. We have chosen to regard Korea's imports and exports of services as significantly different.

(c)   At first glance, it may seem strange that real GDP (a measure of the volume of output) has declined by 0.0768 per cent. Remember that we are holding constant technology and the inputs of labor (years) and capital. Certainly we would not expect a decline in the volume of output if we think in terms of a one sector model with a production function of the form

$$Y \;=\; F(K, L) \,.$$

So what are the reasons for the change in real GDP in this application of the DMR model? It turns out that there are three. First, wage rates per year of labor differ across industries. Second, production taxes per dollar of value added differ across industries. Third, there are tariffs on imports.

Table E4.15.2
Explanation of the Change in Real GDP arising from a 10 per cent Fall in the World Price of Exportable Commodity 8 under the Standard DMR Closure

Industry or commodity	(1) %Δ in employment (ℓ_j)	(2) Employment (L_j)	(3) Change in employment ($\Delta L_j \times 100$)	(4) $\frac{W_j}{GDPR(1-\beta_j)}$	(5) $\frac{100W_j}{GDPR(1-\beta_j)}\Delta L_j$	(6) %Δ in imports (m_j)	(7) Tariff shares in GDP (N_j)	(8) $m_j\,N_j$	(9) gdpr (5)+(8)
1	0.2378	2.959	0.704	0.0642	0.0452	-2.6437	0.0055	-0.0145	
2	-0.0643	0.126	-0.008	0.1845	-0.0015	-1.8147	0.0013	-0.0024	
3	0.0149	0.277	0.004	0.1602	0.0006	-1.5741	0.0021	-0.0033	
4	0.4418	0.124	0.055	0.1781	0.0098	-0.6138	0.0100	-0.0061	
5	0.6047	0.070	0.042	0.1714	0.0072	-0.2778	0.0054	-0.0015	
6	0.5107	0.171	0.087	0.1579	0.0137	-0.0211	0.0000	0.0000	
7	0.0959	0.188	0.018	0.1503	0.0027	-0.5208	0.0000	0.0000	
8	-0.8088	1.115	-0.902	0.1404	-0.1266	-0.5674	0.0003	-0.0002	
Totals		5.030	0.000		-0.0489		0.0246	-0.0280	-0.0769

Using simplified notation we can, in this simulation,[1] write

$$\Delta GDPR = \sum_j (P_j - Q_j) \Delta Z_j + \sum_j \tau_j \Delta M_j \qquad (E4.15.1)$$

where $\Delta GDPR$ is the change in real GDP, P_j is the price per unit of output in industry j, Q_j is the cost of intermediate inputs per unit of output in industry j, ΔZ_j is the change in the number of units of output in industry j, τ_j is the tariff per unit of import of good j, and ΔM_j is the change in the number of units of import of good j. In (E4.15.1), the change in real GDP is calculated by summing the changes in real value-added across industries, and the changes in real tariff collections across imported commodities. The change in real value-added in industry i is assumed to be the change in the industry's output multiplied by its value-added per unit of output in the base period. The change in the real tariff collection on imports of commodity i is assumed to be the change in the volume of these imports multiplied by the base-period tariff rate.

It is not difficult to see why the first term on the right hand side of (E4.15.1) forms part of a measure of real GDP. But what is the intuitive explanation for the tariff term? One way of understanding this term is to imagine that a unit of imports on the domestic market costs $10, including $2 for the tariff. As a nation, to pay for another unit of these imports, we must produce an extra $8 worth of exports. Suppose that this can be done by shifting into export production resources which were initially producing $8 worth of output in some other activity. Then we see that an extra unit of imports leaves us with $2 of extra absorption (a $2 increase in the real value of C+I+G) with no deterioration in the balance of trade (X–M). We get a $2 increase in real GDP because the extra unit of imports, which we value at $10, is paid for by an extra unit of exports, which costs us $8.

---

[1]   It can be shown that (E4.15.1) coincides in the DMR model with the usual expenditure-side measure of the change in real GDP provided that we are assuming no export subsidies, no non-optimizing or rationed behavior and no technological change. The first of these assumptions is implied by the data base in Appendix 4.1, the second is implied by our choice of closure for the current simulation and the third is implied by our choice of zero for the values of the exogenous variables $a_{n+1}^{(1j)}$. The proof of this proposition, although not very difficult, is too space-consuming for inclusion here.

Now returning to our main problem, the explanation of the decline of 0.0768 per cent in real GDP, we note that in the current application of the DMR model, each industry uses labor up to the point where the perceived value to the industry of the output from an extra year of labor equals the costs of employing that labor. In simple notation, we have

$$W_j = \left(P_j(1-T_j) - Q_j\right) MPL_j \qquad (E4.15.2)$$

where W_j is the wage per year of labor in industry j, T_j is the rate of production tax, MPL_j is the marginal product of labor in industry j, and P_j and Q_j are previously defined in (E4.15.1).

With technology and capital held constant in each industry, the change in output in industry j is given by

$$\Delta Z_j = MPL_j\, \Delta L_j \qquad (E4.15.3)$$

where ΔL_j is the change in employment in industry j. On substituting from (E4.15.3) to (E4.15.1) and on using (E4.15.2) we obtain

$$\Delta GDPR = \sum_j \frac{P_j - Q_j}{P_j(1-T_j) - Q_j}\, W_j \Delta L_j + \sum_j \tau_j\, \Delta M_j\ , \qquad (E4.15.4)$$

which can be re-expressed as

$$gdpr = \frac{100}{GDPR} \sum_j \left[\frac{W_j}{1 - \beta_j}\right] \Delta L_j + \sum_j m_j\, N_j\ , \qquad (E4.15.5)$$

where gdpr is the percentage change in real GDP, β_j is the ratio of the production tax to value added in industry j $\left(\text{that is, } \beta_j = T_j\, P_j/(P_j - Q_j)\right)$, m_j is the percentage change in imports of good j, and N_j is the share in GDP accounted for by tariff revenue collected on imports of good j.

From (E4.15.5) we see that if wage rates are the same in each industry:

$$W_j = W \qquad \text{for all j,} \qquad (E4.15.6)$$

production taxes are the same share of value added in each industry:

$$\beta_j = \beta \qquad \text{for all j,} \qquad (E4.15.7)$$

and there are no tariffs,

$$N_j = 0 \qquad \text{for all j,} \qquad (E4.15.8)$$

then

$$gdpr = \frac{W}{(1 - \beta)} \frac{100}{(GDPR)} \sum_j \Delta L_j\ .$$

Thus, if we hold total employment constant, i.e., $\sum_j \Delta L_j = 0$, then gdpr = 0.

This confirms our earlier statement about the three reasons for the decline in real GDP. In absence tariffs and of differences across industries in wage rates and production taxes per dollar of value added, there would, under the assumptions of the present simulation, be no change in real GDP. However, in this simulation, (E4.15.6) – (E4.15.8) are not valid. Thus, as can be seen from (E4.15.5), changes in real GDP can arise from changes in import volumes and from reallocations of labor between industries.

In Table E4.15.2 we have used (E4.15.5) to provide an explanation of the decline in real GDP shown in Table E4.15.1. Column (1) of Table E4.15.2 shows results for employment by industry transcribed from the printout (see Appendix 4.2). Column (2) shows employment by industry in the base period. These numbers can be derived from the wage bill and wage rate matrices in Appendix 4.1. Column (3) was derived by multiplying entries in column (1) by the corresponding entries in column (2). It shows changes in employment by industry multiplied by 100. Notice that the sum of the entries in column (3) is zero. This reflects the assumption underlying the simulation that total employment is constant. In column (4) we have used information from the database (Appendix 4.1) to compute $W_j/[GDPR(1 - \beta_j)]$ for $j = 1,..., 8$. For $j = 2$, for example, we have

$$\frac{W_2}{GDPR(1 - \beta_2)} = \frac{Wage\ bill/Employment}{GDPR(1 - Prod.tax/Value\ added)}$$

$$= \frac{11.77/0.126}{1164.42(1 - 26.42/[11.77 + 8.54 + 26.42])} = 0.1846.$$

Each entry in column (5) is the product of the corresponding entries in columns (3) and (4). It shows the values of the terms in the first sum on the RHS of (E4.15.5). Column (6) contains the results for the percentage changes in imports transcribed from Appendix 4.2 ($m_j \equiv x_{(j2)}$). In column (7) we have used the database to determine the shares in GDP of tariff revenue collection on each commodity. For example,

$$N_1 = (Tariff\ revenue\ on\ commodity\ 1)/GDP$$

$$= (69.94 - 63.58)/1164.42 = 0.0055.$$

Column (8) gives the values of the terms in the second sum on the right hand side of (E4.15.5). It was derived by multiplying entries in columns (7) by the corresponding entries in column (6). Finally, the single entry in column (9) is the sum of the totals from columns (5) and (8). It is the percentage change in real GDP.

Thus, given the changes in industry employment and imports implied by the model, Table 4.15.2 completely explains the change in real GDP. It indicates that about two thirds of the reduction in GDP is due to reallocation of labor with the remainder being associated with reductions in imports.

The final step in the explanation is to discuss why the commodity import and industry employment results look the way they do. On the import results we will merely note that general declines were to be expected. With the exogenously imposed 10 per cent reduction in the world price of export commodity 8, there is a real devaluation of the Korean currency. (Notice that the nominal exchange rate devalues by 1.2411 per cent while the movement in the domestic price level as represented by $\xi^{(1)}$ is zero — see the DMR closure in Table 4.3.5.) Real devaluation is necessary to stimulate exports and restrain imports so that the trade balance can be restored to its initial level. (Recall that ΔB is set exogenously at zero — see Table 4.3.5). With regard to the results on employment by industry we will delay our discussion until part (f).

(d)   From Appendix 4.1 we see that the value of exports of good 8 in the base period data is $16.34 million. Thus, under the given shock, the economy loses $1.634 million of export revenue. Because the balance of trade is exogenous and held to zero change, this loss in export earnings must be offset by increases in export volumes or reductions in imports. Consequently, the reduction in absorption must exceed the reduction in GDP by $1.634 million. In percentage change terms:

$$c_R = (gdpr) \, S_1 - 100 \, (\$1.634/C_R)$$

where c_R is the percentage change in absorption, gdpr is the percentage change in real GDP, and S_1 is the ratio of GDP to absorption in the data set. Consulting Appendix 4.1 we find that GDP is $1164.42 million and absorption is $1262.36 million, so

$$S_1 = 1164.42/1262.36 = 0.9224.$$

From Table E4.15.1 we know that gdpr is 0.0768. Substituting these numbers into the equation above we obtain

$$c_R = -0.20$$

which is the result in Table E4.15.1.

(e)   The shift of absorption toward investment and away from consumption and government spending is probably the most interesting result of this experiment because it is the most unexpected: why should a decline in the world price of exported services actually increase domestic investment?

In trying to understand the absorption results we started by wondering why real consumption and real government spending fall. Equation (4.3.38) shows that consumption is determined by household income and a tax rate. The tax rate is exogenous and set to zero change, so the decline in real consumption must have been caused by a drop in real income. Looking at the simulation results in Appendix 4.2 shows that household real income has indeed fallen. ($y^{(3)} = -0.3171$ and $\xi^{(3)} = 0.0014$.) Similarly, from the equation for government spending, (4.3.39), it is clear that the fall in spending must have been induced by a drop in government real revenue. ($y^{(4)} = -0.2534$ and $\xi^{(4)} = -0.0895$.)

This analysis is fine as far as it goes, but really all we have done so far is to move the burden of explanation from consumption and government spending back one step to incomes. It is a step in the right direction, but far from the end. Focusing on income actually deepens the mystery about investment. Since consumption is proportional to income, so is saving. Therefore, private domestic saving must have fallen. Investment is equal to saving, so this suggests we should expect a drop in investment rather than an increase. Thinking about this for a while eventually leads to the key to the problem: investment is equal to total, not just domestic, saving. Total saving includes net borrowing from foreigners, often called foreign saving, which can be seen from the sectoral balances identity to be equal to the balance of trade deficit.

At first, the existence of foreign saving does not seem to help. The balance of trade is exogenous, and set to zero change, so foreign saving appears to be fixed. However, a careful look at the definition of the trade balance in Table 4.3.2 reveals that it is measured in foreign currency. At the same time, Table E4.15.1 shows that the exchange rate rises (depreciates) significantly. Together, these facts mean that the trade deficit in domestic currency increases by 1.2411 per cent. As a result, the domestic currency value of foreign saving rises by 1.2411 per cent. With the costs of capital goods rising by only 0.1806 per cent (see the result for $\xi^{(2)}$ in Appendix 4.2), this allows a substantial increase in real investment. (Notice from the database that foreign saving is the dominant source of saving, accounting in the base period for $97.94 million in total saving of $159.14 million.)

At this point we have a sound intuitive explanation of what lies behind the puzzling increase in real investment. However, we still need to explain the reductions in real household income and government real revenue which generate the reductions in the real consumption of both the households and the government.

One approach would be to point at our explanation in part (d) of the reduction in real absorption and our explanation here of the increase in real investment. These are certainly sufficient to indicate that in total the real consumption (and therefore income) of households and the government *must* fall. But this doesn't give us a clear picture of mechanisms in the model through which this happens.

The first set of mechanisms are those explained in part (c), generating the fall in real GDP. However, the fall in real GDP is only 0.0768 per cent. This isn't enough to explain falls in real household income and real government revenue of 0.3185 and 0.1639 per cent. The additional mechanism is a reduction in factor prices (wage rates and rentals on capital) relative to the prices of the goods and services absorbed by households and the government. In other words, there is a reduction in real wage and rental rates.

A convenient index of movements in wage and rental rates is the GDP deflator while a convenient index of the prices of goods and services absorbed by households and the government is the absorption deflator.[2] In Table E4.15.1 we see that the GDP deflator falls by 0.2298 per cent while the absorption deflator rises by 0.0137 per cent.

To explain why the GDP deflator decreases relative' to the absorption deflator, we start with equation (E4.14.4). This defines the percentage movement in the expenditure-side GDP deflator as

$$\text{pgdpe} = \sum_i p_{(ic)} N_{(ic)} + \sum_i (\phi + p_{(i3)}^{(w)}) N_{(i3)} - \sum_i (\phi + p_{(i2)}^{(w)}) N_{(i2)},$$

where the terms denoted by N are the shares in GDP of final demands for composite commodities, of exports and of imports. This equation can be rewritten as:

$$\text{pgdpe} = \sum_i p_{(ic)} N_{(ic)} + \sum_i \left(p_{(i3)}^{(w)} N_{(i3)} - p_{(i2)}^{(w)} N_{(i2)} \right) + \phi \sum_i (N_{(i3)} - N_{(i2)}).$$
$$\text{(E4.15.9)}$$

The first term on the right is the percentage movement in the absorption deflator multiplied by the share of absorption in GDP. Appendix 4.1 shows that initial absorption is greater than GDP (since the trade balance is negative), so the first term is larger than the movement in the absorption deflator. However, the difference is small so we can think of it as approximately the movement in the absorption deflator.

---

2   Ideally we should exclude the prices of investment goods from the absorption deflator. However, in the present simulation this would make only a small difference.

The second term is due purely to the deterioration in the terms of trade. Only one foreign price changed, that of exportable good 8, so the summation simplifies to the product of a single price and a share. Since the shock was a fall in $P_{(13)}^{(w)}$ we know the second term will be negative.

The third term is the percentage change in the exchange rate times the share of the original trade balance in GDP. With the exchange rate increasing (devaluing) and the trade balance being negative, this term must be negative.

Since both the second and third terms on the RHS of (E4.15.9) are negative, it is clear that the GDP deflator must fall relative to the absorption deflator.

(f)   The direct impact of the shock is to release labor from industry 8. This occurs because the declining world price of its output causes industry 8 to contract, reducing its demand for labor. However, the economy-wide usage of labor is fixed. Consequently, with employment declining quite sharply in industry 8, we would expect to find positive employment results for most other industries. In fact, the only industry apart from 8 with a negative employment result is 2.

The industries showing the largest employment gains are 5 and 6 (machinery and construction). Both benefit from the expansion in real investment expenditure. Because it faces considerable import competition (see matrix $\tilde{E}$ in Appendix 4.1), industry 5 also benefits from real devaluation which allows it to increase its share of the local market at the expense of imports.

Industry 4 (intermediate goods) has the third largest percentage boost to employment. This industry has no direct sales to investment (see $\tilde{B}$). However, a considerable share of its output is sold to the investment-oriented industries 5 and 6 (see $\tilde{A}$). In addition, industry 4 faces significant import competition (see $\tilde{E}$) and thus benefits from real devaluation.

Industry 1 (primary) has little connection with investment activity. But it faces import competition (see $\tilde{E}$) and has non-negligible exports (see $\tilde{F}$). Thus, like industries 4 and 5, it gains from real devaluation.

The remaining industries, i.e. 2, 3 and 7, have little linkage to investment, face little import competition and have negligible exports. Consequently, in the current simulation, they show relatively weak employment gains or even suffer employment losses. Industry 2 does particularly poorly because its sales are heavily concentrated on households. Household consumption is the component of absorption showing the greatest percentage contraction.

Appendix 4.1   *Tabular Listing of the Input-Output Database and Parameter File for the DMR Model*

Table A4.1.1

Key to Industries, Commodities and Occupations

Industry/ Commodity No.	Description	Occupation No.	Description
1	Primary	1	Small Farmers
2	Food	2	Marginal Labor
3	Other Consumer Goods	3	Organized Labor
4	Intermediate Goods	4	Service Sector Labor
5	Machinery		
6	Construction		
7	Social Overheads		
8	Services		

*   For a key to the structure of the input-output accounts, see Table 4.4.1.

Table A4.1.2[a]

Matrix $\tilde{A}$: Flows of Commodities Used by Industries as Intermediate Inputs ($ million)

Commodity ↓	Using Industry: 1	2	3	4	5	6	7	8	*Total*
1	82.78	84.54	46.58	25.65	1.10	8.76	3.48	3.78	256.67
2	30.71	25.97	11.67	1.10	0.03	0.00	0.01	8.45	77.94
3	10.04	10.83	97.76	16.06	4.90	16.78	6.21	38.30	200.88
4	25.45	3.82	13.32	33.32	17.38	31.91	13.85	11.26	150.31
5	1.15	0.49	1.42	1.07	4.26	3.72	4.64	0.73	17.48
6	0.70	0.49	0.89	0.56	0.40	0.26	0.82	13.42	17.54
7	3.56	5.00	7.03	11.11	1.82	4.61	4.20	10.52	47.85
8	11.94	10.84	30.99	14.82	3.82	7.48	8.01	20.51	108.41
Totals:									
	166.33	141.98	209.66	103.69	33.71	73.52	41.22	106.97	877.08

(a)   All monetary quantities in the DMR database are Korean won converted into millions of US dollars at the 1963 exchange rate.

Table A4.1.3

Matrix $\tilde{B}$: *Flows of Commodities Used by Industries for Capital Formation ($ million)*

Commodity ↓	Using Industry:								Total
	1	2	3	4	5	6	7	8	
1	0.00	0.00	0.00	0.00	0.00	0.00	0.00	0.00	0.00
2	0.00	0.00	0.00	0.00	0.00	0.00	0.00	0.00	0.00
3	0.34	0.05	0.66	0.61	0.20	0.00	0.00	0.00	1.86
4	0.00	0.00	0.00	0.00	0.00	0.00	0.00	0.00	0.00
5	7.50	1.97	15.68	6.33	3.38	0.00	22.54	0.00	57.40
6	11.42	1.37	5.77	3.04	1.70	2.51	16.20	47.17	89.18
7	0.03	0.00	0.03	0.01	0.01	0.00	0.05	0.07	0.20
8	1.40	0.19	1.49	0.67	0.28	0.20	2.59	3.68	10.50
Totals:									
	20.69	3.58	23.63	10.66	5.57	2.71	41.38	50.92	159.14

Table A4.1.4

Matrices $\tilde{E}$ and $\tilde{F}$: *Imports and Exports at Different Valuations ($ million)*

Com-modity	$\tilde{E}$			$\tilde{F}$		
	Minus the c.i.f. Value of Imports		c.i.f. Value of Imports	f.o.b. Value of Exports plus		Minus f.o.b.Value of Exports
	Minus Specific Tariffs	Minus General Tariffs		Specific Sub-sidies	General Sub-sidies	
	(1)	(2)	(3)	(4)	(5)	(6)
1	-69.94	-63.58	63.58	15.66	15.66	-15.66
2	-11.63	-10.12	10.12	6.94	6.94	-6.94
3	-10.60	-8.16	8.16	9.63	9.63	-9.63
4	-58.44	-46.75	46.75	7.44	7.44	-7.44
5	-37.45	-31.21	31.21	1.54	1.54	-1.54
6	0.00	0.00	0.00	2.28	2.28	-2.28
7	-0.96	-0.96	0.96	7.06	7.06	-7.06
8	-4.45	-4.05	4.05	16.34	16.34	-16.34

Table A4.1.5

Matrix $\tilde{G}$: *Wage Bill by Occupation and Industry ($ million)*

Occupation ↓	Employing Industry:								
	1	2	3	4	5	6	7	8	Total
1	185.35	0.00	0.00	0.00	0.00	0.00	0.00	0.00	185.35
2	32.65	7.65	19.97	7.50	2.73	15.27	17.99	25.46	129.22
3	0.00	4.12	29.92	17.47	10.92	15.25	11.98	0.00	89.66
4	0.00	0.00	0.00	0.00	0.00	0.00	0.00	144.53	144.53
Totals:									
	218.00	11.77	49.89	24.97	13.65	30.52	29.97	169.99	548.76

Table A4.1.6

Vector Components of Input-Output Data ($ million)

Vector[†] ↓	Industry/Commodity/Occupation No.[*]								
	1	2	3	4	5	6	7	8	Totals
1 $\tilde{C}'$	452.16	115.45	115.46	57.73	19.24	0.00	28.87	173.17	962.08
2 $\tilde{D}'$	2.82	0.00	4.23	1.41	1.41	2.82	11.29	117.16	141.14
3 $\tilde{H}$	266.46	8.54	58.69	28.22	11.66	6.68	18.41	123.10	521.76
4 $\tilde{J}$	6.57	26.42	3.21	1.58	0.60	1.12	4.72	21.06	65.28
5 $\tilde{T}'$	657.36	188.71	321.45	158.46	59.62	111.84	94.32	421.12	2012.88
6 $\tilde{P}$	20.69	3.58	23.63	10.66	5.57	2.71	41.38	50.92	159.14
7 $\tilde{S}'$	185.35	129.22	89.66	144.53					548.76
8 $\tilde{W}$	−193.47[a]	−164.83[b]	164.83[c]						
9 $\tilde{Y}$	66.89[d]	66.89[e]	−66.89[f]						

† These vectors are:

1	Household Consumption	6	Investment (by industries)
2	Government & Other Consumption	7	Wage Bill (by occupations)
3	Capital Costs	8	Imports
4	Production or Revenue Taxes	9	Exports
5	Total Supplies		

* The column labels denote composite commodities in rows 1 and 2, industries in rows 3 to 6 and occupations in row 7.

(a) The negative of {the c.i.f. value of all imports, plus the commodity-specific tariffs}.

(b) The negative of {the c.i.f. value of all imports, plus the general tariffs}.

(c) The c.i.f. value of all imports.

(d) The f.o.b. value of all exports plus commodity-specific export subsidies.

(e) The f.o.b. value of all exports plus general export subsidies.

(f) The negative of the f.o.b. value of all exports.

Table A4.1.7

Scalar Components of Input-Output Data ($ million)

Item	Description	Value	Item	Description	Value
$\tilde{K}$	Taxes on Households	100.11	$\tilde{L}$	Saving by Households	8.31
$\tilde{U}$	Sum of Household Consumption, Taxes	1070.50	$\tilde{M}$	Saving by Government	52.89
$\tilde{Z}$	Total Taxes	165.39	$\tilde{I}$	Total Domestic Saving	61.20
$\tilde{X}$	Total Capital Costs	521.76	$\tilde{V}$	Sum of Government Saving and Government & Other Consumption	194.03

Table A4.1.8

Parameter File: Substitution and Transformation Elasticities

Parameter†, eqn no. ↓	Industry/Commodity No.							
	1	2	3	4	5	6	7	8
1 $\sigma_j^{(c)}$ (4.3.11)(b)	2.00	1.30	1.10	0.60	0.50	0.33	0.33	0.33
2 $\sigma_j^{(o)}$ (4.3.5)(b)	-1.0244	-1.0382	-1.0309	-1.0493	-1.0265	-1.0208	-1.0809	-1.0404
3 $\sigma_{n+1}^{(1j)}$ (4.3.8)(b)	1	1	1	1	1	2	1	1
4 $\sigma_{(n+1,1)}^{(1j)}$ (4.3.9)(b)	1	1	1	1	1	1	1	1

† These parameters are:

1	Substitution elasticity between domestic and imported commodity j (Armington elasticity)	3	Elasticity of substitution between capital and labor in industry j
2	Elasticity of transformation between the domestic commodity and the export commodity produced by industry j	4	Inter-occupational substitution elasticity in industry j

Table A4.1.9
Other Parameters and Initial Values of Coefficients

Parameter/Coefficient[†]		1	2	3	4	5	6	7	8
	↓ Industry/Commodity No.								
1	γ_j	0	0	0	0	0	0	0	0
2	Ω_j	1	1	1	1	1	1	1	1
3	$R_j + D_j$	40.52	32.30	33.80	33.59	33.69	33.39	4.48	10.82
4	D_j	3.0	5.0	5.0	5.0	5.0	3.5	3.5	3.5
5	$w_j(1)$	0.3266	0.0938	0.1597	0.0787	0.0296	0.0556	0.0469	0.2092
6	$w_j(2)$	0.0000	0.0000	0.0117	0.0000	0.3607	0.5604	0.0013	0.0660
7	$w_j(3)$	0.4700	0.1200	0.1200	0.0600	0.0200	0.0000	0.0300	0.1800
8	$w_j(4)$	0.0200	0.0000	0.0300	0.0100	0.0100	0.0200	0.0800	0.8301
9	h_1	User-selected parameter which allows indexation of wage rates to the consumer price index, Ξ_3. For 100 per cent wage indexation, $h_1 = 1$.							
	h_2	User-selected parameter which allows indexation of rental rates on capital to the consumer price index, Ξ_3. For 100 per cent indexation, $h_2 = 1$.							

† These parameters/coefficients are:

1	Reciprocal of the elasticity of export demand for commodity j	5 – 8	Weights for price index numbers for:
2	Actual import/domestic ratio divided by the desired ratio		total output
3	Gross rate of return in industry j ¶		investment goods
4	Depreciation rate in industry j ¶		consumption
			government expenditure

¶ Units are per cent per year.

Table A4.1.10

Supplementary Data — Initial Wage Rates by Occupation and Industry,

$$\{P_{(n+1,1,k)}^{(1j)}\} \quad (\$ \text{ per year})$$

Occupation, k ↓	Industry, j							
	1	2	3	4	5	6	7	8
1	73.67	73.67	73.67	73.67	73.67	73.67	73.67	73.67
2	73.77	86.78	154.84	174.35	177.03	161.74	146.97	152.12
3	193.39	109.75	201.95	216.86	199.80	198.16	182.13	193.39
4	152.44	152.44	152.44	152.44	152.44	152.44	152.44	152.44

Table A4.1.11

Initial Values of Certain Coefficients Based in Part on Supplementary Data

Parameter†, eqn no. ↓	Industry/Commodity No.*							
	1	2	3	4	5	6	7	8
1 $\eta_{(j1)}^{(zj)}$ (4.3.6)b – see note (a)	0.9762	0.9632	0.9700	0.9530	0.9742	0.9796	0.9251	0.9612
2 $\eta_{(j1)}^{(jc)}$ – see note (b)	0.9017	0.9399	0.9671	0.7210	0.6080	1.000	0.9891	0.9891
3 B_j^K (4.3.34)b – see note (c)	0.26	0.01	0.07	0.03	0.01	0.01	0.16	0.45

† These parameters are:

1	Elasticity of overall output of industry j with respect to output of the domestic commodity produced by j	3	Shares of industry j in the aggregate capital stock
2	Elasticity of output of composite commodity j with respect to input of domestically sourced input j		

(a) Under revenue maximising assumptions, this elasticity is equal to the revenue share $R_{(j1)}$. In the absence of such assumptions, besides the value of $\sigma_j^{(o)}$ and the relevant input-output data, it is necessary also to know the parameter $\gamma_{(j1)}$. See (E4.3.9).

(b) This elasticity relates to input-output data and technological parameters via (E4.8.16). If there is no rationing of imports (i.e., $\Omega = 1$), then $\eta_{(i1)}^{(ic)}$ is equal to the share $S_{(i1)}^{(c)}$, whose value may be found from the input-output data – see (E4.8.17).

(c) For notes on the computation of these shares, see the entry for equation (4.3.34)b in Table 4.3.4.

Appendix 4.2   *Listing of Results from the Simulation in Exercise 4.15* [1]

Commodity (i)	Variable $P_{(i1)}$	$P_{(i2)}$	$P_{(i3)}$	$P_{(ic)}$	(w) $P_{(i3)}$
1	–0.1177	1.2411	1.2411	0.0159	0.0000
2	–0.0872	1.2411	1.2411	–0.0073	0.0000
3	–0.1568	1.2411	1.2411	–0.1108	0.0000
4	–0.0237	1.2411	1.2411	0.3292	0.0000
5	0.0941	1.2411	1.2411	0.5437	0.0000
6	–0.0132	1.2411	1.2411	–0.0132	0.0000
7	–0.1708	1.2411	1.2411	–0.1554	0.0000
8	–0.1142	1.2411	–8.7589	–0.0994	–10.0000

Commodity (i)	Variable $x_{(i1)}$	$x_{(i2)}$	$x_{(i3)}$	$x_{(ic)}$	(w) $x_{(i3)}$
1	0.0739	–2.6437	1.4658	–0.1932	1.4658
2	–0.0880	–1.8147	1.2910	–0.1918	1.2910
3	–0.0364	–1.5741	1.4048	–0.0870	1.4048
4	0.1450	–0.6138	1.4723	–0.0667	1.4723
5	0.2957	–0.2778	1.4731	0.0709	1.4731
6	0.3929	–0.0211	1.6733	0.3929	1.6733
7	–0.0549	–0.5208	1.4713	–0.0600	1.4713
8	–0.1202	–0.5674	–9.1142	–0.1250	–9.1142

Industry (j)	Variable z_j	k_j	$p_K^{(j)}$	r_j	i_j
1	0.1070	0.0000	0.1810	–0.2198	0.4818
2	–0.0373	0.0000	0.2873	–0.7240	0.3755
3	0.0069	0.0000	0.3480	–0.6964	0.3148
4	0.2074	0.0000	0.3064	–0.1467	0.3565
5	0.3261	0.0000	0.3166	0.0325	0.3462
6	0.4190	0.0000	–0.0196	0.0163	0.6825
7	0.0594	0.0000	0.2846	–2.0525	0.3783
8	–0.4691	0.0000	–0.0197	–1.5513	0.6825

[1]   For a key to the notation, see Table 4.3.2.

Appendix 4.2 *(continued)*

Commodity (i)	$f_{(i2)}^{(c)}$	Variable $x_{(ic)}^{(3)}$	$x_{(ic)}^{(4)}$
1	0.0000	−0.3330	−0.2693
2	−0.0000	−0.3098	−0.2461
3	0.0000	−0.2063	−0.1426
4	−0.0000	−0.6463	−0.5826
5	−0.0000	−0.8608	−0.7972
6	−0.0000	−0.3039	−0.2402
7	0.0000	−0.1617	−0.0980
8	0.0000	−0.2177	−0.1540

Industry (i)	$p_{(n+1,1)}^{(1j)}$	Variable $x_{(n+1,1)}^{(1j)}$	$p_{(n+1,2)}^{(1j)}$	$f_{(n+1,2)}^{(1j)}$
1	−0.2603	0.2378	−0.0225	−0.0238
2	−0.2603	−0.0643	−0.3246	−0.3260
3	−0.2603	0.0149	−0.2454	−0.2468
4	−0.2603	0.4418	0.1815	0.1802
5	0.2603	0.6047	0.3443	0.3430
6	−0.2603	0.5107	−0.0050	−0.0063
7	−0.2603	0.0959	−0.1644	−0.1658
8	−0.2603	−0.8088	−1.0692	−1.0705

Industry (j)	Variable $x_{(n+1,1,k)}^{(1j)}$	$p_{(n+1,1,k)}^{(1j)}$
	(the same result for each occupation k, k = 1 , ... , 4)	
1	0.2378	−0.2603
2	−0.0643	−0.2603
3	0.0149	−0.2603
4	0.4418	−0.2603
5	0.6047	−0.2603
6	0.5107	−0.2603
7	0.0959	−0.2603
8	−0.8088	−0.2603

... continued

Appendix 4.2 *(continued)*

Commodity	Variable			
(i)	$x_{(i1)}^{(c)}$	$x_{(i2)}^{(c)}$	$x_{(i1)}^{(c)*}$	$x_{(i2)}^{(c)*}$
1	0.0739	-2.6437	0.0738	-2.6437
2	-0.0880	-1.8147	-0.0879	-1.8147
3	-0.0364	-1.5741	-0.0364	-1.5741
4	0.1450	-0.6138	0.1451	-0.6138
5	0.2957	-0.2778	0.2957	-0.2778
6	0.3929	-0.0211	0.3929	-0.0211
7	-0.0549	-0.5208	-0.0549	-0.5208
8	-0.1202	-0.5674	-0.1202	-0.5674

Industry	Variable	
(j)	$x_{(ic)}^{(1j)}$	$x_{(ic)}^{(2j)}$
	(the same result for each composite commodity i, i =1,...,8)	
1	0.1070	0.4818
2	-0.0373	0.3755
3	0.0069	0.3148
4	0.2074	0.3565
5	0.3261	0.3462
6	0.4190	0.6825
7	0.0594	0.3783
8	-0.4691	0.6825

Variable	Value	Variable	Value
$\xi^{(2)}$	0.1806	m	-1.4528
$\xi^{(3)}$	0.0014	l_1	0.2378
$\xi^{(4)}$	-0.0895	l_2	0.0494
$f_{(n+1,1)}$	-0.2617	l_3	0.2460
$c^{(2)}$	0.6629	l_4	-0.8088
$c^{(3)}$	-0.3171	k	0.0000
$c^{(4)}$	-0.2534		
$y^{(3)}$	-0.3171	$c_R^{(2)}$	0.4822
$y^{(4)}$	-0.2534		
v_{42}	-0.9163	$c_R^{(3)}$	-0.3185
v_{43}	0.0637		
ϕ	1.2411	$c_R^{(4)}$	-0.1639
e	-3.5799	v_{23}	0.9800

Chapter 5

An Introduction to Intertemporal Modeling

5.1 Introduction

Previous chapters have been concerned with models of economies at particular points in time. For long-run models the point of interest is far in the future, when all transient behavior has died out. On the other hand, in short-run models producers are precluded from fully adjusting their capital stocks to changes in their economic circumstances. In both cases, however, only one period is captured by the model: both are essentially static. Because no information is included on how the economy changes over time, it is impossible to solve for the sequence of equilibria between the short- and long-run solutions.

In contrast, intertemporal models include equations describing how the economy evolves. These allow the models to be used to find the economy's trajectory through time. Unfortunately, intertemporal models are somewhat harder to build — and much harder to solve — than static models. However, there are circumstances in which the extra effort is worthwhile. One is when the trajectory itself is of interest apart from the short- and long-run equilibria. Policy makers, for example, are often interested in how fast the economy moves toward the long run, and in whether or not the transition is smooth. This is especially true when the short- and long-run effects of the policy are very different. Furthermore, some models, especially those in which lags play a prominent role, show cycles in certain variables between the short and long runs. It is often important to know the timing and amplitude of the oscillations.

Another reason for building an intertemporal model is to incorporate intertemporal optimization by agents. If some of the agents in the model choose current variables to optimize intertemporal objective functions, even short-run results will require some form of intertemporal modeling. For example, households might be modeled as life-cycle savers whose consumption is based in part on their human wealth, i.e., the discounted sum of expected future labor earnings. Then any shock that changes expected wage rates or hours worked in the future will change human wealth and hence current consumption. Since the life-cycle model is used more and more often as the basis for modeling savings behavior, it has stimulated the development of intertemporal modeling.

Perhaps the strongest motivation for developing intertemporal models has been the desire to integrate recent theories of investment behavior into applied general equilibrium work. In such investment models, each firm chooses its level of investment to maximize the stock-market value of its equity. Market value, in turn, depends on the earnings a firm is expected to generate in the future. Thus, changes in expectations about a firm's prospects can change its market value and hence its level of investment. Investment is an intertemporal decision. Treating it as such in general equilibrium models is appealing.

5.2 Goals, Reading Guide and References

By the time you have finished with this chapter you should be familiar with the basic techniques used in intertemporal modeling and with how they can be applied in building an intertemporal general equilibrium model. You should have developed the skills needed both to understand the intertemporal models which you come across in the literature and to build your own models. In particular, we hope you will:

(1)   be able to discuss what circumstances call for the use of an intertemporal model;

(2)   understand how to build theoretical models of intertemporal decisions from basic assumptions such as arbitrage;

(3)   know about the q-theoretic investment model;

(4)   be able to use graphical techniques such as phase planes to describe in qualitative terms how an intertemporal model will respond to a shock;

(5)   be familiar with numerical methods that can be used to obtain quantitative results from an intertemporal model; and

(6)   know how to integrate intertemporal decisions into general equilibrium models and be able to discuss the costs and benefits entailed.

Reading guide 5 and problem set 5 contain material which will help you to achieve these goals.

Intertemporal modeling uses a number of mathematical methods which you may not have encountered before. The reading guide is intended to help you fill in gaps in your knowledge of optimal control, differential equations, numerical methods and linear algebra. It also includes references to the economic literature on intertemporal analysis.

The problem set is in three parts. In part A you will set up and solve a simple investment problem, By performing qualitative analyses with the investment model in partial equilibrium, you will gain insight into how it works and learn some analytical techniques which are useful in intertemporal modeling. Part B deals with methods of obtaining numerical results from such models. In part C, you will first link the investment problem into a small, static general equilibrium model, thus producing an intertemporal general equilibrium model. Finally, you will be able to use the resulting model to analyze the effects of a number of different policies.

Exercises 5.5 to 5.8 contain a large number of examples of partial equilibrium analyses with different versions of the investment model. Eventually, readers should be sure that they understand these examples but it may not be necessary to complete them all before looking at the later parts of the problem set. At a minimum, questions (a) and (b) of Exercise 5.5 should be completed before proceeding. These establish the difference in the models between the effects of unanticipated and anticipated shocks.

Reading Guide to Chapter 5

Begin

Models of intertemporal decisions usually require methods of optimization beyond the Lagrangian multiplier approach used in static problems. Two frequently used techniques are optimal control and the calculus of variations. Optimal control is a fairly recent generalization of the calculus of variations, and can be used to solve any problem that can be solved by the older technique. However, because some models are more easily formulated as calculus-of-variations problems, it is helpful to understand both techniques. For an applications-orientated approach, a good reference is Kamien and Schwartz (1981). It includes clear, detailed expositions of both methods and has scores of interesting examples. For a more theoretical treatment, see Leitmann (1981).

Interested in using optimal control in stochastic problems?

yes

no

See Bryson and Ho (1975). It also discusses feedback control and optimal filtering methods such as the Kalman filter, that can be used when the values of state variables are uncertain.

The first-order conditions obtained from intertemporal optimization problems almost always involve differential equations, so some background in that area is essential. It is important to understand first order linear differential equations with constant coefficients. Not all models fall into that class, but understanding it is the key to understanding more difficult kinds of differential equations. For an elegant treatment at the intermediate level, see Birkhoff and Rota (1978), particulary chapters 1,3 and 5.

Reading guide to Chapter 5 (continued)

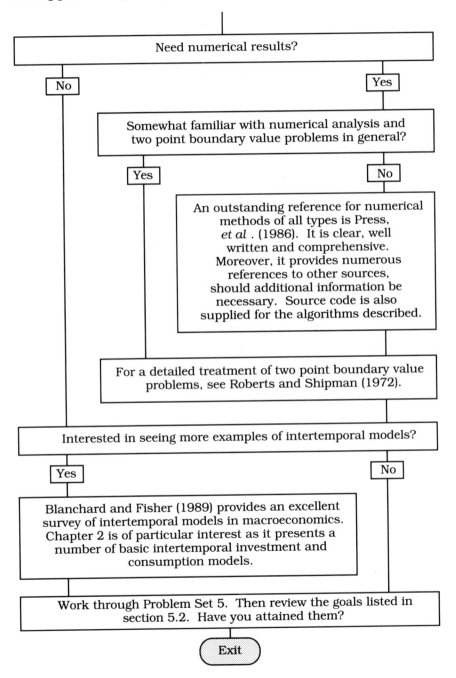

Need numerical results?

No

Yes

Somewhat familiar with numerical analysis and two point boundary value problems in general?

Yes

No

An outstanding reference for numerical methods of all types is Press, *et al* . (1986). It is clear, well written and comprehensive. Moreover, it provides numerous references to other sources, should additional information be necessary. Source code is also supplied for the algorithms described.

For a detailed treatment of two point boundary value problems, see Roberts and Shipman (1972).

Interested in seeing more examples of intertemporal models?

Yes

No

Blanchard and Fisher (1989) provides an excellent survey of intertemporal models in macroeconomics. Chapter 2 is of particular interest as it presents a number of basic intertemporal investment and consumption models.

Work through Problem Set 5. Then review the goals listed in section 5.2. Have you attained them?

Exit

References for Chapter 5

Birkhoff, Garrett, and Gian-Carlo Rota (1978), *Ordinary Differential Equations*, New York: John Wiley and Sons.

Blanchard, Olivier Jean, and Stanley Fischer (1989), *Lectures on Macroeconomics*, Cambridge: MIT Press.

Bryson, Arthur E. Jr, and Yu-Chi Ho (1975), *Applied Optimal Control: Optimization, Estimation and Control*, Washington: Hemisphere.

Fair, Ray C. (1979), "An Analysis of a Macro-Econometric Model with Rational Expectations in the Bond and Stock Markets", *American Economic Review*, 69(4): 539-552.

Fair, Ray C., and John B. Taylor (1983), "Solution and Maximum Likelihood Estimation of Dynamic Nonlinear Rational Expectations Models", *Econometrica*, 51(4): 1169-1185.

Fox, L. (1962), *Numerical Solution of Ordinary and Partial Differential Equations*, London: Addison-Wesley.

Hayashi, F. (1982), "Tobin's Marginal q and Average q: A Neoclassical Interpretation", *Econometrica*, 50(1): 213-224.

Isaacson, E., and H.B. Keller (1966), *Analysis of Numerical Methods*, New York: John Wiley and Sons.

Kamien, Morton I., and Nancy L. Schwartz (1981), *Dynamic Optimization: The Calculus of Variations and Optimal Control in Economics and Management*, Amsterdam: North-Holland.

Leitmann, G. (1981), *The Calculus of Variations and Optimal Control: An Introduction*, New York: Plenum Press.

Lipton, D., J. Poterba, J. Sachs and L. Summers (1982), "Multiple Shooting in Rational Expectations Models", *Econometrica*, 50(2): 1329-1333.

McLaren, Keith (1989), "A Reappraisal of the Neoclassical Approach to Modelling Business Investment", mimeo, Department of Econometrics, Monash University, Clayton, 3168, Australia.

Modigliani, Franco and Merton Miller (1958), "The Cost of Capital, Corporation Finance and the Theory of Investment", *American Economic Review*, 76(3): 297-313.

Press, W., B. Flannery, S. Teukolsky, and W. Vetterling, (1986), *Numerical Recipes*, New York: Cambridge University Press.

Roberts, S.M. and J.S. Shipman (1972), *Two-Point Boundary Value Problems: Shooting Methods*, New York: American Elsevier.

Strang, Gilbert (1980), *Linear Algebra and Its Applications*, New York: Academic Press.

Summers, L. H. (1981), "Taxation and Corporate Investment: A q-Theory Approach", *Brookings Papers on Economic Activity*, 1: 67-127.

Wilcoxen, P.J. (1985), "Numerical Methods for Investment Models with Foresight", *Impact Preliminary Working Paper* No. IP-23, mimeo, 47pp.   Available from Impact Information Officer, Industry Commission, P.O. Box 80, Belconnen ACT 2616, Australia.

Wilcoxen, P.J. (1987), "Investment with Foresight in General Equilibrium", *Impact Project Preliminary Working Paper* No. IP-35, mimeo, 50pp.   Available from Impact Information Officer, Industry Commission, P.O. Box 80, Belconnen ACT 2616, Australia. .

Wilcoxen, P.J. (1988), "The Effects of Environmental Regulation and Energy Prices on U.S. Economic Performance", Ph.D. Thesis, Harvard University.

PROBLEM SET 5

A.   A SIMPLE INTERTEMPORAL MODEL OF INVESTMENT

We begin building our intertemporal model of investment by making two assumptions: first, that each firm chooses its level of investment to maximize its stock-market value, and second, that an arbitrage equation governs the relationship between returns on debt and returns on equities. The first assumption establishes the basis for the firm's investment behavior. The second is needed to define how the firm's market value is determined by asset holders. Together, the two assumptions will allow us to construct the firm's objective function.

Exercise 5.1   *The value of the firm*

In setting up the model we must choose a particular arbitrage equation. In this exercise, we will use:

$$r(t)V(t) = D(t) + V'(t) , \qquad (E5.1.1)$$

where V(t) is the value of the firm at time t, r(t) is the rate of interest on bonds at t, D(t) is the dividend paid by the firm, and V'(t) is the derivative of the firm's value with respect to time[1]. The left side of the equation gives the return that could be earned at time t by holding V dollars of bonds. The right side is the return received by holding the firm's equity and is equal to dividends plus capital gains. At this stage we assume that no taxes are levied on interest, dividends or capital gains. Arbitrage will occur as long as the returns on the two assets differ, ensuring that, in equilibrium, equation (E5.1.1) must hold.

Next, we assume that investors have information allowing them to form expectations about the future path of dividends, and that they believe that the arbitrage condition (E5.1.1) will always hold. Assume that investors at time τ have an information set Ω_τ that leads them to expect the path of dividends at all future times $t \geq \tau$ up to an arbitrary time horizon at T to be given by a function $D(t;\Omega_\tau)$. That is, $D(t;\Omega_\tau)$ is the dividend expected for time t given information set Ω_τ. Similarly, assume that they expect the value of the firm at time T to be $V(T;\Omega_\tau)$.[2]

(a)   Derive an expression for $V(\tau;\Omega_\tau)$, the expected value of the firm at τ given information Ω_τ.

(b)   Unfortunately, for most points in the future, we do not know *a priori* what investors expect the firm's value to be, i.e., we do not have an appropriate value of $V(T;\Omega_\tau)$. One solution, however, is to assume that $V(T;\Omega_\tau)$ remains bounded as T→∞. Under this assumption, derive an expression for $V(\tau;\Omega_\tau)$ which does not involve $V(T;\Omega_\tau)$.

Answer to Exercise 5.1

(a)   From (E5.1.1) we have

$$V'(t) - r(t)V(t) = -D(t) .$$

(E5.1.2)

When r is constant[3], we can multiply both sides of (E5.1.2) by an integrating factor, e^{-rt}, producing the following:

$$\left(V'(t) - rV(t)\right) e^{-rt} = -D(t)e^{-rt} .$$

(E5.1.3)

---

1   For typographical convenience we will denote time derivatives using the prime symbol (') rather than the usual dot.

2   In the remainder of the chapter, the values of variables in future periods will always be expectations based on an information set Ω_τ. To keep our notation simple, we will often suppress Ω_τ and write, for example, $V(t;\Omega_\tau)$ as $V(t)$.

3   When r is not constant, the integrating factor becomes more complicated; for this model it would be $exp(-\int^t r(v)dv)$. However, none of the subsequent results would change significantly.

The left side of (E5.1.3) is the differential of the product of V and the integrating factor. Hence, the equation can be rewritten as:

$$\frac{d(\,V(t)e^{-rt}\,)}{dt} = -D(t)e^{-rt} . \tag{E5.1.4}$$

Equation (E5.1.4) shows how the value of the firm must change over time if the arbitrage equation is to hold. Introducing investors' expectations and integrating both sides of (E5.1.4) from τ to T (and rearranging slightly) gives:

$$V(\tau;\Omega_\tau) = V(T;\Omega_\tau)e^{-r(T-\tau)} + \int_\tau^T D(t;\Omega_\tau)e^{-r(t-\tau)}\, dt . \tag{E5.1.5}$$

If we let τ be the present ("today"), then the left term in (E5.1.5), $V(\tau;\Omega_\tau)$, is the value of the firm today, given today's information. $V(T;\Omega_\tau)$ is the expected value of the firm at time T given information available today. Hence, the first term on the right side is the present value today of owning the firm at T. Finally, the rightmost term is the present value of the dividends expected to be paid between τ and T. Thus, equation (E5.1.5) shows the value of the firm today as the present value of owning it at T plus the present value of the dividends it is expected to pay between τ and T.

(b) Observe that when T goes to infinity, the middle term in (E5.1.5) becomes:

$$\lim_{T \to \infty} V(T;\Omega_\tau)e^{-r(T-\tau)} . \tag{E5.1.6}$$

As long as $V(T;\Omega_\tau)$ remains bounded as T→∞, (E5.1.6) will be zero. Thus, if V remains bounded for all time, the middle term in (E5.1.6) can be dropped from the equation. In fact, (E5.1.6) will be zero under the more general condition that as T goes to infinity, the rate of growth of V is strictly less than the interest rate. That is, (E5.1.6) will be zero as long as:[4]

$$\lim_{T \to \infty} \frac{V'(T;\Omega_\tau)}{V(T;\Omega_\tau)} < r . \tag{E5.1.7}$$

Thus, if we are willing to assume that (E5.1.7) holds, we can write the value of the firm at time τ as:

$$V(\tau;\Omega_\tau) = \int_\tau^\infty D(t;\Omega_\tau)e^{-r(t-\tau)}\, dt . \tag{E5.1.8}$$

---

4   In fact, the following analysis can also be applied, with slight modifications, when (E5.1.7) holds with equality.

This says that the value of the firm today is the present value of the dividend stream it is expected to pay in the future, given today's information.

Expression (E5.1.7) is known as a transversality condition. It is an assumption made in order to obtain equation (E5.1.8), and is not an implication of the model; there is nothing in the problem we have specified so far that requires (E5.1.7) to hold. However, it has a sensible economic interpretation, and is not an unreasonable assumption. In essence, it rules out Ponzi schemes that go on forever.[5] To see why, notice that if (E5.1.7) is violated, the arbitrage condition can hold only if the firm pays negative dividends. Otherwise, (if dividends were zero or positive) the return on equity would be higher than the return on debt and no one would be willing to hold bonds. This would force the interest rate up until (E5.1.7) held. If the arbitrage equation is to hold, (E5.1.7) can be violated only if investors are willing to pay money into a firm forever without receiving any dividends. Thus, assuming that (E5.1.7) holds rules out infinitely-lived Ponzi schemes.

Exercise 5.2   *Conditions for solving the firm's investment problem*

In Exercise 5.1, we derived an objective function for the firm's investment problem: (E5.1.8) gives the firm's value as the present value of its dividend stream. The next step in setting up the investment problem is to specify how dividends depend on the firm's choice variables. We will also introduce some taxes.

We assume that the firm pays out everything it earns except what it uses for investment. In addition, we assume that all investment is internally financed: the firm does not issue new debt or equity to pay for investment.[6] Under these assumptions, pre-tax dividends are equal to the difference between the firm's revenue and the total of its variable costs and its investment costs. To put this symbolically, if K is a vector of capital stocks, L is a vector of variable inputs, I is a vector of gross investments in the capital stocks and P is a vector of prices and wages, pre-tax dividends are given by some function D(K,L,I,P). We assume that D is additively separable into a short-run profit function and an

---

5   Ponzi schemes take their name from Charles Ponzi who perpetrated a famous chain letter swindle in the 1920s. Today the term is used for any pyramid scheme that operates by continually drawing in new people at the bottom.

6   Introducing other means of finance, such as corporate bonds or new share issues, alters the problem relatively little. In fact, the financial decision makes no difference at all if capital markets are perfect. This is a consequence of the Modigliani-Miller theorem, first described in Modigliani and Miller (1958). Blanchard and Fischer (1989, chapter 6) provides a discussion of this point.

investment-cost function.[7] The short-run profit (or earnings) function (E) gives the profit on a particular vector of capital stocks after variable inputs are chosen optimally. Using C to represent the investment-cost function, pre-tax dividends can be written as:

$$D = \left(E(K,P) - C(I,P)\right). \tag{E5.2.1}$$

We will assume there is no sign constraint on dividends (or that if there is one, it is never binding). That is, we will not prohibit the firm from spending more on investment than it earns at a particular date. For this exercise, we will assume that a tax is levied on dividends at the *ad valorem* rate T^d but that there are no taxes on interest or capital gains.

We can now set up the firm's investment problem. Inserting (E5.2.1) into (E5.1.8) and including the tax term, gives us the firm's objective function. In addition, the firm is subject to an accumulation constraint which specifies how the capital stock evolves as a consequence of the firm's investment. We make the usual assumption that the time derivative of the capital stock is given by the difference between gross investment and depreciation. Thus, the firm's investment problem at time τ is to choose a path of investment, I(t) for $t \geq \tau$, that solves:[8]

$$\max \int_{\tau}^{\infty} \left(E(K,P) - C(I,P)\right)(1-T^d)e^{-r(t-\tau)}\, dt \, ,$$

subject to

$$K' = I - \delta K \, , \tag{E5.2.2}$$

where δ is the rate of depreciation which we assume is positive[9].

Show that the necessary conditions for the solution of problem (E5.2.2) are:

$$\lambda = \frac{\partial C}{\partial I}(1-T^d) \, , \tag{E5.2.3}$$

$$\lambda' = (r+\delta)\lambda - \frac{\partial E}{\partial K}(1-T^d) \, , \tag{E5.2.4}$$

and

$$I - \delta K = K' \, , \tag{E5.2.5}$$

where λ is a multiplier. What is the interpretation of the multiplier?

---

7   Formally, we have assumed that the short-run variable input decision is separable from the long-run decision on investment, and also that the capital stock does not enter the investment-cost function.

8   In writing the problem this way we have implicitly assumed that any constraint on the sign of investment would not be binding. Moreover, we have also ignored certain boundary conditions (such as the initial capital stock) which constrain the firm. We will discuss the boundary conditions in detail in Exercise 5.4.

9   See Exercise 5.4 (c).

Answer to Exercise 5.2

Problem (E5.2.2) can be solved using the method of optimal control (Kamien and Schwartz, 1981) in the following way. The problem has the form:

$$\max \int f(s,c,t) \, dt \ ,$$

subject to

$$s' = g(s,c,t) \ ,$$

where s and c are variables and t indicates time. It is customary to refer to s as the problem's "state variable" and c as its "control variable". In problem (E5.2.2), the state variable is the capital stock (K) and the control variable is the rate of investment (I). To find necessary conditions for an optimum, we first form the problem's Hamiltonian function, H:

$$H = f(s,c,t) + \Lambda(t)g(s,c,t) \ ,$$

where $\Lambda(t)$ is a multiplier (also called a costate variable) much like the Lagrangian multiplier of static problems.[10] Then necessary conditions for a solution of the optimization problem are:

$$\frac{\partial H}{\partial c} = 0, \qquad \frac{\partial H}{\partial s} = -\Lambda', \qquad \frac{\partial H}{\partial \Lambda} = s' \ .$$

To apply these conditions in our current problem, we start by constructing the Hamiltonian for (E5.2.2):

$$H = (E-C)(1-T^d)e^{-r(t-\tau)} + \Lambda(I-\delta K) \ . \tag{E5.2.6}$$

Thus, the necessary conditions for optimality are:

$$\frac{\partial H}{\partial I} = 0 \ , \tag{E5.2.7}$$

$$\frac{\partial H}{\partial K} = -\Lambda' \ , \tag{E5.2.8}$$

$$\frac{\partial H}{\partial \Lambda} = K' \ . \tag{E5.2.9}$$

Differentiating (E5.2.6) as required by (E5.2.7) - (E5.2.9) produces the first-order conditions for the problem:

$$-\frac{\partial C}{\partial I}(1-T^d)e^{-r(t-\tau)} + \Lambda = 0 \ , \tag{E5.2.10}$$

$$-\frac{\partial E}{\partial K}(1-T^d)e^{-r(t-\tau)} + \delta\Lambda = \Lambda' \ , \tag{E5.2.11}$$

and (E5.2.5).

---

[10]   Unlike the static case, however, a dynamic optimization problem will have a whole sequence of multipliers, one for each point in time. Hence, Λ is a function of t.

For convenience, we can introduce a new function, $\lambda(t)$, which is defined by:

$$\Lambda(t) = \lambda(t) e^{-r(t-\tau)} . \tag{E5.2.12}$$

Using this to eliminate Λ from (E5.2.10) and (E5.2.11) and rearranging produces (E5.2.3) and (E5.2.4).

Several conclusions can be drawn. Starting with (E5.2.3), if we assume that investment costs are a continuous, strictly convex function of I (so that C_I and C_{II} are positive), then we know from the implicit function theorem that there must be an inverse function F such that:

$$I = F(\lambda, T^d, P) . \tag{E5.2.13}$$

Thus, (E5.2.3) determines the level of investment as an implicit function of λ: if λ were known, I could be calculated from (E5.2.13).[11]

Equation (E5.2.4) on the other hand is a first-order differential equation in λ which does not depend on I. It can be solved using the method of integrating factors described above for the arbitrage equation.[12] In this case, the resulting expression is:

$$\lambda(t) = \int_t^{\infty} \frac{\partial E}{\partial K} (1 - T^d) e^{-(r+\delta)(s-t)} ds. \tag{E5.2.14}$$

Equation (E5.2.14) can be used to interpret λ. It shows that λ is the present value at time t of the additional future post-tax earnings which would be generated by an extra unit of capital received at time t. That is, (E5.2.14) shows that λ is the stock market value of an extra unit of capital.

Exercise 5.3   *Earnings functions and investment-cost functions*

The next step in building the investment model is to derive the earnings and investment-cost functions for a firm with a particular technology.

---

11   This property has spawned dozens of empirical papers. Under conditions derived in Hayashi (1982), λ can be linked to stock market data, and hence can be observed. (This will be discussed in Exercise 5.8). Thus, if λ can be taken to be exogenous, choosing a particular functional form for C allows the adjustment cost model to be tested econometrically using only the first of the necessary conditions, in this case the rewritten expression (E5.2.3); one such example is Summers (1981). What is often overlooked in these papers, however, is that since λ and I are simultaneously determined, it is inappropriate to assume that λ is exogenous. See McLaren (1989) for a more complete discussion.

12   Here we assume that $\lambda(T) e^{-(r+\delta)(T-t)}$ goes to zero as T goes to infinity.

(a)   Suppose the firm's output is produced according to a constant-returns-to-scale Cobb-Douglas function of labor and capital:

$$q = L^{\varepsilon}K^{1-\varepsilon} . \qquad (E5.3.1)$$

In the short run, the capital stock is fixed. Derive the firm's earnings function, E(K,P).

(b)   Assume that new capital goods have to be installed before they can be used in production. Each firm produces its own installed capital goods by buying raw capital goods and hiring workers to install them. Raw capital goods and installation services have to be combined in fixed proportions, i.e., the production functions for installed capital goods are of the following form:

$$I \;=\; \min \{X_k, S\} , \qquad (E5.3.2)$$

where X_k is the quantity of raw capital goods, and S is a measure of installation services. Next, assume that S is produced from labor as follows:

$$S \;=\; (L^i/\theta)^{1/2} , \qquad (E5.3.3)$$

where L^i is the labor hired for installation and θ is a positive parameter. If the firm chooses X_k and L^i to minimize the total cost of attaining any particular level of I, what is its investment-cost function, C(I,P)?   What are the signs of its first two derivatives with respect to the level of investment?

(c)   Insert the earnings function and the investment-cost function derived in (a) and (b) into conditions (E5.2.3) – (E5.2.5) to produce the necessary conditions for the solution of the investment problem under conditions (E5.3.1) – (E5.3.3).

(d)   Solve the conditions derived in (c) for the equations of motion characterising the firm's investment problem, i.e., find a pair of differential equations in λ and K that are necessary conditions for the solution of the investment problem under (E5.3.1) – (E5.3.3)

Answer to Exercise 5.3

(a)   The firm chooses its labor input and its output to maximize the difference between its revenue and its variable costs. That is, it solves the following problem:

$$\max \quad (pq - wL),$$

subject to

$$q \;=\; L^{\varepsilon}K^{1-\varepsilon} . \qquad (E5.3.4)$$

The earnings function E can be found by inserting the optimal labor input and optimal output into the maximand. The result is :

$$E(K,P) \;\; = \;\; \left(\frac{1-\varepsilon}{\varepsilon}\right)\left(\frac{\varepsilon p}{w}\right)^{1/(1-\varepsilon)} wK \;. \tag{E5.3.5}$$

For convenience, we can define a function β which captures the price and wage effects, so (E5.3.5) can be rewritten as:

$$E(K,P) = \beta(P)K \;, \tag{E5.3.6}$$

where P is a vector of wages and prices. The function $\beta(P)$, which gives the short-run return on a unit of capital, can be thought of as the rental price of the capital stock. We will often refer to earnings functions that are linear in K as having constant returns to scale.

(b) The total cost of investment is the expenditure on raw capital goods plus the cost of labor for installation. If the firm chooses X_k and L^i to minimize the cost of attaining any particular level of I, the investment cost function is :

$$C(I,P) \;\; = \;\; P_k I \;+\; \theta w I^2 \;. \tag{E5.3.7}$$

As long as θ and I are greater than zero, C(I,P) in (E5.3.7) is positive as are its first two derivatives. This means that investment is costly, and that its marginal cost is positive and increases as I rises. That is, there are costs of adjustment in investment.

(c) The conditions derived by insertion of (E5.3.6) and (E5.3.7) into (E5.2.3) – (E5.2.5) are:

$$\lambda \;\; = \;\; (P_k + 2w\theta I) \; (1-T^d) \;, \tag{E5.3.8}$$

$$\lambda' \;\; = \;\; (r + \delta)\lambda - \beta(P) \; (1-T^d) \;, \tag{E5.3.9}$$

and

$$K' \;\; = \;\; I - \delta K \;. \tag{E5.3.10}$$

(d) (E5.3.8) can be solved for the optimal level of investment given a value of λ:

$$I \;\; = \;\; \frac{1}{2w\theta}\left(\frac{\lambda}{1-T^d} - P_k\right). \tag{E5.3.11}$$

Equation (E5.3.11) can be used to eliminate I from (E5.3.10), producing a final pair of differential equations in λ and K: (E5.3.9) and

$$K' \;\; = \;\; \frac{\lambda}{2w\theta(1-T^d)} - \delta K - \frac{P_k}{2w\theta}\;. \tag{E5.3.12}$$

Equations (E5.3.9) and (E5.3.12) characterize the solution to the firm's investment problem. Solving them simultaneously produces paths of λ and K that are consistent with the necessary conditions (E5.3.8)–(E5.3.10).

Exercise 5.4   *Graphical analysis*

Ideally we would like to solve differential equations (E5.3.9) and (E5.3.12) for the time paths of λ and K, insert the resulting λ into (E5.3.11), and solve for the path of investment over time. However, some of the terms in (E5.3.9) and (E5.3.12) such as tax rates, can be arbitrary functions of time. That means that (E5.3.9) and (E5.3.12) must be solved explicitly for each policy to be modeled. For most policies, it will be difficult or impossible to solve the equations analytically, hence numerical methods must be used to obtain explicit results for investment. On the other hand, (E5.3.9), (E5.3.11) and (E5.3.12) do contain all relevant economic information about the solution, albeit implicitly. This makes it possible to explore many properties of the model without solving for the explicit path of investment. In this exercise, you will discover how such an analysis might proceed. The methods we use are routine analytical tools in the study of differential equations and can be found in textbooks such as Birkhoff and Rota (1978).

(a)   Suppose that the exogenous variables in (E5.3.9) and (E5.3.12) eventually settle down to stable values P^{ss}, Td^{ss}, w^{ss} and P^{ss}_k. Find equations for the corresponding steady-state values (λ^{ss} and K^{ss}) of the endogenous variables. What is the equation for the steady-state level of investment?

(b)   Using the steady-state equations derived in (a), find the effects on the steady-state of increases in the dividend tax (Td^{ss}), the price of capital (P^{ss}_k), the output price (p^{ss}) and the wage rate (w^{ss}).

(c)   Knowing how the steady state responds to changes in the exogenous variables is helpful, but it does not provide any information about the model's dynamic behavior. For that, another tool can be used: the Poincaré phase plane. A phase plane is a two-dimensional graph of a model's dynamic behavior that is constructed in the following way. Two of the model's variables are chosen to be axes. Usually these will be the two variables of most dynamic interest; in the investment model above, they would be λ and K. Then, given the values of the exogenous variables, for each point in the plane, the time derivatives of the two variables are evaluated. Again using the investment model as an example, these would be λ' and K'. Together, these derivatives define a vector which indicates the direction in which the system would move if it ever happened to reach that point. Thus, by using the finished phase plane, it is possible to trace out the complete trajectory of the system given initial values of the dynamic variables. But it would be a tedious, if straightforward, process: start at the given point, evaluate the derivatives, take a small step in the indicated direction, and repeat. As a practical matter, computing the derivatives of the dynamic variables at all points in the plane usually is unnecessary. Most of the details of the model's dynamic behaviour can be discovered by plotting the loci at which the derivatives of the dynamic variables are zero. Plot these loci in a phase plane for the investment model developed in Exercises 5.1–5.3.

(d)   The loci plotted in the phase diagram (Figure E5.4.1) in (c) allow the model's dynamic behavior to be inferred without solving for the system's direction of motion at every point in the plane. The loci divide the plane into four regions, marked I–IV in Figure E5.4.1. In each of these regions plot arrows indicating the directions in which λ and K would move from an arbitrary point in the region.

(e)   What will be the dynamic paths of the model from different points in the phase plane? Are there any stable paths, i.e., dynamic paths which lead to the steady state?

(f)   At least near the steady state, most interesting economic models possess a characteristic known as "saddle-path stability" which guarantees uniqueness of the stable path. This uniqueness turns out to be essential in many models because it allows the transversality condition discussed in Exercise 5.1 (b) to be used to tie down the value of the firm immediately after a change in the information set Ω_τ. If there were many paths leading to the steady state, the transversality condition alone would not be enough to determine the value of the firm at an earlier point in time. Why not?

(g)   Showing that a particular model has a unique stable path is a fairly technical exercise in linear algebra and differential equations. Can you sketch how it can be done? (The material in this exercise is not needed to understand the rest of the chapter. If you are not comfortable with differential equations, we suggest you skip to Exercise 5.5.)

Answer to Exercise 5.4

(a)   The difficult integration required to solve (E5.3.9) and (E5.3.12) becomes easy when the model reaches the steady state.   If the exogenous variables have settled down to stable values P^{ss}, $T^{d\,ss}$, w^{ss} and P_k^{ss} we can find the steady state corresponding to these by setting λ' and K' to zero in (E5.3.9) and (E5.3.12) and solving the equations simultaneously. This produces:

$$\lambda^{ss} \;=\; \beta(P^{ss})\left(\frac{1-T^{d\,ss}}{r+\delta}\right), \tag{E5.4.1}$$

$$K^{ss} \;=\; \frac{1}{2\theta\delta w^{ss}}\left(\frac{\beta(P^{ss})}{r+\delta} - P_k^{ss}\right). \tag{E5.4.2}$$

Steady-state investment can be found by inserting (E5.4.1) into (E5.3.11). As might be expected, the result confirms that

$$I^{ss} = \delta K^{ss}. \tag{E5.4.3}$$

(b)   Equations (E5.4.1) and (E5.4.2) can be used to examine the effects of different shocks on the model's steady state. This can be accomplished most easily by total differentiation of both expressions with respect to prices and taxes:

$$d\lambda^{ss} \;=\; \left(\frac{1-T^{d\,ss}}{r+\delta}\right) d\beta \;-\; \frac{\beta(P^{ss})}{r+\delta}\,dT^{d\,ss}, \tag{E5.4.4}$$

$$dK^{ss} = \frac{d\beta}{2\theta\delta(r+\delta)w^{ss}} - \frac{1}{2\theta\delta(w^{ss})^2}\left(\frac{\beta(P^{ss})}{r+\delta}-P_k^{ss}\right)dw^{ss} - \frac{1}{2w^{ss}\theta\delta}dP_k^{ss}, \tag{E5.4.5}$$

From (E5.4.4) and (E5.4.5) we can see what happens when one of the model's exogenous variables changes. For example, if the dividend tax, $T^{d\,ss}$, were to rise, steady-state λ would fall, while the capital stock would be unchanged. Capital is unaffected because T^d is a pure profits tax in the long run, falling only on profits and not affecting any decisions at the margin. In contrast, if the price of capital, P_k^{ss}, were to rise, the steady-state capital stock would fall while λ^{ss} would be unchanged. λ^{ss}, which is the present value of future earnings on an additional unit of capital, is not affected by a change in the cost of new capital goods, P_k. When the price of capital increases with no accompanying rise in λ, the capital stock must fall.   Finally, changes in the prices and wages embodied in vector P also affect λ and K. For example, from (E5.3.5) and (E5.3.6) it can be seen that an increase in the firm's output price would increase β. Hence, it would increase the steady-state values of both λ and K. On the other hand, a rise in the wage rate would lower β and decrease both λ and K. (Notice that the coefficient on dw^{ss} in (E5.4.5) is positive — it is K^{ss}/w^{ss}.)

This sort of analysis can be applied to any model with an explicit steady state or which can be transformed to have a steady state. For example, if the original model did not have a steady state because of exogenous population growth, it could be transformed to a per-capita basis which would then have a steady state. Models which do not themselves have steady states but which can be transformed to have them are often said to attain balanced growth in the long run. Thus, steady-state analysis can be applied both to models with steady states, and to models with long-run balanced growth. Moreover, this is likely to encompass all models with interesting long-run behavior, since any model which does not attain balanced growth asymptotically will eventually exhibit peculiar features (such as negative budget shares in consumption).

(c)   For the axes of the phase diagram of the investment model, we will use λ and K, the variables of most dynamic interest. At the model's steady state, the derivatives of both λ and K are zero. Hence, the system will stay there if it ever gets there. The two loci of points, one where λ' is zero and the other where K' is zero, each include the steady state. These loci divide the plane up into several regions. In each region the derivatives of the dynamic variables have a particular sign, implying that if the system ever enters that region, it will evolve unambiguously in a particular direction. From this it is possible to conclude a great deal about qualitative aspects of the model's dynamics.

We solve for the loci of points for which the time derivatives of λ and K are zero by setting the right sides of (E5.3.9) and (E5.3.12) to zero and totally differentiating with respect to λ and K. This produces equations showing what changes must be made in λ in order to keep λ' and K' at zero when K changes:

$$0 = (r+\delta)d\lambda , \qquad\qquad (E5.4.6)$$

and

$$0 = \frac{1}{2w\theta(1-T^d)} d\lambda - \delta d K . \qquad\qquad (E5.4.7)$$

Thus, the $\lambda'= 0$ locus given by (E5.4.6) is a horizontal line through the steady state. The $K' = 0$ locus given by (E5.4.7) is upward sloping with slope:

$$\frac{d\lambda}{dK} = 2w\theta(1-T^d)\delta . \qquad\qquad (E5.4.8)$$

It also includes the steady state and hence must intersect the $\lambda'= 0$ locus. The loci must look like those plotted in Figure E5.4.1. As we saw

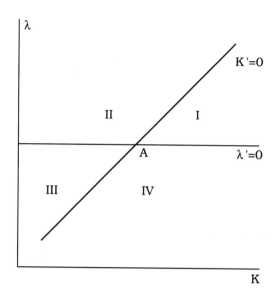

Figure E5.4.1 Constructing a phase diagram: step one

from equations (E5.4.1) and (E5.4.2), the model has a unique steady state, (λ^{SS}, K^{SS}), which is plotted in Figure E5.4.1 as point A.

It is clear from (E5.4.8) that our assumptions that the firm faces adjustment costs ($\theta > 0$) in investment and that capital depreciates ($\delta > 0$) are both crucial to the model. If either θ or δ were zero the $K' = 0$ locus in Figure E5.4.1 would be horizontal and the model would have either no steady state or an infinity of them. The same problem would arise were a 100 per cent dividend tax ($T^d = 1$) to be levied.

(d)   Consider the two loci in turn. By construction, the $\lambda' = 0$ locus contains all points in the plane where λ' is zero. Points not on the locus, therefore, have non-zero λ derivatives. Since both equations in the system are continuous in λ and K, regions of positive and negative λ derivatives must be separated by the $\lambda' = 0$ locus. Thus, the derivative of λ must have the same sign in regions I and II, and must be non-zero. Similarly, λ' in regions III and IV must be nonzero, and of the opposite sign to that of regions I and II.[13] Inserting an arbitrary value of λ greater than λ^{SS} into equation (E5.3.9) reveals that λ' is positive when λ is above its steady-state value. In the same way it can be shown that λ' is negative for values of λ below the steady state. These facts can be

---

13   We assume the $\lambda' = 0$ locus does not lie along a local extremum.

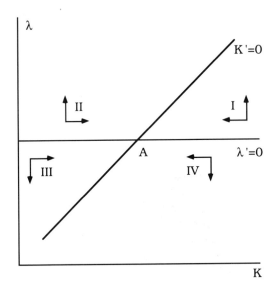

Figure E5.4.2 Constructing a phase diagram: step two

summarized on Figure E5.4.2 by small arrows pointing up in regions I and II, and down in regions III and IV.

The same technique can be applied to the K′= 0 locus. Points to the right of K′=0, in regions I and IV, must have the same sign for K′. Inserting an arbitrary value of K above its steady state into (E5.3.12) shows that K′ must be negative in those regions. Similarly, it can be shown that the derivative of K must be positive in regions II and III. This information can be included in the phase diagram by small arrows pointing to the right in regions II and III and to the left in regions I and IV. The results are shown in Figure E5.4.2.

(e)   Suppose that initially the economy is somewhere in region II. We know from the analysis of (d), as summarized by the arrows drawn in region II, that the system will move upward and to the right as long as it is in that region. This means that λ and K will both grow indefinitely and the system will move farther and farther away from the steady state as long as it remains in region II. The only event which could possibly change the trajectory would be for the system to move into one of the other regions. But no such move is possible. The system cannot move from region II into either region III or region IV because in region II the derivative of λ is strictly positive. Thus, the system can only move upward. On the other hand, since the derivative of K is positive in region II, the model could move to the right, toward quadrant I. However, if the system ever reached the $K'= 0$ locus, it would cease moving to the right. The upward motion of increasing λ would then push the system back into region II.

From this argument, we know that if the system ever entered region II it would move upward and to the right forever. Similar reasoning shows that if the model entered region IV, it would move down and to the left forever. Regions I and III are a little more difficult because it turns out that the system does leave those sectors eventually, but in both cases it is possible to show that it will move farther and farther away from the steady state as time goes on. For example, starting in region I, the system would move into region II — its leftward motion would attenuate as it approached the $K'= 0$ locus, but its upward motion would be enough to carry it into region II. Once in region II it would move upward and to the right forever, as we argued above. Similarly, from region III the system would move into region IV and then downward and to the left forever.

Are there any dynamic paths that lead to the steady state? So far, we have established that no such paths can run through any of the regions I through IV because we have established that once the model enters those regions it will never return to the steady state. However, two possible paths remain: the $\lambda'= 0$ locus and the $K'= 0$ locus. Of these, the $K'= 0$ locus can be ruled out. Provided the system is not at its steady state, λ tends to move away from its steady-state value at each point on the $K'= 0$ locus. On the other hand, along the $\lambda'= 0$ locus the system would eventually converge to the steady state. Thus, only a single path leads to the steady state and it lies along the $\lambda'= 0$ locus. This is illustrated in the finished phase diagram, Figure E5.4.3, by a heavy line with several arrows.

A trajectory leading to the steady state is usually called a "stable path" The stable path plays a crucial role in the dynamic behavior of the model. In most models it is unique. That is, it associates a single value of λ with each value of the capital stock. Moreover, if the system starts at some point on the stable path, as time passes it will remain on the path and move closer to the steady state. If it starts somewhere off the stable path, it never attains the steady state. Together, these properties mean that if the system is to attain the steady state from an arbitrary initial capital stock, there will be a unique value of λ associated with that stock. That is, the marginal value of an additional unit of capital is unique at any particular capital stock. The essence of dynamic modeling is to determine the stable path, and hence the initial value of λ.

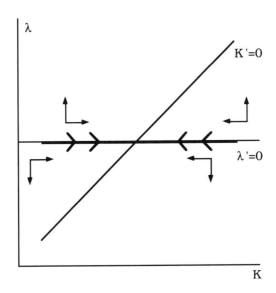

Figure E5.4.3 The finished phase diagram

(f)   To understand the role of the transversality condition more deeply, and to see why it is important that the stable path be unique, it is useful to think about exactly what the equations of motion tell us. As a group, they describe how the model would evolve from any particular point in the (λ, K) plane, given an underlying information set Ω_τ. Thus, if we knew where the system was at a particular moment, and no news had occurred to change Ω_τ, the equations of motion would tell us where the system was going next.   However, at the instant that new information arrives, investors may change their expectations about the firm's prospects. If they do, λ will change discontinuously from its value under the old information set, say $\lambda(\tau;\Omega_\tau^1)$ to a new value, say $\lambda(\tau;\Omega_\tau^2)$.   The path of λ up to the instant at which news arrives provides no guidance about what the value of λ will be just after a shock. Moreover, the size of the jump cannot be determined from the equations of motion alone; an additional piece of information is needed. Formally, one of the problem's boundary conditions is missing.

The role of boundary conditions is to determine the constants of integration that arise in solving (integrating) the model's equations of motion.   If the model consists of two differential equations, two constants of integration will appear and two boundary conditions will be needed. Sometimes these conditions can be derived from fairly obvious facts. In particular, since state variables, such as the capital stock, do not change discontinuously, their values should not change at the instant of the shock. Since the initial post-shock values of state variables should be exactly equal to their values just before the shock, the pre-shock values of state variables provide some of the needed boundary conditions.

Unfortunately, state variables alone do not provide enough information. In the investment model, for instance, two boundary conditions are required but there is only one state variable. Since costate variables, such as λ, can change discontinuously when news arrives and their values before the shock provide no information about the condition of the model just after the shock (i.e., the initial condition for λ is unknown), we must look for another boundary condition.

One possibility is to impose something on the long-run behavior of the model. We may not know the initial value of λ, but we might be willing to assume that in the long run λ will eventually approach its steady-state value. This is another transversality condition like (E5.1.7). (In fact, it is the same condition slightly disguised.) If the stable path is unique, transversality conditions can be used to provide the missing boundary conditions. On the other hand, transversality conditions are inadequate when there are several stable paths leading to the steady state — then steady-state properties alone cannot determine which stable path the model will follow.

To see this, consider Figure E5.4.4 which is a phase diagram for a hypothetical model with a state variable S, a costate variable λ and two stable paths. We can think of this figure as being a picture of the situation immediately after a shock which has left the state variable at S_I, away from its new steady state . With two stable paths, P_1 and P_2, the assumption that λ eventually reaches its steady-state value (the transversality condition) is not sufficient to determine whether the immediate post-shock value of λ will be λ_1 or λ_2. Thus we do not have sufficient information to know whether the system will follow path P_1 or P_2. However, if there is only one stable path, P_1, then the transversality condition does supply the second boundary condition. It implies that the immediate post-shock value of λ is λ_1 and that the system will follow the path P_1. Thus, uniqueness of the stable path is an important property of a model because it allows information about the steady state to be used to determine some of the model's integration constants. If the stable path is unique, there will be a single immediate-post-shock value allowable for each costate variable, making it is possible to determine the dynamic path the system will follow after a shock.

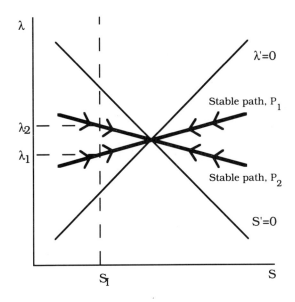

Figure E5.4.4 Phase diagram for hypothetical model with two
stable paths

(g) All models discussed in this chapter, and virtually all rational-expectations models appearing in the literature, have saddle-path stability, i.e., they have unique stable paths. Saddle-path stability holds when the linear form of the model has eigenvalues which are distinct, non-zero and of mixed sign.[14] Hence, to check whether a model has a unique stable path we must solve for its eigenvalues. Suppose that the model is a system of first-order differential equations which can be written in the form:

$$x' = Ax + b , \qquad (E5.4.9)$$

where x is a vector of variables whose time derivatives are given by x', A is a matrix and b is a vector (both A and b may be functions of time). The eigenvalues which we require are those of the matrix A. For example, to see if the model of Exercises 5.1–5.3 has a unique stable path, we would write equations (E5.3.9) and (E5.3.12) as:

---

14 Strictly speaking, these are sufficient conditions for saddle path stability. For a review of the properties of eigenvalues, or of linear algebra in general, see Strang (1980). In this context, we are using "linear" in the differential equations sense only.

$$\begin{bmatrix} \lambda' \\ K' \end{bmatrix} = \begin{bmatrix} r+\delta & 0 \\ \dfrac{1}{2w\theta(1-T^d)} & -\delta \end{bmatrix} \begin{bmatrix} \lambda \\ K \end{bmatrix} + \begin{bmatrix} -\beta(P)(1-T^d) \\ -P_k/2w\theta \end{bmatrix}. \quad (E5.4.10)$$

The eigenvalues of this equation are $r+\delta$ and $-\delta$, which are distinct, non-zero and have mixed signs. The model in Exercises 5.1–5.3, therefore, has the saddle-path property.

To see why the eigenvalues are so important, consider solving (E5.4.9) near the steady state (so that A and b are essentially constant). The first step is to look for a solution to the homogeneous form of the problem in which b is zero:

$$x' = Ax. \quad (E5.4.11)$$

If all of the eigenvalues of A are distinct and non-zero, then any vector x can be written as a linear combination of the eigenvectors of A. Thus, if Γ is a matrix whose columns are the eigenvectors, it must be true that:

$$x = \Gamma c, \quad (E5.4.12)$$

where c is a vector of coefficients. Since Γ is constant near the steady state (because A is constant), differentiating (E5.4.12) with respect to time gives the following:

$$x' = \Gamma c'. \quad (E5.4.13)$$

Substituting (E5.4.12) and (E5.4.13) into (E5.4.11) gives:

$$\Gamma c' = A\Gamma c. \quad (E5.4.14)$$

However, since Γ is composed of the eigenvectors of A, it must be the case that:

$$A\Gamma = \Gamma \psi, \quad (E5.4.15)$$

where ψ is a diagonal matrix of eigenvalues. Inserting (E5.4.15) into (E5.4.14) and multiplying through by the inverse of Γ produces the following:

$$c' = \psi c. \quad (E5.4.16)$$

Thus, the original differential equation can be transformed into (E5.4.16), which is easy to solve: ψ is diagonal, so (E5.4.16) is nothing more than a collection of unrelated differential equations, each of which can be solved by the method of integrating factors. The solution is:

$$c = e^{\psi t}\gamma, \quad (E5.4.17)$$

where $e^{\psi t}$ is the diagonal matrix the ii th component of which is $e^{\psi_{ii}t}$ and γ is a vector of integration constants. Together (E5.4.17) and (E5.4.12) imply that x has the solution:

$$x = \Gamma e^{\psi t}\gamma. \quad (E5.4.18)$$

The complete solution to the original equation (E5.4.9) is the sum of (E5.4.18), which solves the homogeneous equation, and a particular solution to (E5.4.9), such as the steady state. Thus, a final expression for x is the following:

$$x = \Gamma e^{\psi t}\, \gamma + x^{ss}. \qquad\qquad (E5.4.19)$$

Equation (E5.4.19) allows us to infer a great deal about the behavior of the solution from the eigenvalues alone. For example, if all the eigenvalues had positive real parts, then the model would converge to x^{ss} only if every element of γ were zero. A model whose eigenvalues were all positive, therefore, could only reach the steady state if it started out there initially. For this reason, such models are said to be "unstable". On the other hand, if the eigenvalues all had negative real parts, the solution would converge to the steady state from any starting vector. This comes about because the first term on the left in (E5.4.19) will always approach zero as time tends to infinity when the eigenvalues are negative. Models with this property are said to be "globally stable".

Many economic models, however, have a mixture of positive and negative eigenvalues. Since they are neither unstable nor globally stable, such models are often said to be "saddle-path stable". Saddle-path stability means that a model will converge to its steady state from some initial vectors but not from others. In a sense, this is intermediate between the unstable and globally stable cases: an unstable model will only reach the steady state from a single point — the steady state itself — while a globally stable model will get there from any starting point.

To put this more formally, suppose x is a vector of length n in $\mathbf{R}^n$. If all the eigenvalues are distinct, there will be n of them. In general, if m of the eigenvalues have negative real parts, the model will converge to the steady state from an m dimensional subspace of $\mathbf{R}^n$. This means that if we want the system to converge to the steady state, we can only choose m elements of x independently — the other n–m terms will be implied by the model. If all n eigenvalues are positive (m = 0), the model will converge to the steady state from a subspace of dimension 0 — a single point. This is the unstable case discussed above. If all n eigenvalues are negative (m = n), the steady state can be reached from any point in $\mathbf{R}^n$, so the model will be globally stable.

The property of saddle-path stability is a useful one for a model to possess because we usually do not know the initial values of all elements of the vector x. In the model of Exercises 5.1–5.3, for example, we do not know the value of λ immediately after a shock. Since the model is saddle-path stable, however, we know that it can only attain the steady state from certain (λ, K) pairs. Furthermore, because one of the model's two eigenvalues is negative, we know that if we choose a value for either λ or K, the value of the other will be implied. Thus, knowing the initial value of K and requiring that the model eventually attain the steady state is enough (in principle) to let us calculate the value of λ. As you will discover in Exercise 5.9, however, computing λ usually requires numerical integration.

In summary, that a particular model has a unique stable path can be checked by computing the model's eigenvalues and verifying that they are distinct, non-zero and of mixed sign. If the stable path is unique, features of the steady state can be imposed on the solution as boundary conditions. For models with foresight, this is often essential.

Exercise 5.5   *Analyzing experiments*

The phase diagram facilitates qualitative descriptions of the effects of changes in the exogenous variables. It does not provide numerical results. You will investigate numerical analysis in Section B of the problem set.

Intertemporal models deal with complete time paths of variables. In assessing the effects of a change in a tax rate, for example, the entire path of the tax rate over time matters. Experiments with such a model fall into four categories depending on: (1) whether the shock is permanent or temporary, and (2) whether it is announced in advance or implemented immediately. A given shock can have substantially different effects depending on how it is enacted over time. A temporary tax increase, for example, can produce effects which are completely different from the effects of a permanent increase.

All four categories of experiment can be analyzed using phase diagrams. The first step in using the phase plane is to determine how the shock affects the zero-derivative loci. Most shocks will shift one or both of the loci, resulting in a new steady state. The second step is to find the new stable path. Usually this will be straightforward once the new loci have been found. At this point, the post-shock phase diagram is complete. It governs the motion of the system when all of the exogenous variables have their post-shock values. Thus, the overall diagram consists of two superimposed phase planes: one which applies when the exogenous variables have their initial values, and one which applies after the shock.

The remaining step is to trace out on the phase diagram the motion of the system. At the instant the shock occurs, the state variables (K in the model developed in Exercises 5.1–5.4) are fixed and cannot jump. This means that if the economy is ever to get to the new steady state, the costate variables (λ in the model) must jump immediately to the new stable path. Once on the stable path, the economy evolves over time toward the steady state.

(a)   Use a phase diagram to show the effects of an immediate, permanent increase in the dividend tax in the model of Exercises 5.1–5.4. Assume that the model was initially at a steady state.

(b)   Suppose that instead of implementing the tax increase immediately, the government announces that it will occur after three years. Use a phase diagram to show the effects of the announced tax change. Compare the results with those obtained in (a).

(c)   Using a phase diagram, show the effects of an unexpected, immediate, permanent increase in the price of the firm's output. Sketch the paths of the multiplier (λ), investment and the capital stock over time.

(d)   Using a phase diagram, show the effects of a permanent increase in the firm's output price expected to occur in two years. Again, sketch the time paths of the model's variables.

(e)   Use a phase diagram to analyze the effects of an immediate increase in the price of the firm's output which is anticipated by investors (correctly) to last for three years. That is, the price rises immediately and investors believe (correctly) that it will stay high for three years and then fall back to its original value. Sketch the paths of the variables.

(f)   Using a phase diagram, explain the consequences of an unexpected, immediate, permanent fall in the price of capital goods. Sketch the paths of λ, investment and the capital stock over time.

(g)   Use a phase diagram to illustrate what happens if the fall in P_k is anticipated several years in advance. Are the results what you expected?

Answer to Exercise 5.5

(a)   First, consider what happens to the $\lambda'=0$ locus defined by equation (E5.3.9). As T^d rises, the rightmost term in equation (E5.3.9) becomes closer to zero. For λ' to remain zero, therefore, λ must fall. Thus, the $\lambda'=0$ locus must shift downward. The new location of the locus can be found by solving for the new steady-state value of λ. To find the effect of the tax increase on the $K'=0$ locus, we begin with equation (E5.3.12). The increase in T^d causes the leftmost term on the right hand side to rise. For K' to remain zero at constant λ, K must rise. Thus, the $K' = 0$ locus shifts to the right. From (E5.4.9) we see that the tax increase also reduces its slope.

As we noted in Exercise 5.4(b), in this model, the dividend tax does not change the steady-state value of the capital stock. This can be verified by solving for λ^{ss}, inserting it into equation (E5.3.12), and solving for K^{ss}. Thus, the shifts in the two loci caused by an increase in T^d are as indicated in Figure E5.5.1 with the new intersection point directly below the old one.

The movement of the system arising from the increase in T^d is simply that λ jumps down to the new stable path. With the capital stock already at its steady-state level, the jump in λ brings the model instantly to the new steady state. This path is shown in Figure E5.5.2 by a grey arrow.

(b)   The results are different when the shock is anticipated. If, instead of implementing the tax increase immediately, the government announces that it will occur after three years, the initial and final steady states are the same as in the previous case. Hence, the shifts in the zero-derivative loci are the same as Figure E5.5.1. The path of the model over time, however, is more complicated.

When the policy is announced, λ falls part of the way toward its new steady-state value, but not as far as it would if the policy took effect immediately. It stays higher initially because for the three years during which the dividend tax stays at its old value, dividends will not be taxed any more heavily than they were before. However, λ does drop below its original value because the firm will eventually pay lower dividends.

After the drop in λ, the system initially evolves according to the equations of motion associated with the original steady state. The motion of the system depends only on current tax rates. Thus, the system moves down and to the left. It continues to move in that direction until the tax change occurs after year three. At that time, the model becomes governed by the new equations of motion. These have the same form as the original equations, but are evaluated at the new value of T^d. Since the model is required to attain the steady state eventually, it must be on the new stable path when the tax change is implemented in year three. After year three, the system evolves along the stable path toward the new steady state. The path of the model is shown in Figure E5.5.3.

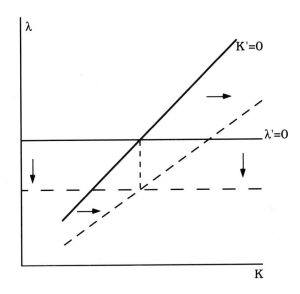

Figure E5.5.1 Effects of a permanent increase in the dividend tax rate: shifting the loci

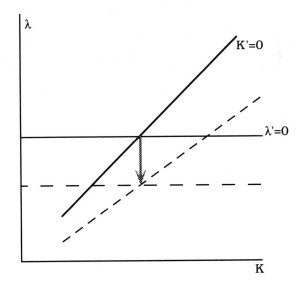

Figure E5.5.2 Effects of an immediate, permanent increase in the dividend tax rate: finding the dynamic path

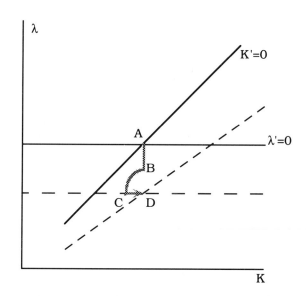

Figure E5.5.3 Effects of an anticipated, permanent increase in the
dividend tax rate: finding the dynamic path

Notice that Figure E5.5.3 shows no jump in λ at the instant when the tax is implemented. Instead, λ evolves smoothly, reaching the new stable path precisely at the moment of implementation. This reflects an important feature of intertemporal models with perfect foresight: there are no windfall gains or losses from the *implementation* of anticipated policies. There can be windfalls associated with the *announcement* of a policy — in this example, λ jumps down at the announcement — but there are no windfalls from events that have been anticipated.

This point can be understood intuitively by thinking about what happens to λ near implementation. Recall from equation (E5.2.14) that λ is the present value of the after-tax earnings of a marginal unit of capital. Once the tax has actually increased, all subsequent earnings are evaluated at the new rate. Shortly before implementation, however, the value of an extra unit of capital is what it will earn after implementation plus a small amount obtained before the tax change. As implementation is approached, this extra amount of earnings becomes smaller and smaller and λ approaches its post-implementation value smoothly.

To demonstrate this mathematically, let the time of implementation be τ and the value of λ at that point be $\lambda(\tau)$. Now consider the value of λ at an instant Δ before implementation. Equation (E5.2.14) can be written:

$$\lambda(\tau-\Delta) = \int_{\tau-\Delta}^{\tau} \frac{\partial E}{\partial K}(1-T^d) e^{-(r+\delta)(s-\tau+\Delta)} \, ds + \lambda(\tau) e^{-(r+\delta)\Delta} . \qquad (E5.5.1)$$

As Δ approaches zero, the first term on the right side of (E5.5.1) approaches zero. (There are no jumps in any of the variables in the expression being integrated.) Thus, $\lambda(\tau-\Delta)$ approaches $\lambda(\tau)$, implying that λ must be continuous at implementation and cannot jump. Notice that this argument does not depend on features of the model such as the form of the earnings or investment-cost functions. It is a general property of perfect-foresight models.

Figure E5.5.3 shows that the capital stock falls during the period between announcement and implementation of the policy. This occurs because firms respond to the policy by paying higher dividends before implementation while the dividend tax is low. Higher dividends limit investment and drive down the capital stock. Once the tax is in place, investment increases, dividends drop and the amount of capital rises. This causes the value of the firm to increase and allows investors to receive part of their return as capital gains.[15] Since the capital gains tax is unchanged (and zero), investors benefit from shifting part of their return from heavily taxed dividends to lightly taxed capital gains.

The difference between the effects of implementing the dividend-tax increase immediately and announcing the change in advance could not have been discovered using a static model. Since it is rare for shocks to the economy to come as a complete surprise, explicit modeling and analysis of announcement effects may be important in understanding the impacts of government policies and of other kinds of shocks.

(c) The phase diagram and time paths of the variables for a surprise, permanent increase in the price of the firm's output are shown in Figure E5.5.4. As shown in the top panel, the $\lambda' = 0$ locus shifts vertically upwards, while the $K' = 0$ locus is unaffected. The increased output price immediately raises the marginal value of additional capital, λ, to its new steady-state level. This causes the system to jump from point A to point B. As shown in the bottom panel, investment jumps to its new steady-state level. With higher investment, the capital stock rises asymptotically toward its new steady-state level at C.

---

15 Refer to the arbitrage condition shown in equation (E5.1.1).

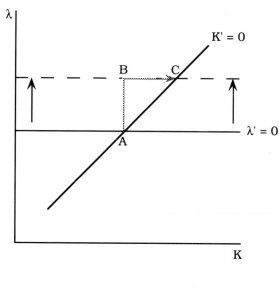

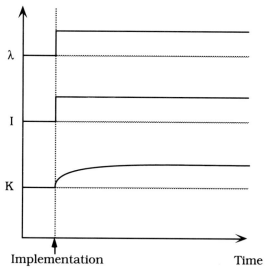

Figure E5.5.4 Effects of a surprise increase in the price of output

(d) The phase diagram and graphs of the dynamic variables for the case of an anticipated permanent increase in the firm's output price are shown in Figure E5.5.5. When news of the price increase first arrives, λ jumps part way toward its new steady-state value. It does not jump all the way, however, because the higher price will not be obtained for two years. In the period between announcement and implementation of the new price, λ rises exponentially toward the new stable path, arriving there just as the price increase occurs. Investment follows the path of λ, jumping upward at the announcement and then rising steadily toward its new steady-state value, which it reaches at the implementation date. The capital stock is drawn upward by the higher level of investment. After investment reaches its new steady state, the capital stock continues to grow, but at a decreasing rate. Over time, it asymptotically approaches its new steady state.

(e) The phase diagram and variable paths for the case of an immediate, temporary price rise are shown in Figure E5.5.6. The temporary increase in the output price leads immediately to an upward jump in λ from point A to B. This occurs because the increased output price raises the returns to capital for a while. In contrast to exercises (c) and (d), the steady-state value of λ is unaffected. It remains at its initial value because eventually the firm's output price returns to its initial level.

After the initial jump, the system moves downward and to the right under the control of the equations of motion holding at the higher price. The reason is that when λ jumps, so does investment. Higher investment leads to growth in the capital stock, moving the system toward the right. At the same time, the remaining period of higher prices becomes steadily shorter, causing λ to fall back toward its initial value. However, as λ falls, so does investment. Eventually, a point is reached where investment just covers depreciation of the higher capital stock. On the phase diagram, that point occurs where the dynamic path crosses the $K' = 0$ locus, as indicated by point C in the figure.

At point C, the system is moving straight down. Investment is just enough to maintain the capital stock, but λ is still declining. Past C, the model begins moving downward and to the left. The value of λ has fallen so much that investment is no longer enough to offset depreciation and the capital stock begins to erode. This continues until the price finally returns to its original value. At that time the system will have reached point D. At D, λ and investment are back to their

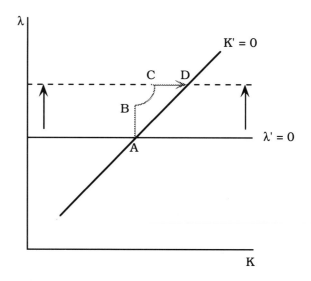

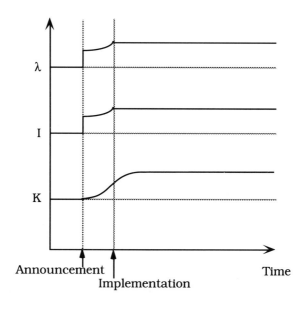

Figure E5.5.5 Effects of an announced increase in the price of output

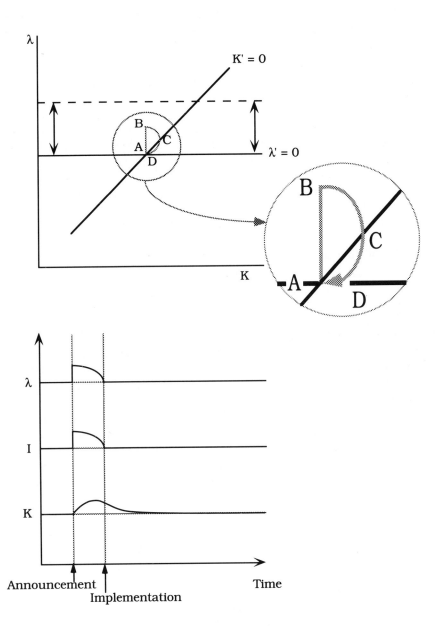

Figure E5.5.6 Effects of a temporary increase in the price of output

original values, but the capital stock is somewhat higher than its steady-state value. Thus, K continues to erode, gradually returning to its initial value.

A feature of this experiment is that the dynamic path crosses the $K'=0$ locus. This demonstrates that the loci do not necessarily confine the model to a particular quadrant. However, as the system crosses a locus, the derivative of the corresponding variable must be zero (by definition of the locus). In this experiment, for example, the derivative of the capital stock at point C must be zero. The dynamic path can only cross the $K'=0$ locus while moving vertically. This feature also allows us to deduce that point D cannot lie to the left of the initial steady state. If it did, the system would have to cross the $K' = 0$ locus a second time. Since that can only occur while the path is moving vertically, λ would have to be rising. However, λ falls continuously after its initial jump. Hence, the dynamic path must intersect the original stable path at or to the right of the original steady state.

(f)   As can be seen from equations (E5.3.12) and (E5.3.9), a fall in the price of capital goods generates a parallel rightward shift in the $K' = 0$ locus and leaves the $\lambda' = 0$ locus unaffected. This is shown in Figure E5.5.7. Thus, λ is already at its new steady-state value and does not jump when the price change occurs. From equation (E5.3.11), the lower price of capital leads to a higher level of investment, even with no change in λ. This, in turn, leads to capital accumulation, causing the system to move gradually from the initial steady state at A to the new steady state at B.

(g)   Knowing about the price decline in advance does not change the firm's behavior in the pre-implementation period. The model remains at the initial steady state until the change actually occurs. After that, it proceeds in the manner described in (f). Thus, the appropriate diagrams are as in Figure E5.5.7 except that in the lower diagram, the announcement time could be marked on the time axis to the left of the implementation time.

At first this result may appear peculiar. Intuitively, it seems as though the firm should be able to gain by postponing some investment just before the price decline and doing more investment later. It is true that the firm will increase its investment when the price fall takes effect. As in (f), investment after the price change proceeds until adjustment costs rise just enough to make the cost of installed capital equal to λ, which is unaffected by the shock. However, because λ is unaffected, investment in the pre-implementation period which would

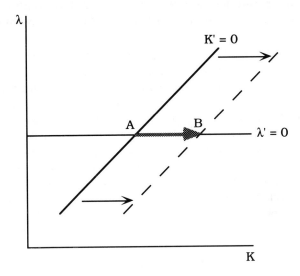

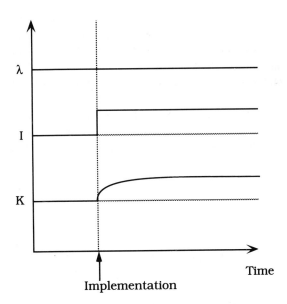

Figure E5.5.7 Effects of a surprise drop in the price of capital
goods

have been profitable had no price change been announced is still profitable after the announcement. Because of adjustment costs, the marginal cost of investment in the new equilibrium after the price change is the same as the marginal cost before the change, i.e., it is equated to the unchanged value of λ.

Exercise 5.6   *Adding more taxes to the investment model*

Now consider an economy in which there are two financial assets: government bonds and equities issued by corporations. Bonds pay a fixed rate of return and there is no inflation. The government levies three taxes: the dividend tax, a tax on interest payments, at the *ad valorem* rate T^i, and a tax on capital gains at the *ad valorem* rate T^c. The earnings (short-run profits) of firms are functions of wages, prices and the capital stock, but not of investment. On the other hand, investment costs depend on wages, prices and investment, but not on the capital stock. Firms take wages, prices, tax rates and the interest rate to be exogenous. Thus, this economy is similar to that of Exercises 5.1–5.3, except that there are two additional taxes.

(a)   Write the arbitrage equation for this economy and explain what it means. Using the arbitrage equation, solve for an explicit expression for the value of the firm in terms of the earnings and investment cost functions and the model's exogenous variables. What transversality equation did you use? How should it be interpreted?

(b)   Assuming that the firm chooses investment to maximize its stock-market value, write down the investment problem, form the Hamiltonian, and find the first-order conditions (i.e., necessary conditions for an optimum derived by differentiating the Hamiltonian).

(c)   Suppose that the earnings function has the form (E5.3.6) and that the investment-cost function is:

$$C = P_k I^2/2\theta, \tag{E5.6.1}$$

giving:

$$D(K(s),I(s),P(s)) = \beta(P(s))K(s) - P_k(s)I^2(s)/2\theta, \tag{E5.6.2}$$

where, as in Exercise 5.3, P_k is the price of capital goods, I is the level of gross investment and θ is a positive parameter. Using this information and the results obtained in (b), show that the model's equations of motion are :

$$\lambda' = \left(r\,\frac{1-T^i}{1-T^c} + \delta \right)\lambda - \beta(P)\,\frac{1-T^d}{1-T^c}, \tag{E5.6.3}$$

and

$$K' = \frac{\lambda\theta}{P_k} \left(\frac{1-T^c}{1-T^d}\right) - \delta K .$$
(E5.6.4)

(d)   Construct a phase diagram for the model.

(e)   Assuming that the model is initially at a steady state, use a phase diagram to analyze the effects of an unexpected, permanent decrease in the capital gains tax. Show the initial and final steady states and the transition path. Sketch the paths of the multiplier (λ, the costate variable), investment and the capital stock over time and interpret the solution.

(f)   Use a phase diagram to illustrate the effects of a permanent decrease in the capital gains tax announced several years in advance. Sketch the paths of the multiplier, investment and the capital stock and interpret the solution. Does anticipation of the shock lead to any interesting or perverse effects?

(g)   Finally, suppose that the government surprises investors with a temporary drop in the capital gains tax. The tax is lowered immediately, kept low for several years, and then returned to its original level. Investors understand the new policy, and realize that the tax change is temporary. Analyze this shock using a phase diagram.

Answer to Exercise 5.6

(a)   Arbitrage will equate after-tax returns on bonds and equity, implying that in equilibrium:

$$(1-T^i)rV = D(1-T^d) + V'(1-T^c) .$$
(E5.6.5)

The left side of (E5.6.5) is the after-tax return on V dollars of bonds, while the right side is the after-tax return on V dollars of equity.

From (E5.6.5) we obtain:

$$V' - \frac{1-T^i}{1-T^c} rV = -\frac{1-T^d}{1-T^c} D .$$
(E5.6.6)

This form suggests that the equation can be solved using the integrating factor $e^{-R(0,t)}$, where $R(a,b)$ is defined by:

$$R(a,b) = \int_a^b r(q) \frac{1-T^i(q)}{1-T^c(q)} dq .$$
(E5.6.7)

Expression (E5.6.7) takes the form of an integral because the two tax rates (and the interest rate) are not necessarily constant over time. If they were, (E5.6.7) would simplify to:

$$R(a,b) = r \frac{1-T^i}{1-T^c} (b-a) .$$

(E5.6.8)

On recognizing that:

$$\left(V'(s) - \frac{1-T^i(s)}{1-T^c(s)} r(s)V(s)\right) e^{-R(0,s)} = \frac{d(V(s)e^{-R(0,s)})}{ds} ,$$

(E5.6.9)

we find from (E5.6.6) that:

$$\lim_{T \to \infty} V(T)e^{-R(0,T)} - V(t)e^{-R(0,t)} = -\int_t^\infty \frac{1-T^d(s)}{1-T^c(s)} D(K(s),I(s),P(s))e^{-R(0,s)}ds.$$

(E5.6.10)

We assume that the limit in the left-most term of (E5.6.10) is zero. This transversality condition will be valid as long as the rate of growth of the value of the firm is less than the tax-adjusted interest rate as time tends toward infinity. The best way to interpret it is to look at what behavior it rules out. If the value of the firm were to grow at a rate higher than the interest rate, for the arbitrage condition (E5.6.5) to hold, the firm would have to pay *negative* dividends. Thus, the transversality condition rules out firms whose values grow more rapidly than the tax-adjusted interest rate forever even though they pay negative dividends.

After applying the transversality condition and rearranging slightly, we obtain an explicit equation for the value of the firm at any time t:

$$V(t) = \int_t^\infty \frac{1-T^d(s)}{1-T^c(s)} D((K(s),I(s),P(s))e^{-R(t,s)}ds .$$

(E5.6.11)

Note that use has been made of the following

$$e^{-R(0,s)} \times e^{R(0,t)} = e^{-R(t,s)} ,$$

(E5.6.12)

which can be shown to be true from the definition of R(a,b).

(b)   From (E5.6.11) and the capital-accumulation constraint, the firm's problem at time t can be stated as follows:

$$\max \int_t^\infty \frac{1-T^d}{1-T^c} D((K(s),I(s),P(s))e^{-R(t,s)}ds ,$$

(E5.6.13)

subject to

$$K' = I - \delta K .$$

(E5.6.14)

The Hamiltonian for this problem is:

$$H = \frac{1-T^d}{1-T^c} De^{-R(t,s)} + \Lambda(I-\delta K) .$$

(E5.6.15)

The first-order conditions obtained by differentiation are:

$$\frac{\partial H}{\partial I} = \frac{\partial D}{\partial I} \left(\frac{1-T^d}{1-T^c}\right) e^{-R(t,s)} + \Lambda = 0 , \qquad (E5.6.16)$$

$$\frac{\partial H}{\partial K} = \frac{\partial D}{\partial K} \left(\frac{1-T^d}{1-T^c}\right) e^{-R(t,s)} - \delta\Lambda = -\Lambda' \qquad (E5.6.17)$$

and

$$\frac{\partial H}{\partial \Lambda} = I - \delta K = K' . \qquad (E5.6.18)$$

It is convenient to introduce the following transformation of Λ to eliminate the discount factors:

$$\Lambda(s) = \lambda(s) e^{-R(t,s)} . \qquad (E5.6.19)$$

Differentiating this with respect to future time s gives:

$$\Lambda'(s) = \left(\lambda'(s) - r(s)\frac{1-T^i(s)}{1-T^c(s)}\lambda(s) \right) e^{-R(t,s)} . \qquad (E5.6.20)$$

Inserting (E5.6.19) and (E5.6.20) into (E5.6.16) and (E5.6.17) gives:

$$\frac{\partial D}{\partial I} \left(\frac{1-T^d}{1-T^c}\right) + \lambda = 0 , \qquad (E5.6.21)$$

$$\frac{\partial D}{\partial K} \left(\frac{1-T^d}{1-T^c}\right) - \delta\lambda = -\lambda' + r \frac{1-T^i}{1-T^c} \lambda . \qquad (E5.6.22)$$

Equations (E5.6.18), (E5.6.21) and (E5.6.22) are the model's first-order conditions.

(c)   From (E5.6.2) we have

$$\frac{\partial D}{\partial I} = -\frac{P_k I}{\theta} , \qquad (E5.6.23)$$

and

$$\frac{\partial D}{\partial K} = \beta(P) . \qquad (E5.6.24)$$

Inserting these into (E5.6.21) and (E5.6.22), and rearranging produces:

$$\lambda = \frac{P_k I}{\theta} \left(\frac{1-T^d}{1-T^c}\right) \qquad (E5.6.25)$$

and (E5.6.3). Equation (E5.6.25) can be solved for investment as a function of K and λ:

$$I = \frac{\lambda\theta}{P_k} \left(\frac{1-T^c}{1-T^d}\right). \qquad (E5.6.26)$$

Equation (E5.6.3) is one of the model's equations of motion. By using (E5.6.26) to eliminate investment from (E5.6.14) we can confirm that (E5.6.4) is the other equation of motion.

(d)   The phase diagram for the model is shown in Figure E5.6.1. It is very similar to the phase diagram derived in Exercise 5.4(c)–(e), except that the loci are in different positions due to the additional taxes. The position of the $\lambda' = 0$ locus can be established by setting λ' in (E5.6.3) to zero and solving for λ, yielding:

$$\lambda = \frac{\beta(P)\left(\dfrac{1-T^d}{1-T^c}\right)}{\left(r\dfrac{1-T^i}{1-T^c}+\delta\right)} . \qquad (E5.6.27)$$

Setting K' in (E5.6.4) to zero yields:

$$\lambda = \frac{\delta P_k}{\theta}\left(\frac{1-T^d}{1-T^c}\right) K. \qquad (E5.6.28)$$

This confirms that the $K' = 0$ locus is an upward sloping ray through the origin. Its slope is:

$$\frac{d\lambda}{dK} = \frac{\delta P_k}{\theta}\left(\frac{1-T^d}{1-T^c}\right). \qquad (E5.6.29)$$

(e)   The phase diagram and the intertemporal paths of capital, the multiplier (λ) and investment for the case of an unexpected, permanent decline in the capital gains tax are shown in Figure E5.6.2. Under this shock, the $\lambda' = 0$ locus falls. A given drop in T^c reduces the numerator of the right side of (E5.6.27) by a greater proportion than it reduces the denominator. At the same time, the $K' = 0$ locus rotates to the right, i.e., the drop in T^c reduces the slope (E5.6.29). From a comparison of (E5.6.28) and (E5.6.27) it is clear that, at the initial steady-state capital stock, the fall in λ on the $K' = 0$ locus is greater than the fall in λ on the $\lambda' = 0$ locus. Hence, as can be seen in the upper panel of Figure E5.6.2, the new steady state is to the right of the initial one.

With the reduction in T^c, λ immediately jumps down to its new steady-state value. The capital stock rises because, even though the reduction in the capital gains tax reduces λ, the implicit cost of investment drops more. In terms of equation (E5.6.26), investment increases because the drop in T^c increases the term $(1-T^c)$ by a greater percentage than it reduces λ via (E5.6.27).

(f)   The diagrams for the case of an anticipated permanent decrease in the capital gains tax are shown in Figure E5.6.3. The shift in the steady state is precisely the same as in (e) but announcement of the policy alters the dynamic path. On announcement, λ jumps down from point A to point B, but not all the way to its new steady-state value. (An upward jump in λ or a downward movement to or beyond the post-implementation $\lambda' = 0$ locus would be incompatible with λ being at its new steady state value at implementation date). The capital stock

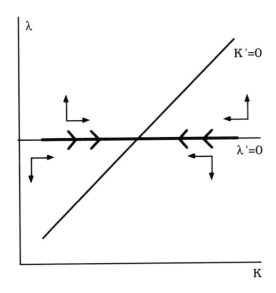

Figure E5.6.1 Phase diagram for a model with taxes on dividends, interest and capital gains

declines after the policy is announced but before it is implemented. The intuition behind this result is exactly the same as in the case of an announced dividend tax: after the policy has been implemented, the tax rate on capital gains relative to dividends will be lower, so firms will find it optimal to shift shareholder returns toward capital gains and away from dividends. This is accomplished by paying higher dividends before the policy is implemented, which drives down the capital stock, allowing it to grow more rapidly after implementation.

This could be described as a perverse effect because the policy causes a short-term deterioration in K, even though it increases K in the long run. Thus, anticipation causes the short- and long-term effects to have opposite sign.

(g) The diagrams for the case of an unanticipated, temporary drop in the capital gains tax are shown in Figure E5.6.4. When the tax change is only temporary, there is no permanent effect on the capital stock. However, in the short run there will be a burst of growth in K until the tax is returned to its initial level. At that point, the capital stock begins to decline back to its original value. The intuition behind this is another variation on the theme discussed in (f): the temporary drop in the capital gains tax makes capital gains (rather than dividends) a more effective way of transferring earnings to the stockholders. Thus, when

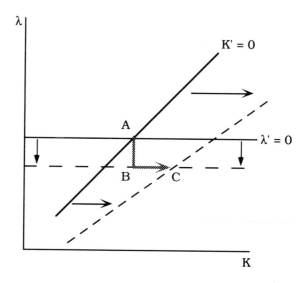

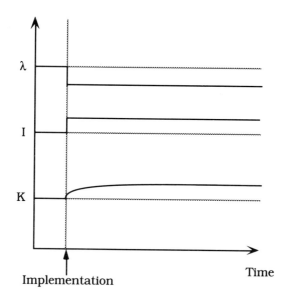

Figure E5.6.2 Effects of an unexpected decline in the capital gains tax

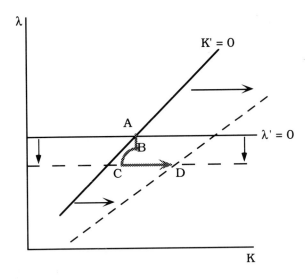

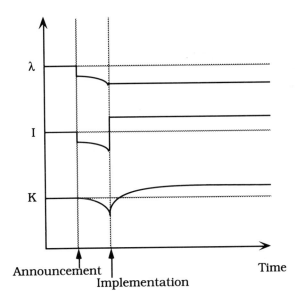

Figure E5.6.3 Effects of an announced decline in the capital gains tax

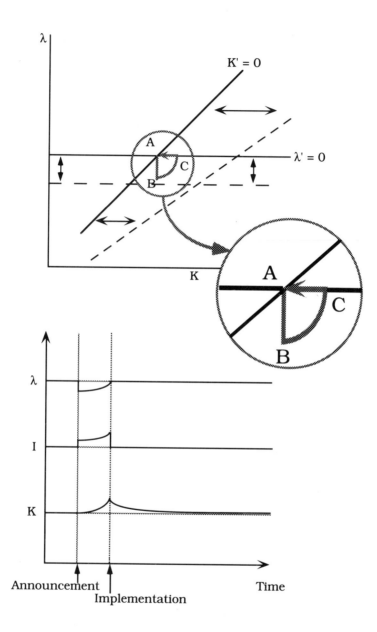

Figure E5.6.4 Effects of a temporary decline in the capital gains tax

the tax is low, firms increase investment, raising the capital stock and producing capital gains for the stockholders. Once the tax is removed, investment returns to its original level and the capital stock begins to decline back to the initial steady state.

Exercise 5.7   *Introducing diminishing returns into the model*

Now consider a model similar to that of Exercise 5.6 but with diminishing returns to capital in the earnings function. In particular, suppose that, instead of (E5.3.6), earnings are given by:

$$E = \beta(P)\ln(K) \ , \tag{E5.7.1}$$

where β, P and K have the same interpretation as before. Since K has been replaced by its natural logarithm, the second derivative of the earnings function is negative. This means that marginal earnings decrease as the capital stock increases. From the firm's point of view, there are diminishing returns to capital.

(a)   Starting from the general results obtained in Exercise 5.6(b), derive the firm's first-order conditions. Solve for investment as a function of other variables and find the model's equations of motion.

(b)   Construct a phase diagram for the model and compare it with the one obtained in Exercise 5.6(d).

(c)   Assume that the initial situation is a steady state. Using a phase diagram, analyze the effects of an unexpected permanent increase in the tax on interest payments. Show the initial and final steady states, and also the transition path. Sketch the paths of the multiplier (λ), investment and the capital stock over time.

(d)   Again starting from a steady state, use a phase diagram to illustrate the effects of a permanent increase in the interest tax announced several years in advance. Sketch the paths of important variables and interpret the solution.

Answer to Exercise 5.7

(a)   In Exercise 5.6(b), the first-order conditions for optimization were shown to be: (E5.6.18), (E5.6.21) and (E5.6.22). To obtain the first-order equations for the model incorporating diminishing returns, first construct the pre-tax dividend function. As in Exercise 5.6(c), pre-tax dividends are earnings less investment costs. Applying (E5.7.1) and (E5.6.1) gives:

$$D = \beta(P)\ln(K) - \frac{P_k I^2}{2\theta} . \tag{E5.7.2}$$

Differentiating (E5.7.2) provides the terms needed in equations (E5.6.21) and (E5.6.22): (E5.6.23) and

$$\frac{\partial D}{\partial K} = \frac{\beta(P)}{K}.$$

(E5.7.3)

Since $\partial D/\partial I$ is the same as in Exercise 5.6, the investment function and the capital-accumulation equation are identical to (E5.6.26) and (E5.6.4). However, the difference in $\partial D/\partial K$ changes the other equation of motion from (E5.6.3) to:

$$\lambda' = \left(r \frac{1-T^i}{1-T^c} + \delta \right)\lambda - \frac{\beta(P)}{K}\left(\frac{1-T^d}{1-T^c}\right).$$

(E5.7.4)

Thus (E5.6.26) is the investment function for this model, while (E5.6.4) and (E5.7.4) are its equations of motion.

(b)   The phase diagram for this model is Figure E5.7.1. It differs from Figure E5.6.1 in two respects: both the $\lambda'= 0$ locus and the stable path are now downward sloping. The $\lambda'= 0$ locus is hyperbolic because of the $1/K$ term in equation (E5.7.4). This reflects the fact that marginal earnings decrease as the capital stock becomes larger.

When the $\lambda'= 0$ locus changes, so does the stable path. To see why, consider where the model would go from an arbitrary point located horizontally to the left of the steady state. Such a point is no longer on the $\lambda'= 0$ locus. Instead, it is in a region where λ' is negative. With K' positive, the system moves downward and to the right. Moreover, it will continue moving downward forever. Similarly, from points to the right of the steady state, the value of λ will increase forever. The stable path, therefore, is no longer horizontal. In fact, it must be downward sloping, and will lie between the $\lambda'=0$ locus and a horizontal line through the steady state. Only from points along such a path could the model eventually reach the steady state. The path will be unique under the conditions discussed in Exercise 5.4 (f) and (g).

(c)   An increase in the tax on interest payments shifts the $\lambda'=0$ locus upward (cf. (E5.7.4)) but leaves the $K'=0$ locus unchanged (cf. (E5.6.4)). The steady state moves upward and to the right, from point A to point C in the upper panel of Figure E5.7.2. Since the tax change is permanent and occurs immediately, the model jumps instantly from the original steady state, point A, to point B on the new stable path. Then, as time passes, the system moves downward and to the right along the stable path from B to C. This produces the time paths of λ, I and K shown in the lower panel of Figure E5.7.2.

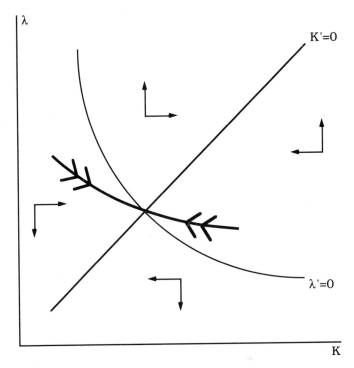

Figure E5.7.1 Phase diagram for a model with diminishing returns

Why should the tax increase lead to a rise in the capital stock? This can be best understood from equation (E5.6.5), the arbitrage condition for the model. When the tax on interest payments rises, the after-tax return on bonds falls. The tax does not apply to dividends or capital gains, however, so the return on equity is unchanged. Thus, the initial effect of the policy is to make the after-tax return on equity higher than the return on bonds. This produces a windfall gain to the holders of equity, which shows up in Figure E5.7.2 as a jump from A to B. Note from equations (E5.6.11) and (E5.6.7) that the rise in the interest-tax rate reduces the discount rate used in calculating the value of the firm. The increase in λ induces a rise in investment, increasing the capital stock toward its new steady state at C.

(d) When the tax increase is announced in advance, the system follows the path shown in Figure E5.7.3. At the moment of the announcement, the model jumps from A to B because of the windfall benefit to holders of equity. It does not, however, move all the way to

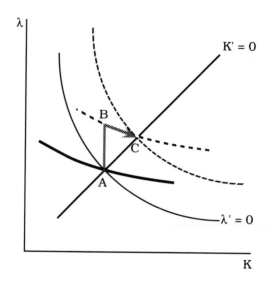

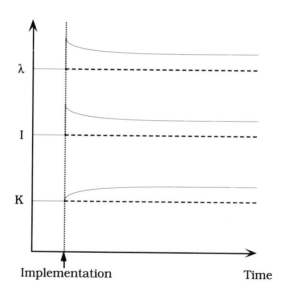

Figure E5.7.2 Effects of a surprise increase in the tax on interest

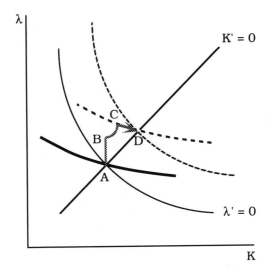

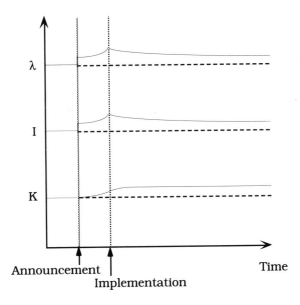

Figure E5.7.3 Effects of an announced increase in the tax on interest

the new stable path because the tax change will not occur for some time. From point B the model evolves according to the original equations of motion (since the tax has not yet changed). It reaches point C at the instant the tax change is implemented. After that, the model moves along the new stable path toward the steady state at D. The paths of the model's variables over time are shown at the bottom of the figure.

Exercise 5.8   *The stock market and the costate variable*

Intertemporal investment models, such as the ones discussed in this chapter, often generate equations giving the optimal value of investment as a function of the capital stock, a costate variable (or multiplier) and variables which the firm takes as given. In the model of Exercises 5.1–5.3, for example, equation (E5.3.11) gives investment as a function of λ and a number of prices. If λ were observable, equations such as (E5.3.11) could be estimated econometrically, allowing values to be obtained for parameters such as θ. It would also allow the statistical performance of the model to be assessed.

Hayashi (1982) presented conditions under which the value of an additional unit of capital (λ, in the notation of this chapter) would be equal to the average value of units of capital (V/K). This allowed observable stock-market data to be used to construct the unknown variable λ, which in turn allowed investment equations such as (E5.3.11) to be estimated. A number of studies along those lines have been conducted, e.g., Summers (1981). This exercise asks you to derive the Hayashi result.

So far in this chapter, we have always assumed that dividends were additively separable into an earnings function, which was independent of investment, and an investment cost function, which was independent of the capital stock. Now we will relax that assumption and solve the investment problem under more general conditions. Assume that dividends are a function of capital, investment, and a vector of short-run variables, P, which the firm takes as given, i.e., that:

$$D = D(K,I,P) . \tag{E5.8.1}$$

A single restriction will be imposed on D: it must be homogeneous of degree one in capital and investment.[16] For convenience, assume that the interest rate is constant and that there are no taxes.

---

[16]   The dividend functions used previously in this chapter do not have this property, but it is easy to construct ones that do. For example, the following is homogeneous in I and K:

(a) Write down the firm's investment problem and derive the corresponding first-order conditions.

(b) Differentiate the following function with respect to future time s, where λ, as usual, is the current-value multiplier associated with the capital-accumulation constraint:

$$F(s) = \lambda(s)Ke^{-r(s-t)} . \qquad (E5.8.2)$$

Use the conditions found in part (a) to eliminate the terms in λ, λ' and K'. Then, apply Euler's theorem to simplify the result.

(c) Integrate the result from part (b) over the interval $[t,\infty)$ and discuss the result.

Answer to Exercise 5.8

(a) The arbitrage condition (E5.1.1) applies. The firm's value function can be obtained by inserting (E5.8.1) into (E5.1.8) to give:

$$V(t) = \int_{t}^{\infty} D(K,I,P)e^{-r(s-t)}ds . \qquad (E5.8.3)$$

Thus, the firm's investment problem is to choose I to maximize (E5.8.3) subject to the capital accumulation constraint. The Hamiltonian for this problem is:

$$H = D(K,I,P)e^{-r(s-t)} + \Lambda(I-\delta K) . \qquad (E5.8.4)$$

Taking first-order conditions and converting the multiplier to its current-value equivalent produces:

$$\frac{\partial D}{\partial I} + \lambda = 0 , \qquad (E5.8.5)$$

$$\frac{\partial D}{\partial K} - \delta\lambda = -\lambda' + r\lambda \qquad (E5.8.6)$$

and

$$I - \delta K = K' . \qquad (E5.8.7)$$

Equations (E5.8.5)–(E5.8.7) must hold along the optimal path of investment.

$$D(K,I,P) = \beta K - P_kI(1+\phi\frac{I}{K})$$

This formulation would be appropriate if adjustment costs arise from rapid growth of the firm rather than just from high levels of investment. We have not imposed homogeneity elsewhere in the chapter because it causes the model's equations of motion to become nonlinear — making them much harder to analyze — without changing the basic substance of our argument. If you are interested in how the methods we discuss would change if the model's equations of motion were nonlinear, refer to Birkhoff and Rota (1978).

(b)   Differentiating F with respect to s produces:

$$\frac{dF}{ds} = (\lambda'K + \lambda K' - r\lambda K)e^{-r(s-t)} . \tag{E5.8.8}$$

Using (E5.8.6) to eliminate λ', (E5.8.5) to eliminate λ, and (E5.8.7) to eliminate K' gives:

$$\frac{dF}{ds} = -\left(\frac{\partial D}{\partial K}K + \frac{\partial D}{\partial I}I\right)e^{-r(s-t)} . \tag{E5.8.9}$$

Since D is homogeneous of degree one, Euler's theorem implies that:

$$\frac{\partial D}{\partial K}K + \frac{\partial D}{\partial I}I = D(K,I,P) . \tag{E5.8.10}$$

Thus, (E5.8.9) can be simplified to:

$$\frac{dF}{ds} = -D(K,I,P)e^{-r(s-t)} . \tag{E5.8.11}$$

(c)   Integrating (E5.8.11) over an interval [a,b] and using (E5.8.2) produces:

$$\lambda(b)K(b)e^{-r(b-t)} - \lambda(a)K(a)e^{-r(a-t)} = -\int_a^b D(K,I,P)e^{-r(s-t)}ds. \tag{E5.8.12}$$

Choosing the limits of integration to be t and ∞, and making use of the usual transversality condition on the behavior of λ as time tends toward infinity gives:

$$\lambda(t)K(t) = \int_t^\infty D(K,I,P)e^{-r(s-t)}ds . \tag{E5.8.13}$$

Since the right side of this equation is exactly the same as the right side of equation (E5.8.3), it must be true that:

$$\lambda(t)K(t) = V(t) . \tag{E5.8.14}$$

Thus, $\lambda(t)$ can be calculated using the formula:

$$\lambda(t) = \frac{V(t)}{K(t)}. \tag{E5.8.15}$$

Equation (E5.8.15) shows that under the assumptions made above, the marginal value of a unit of capital, λ, is equal to the average value of a unit of capital, V/K. Thus, λ can be calculated by simply dividing the firm's stock-market value by its capital stock. Assuming that the capital stock can be observed or computed, (E5.8.15) provides a way of obtaining the multiplier, λ. However, this approach depends on the assumption that the dividend function is homogeneous of degree one in capital and investment. If it is not, the average and marginal values of the capital stock will differ.

B.   NUMERICAL METHODS

To solve our investment model numerically, we must obtain numerical paths for the dynamic variables (λ and K). Once these are known, the paths of other variables can be found easily by applying equations from the model. For example, in Exercise 5.3 investment can be calculated from λ using equation (E5.3.11). Finding a numerical solution to the model boils down to solving the model's equations of motion which are a set of simultaneous differential equations. Solving them requires numerical integration.

In Exercise 5.3, the equations of motion are (E5.3.9) and (E5.3.12). These would be easy to solve if the initial values of λ and K were known. Differential equations for which all boundary conditions are known at the initial point in time are called initial value problems. There are many methods available to solve them (see Press, *et al.*, 1986). A simple, intuitive approach is Euler's method, which works in the following way.[17] Let the first instant after the shock be called time 0. If λ and K were known to take values λ_0 and K_0 at t = 0, those values could be used in (E5.3.9) and (E5.3.12) to calculate $\lambda'(0)$ and $K'(0)$. Multiplying the derivatives by a tiny increment of time, say Δt, would show approximately how much λ and K changed over that interval. Adding these changes to λ_0 and K_0 would give approximate values for λ and K at time Δt. These could then be used in (E5.3.9) and (E5.3.12) to obtain $\lambda'(\Delta t)$ and $K'(\Delta t)$. By applying this process repeatedly, the entire future path of λ and K could be calculated. Moreover, the solution could be made arbitrarily accurate by making Δt sufficiently small.

Unfortunately, the initial post-shock values of any costate variables in the model (such as λ) will usually be unknown. As we saw in Exercises 5.4–5.7, the costate variable may jump initially, taking on a new value which cannot be determined without solving the entire model. This leaves the model without enough boundary conditions to determine the solution uniquely. To understand this intuitively, recall the phase diagram in Figure E5.6.3. If $\lambda(0)$ is not known, there is no way to determine where the system will be immediately after the shock, except that it will be somewhere in the vertical line through the point A. Since different points on this line lead to different paths of the variables over time, the solution is not completely determined.

Fortunately, this indeterminacy can be eliminated for models having the saddle-path property discussed in Exercise 5.4 (f) and (g).

---

17   Although it is intuitively appealing, Euler's method is not usually satisfactory in practice. For a complete discussion, refer to Press, *et al.* (1986).

Any absent initial conditions can be replaced by conditions on the long-run behavior of the costate variables. Typically this is accomplished by imposing transversality conditions which require the costate variables to approach their steady-state values as time tends to infinity. This allows the solution to be determined uniquely in a system in which some of the boundary conditions hold at the initial time and some at the steady state. When the boundary conditions are scattered among several points in time, the system is a "two-point boundary value problem".

The next few exercises introduce you to some methods for solving two-point boundary value problems. We will focus on economic models which have a single costate variable, λ, such as the model in Exercises 5.1–5.3. However, all of the methods can be extended to handle models with multiple costate variables.

Exercise 5.9   *Shooting*

One way to solve a two-point boundary value problem is to guess the missing initial condition, integrate the system forward as though solving an initial value problem, and check whether the transversality condition is satisfied. If not, the guessed condition is revised and the entire process repeated. Eventually an initial condition is found which leads to the steady state when the system is integrated forward. This approach, which has been used extensively in engineering and in the physical sciences, is known as "shooting". (See, for example, Press, *et al.*,1986 or Roberts and Shipman, 1972).

In practice, shooting is usually implemented in the following way. Let the missing initial condition be denoted by λ_0. For each guess of λ_0, the model is integrated forward using Euler's method to a large but finite time T. This generates a $\lambda(T)$ which we will refer to as an "achieved" value and denote λ_T^a. Next, the transversality condition is tested by comparing λ_T^a with the steady-state value (λ^{ss}) of λ, calculated by using the approach discussed in Exercise 5.4(a). We can define a function M which measures how close the solution is to the steady state:

$$M(\lambda_0) = \lambda_T^a(\lambda_0) - \lambda^{ss} . \qquad (E5.9.1)$$

When a guess of λ_0 has been found for which M is less than a specified tolerance, a solution has been obtained.

(a)   The object of shooting is to choose a value of λ_0 that sets M in (E5.9.1) to zero. Suggest a method to update the guess of λ_0 at each iteration.

(b)   Unfortunately, in economic applications shooting often suffers from numerical instability and can rarely be used. Small errors made in the guess of the initial value of the costate variable lead to paths that move far from the steady state after only a few years. Why might this problem occur in the model of Exercises 5.1–5.3?

Answer to Exercise 5.9

(a)   Newton's method is a possible updating procedure. The Taylor series expansion,

$$M(\lambda_0^{k+1}) = M(\lambda_0^k) + \frac{dM(\lambda_0^k)}{d\lambda}(\lambda_0^{k+1} - \lambda_0^k) + \text{(higher order terms)}, \quad (E5.9.2)$$

suggests that we set λ_0^{k+1} according to

$$\lambda_0^{k+1} = \lambda_0^k - \frac{M(\lambda_0^k)}{dM(\lambda_0^k)/d\lambda}. \quad (E5.9.3)$$

If the higher order terms are in (E5.9.2) zero, then under (E5.9.3), $M(\lambda_0^{k+1})$ is zero. The use of (E5.9.3) requires evaluation of both M and its first derivative at λ_0^k. M is evaluated as $\lambda_T^a(\lambda_0^k) - \lambda^{ss}$. Evaluation of the first derivative requires another evaluation of M at a point close to λ_0^k. This enables us to approximate the derivative by

$$\left[M(\lambda_0^k + \Delta) - M(\lambda_0^k) \right]/\Delta$$

where Δ is a small number.

(b)   Recall equation (E5.3.9), one of the model's equations of motion. If the true post-shock value of λ_0 were inserted on its the right side, the true value of $\lambda'(0)$ could be calculated and the system integrated forward toward the steady state. On the other hand, if the guess of λ_0 were too high, evaluating (E5.3.9) would give a value of λ' that is also above its true value. Thus, if λ starts out too high, it will grow too fast as well. As it grows, λ' increases and so λ moves farther and farther away from the stable path. Similarly if λ starts out too low, it will grow too slowly as well and move farther and farther away from the stable path.

To give a quantitative illustration of the potential instability of shooting, imagine that we guess $\lambda(0)$ in (E5.3.9) at $\bar{\lambda}(0)$. Assume also that P, T^d, r and δ are constant through time. Then the path of λ can be found by integrating (E5.3.9) to give

$$\lambda(t) = \left[\bar{\lambda}(0) - \frac{\beta(P)(1-T^d)}{(r+\delta)} \right] e^{(r+\delta)t} + \frac{\beta(P)(1-T^d)}{r+\delta}. \quad (E5.9.4)$$

If our guess of $\lambda(0)$ differs from the true value [which in this example is $\beta(P)(1-T^d)/(r+\delta)$] by Δ, then (E5.9.4) will give a value for $\lambda(T)$ which differs from the true value by $\Delta e^{(r+\delta)T}$. For example, if the interest rate were 5 percent and the depreciation rate 10 percent, after 100 years the error in λ would be $3.27\Delta \times 10^6$. The extreme sensitivity of $\lambda(T)$, for T large, to the value chosen for $\bar{\lambda}(0)$, makes shooting very vulnerable to the rounding errors introduced by computer programs and prevents it from being useful for most economic models.

Exercise 5.10   *Multiple Shooting*

Multiple shooting is a refinement of simple shooting which helps to control models with explosive tendencies. (See Lipton, *et al.*, 1982 and Roberts and Shipman, 1972). The full period over which a solution is to be computed is divided into a number of subintervals and the model is then shot over each subperiod. Shooting over shorter periods keeps the model from drifting too far from the stable path in any one interval. This limits the numerical damage done by rounding errors. However, using more intervals means that rather than searching for a single missing initial condition, the algorithm must find a vector of such conditions spread out across time.

Like simple shooting, multiple shooting is an iterative procedure. As an example of how multiple shooting is used, consider solving the investment model over two adjoining intervals: $[0,\tau]$ and $[\tau,T]$. The first step is to guess what values λ will take at 0 and τ. Denote the guesses at iteration k by λ_0^k and λ_τ^k. The next step is to integrate the model forward from 0 to τ starting at the known initial capital stock, K_0, and the guess λ_0^k. This produces a pair of achieved values, K_τ^a and λ_τ^a. Using K_τ^a and λ_τ^k as initial conditions, the model is then integrated forward from τ to T. From this, an achieved value of λ at T is obtained.

The key feature of multiple shooting is that the integration over $[\tau,T]$ starts from the guess λ_τ^k, and not from λ_τ^a, the achieved value from the first integration. Starting from the achieved value of λ would be exactly the same as integrating the model over $[0,T]$, which is ordinary shooting. When the guess of λ_0^k is incorrect, λ may have drifted very far from its true value by time τ. This may make λ_τ^a a very bad estimate of what λ should be at τ. Replacing it with a guessed value — even a bad guess — may reduce error in the second integration.

(a)   Explain how multiple shooting might help in the example of error propagation described in Exercise 5.9 (b).

(b)   Suggest a revision rule to be used in generating new guesses at each iteration in a multiple-shooting calculation.

Answer to Exercise 5.10

(a)   In Exercise 5.9(b), after T years, an initial error Δ had compounded to a miss distance of $\Delta e^{(r+\delta)T}$. With the period $[0,T]$ divided into two subintervals of equal length, an error Δ in the guess of λ_τ only grows to $\Delta e^{(r+\delta)T/2}$ by year T. Thus, dividing the interval into two equal parts means that instead of having to deal with a miss distance M, we face two miss distances each of roughly $(\Delta M)^{1/2}$. When M is large, this can be an enormous improvement. Moreover, the number of subintervals is not limited to two. Using more subintervals will reduce the error propagation problem even further, allowing any explosive tendencies of the model to be controlled.

(b)   Since the costate variable has to be guessed at the beginning of each interval, the revision rule used to generate new guesses at each iteration is more complicated than the one used for simple shooting. In the case of two subintervals, the guess of λ for the beginning of the second interval, λ_τ, would be revised until M_2 in following equation became zero:

$$M_2(\lambda_0,\lambda_\tau) = \lambda^a_T(\lambda_0,\lambda_\tau) - \lambda^{ss}. \qquad (E5.10.1)$$

As with ordinary shooting, M_2 is a miss distance. The subscript 2 has been added to indicate that it is the miss distance for the second interval. Just as in shooting, M_2 and λ^a_T both depend on λ_τ, the guess of λ at the beginning of the interval. However, they now also depend on the guess for the earlier period, λ_0. This occurs because λ_0 affects K_τ, the starting capital stock for the second interval.

A second rule is needed to guide revision of λ_0. Since the model will not necessarily have reached the steady state by τ, a rule involving λ^{ss} would be inappropriate. Instead, λ_0 is revised until M_1 in the expression below becomes zero:

$$M_1(\lambda_0,\lambda_\tau) = \lambda^a_\tau - \lambda_\tau. \qquad (E5.10.2)$$

That is, λ_0 is varied until a value is found that can be integrated forward to attain the starting guess of λ for the next interval. When the correct value of λ_τ has been found (so that M_2 in (E5.10.1) is zero), a value of λ_0 that makes M_1 in (E5.10.2) zero must be the true initial value of λ; if it were inserted into the model's equations of motion, the system could be integrated forward to time T and the transversality condition would be satisfied.

Thus, dividing the original period into two subintervals means that two variables (λ_0 and λ_τ) must now be chosen to satisfy two equations ($M_1 = 0$ and $M_2 = 0$). This suggests using the multivariate version of Newton's method to compute an updated vector of guesses at each step of the algorithm. If λ^k is the vector of guesses at iteration k, then a new guess could be constructed as follows:

$$\lambda^{k+1} = \lambda^k - J^{-1}M(\lambda^k) , \qquad (E5.10.3)$$

where J is the Jacobian matrix of partial derivatives of M evaluated at λ^k and λ^k itself is the guess of λ at iteration k. Equation (E5.10.3) can be used with any number of shooting intervals, and with multiple costate variables.

Unfortunately, multiple shooting consumes a great deal of computer time. Moreover, like all algorithms based on Newton's method, it is not guaranteed to converge. Worse yet, it is particularly unsuitable for intertemporal general equilibrium models because it requires solving the intraperiod part of the model thousands of times in the course of finding a full intertemporal solution.[18] A single intraperiod equilibrium solution requires solving a static short-run general equilibrium model, which for even moderate sized models will require a noticeable amount of computer time. Having to compute thousands of these solutions makes multiple shooting of limited use for general equilibrium work.

Exercise 5.11   *The Fair-Taylor Method*

A third method for solving two-point boundary-value problems, and one which is often used for intertemporal general equilibrium models, is known as the Fair-Taylor algorithm.[19] It is much easier to use than multiple shooting, controls explosive tendencies in the solution equally well, and requires somewhat less computer time.

First, a guess is made of the entire path of the costate variable. That is, instead of guessing a single λ as in shooting, or a handful of λ's

---

[18]   Thousands of intratemporal solutions are needed because each iteration of the algorithm requires solving every period in the time interval several times. If the model is to be solved at yearly intervals over 100 years, for example, 101 intraperiod solutions are required just to integrate the path forward from 0 to T once. Much worse, however, is that the Jacobian matrix will usually have to be computed numerically. That requires perturbing each of the elements of λ and computing an entire solution path from 0 to T. If there are five shooting intervals, the entire path of 101 intratemporal solutions would have to be computed six times in order to evaluate M and J. Since over 600 intraperiod solutions would have to be found for a single iteration of the intertemporal algorithm, the method is not useful for more than very small models.

[19]   The Fair-Taylor algorithm was originally proposed by Fair (1979), and later extended by Fair and Taylor (1983). This problem is concerned with Fair and Taylor's "type II" iteration. They also proposed a "type III" procedure which can be used when the terminal condition cannot be computed easily.

as in multiple shooting, values of λ are guessed for each point in the set $\{0,1, ..., T\}$. Let the guess at iteration k be denoted by the vector λ^k. If T is chosen to be year 100, λ^k will usually have 101 elements.[20] The final element is always chosen to satisfy the transversality condition. Using λ^k and the equation of motion of the capital stock, the model is integrated forward from the initial point to the terminal point. During this process, the costate variable's equation of motion is temporarily ignored. The result is a vector of the capital stocks, K^k for iteration k, that is consistent with λ^k. It is the path K would follow if λ actually had the sequence of values in λ^k. However, it is not necessarily a solution to the model because λ^k does not necessarily satisfy λ's equation of motion. The algorithm must iterate over λ vectors until one is found that satisfies both equations of motion.

Revising the guess vector between iterations is accomplished by using the equation of motion for λ in a special way. Consider a slightly generalized version of the model introduced in Exercises 5.1–5.3 with one state variable (K), one costate variable (λ), a vector of exogenous variables (Z), and two equations of motion, one in K' and one in λ'. The equation of motion for λ has the form:

$$\lambda'_t = f(\lambda_t, K_t, Z_t) . \tag{E5.11.1}$$

Equation (E5.3.9), for example, is a special case of (E5.11.1) in which a particular functional form has been imposed for f. The derivative of λ at time t can be approximated by the difference between two consecutive values of λ (see also Exercise 5.13):

$$\lambda'_t \approx \lambda_{t+1} - \lambda_t . \tag{E5.11.2}$$

Inserting this into (E5.11.1) produces:

$$\lambda_{t+1} - \lambda_t \approx f(\lambda_t, K_t, Z_t) . \tag{E5.11.3}$$

This expression holds at all points along the path of λ. Rearranging it slightly and dropping the implied error terms produces the following:

$$\lambda_t = \lambda_{t+1} - f(\lambda_t, K_t, Z_t) . \tag{E5.11.4}$$

(a)   Equation (E5.11.4) must hold at all points along the solution path. In light of (E5.11.4), suggest a revision rule for λ which leaves the known value for λ_T undisturbed.

(b)   Compare the Fair-Taylor method with multiple shooting.

---

20   Simulating periods one year apart is not necessary for the Fair-Taylor algorithm to work. However, it is the most common approach.

Answer to Exercise 5.11

(a)   By inserting values of λ_{t+1}, λ_t and K from iteration k into the right side of (E5.11.4), an implied value of λ_t could be calculated. This achieved value, λ^{ka}_t, could be computed as:

$$\lambda^{ka}_t = \lambda^k_{t+1} - f(\lambda^k_t, K^k_t, Z_t) \quad \text{for } t = 0,...,T-1. \tag{E5.11.5}$$

At the solution, λ^{ka}_t will be equal to λ^k_t because the solution vector must satisfy λ's equation of motion. Away from the solution, however, λ^{ka}_t will not be the same as λ^k_t. Leaving λ^{k+1}_T at the known value of λ_T, the Fair-Taylor algorithm uses λ^{ka}_t to update the guess of λ_t for t = 0,...,T–1 in the following way:

$$\lambda^{k+1}_t = \alpha\lambda^k_t + (1-\alpha)\lambda^{ka}_t, \tag{E5.11.6}$$

where α is a parameter used to ensure the algorithm converges smoothly. It takes values in the interval [0,1] and is typically around one-half. The choice of α is important. Choosing α too close to zero puts undue emphasis on λ^{ka}_t, which is not necessarily closer to the true solution than λ^k_t. That is, the true value of λ_t may lie between λ^k_t and λ^{ka}_t, but be much closer to λ^k_t than λ^{ka}_t. In that case, $\alpha\approx 0$ would tend to make the algorithm diverge. On the other hand, if α is chosen too close to one, the algorithm will converge very slowly. The solution has been obtained when the guessed and achieved values of λ differ by less than a given tolerance.

(b)   On the surface, the Fair-Taylor technique seems very different from multiple shooting. At a deeper level, however, the algorithms are quite similar. Multiple shooting proceeds by guessing λ at a handful of points, integrating forward, and employing a fairly sophisticated updating rule. Fair-Taylor works by guessing λ at a vast number of points, integrating forward, and using a very simple updating rule. In a sense, the Fair-Taylor algorithm is a version of multiple shooting in which there are T shooting intervals — one for each year of the solution. It can, however, be somewhat faster than multiple shooting because it does not require computing the Jacobian matrix of the miss distances at each iteration. In practice, this means that Fair-Taylor will require more iterations to converge than multiple shooting, but each iteration will be much faster to compute.

Exercise 5.12   *Finite Differences*

A fourth approach to solving two-point boundary-value problems is the finite-difference method which has been applied to economic models by Wilcoxen (1985). It differs from the three previous algorithms because it does not operate by guessing the initial value of the costate variable and integrating forward to see if the transversality condition is satisfied. Instead, a system of overlapping difference equations is constructed which approximates the model's equations of motion. This system is then solved simultaneously to give the paths of the model's dynamic variables. The initial and terminal conditions will both be satisfied and the algorithm is immune to the numerical instability that plagues shooting methods. In addition, since the algorithm is not iterative[21], it will always find a solution if one exists.

The first step in using finite differences is to replace all of the derivatives in the model by finite-difference formulae. These formulae are approximations to derivatives and are constructed from Taylor-series expansions:

$$f(t+h) \;=\; f(t) + f'(t)h + O(h^2) \,, \qquad (E5.12.1)$$

where $O(h^2)$ represents the Taylor-series terms of order h^2 and above. Rearranging (E5.12.1) and dropping the higher-order terms shows that:

$$f'(t) \;\approx\; \frac{f(t+h) - f(t)}{h}. \qquad (E5.12.2)$$

The term on the right is a finite-difference approximation to the derivative of f evaluated at time t. Since it was constructed using current and future values of f, it is known as a forward difference. Dividing through by h reduced the terms that were dropped to $O(h)$, implying that the approximation will be accurate to that order.[22] Hence, if (E5.12.2) were used to replace a derivative, the resulting equation would be accurate only when h was fairly small. Thus, it is inappropriate to use a single-difference equation to approximate the original model over a long period of time.

Long periods of time can, however, be modeled using a series of expressions like (E5.12.2), holding over successive intervals of time. A total period of 100 years, for example, could be broken up into two intervals of fifty years each. Then, one equation like (E5.12.2) could link years 0 to 50, while another connected years 50 to 100. Because 50 years is still a very large value for h, it would usually be necessary to break the original interval up into smaller segments using many more equations. If necessary, the solution can be made arbitrarily accurate by using a sufficiently small step size h. No matter how many intervals are used, in the end the original differential equation will have been

---

21 Although finite differences is not iterative in the sense that multiple shooting iterates over guesses of the costate variable, it may require iteration to solve the difference equations if they are nonlinear.

22 A number of other difference formulae, some of which are accurate to higher orders, will be discussed in Exercise 5.13.

replaced by a system of difference equations which link values of f at different points in time. Solving this system simultaneously yields the entire path of f. Since for many models the equations will be linear or easily linearized, often the solution can be found using a variant of Gaussian elimination. This makes finite differences very fast and a natural choice for use with general equilibrium models that employ the Johansen method which was the subject of Chapter 3.[23]

(a)   Consider a model with equations of motion of the form

$$\lambda'(t) = a(t)\lambda(t) + b(t)K(t) - c(t) , \qquad (E5.12.3)$$

$$K'(t) = d(t)\lambda(t) + e(t)K(t) - f(t) . \qquad (E5.12.4)$$

(The model of Exercises 5.1 - 5.3 is a special case of this in which b(t)=0.) Assume that the model is to be solved over the interval $[t^0, T]$ where $K(t^0)$ and $\lambda(T)$ are known. Replace the left hand sides of (E5.12.3) and (E5.12.4) with finite-difference approximations. Then show how, by the use of matrix manipulations, approximate solutions can be computed for K(t) and $\lambda(t)$ for values of t spaced h time units apart, i.e., show how we can compute approximate values for $K(t^0+ih)$ and $\lambda(t^0+ih)$, i=0,1,...,N where $N=(T-t^0)/h$.

(b)   Since approximations are used for derivatives, the results obtained using finite differences will contain truncation errors arising from dropping high-order terms in the Taylor-series expansions used to form the difference approximations. Explain why truncation errors are reduced by using a finer time grid (smaller value of h). Can you see a possibility for reducing truncation errors by using a non-uniform grid, i.e., by having different lengths of time between adjacent points in the solution?

Answer to Exercise 5.12

(a)   Converting (E5.12.3) and (E5.12.4) into finite-difference form using forward differences produces the following:

$$\frac{\lambda(t+h)-\lambda(t)}{h} = a(t)\lambda(t) + b(t)K(t) - c(t) , \qquad (E5.12.5)$$

---

[23]   It results in a system of equations which can be integrated directly into the Johansen solution procedure. This approach to intertemporal general equilibrium modeling is due to Wilcoxen (1987).

$$\frac{K(t+h)-K(t)}{h} = d(t)\lambda(t) + e(t)K(t) - f(t) \quad . \tag{E5.12.6}$$

Equations (E5.12.5) and (E5.12.6) can be written in matrix notation as:

$$\begin{bmatrix} a(t)+\dfrac{1}{h} & b(t) & \dfrac{-1}{h} & 0 \\[2ex] d(t) & e(t)+\dfrac{1}{h} & 0 & \dfrac{-1}{h} \end{bmatrix} \begin{bmatrix} \lambda(t) \\[1ex] K(t) \\[1ex] \lambda(t+h) \\[1ex] K(t+h) \end{bmatrix} = \begin{bmatrix} c(t) \\[1ex] f(t) \end{bmatrix} \quad . \tag{E5.12.7}$$

This system approximates the true equations of motion, (E5.12.3) and (E5.12.4), in the neighborhood of t. The complete solution requires a set of such equations, one for each interval of time. If there are N intervals each of length h, collecting the approximations together produces a set of equations with the structure:

$$\begin{bmatrix} a(t^0)+\dfrac{1}{h} & b(t^0) & \dfrac{-1}{h} & 0 & 0 & 0 & \cdots \\[2ex] d(t^0) & e(t^0)+\dfrac{1}{h} & 0 & \dfrac{-1}{h} & 0 & 0 & \cdots \\[2ex] 0 & 0 & a(t^1)+\dfrac{1}{h} & b(t^1) & \dfrac{-1}{h} & 0 & \cdots \\[2ex] 0 & 0 & d(t^1) & e(t^1)+\dfrac{1}{h} & 0 & \dfrac{-1}{h} & \cdots \\[2ex] & & & \cdots & & \cdots & \end{bmatrix} \begin{bmatrix} \lambda(t^0) \\[1ex] K(t^0) \\[1ex] \lambda(t^1) \\[1ex] K(t^1) \\[1ex] \cdots \\[1ex] \lambda(t^N) \\[1ex] K(t^N) \end{bmatrix} = \begin{bmatrix} c(t^0) \\[1ex] f(t^0) \\[1ex] c(t^1) \\[1ex] f(t^1) \\[1ex] \cdots \\[1ex] c(t^{N-1}) \\[1ex] f(t^{N-1}) \end{bmatrix} .$$

$$\tag{E5.12.8}$$

where $t^i = t^0 + ih$ for $i=0,\dots,N$. This is a system of 2N equations and 2(N + 1) variables. However, two of the variables are known from the model's boundary conditions: $K(t^0)$ and $\lambda(t^N)$ (using λ^{ss} as the approximate value of $\lambda(t^N)$). Moving the corresponding columns over to the right side of the equation and simplifying produces:

$$
\begin{bmatrix}
a(t^0)+\dfrac{1}{h} & \dfrac{-1}{h} & 0 & 0 & 0 & \cdots \\[2ex]
d(t^0) & 0 & \dfrac{-1}{h} & 0 & 0 & \cdots \\[2ex]
0 & a(t^1)+\dfrac{1}{h} & b(t^1) & \dfrac{-1}{h} & 0 & \cdots \\[2ex]
0 & d(t^1) & e(t^1)+\dfrac{1}{h} & 0 & \dfrac{-1}{h} & \cdots \\[2ex]
& & \cdots & & \cdots &
\end{bmatrix}
\begin{bmatrix}
\lambda(t^0) \\[1ex]
\lambda(t^1) \\[1ex]
K(t^1) \\[1ex]
\cdots \\[1ex]
\lambda(t^{N-1}) \\[1ex]
K(t^{N-1}) \\[1ex]
K(t^N)
\end{bmatrix}
=
\begin{bmatrix}
c(t^0)-b(t^0)K(t^0) \\[1ex]
f(t^0)-\left\{e(t^0)+\dfrac{1}{h}\right\}K(t^0) \\[1ex]
c(t^1) \\[1ex]
f(t^1) \\[1ex]
\cdots \\[1ex]
c(t^{N-1})+\dfrac{\lambda(t^N)}{h} \\[1ex]
f(t^{N-1})
\end{bmatrix}
$$

$$\text{(E5.12.9)}$$

This direct use of the boundary conditions eliminates the need for iteration and removes the numerical instability associated with shooting methods. Equation (E5.12.9) can be written compactly as:

$$\Theta F = B, \qquad \text{(E5.12.10)}$$

where Θ is a matrix of coefficients, F is a vector of unknown values of λ and K, and B is the vector on the right hand side of (E5.12.9) which results from applying the boundary conditions. Solving the model requires finding the unknown values of F, which could be accomplished by computing:

$$F = \Theta^{-1}B. \qquad \text{(E5.12.11)}$$

In practice, the solution would never be computed using (E5.12.11). Instead, because it is much faster than matrix inversion, Gaussian elimination would be applied to (E5.12.10).

(b)   For the difference formula (E5.12.2), the truncation error is $O(h)$. Thus, doubling the density of the grid, i.e., doubling the number of intervals or cutting h in half, would reduce the error at each point by roughly a factor of two. Moreover, comparing solutions on grids of N and $2N$ intervals gives a good indication of the extent to which truncation error has affected the results. It is possible to use Richardson's extrapolation[24] to exploit this fact to obtain more accurate results.

---

24   See Exercise 3.7 or Birkhoff and Rota (1978).

As the distance between grid points approaches zero, a finite-difference approximation converges to the true solution (Isaacson and Keller, 1966). With enough grid points, the results can be made arbitrarily accurate. However, the number of equations in the system goes up with 1/h. As a practical matter there will be an upper limit on the number of grid points that can be used.

Another way to reduce truncation error is to abandon using a uniform grid. It is often possible to make a solution much more accurate by rearranging the locations of the grid points in time. This has the advantage of keeping the size of the problem small. Over certain periods of time, often late in the solution as the model nears the steady state, the model's dynamic variables will be changing very slowly. Moving grid points from these regions to periods where the variables are changing more rapidly improves the ability of the finite-difference approximation to capture the model's dynamic behavior.

Shifting grid points around is an extremely powerful tool for improving the accuracy of finite-difference solutions. This stems from the Taylor series expansions used to construct the difference formulae. Consider the Taylor series expansion:

$$f(t+\varepsilon) \;=\; f(t) \;+\; f'(t)\varepsilon \;+\; \frac{f''(t)\varepsilon^2}{2!} \;+\; \dots \; . \qquad (E5.12.12)$$

In forming the forward-difference formula, the terms above first order were discarded. This introduced the error:

$$\frac{f''(t)\varepsilon^2}{2!} \;+\; \dots \; . \qquad (E5.12.13)$$

On a uniform grid, truncation error would be highest where f'' was largest. Similarly, the solution would be very accurate in regions where f'' was small. Thus, shifting points from regions of low curvature to regions of high curvature would improve the solution by reducing overall truncation error. Another approach would be to move points from uninteresting parts of the solution to periods of more interest. Most of the time, these two reallocations will be about the same.

Exercise 5.13   *Constructing finite-difference formulae*

In Exercise 5.12, you replaced the derivatives in a model by the forward-difference formula (E5.12.2). The finite-difference approach can be implemented with the other difference formulae for approximating derivatives. Difference formulae accurate to high orders can be constructed by using combinations of Taylor series expansions at several adjacent points. For example, a first-order difference accurate to $O(h^2)$ can be constructed by subtracting the expansion for $f(t-h)$ from that for $f(t+h)$. This is known as a "central" difference. Using more expansions, it is possible to construct formulae accurate to even higher orders.

It is also possible to construct difference approximations to higher-order derivatives. This is done by applying the method used for first-order differences recursively. For example, an approximation for a second-order derivative could be constructed by first building a difference formula for f'' in terms of f' and then inserting an appropriate difference formula for f'.

Finally, difference formulae can also be constructed for unevenly spaced grids in which adjacent points are separated by varying distances. This is done in exactly the same manner as for uniform grids, but with the appropriate distances inserted wherever h appears. As you discovered in Exercise 5.12, uneven grid spacing can be a useful device for reducing truncation error. However, as you will find in this exercise, it does introduce an additional source of truncation error at points where there are sharp changes in grid spacing.

(a) Construct a first-order central-difference formula. How does its accuracy compare with the forward-difference presented in Exercise 5.12?

(b) Using the results of part (a), construct a second-order central-difference formula (i.e., an approximation for $f''(t)$). What is its order of accuracy?

(c) Construct the analog of a first-order central-difference for an unevenly spaced grid. Discuss its order of accuracy.

Answer to Exercise 5.13

(a) A first-order central difference is constructed from Taylor-series expansions around time t for times t+h and t–h. To the fourth order, these expansions are the following:

$$f(t+h) = f(t) + hf'(t) + \frac{h^2 f''(t)}{2!} + \frac{h^3 f'''(t)}{3!} + \frac{h^4 f''''(t)}{4!} + O(h^5) , \quad (E5.13.1)$$

$$f(t-h) = f(t) - hf'(t) + \frac{h^2 f''(t)}{2!} - \frac{h^3 f'''(t)}{3!} + \frac{h^4 f''''(t)}{4!} + O(h^5) . \quad (E5.13.2)$$

Subtracting produces:

$$f(t+h) - f(t-h) = 2hf'(t) + \frac{2h^3 f'''(t)}{3!} + O(h^5) . \quad (E5.13.3)$$

Rearranging (E5.13.3) and dividing through by 2h gives

$$f'(t) = \frac{f(t+h)-f(t-h)}{2h} - \frac{h^2 f'''(t)}{3!} + O(h^4) . \qquad \text{(E5.13.4)}$$

The central difference formula for $f'(t)$ is the first term on the right side of (E5.13.4). This is accurate to $O(h^2)$, an order more accurate than the simple forward differences presented in Exercise 5.12.

(b)   To construct a second-order central difference, start by expanding $f'(t+a)$ and $f'(t-a)$ around $f(t)$:

$$f'(t+a) = f'(t) + af''(t) + \frac{a^2 f'''(t)}{2!} + \frac{a^3 f''''(t)}{3!} + \frac{a^4 f'''''(t)}{4!} + O(a^5) , \quad \text{(E5.13.5)}$$

$$f'(t-a) = f'(t) - af''(t) + \frac{a^2 f'''(t)}{2!} - \frac{a^3 f''''(t)}{3!} + \frac{a^4 f'''''(t)}{4!} + O(a^5) . \quad \text{(E5.13.6)}$$

Subtracting these, dividing through by $2a$, and rearranging produces an expression analogous to (E5.13.4):

$$f''(t) = \frac{f'(t+a) - f'(t-a)}{2a} - \frac{a^2 f''''(t)}{3!} + O(a^4) . \qquad \text{(E5.13.7)}$$

Substituting (E5.13.4) for the derivatives produces:

$$f''(t) = \frac{1}{2a} \left(\frac{f(t+2a)-f(t)}{2a} - \frac{f(t)-f(t-2a)}{2a} - \frac{a^2}{3!} \left(f'''(t+a) - f'''(t-a) \right) + O(a^4) \right)$$
$$- \frac{a^2 f''''(t)}{3!} + O(a^4) . \qquad \text{(E5.13.8)}$$

Setting h equal to $2a$, we see that (E5.13.8) implies that $f'(t)$ can be approximated as

$$f''(t) \approx \frac{f(t+h)-2f(t)+f(t-h)}{h^2} . \qquad \text{(E5.13.9)}$$

On recognizing that $(a^2/3!)[f'''(t+a)-f'''(t-a)]$ is $O(a^3)$, we find that the error in approximation (E5.13.9) is $O(h^2)$.

(c)   A first-order central difference for a non-uniform grid is constructed almost exactly as shown in part (a), except that care must be taken about the spacing of the points. The first step is to construct Taylor-series expansions around t for $t+a$ and $t-b$. To the third order, these expansions are:

$$f(t+a) = f(t) + af'(t) + \frac{a^2 f''(t)}{2!} + \frac{a^3 f'''(t)}{3!} + O(a^4) , \qquad \text{(E5.13.10)}$$

$$f(t-b) = f(t) - bf'(t) + \frac{b^2 f''(t)}{2!} - \frac{b^3 f'''(t)}{3!} + O(b^4) . \qquad \text{(E5.13.11)}$$

Subtracting these produces:

$$f(t+a)-f(t-b) = \left(f(t) + af'(t) + \frac{a^2 f''(t)}{2!} + \frac{a^3 f'''(t)}{3!} + O(a^4) \right)$$

$$- \left(f(t) - bf'(t) + \frac{b^2 f''(t)}{2!} - \frac{b^3 f'''(t)}{3!} + O(b^4) \right). \quad \text{(E5.13.12)}$$

Rearranging (E5.13.12) and dividing through by a+b produces the following:

$$\frac{f(t+a)-f(t-b)}{a+b} = f'(t) + \frac{1}{2!}(a-b)f''(t) + \frac{1}{3!}\left(\frac{a^3+b^3}{a+b}\right)f'''(t) + \dots . \quad \text{(E5.13.13)}$$

This suggests using the difference formula:

$$f'(t) \approx \frac{f(t+a)-f(t-b)}{a+b}, \quad \text{(E5.13.14)}$$

which will have an error term given by :

$$\frac{1}{2!}(a-b)f''(t) + \frac{1}{3!}\left(\frac{a^3+b^3}{a+b}\right)f'''(t) + \dots . \quad \text{(E5.13.15)}$$

When a and b are close in magnitude, the even-order terms in (E5.13.15) will be negligible. In that case, the error will be essentially $O(a^2)$ (or $O(b^2)$, since a≈b), which is the same as for a uniform grid. On an uneven grid, in regions where the spacing between points changes suddenly, a and b may differ substantially. When that occurs, the first term in (E5.13.15) will be significant, so the error will be more like $O(a)$. This effect can be minimized by avoiding sharp jumps in grid spacing, and by locating any such changes in the regions where f''(t) is small. By constructing more elaborate difference formulae, the term in (a–b) can be eliminated entirely. For more discussion of difference formulae refer to Fox (1962).

C.   AN INTERTEMPORAL GENERAL EQUILIBRIUM MODEL

We now turn to the inclusion of intertemporal behavior in a general equilibrium model. We will build a five-sector general equilibrium model with intertemporal investment. Subsequent exercises cover the structure of the model, its solution and a number of simulations showing how the inter- and intra-temporal parts of the model interact. The simulation results demonstrate that general equilibrium effects have a strong impact on investment behavior, and that changes in investment brought about by intertemporal optimization have a significant effect on general equilibrium variables.

Exercise 5.14 *The structure of the model*

The model consists of a sequence of short-run general equilibrium models linked by an adjustment-cost investment model. All of the general equilibrium models have the same structure, but each represents the economy at a different point in time.

There are five sectors of production denoted A, B, 1, 2, and 3. Sectors A, 1 and 2 produce consumption goods which are sold to a single consumer. Sector B produces capital services, and sector 3 produces raw capital goods. There is one type of labor, L, and there are two types of capital, K_a and K_b. K_a is created by industry A's investment and is used solely in the production of good A. K_b is created by sector B's investment and is rented out to sectors 1, 2 and 3. Sectors 1, 2 and 3 do not do any investment. The sectors are shown schematically in Figure 5.14.1. Their attributes are summarized in Table E5.14.1.

Sector A is fully integrated into both the general equilibrium and investment models. It must solve both a short-run production and a long-run investment problem. Sector B, however, operates more like a bank. It invests to build capital which it then rents out to other industries for use in production. Thus, sector B solves a long-run investment problem but its short-run problem is trivial — it rents out whatever it has.[25] Sectors A and B, both of which determine investment via intertemporal optimization, account for all investment in the model.

Derive the structural equations of the model by solving the following problems:

(a)   Assume that the production function in sector A is

$$X_a(t) = (L_a^P(t))^{\varepsilon a}(K_a(t))^{1-\varepsilon a} \qquad (E5.14.1)$$

where $X_a(t)$ is output of good a at time t, $L_a^P(t)$ is labor input, $K_a(t)$ is capital input and ε_a is a positive parameter less than one. Assume that sector A also produces units $[I_a(t)]$ of its own capital good by purchasing raw capital $[X_3^a(t)]$ and hiring labor $[L_a^I(t)]$ to install it. The amount of labor required is proportional to the square of the amount of raw capital. This can be summarized by the Leontief production function:

$$I_a(t) = \min\left\{X_3^a(t), \ \left[L_a^I(t)/\theta_a\right]^{1/2}\right\}, \qquad (E5.14.2)$$

---

25   By requiring that sector B always rent out all of its capital we are ruling out monopolistic behavior on its part.

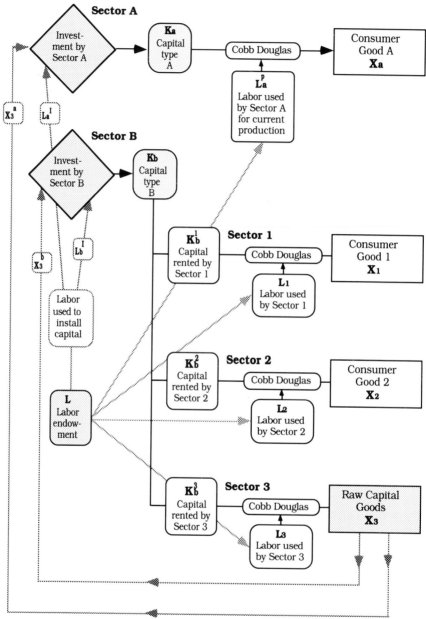

Figure E5.14.1 The structure of the model

Table E5.14.1

Characteristics of the Sectors

Sector	Invests In	Capital Used	Output Produced
A	K_a	K_a	Consumption good A
B	K_b	—	K_b capital services
1	—	K_b	Consumption good 1
2	—	K_b	Consumption good 2
3	—	K_b	Raw capital goods

where θ_a is a positive parameter. Assume that an investment subsidy is paid at the *ad valorem* rate, $T^S(t)$. Where $P_a(t)$ is the price of the sector's output, $W(t)$ is the wage rate, $P_3(t)$ is the price per unit of raw capital, write for sector A:

(i)   its earnings or short-run profit function per unit of capital;

(ii) its investment cost function;

(iii) its pretax dividend function, assuming that dividends are short-run profits less investment expenditure;

(iv) its demand for labor as an input to current production, i.e., $L_a^P(t)$ as a function of $P_a(t)$, $W(t)$ and $K_a(t)$; and

(v)   its demand for labor in capital assembly, i.e., $L_a^I(t)$ as a function of $I_a(t)$.

(b)   Sector B sells capital services at a price $\rho(t)$. Revenue from these sales is $\rho(t)K_b(t)$, where $K_b(t)$ is sector B's capital stock. The sector uses no labor in current production. Assume, however, that it uses labor to create new units of capital stock out of raw capital according to the function

$$I_b(t) = \min\left\{ X_3^b(t), \ \left[L_b^I(t)/\theta_b\right]^{1/2} \right\}. \tag{E5.14.3}$$

Answer questions (iii) and (v) from part (a) for sector B.

(c)   Assume that there is a dividend tax at the *ad valorem* rate $T^d(t)$ and that sectors A and B choose their investment paths to maximize the present values of their post-tax dividend streams. Assume that the interest rate remains fixed at r and that both sectors are price takers. This last assumption means that they do not expect their investment decisions to affect prices of outputs $(P_a(t)$ and $\rho(t))$ or inputs $(W(t)$ and $P_3(t))$. For both sectors write down the first-order conditions for the solution of their investment problems and equations for the steady-state values of the associated multipliers $(\lambda_a$ and $\lambda_b)$. In answering this question, assume that both sectors have perfect foresight, i.e., that they make their investment plans on the basis of actual future values for P_a, ρ, W, P_3, T^d and T^s. In Exercise 5.15 we ask you to introduce a distinction between actual outcomes and expected outcomes.

(d)   Industries 1, 2 and 3 rent their capital from industry B at price ρ and do not invest. Assume that their production functions are Cobb-Douglas, i.e.,

$$X_i(t) = \gamma_i(t) \left(L_i(t)\right)^{\varepsilon_i} \left(K_b^i(t)\right)^{1-\varepsilon_i}, \qquad i=1,2,3. \qquad (E5.14.4)$$

Derive their factor-demand equations, i.e., express $L_i(t)$ and $K_b^i(t)$ as functions of $X_i(t)$, $\rho(t)$ and $W(t)$ under cost minimizing assumptions. Treat $\gamma_i(t)$ as an exogenously given technological-change variable.

(e)   Assume that sectors 1, 2 and 3 receive $P_1(t)$, $P_2(t)$ and $P_3(t)/\left[1+T_s^3(t)\right]$ per unit for their outputs. $P_1(t)$ and $P_2(t)$ are producer or basic prices. $P_3(t)$ is a purchasers' price and $T_s^3(t)$ is an *ad valorem* sales tax. Write zero-pure-profit conditions for sectors 1, 2 and 3, that is, equate their revenues with their costs.

(f)   The single consumer in the model supplies labor $[L(t)]$ and owns all the economy's capital. The consumer's income includes wages, dividends and lump-sum payments $[LS(t)]$ from the government. Assume that a tax is levied on wages at the *ad valorem* rate $T^w(t)$. There is no explicit saving — household disposable income in each period is spent entirely on consumption — but implicitly the consumer saves whatever earnings firms retain for new investment. Write down the consumer's budget constraint. Assume that, subject to the budget constraint, the consumer maximizes a Cobb-Douglas utility function of the consumption of goods A, 1 and 2, and that labor is supplied inelastically. Assume also that sales taxes are levied on goods A, 1 and 2 at the *ad valorem* rates T_s^a, T_s^1, and T_s^2. Derive the consumer's demand system.

(g)   Write down the government's budget constraint. Assume that the government maximizes a Cobb-Douglas utility function of goods A, 1 and 2 subject to its budget constraint. Assume that in this maximization the government treats commodity prices inclusive of sales taxes as being beyond its control. Derive the government's demand equations.

(h)   Write down market-clearing equations for goods A and 1-3, for labor and for general-purpose capital services produced by sector B.

(i)   Write down the equation for a price deflator, ζ, defined as the current cost of the bundle of consumption and government goods divided by its cost at the prices of a base period.

Answer to Exercise 5.14

The answers are in Appendix 5.1 which sets out the model's equations. Except for the dynamic equations, we have, for notational convenience, suppressed t. For some variables we have appended an e subscript meaning expectation. This is explained in Exercise 5.15. At first reading you may ignore the e's and assume that expected values of variables are actual values.

(a)   (i) Sector A's earnings function per unit of capital (β) is given by equation (A5.1.7). This is the same form as in (E5.3.5)

(ii) Sector A's investment-cost function is

$$C_a = (P_3 I_a + \theta_a W I_a^2)(1 - T^s) \quad . \qquad (E5.14.5)$$

This type of investment-cost function was discussed in Exercise 5.3(b). In the equation list in Appendix 5.1, C_a has been eliminated. (Notice that in A's dividend function, (A5.1.12), C_a is represented by the right hand side of (E5.14.5) after the elimination of $\theta_a I_a^2$ by use of (A5.1.11)).

(iii) Sector A's pretax dividend function is given in Appendix 5.1 as equation (A5.1.12). Other representations are possible. For example, we could write

$$D_a = \beta K_a - C_a \quad . \qquad (E5.14.6)$$

(Can you show in the context of the system of equations in Appendix 5.1 that (A5.1.12) and (E5.14.6) are equivalent?)

(iv) and (v) Sector A's labor-demand functions are given by equations (A5.1.10) and (A5.1.11), see Exercises 5.3(a) and (b).

(b)   The required functions are given by (A5.1.15) and (A5.1.14).

(c)   The first-order conditions are expressed in Appendix 5.1 as equations (A5.1.1) - (A5.1.4), (A5.1.8) and (A5.1.13). If you are having difficulty in deriving these, you should rework Exercise 5.3. Notice that on the left hand sides of (A5.1.1) - (A5.1.4), we have replaced λ'_a, λ'_b, K'_a and K'_b by finite-difference approximations. This takes our representation of the model closer to the form used in computations. The steady-state values of λ_a and λ_b are given by (A5.1.5) and (A5.1.6). If you need an explanation of these, refer to Exercise 5.4(a).

(d)   The input demand functions for industries 1, 2 and 3 are given by (A5.1.16) and (A5.1.17). Notice that we have not included the production functions (E5.14.4) in the equation list in Appendix 5.1. These are implied by (A5.1.16) and (A5.1.17). On the other hand, we have included sector A's production function, see (A5.1.9). For sector A, we have not included an explicit demand-for-capital function. Sector B's production function has the form

$$X_b = K_b \tag{E5.14.7}$$

This equation has been used to eliminate X_b from the equation list.

(e)   The required conditions are (A5.1.18) and (A5.1.19).[26]

(f)   The consumer's budget constraint is given by (A5.1.22) where C is both household disposable income and consumer spending. With a Cobb-Douglas utility function, the consumer demand system is

$$P_i(1+T_s^i)C^i = \alpha_C^i C \quad , \quad i=A, 1, 2 \quad . \tag{E5.14.10}$$

where C^i is the consumer's demand for i and the α's are exogenously given budget shares. In the equation list in Appendix 5.1, the C^is have been eliminated — see the right hand side of (A5.1.24).

(g)   The government's budget constraint is given by (A5.1.23) where G is both government expenditure and government revenue net of subsidies and lump sum payments. The government's demand equations are similar to those of the consumer and have been eliminated from the equation list — see the right hand side of (A5.1.24).

---

26   Notice that our equation list does not include explicit zero-pure-profits conditions for sectors A and B. We could have included such conditions by writing

$$P_a X_a = WL_a^p + \beta K_a \tag{E5.14.8}$$

and

$$\rho X_b = \beta_b K_b \tag{E5.14.9}$$

where β_b is the profit per unit of capital in sector B. However, equation (E5.14.8) is implied by (A5.1.9), (A5.1.10) and (A5.1.7) and we can think of equation (E5.14.9) as having been used to eliminate β_b.

(h)   The market-clearing equations for goods A, 1 and 2, for labor and for general-purpose capital are given by (A5.1.24), (A5.1.20) and (A5.1.21). (In (A5.1.24) we equate the purchasers' value of the supply of good i to the purchasers' value of demand. This is equivalent to the usual representation where quantities supplied are equated to quantities demanded.)

The market-clearing equation for good 3 can be written as

$$X_3 = I_a + I_b \qquad \text{(E5.14.11)}$$

However, we have not included this in our list of equations in Appendix 5.1. It can be deduced from the other equations by Walras' Law.

(i)   The price deflator is given by (A5.1.25) where the bars denote base-period values.

Exercise 5.15   *Expectations*

The investment models for sectors A and B are embedded in our intertemporal general equilibrium model via equations (A5.1.1) - (A5.1.6), (A5.1.8) and (A5.1.13). These equations arise from the sectors' investment-optimization problems.   What should appear in these problems are *expectations* of the variables that the sectors treat as exogenous.   In recognition of this, we have appended superscript e's, denoting expectations, to the variables P_a, ρ, W, P_3, T^d and T^s wherever they appear in equations (A5.1.1) -   (A5.1.6), (A5.1.8) and (A5.1.13).[27] We have also added e's to these variables in (A5.1.7) so that β is the *expected* short-run profit of a unit of capital of type a.   With the e's in place, we must make assumptions about how expectations are formed if we are to link the investment models with the intraperiod general equilibrium models.

One possibility is to assume that the expectations are rational, i.e., that in the absence of any unforeseen shocks, firms can predict the course of the economy perfectly.   To implement rational expectations, the variables needed in the investment models could be taken directly from their counterparts in the short-run general equilibrium models.   The price of capital appearing in the investment models, for example, would be equal to the price generated by the general equilibrium model for the appropriate date.   Solving the complete model simultaneously would yield paths of wages and prices consistent with firms' capital stocks, and capital-accumulation plans consistent with wages and prices.

---

27   We could append an e to the interest rate r. For simplicity, we have assumed that this variable is forseen with perfect foresight, i.e., actual outcomes equal expected outcomes.

In our implemented version of the model, we have added equations (A5.1.26) - (A5.1.31). These allow for departures from complete rationality in the formation of expectations. In each of these equations, an expectation is formed by combining a variable's true general equilibrium value with an exogenous component. The six equations contain two weighting parameters. The first of these, ϕ_n, is used in the formation of expectations of market variables. The second, ϕ_x, is used for policy variables.

Explain how different settings of the ϕ parameters imply different assumptions about the formation of expectations.

Answer to Exercise 5.15

Parameters ϕ_n and ϕ_x allow simulations to be run under different assumptions about the extent to which firms can predict the future values of variables. When both ϕ_n and ϕ_x are set to 1, firms have perfect foresight. On the other hand, if $\phi_n = 0$ and $\phi_x = 1$, firms know what tax changes are planned for the future, but are unable to predict the general equilibrium consequences. The possibility that $\phi_n = 1$ and $\phi_x = 0$ is not very appealing — it implies that firms can predict market variables correctly even though they do not predict future tax changes.

Setting both ϕ_n and ϕ_x to zero converts the model to one in which firms expect no changes in the variables which drive their investment decisions. Hence, the model becomes a set of linked static equilibria in which investment does not vary between periods.

In Exercise 5.18 you will compare results from the perfect foresight model (ϕ_n and ϕ_x both set to 1) with results generated under the assumption that firms anticipate only changes in tax rates, not changes in market variables ($\phi_n = 0$ but $\phi_x = 1$). The comparisons give some insights into the implications of the perfect-foresight assumption.

What is the appropriate way to model expectations is an empirical issue. We do not attempt to compare the performance perfect-foresight models with models using other commonly proposed expectation specifications — adaptive expectations, for example.

Exercise 5.16   *Implementing the model*

We have now completed the economic specification of our intertemporal general equilibrium model. Before it can be used to generate numerical results it must be implemented on a computer.

There are four tasks to accomplish in implementing a model: selecting the solution algorithm, constructing the data set, partitioning the variables into endogenous and exogenous sets, and testing the final program.

(a)   Solving the two investment problems requires solving systems of differential equations, while solving the short-run general equilibrium models requires solving systems of nonlinear equations. These components of the model must be solved simultaneously. Describe how this could be done by combining the finite-difference approach (see Exercise 5.12) with the Johansen approach (see the introductory section of Chapter 3). In Chapter 3, we saw that application of the Johansen approach in a one-period model requires a data base giving an initial or base-case solution. Does this present any difficulties in an intertemporal model?

(b)   Once the solution algorithm and the data set have been prepared, the next step is to decide on a partitioning of the model's variables into endogenous and exogenous sets, i.e., to select a closure. One of the advantages of using the Johansen approach is that it is easy to change the closure for different experiments. Consult Appendix 5.1 and decide how many exogenous variables are required to close the model. Table A5.1.3 shows the list of exogenous variables used in the experiments discussed in Exercises 5.17 and 5.18. Comment on this closure.

(c)   A number of experiments using the closure in Table A5.1.3 can be run to check that the model was programmed correctly. Three such simulations are: a 10 per cent increase at all points of time in the price deflator, government expenditure and the exogenous expectations variables W^X, ρ^X, P_3^X and P_a^X; the imposition at time zero of a surprise, permanent increase in the dividend tax[28]; and an increase in the tax on wages. Explain why these simulations are suitable tests. What results do you anticipate from each?

Answer to Exercise 5.16

(a)   In the model's equations listed in Appendix 5.1, we have already replaced derivatives with finite differences. This enables us to represent the dynamic equations, (A5.1.1) - (A5.1.4), by

$$G_D \left[Z(t^i) , Z(t^{i+1}) \right] = 0, \quad i=0, ..., N-1, \qquad \text{(E5.16.1)}$$

where $Z(t)$ is the vector of values of the model's n variables at time t, and t^0, t^1, ..., t^N are a selection of N time points with t^0 being the initial

---

[28]   Assume that ϕ_x is set at one so that the increase in T^d produces an equivalent increase in T^{de}.

time and t^N being a distant time at which it is reasonable to assume that the steady state has been reached. In (A5.1.1) - (A5.1.4) we have implied that the t^is are spaced uniformly at intervals of h time units. Here, however, we will allow for a non-uniform time grid. Notice also that (A5.1.1) - (A5.1.4) contain only a small subset of the model's variables. In (E5.16.1) we allow all variables to appear but we do not rule out the possibility that many may have zero coefficients.

Next, we represent the intraperiod and expectation equations, (A5.1.7) - (A5.1.31), by

$$G_I \left[z(t^i) \right] = 0, \quad i=0, ..., N .$$
(E5.16.2)

Finally, the boundary conditions, (A5.1.5) and (A5.1.6), can be written as

$$G_B \left[z(t^N) \right] = 0 .$$
(E5.16.3)

Notice that in Appendix 5.1 we have not included the initial conditions on K_a and K_b in the equation list. Instead, we always treat $K_a(t^0)$ and $K_b(t^0)$ as exogenous variables, see part (c).

Assume that we can find an initial solution for the system (E5.16.1) - (E5.16.3), i.e., assume that we can find

$$\bar{Z} = \left(\bar{Z}(t^0), ..., \bar{Z}(t^N) \right)$$

to satisfy these equations. Then we can apply the Johansen approach to obtain a linear system of the form

$$
\begin{bmatrix}
\psi(\bar{Z}(t^0),\bar{Z}(t^1)) & & & & & \\
& \psi(\bar{Z}(t^1),\bar{Z}(t^2)) & & & & \\
& & \cdots & & & \\
& & & \psi(\bar{Z}(t^{N-1}),\bar{Z}(t^N)) & \\
\Theta(\bar{Z}(t^0)) & & & & \\
& \Theta(\bar{Z}(t^1)) & & & \\
& & \cdots & & \\
& & & \cdots & \\
& & & \Theta(\bar{Z}(t^{N-1})) & \\
& & & & \Theta(\bar{Z}(t^N)) \\
& & & & \Xi(\bar{Z}(t^N))
\end{bmatrix}
\begin{bmatrix}
z(t^0) \\
z(t^1) \\
z(t^2) \\
\cdots \\
\cdots \\
z(t^{N-1}) \\
z(t^N)
\end{bmatrix}
= \underline{0}
$$
(E5.16.4)

where the $z(t^i)$ are vectors of changes, log changes or percentage changes in the components of $Z(t^i)$ away from $\bar{Z}(t^i)$, and ψ, Θ and Ξ are coefficient matrices of dimensions $M_D \times 2n$, $M_I \times n$ and $M_B \times n$ arising from the linearizations of (E5.16.1), (E5.16.2) and (E5.16.3). M_D, M_I and M_B are the numbers of dynamic, intraperiod and boundary equations. Although system (E5.16.4) is likely to be large, Gaussian elimination will normally provide a practical solution method.

How do we obtain $\bar{Z}$, the base-case solution? In the one-period models of Chapters 3 and 4, the base-case solution was derived mainly from the input-output data of the base year. Here we need an entire string of equilibria stretching far into the future. These cannot be observed. They must be constructed.

The easiest base case to construct, and the one which has dominated intertemporal modeling to date, is a steady state. In this approach, the base-case values of future exogenous variables are set to particular constants. Then, the data set for the first year of the base case (which is usually obtained from historical data) is adjusted so that the model will replicate itself from year to year as long as the exogenous variables remain at their original values. The result is a base case which consists of an arbitrary string of future periods which are identical to the initial year.

For many experiments, a steady-state base case is acceptable. Often the most important question about a particular shock is how far it pushes the economy away from the base case, not how the base case itself is evolving. In this situation, starting from a steady state is a minor liability which is more than offset by the ease with which the base case can be constructed. For this reason, we have chosen to use a steady-state base case for the simulations presented below. The data we used are presented in Appendix 5.1 Methods for building other kinds of base cases are discussed in Wilcoxen (1988).

Solutions derived from systems such as (E5.16.4) entail Taylor series expansions in both time (finite differences) and variables (linearization). Hence, they are only approximate, and care must be taken to ensure that truncation error is kept small. The results may be made arbitrarily accurate by decreasing the step size used in each expansion. We return to this topic in Exercise 5.17.

(b) From Appendix 5.1 we can count the model's equations and variables. In Table A5.1.1 it can be seen that the complete model has 56 variables at each grid point, or $56(N+1)$ in all. Adding up the number of dynamic, boundary, intraperiod and expectations equations gives a total of 36N+34.   Subtracting this from 56(N+1) gives 20(N+1)+2 as the number of variables which must be set exogenously. This is the number of variables shown in Table A5.1.3. Hence, we have a *prima facie* case that the model is properly closed by that selection.

Most of the variables listed in Table A5.1.3 are initial conditions, tax rates, technical-change variables or exogenous-expectations variables. All of these are naturally exogenous. We will confine our comments to the price deflator, the labor supply, government spending and the interest rate.

Since the price deflator is exogenous, it can be the model's numeraire, setting the rate of pure inflation in addition to the overall price level. There are are no equations describing the demand and supply for money or any other mechanisms for determining the price level and the inflation rate. Instead, these are set exogenously by the path of ζ. If ζ were constant (as it is in the base-case data), there would be no pure inflation — the price of the aggregate consumption bundle would be constant from one year to the next. On the other hand, if the base-case numeraire rose by 5 percent a year, the model would include a 5 percent rate of pure inflation. Besides ζ, there are several other nominal exogenous variables in Table A5.1.3: G, r, W^X, ρ^X, P_3^X and P_a^X. Thus, in choosing a path for ζ, we need to think about the implied values for *real* government expenditure, the *real* interest rate and the exogenous expectations for various *real* prices.

The household is assumed to be the supplier of labor, but there is no specification of how labor supply might respond to other variables: no specification of labor-leisure choice, for example. In this context, setting labor supply exogenously, with the wage rate endogenous, is one obvious option. Another is to set the wage rate exogenously, with labor supply endogenous.

Since government spending is exogenous and the lump sum payment is endogenous, any revenue accruing from changes in tax rates will be passed back to households. This is convenient for the simulations which we discuss in the subsequent exercises, but there are other alternatives. In some applications, for example, it may be more useful to make the lump-sum tax exogenous and government spending endogenous.

The final noteworthy feature of Table A5.1.3 is the inclusion of the interest rate. Exogenous treatment is dictated by the structure of the consumer problem described in Exercise 5.14(f). Since, at any interest rate, the consumer will save whatever the firms want to invest, the consumer's saving-supply curve is coincident with the firms' demand-for-savings curve. Thus, we have little choice but to make the interest rate exogenous. If we wanted the specification of the financial market to be more realistic, we could introduce an upward-sloping savings supply curve by changing the consumer model to include intertemporal optimization.

(c) As was pointed out in Exercise 4.13, one way to check for computational errors is to run simulations for which the solution is known *a priori* from the theoretical structure of the model.

In the first of the three suggested simulations, the effect should be to raise all prices (including λ's), profits (including β, D_a and D_b), revenues and expenditures (including C and LS) by 10 per cent while leaving all real variables and the interest rate unchanged. To check this, work through equations (A5.1.1) to (A5.1.31). We see that under the proposed solution, both the left and right hand sides of (A5.1.1) are raised by 10 per cent; both the left and right hand sides of (A5.1.2) are unchanged, etc...

As noted in Exercises 5.4(b) and 5.5(a), an increased dividend tax at time zero acts as a pure profits tax. As such, it should have no effect on the capital stock or output of any industry, although the λ's should fall by the amount of the tax. There should also be a shift of income from consumers to the government. However, with G constant, this will be offset by an increase in LS. Work through equations (A5.1.1) - (A5.1.31) assuming that there are 10 per cent falls in $(1-T^{de})$, $(1-T^d)$, λ_a and λ_b. Allow for a suitable increase in LS. Convince yourself that if you are starting from a solution, you will still have a solution.

The final test is an increase in the wage tax paid by consumers. Since labor supply is completely inelastic, the effect of a wage tax should be simply to transfer income to the government. Again, this will be offset by an increase in LS with no effects on any other variables.

Exercise 5.17 *A further implementation test, numerical accuracy and grid spacing*

Under our computational approach, the complete model is a system of partial differential equations in time and variables which are solved by integrating over time using finite differences and over variables using Euler's method.[29] Apart from a few special cases, of which the test simulations in Exercise 5.16(c) are examples, the accuracy of solutions depends on the step size used in these

---

29   See part B of Problem Set 3 for an explanation of how Johansen linearization is related to Euler's method.

integrations: computed solutions will approach true solutions as the step size in both time and variables is made smaller.[30] Consequently, another test of the implementation of the model is to show, for an experiment subject to truncation error, that the computed solution can be made arbitrarily close to the true solution as the step sizes are decreased.

Using the data, parameter values and closure given in Tables A5.1.1 to A5.1.3, and setting t^N at 100 years, we have computed the effects of a permanent increase in the dividend tax rate from 10 percent to 20 percent, to take effect ten years in the future. The expectation parameters discussed in Exercise 5.16 were set to $\phi_n=0$ and $\phi_x=1$. Thus, firms are assumed to ignore any feedback effects from their actions to the price variables in their investment decisions. This allows us to solve the investment models independently of the intraperiod general equilibrium models. The qualitative results of a similar experiment were discussed in Exercise 5.5(b).

To assess the accuracy of different numerical solutions, we examined how well they captured the true values of the capital stocks of sectors A and B in year ten. This is a good indication of the overall accuracy of a solution because the true paths of the capital stocks have cusps at that point. Recall from Exercise 5.12 that truncation error will be large in regions where the high-order derivatives dropped from the difference formulae are large. At a cusp, the first derivative changes discontinuously and the second derivative goes through infinity. In a numerical simulation, this will manifest itself as rounding of the solution near where the cusp should be.

The results of several experiments are shown in Table E5.17.1.[31] The rows indicate how many steps were used to impose the exogenous shock, while the columns show how many grid intervals were used in the finite-difference approximation. Each entry gives the value of $K_a(10)$ obtained with a particular combination of steps and grid points. Since step sizes decrease downward and to the right, the solution should become more accurate in those directions. The bottom row was obtained by solving the investment models without linearizing.

---

30 As shown in Chapter 3, truncation errors in the Johansen linearization can be made arbitrarily small by applying the shock in a series of small steps.

31 The values in this and subsequent tables were computed using slightly different difference formulae from those shown for the dynamic equations in Appendix 5.1. Implementing the model as it is described in this chapter would produce slightly different, but qualitatively similar, results.

Table E5.17.1

The Effect of Grid Density and Step Number on the Computed Capital Stock of Sector A at Period 10*

No. of steps	Number of Grid Intervals			
	10	20	40	80
1	.9623	.9376	.9247	.9180
2	.9605	.9361	.9236	.9174
4	.9596	.9353	.9233	.9171
8	.9591	.9350	.9229	.9169
∞	.9586	.9346	.9227	.9168

*   The steady state value of K_a in the data base is 1. Thus, for example, the first entry indicates that the increase in the dividend tax reduces capital in year 10 to 96.23 per cent of the level it otherwise would have been. With the data and parameter values given in Appendix 5.1, sector B's capital stock is 10 times larger than that in sector A, and in the simulation under consideration, the proportionate effects of the dividend-tax increase are identical in the two sectors. Thus, the first entry in the table implies that sector B's capital falls to 9.623, i.e., to 96.23 per cent of the level it otherwise would have been.

Since that is equivalent to using an infinitesimal step size, the row is labeled "infinite" iterations.

(a)   Can you calculate the true value of $K_a(10)$ in this experiment using a pocket calculator? (This is not the main point of the exercise. Consequently if you are having difficulty, refer to our answer without too much delay.)

(b)   What light does Table E5.17.1 throw on the accuracy of our numerical method?

(c)   As noted in Exercise 5.12, for large models it may not be feasible to eliminate finite-difference truncation error by using a large number of grid points. For such models, however, it may be possible to improve the approximation by shifting grid points from regions of low curvature to regions of high curvature. Table 5.17.2 shows five possible allocations of nine points to times between 0 and 100 years. How would you expect the numerical accuracy of the solutions for $K_a(10)$ to be affected by these different grids?

Table E5.17.2

A Selection of Grid Spacings

Point	Grid				
	A	B	C	D	G
0	0	0	0	0	0
1	10	5	5	5	5
2	20	10	7	7	7
3	30	20	10	9	9
4	40	30	20	10	10
5	50	40	30	20	15
6	60	50	40	30	20
7	70	60	50	40	35
8	80	70	60	50	50
9	90	80	70	60	75
10	100	100	100	100	100

Answer to Exercise 5.17

(a)   With the announced change in the dividend tax causing no change in investor expectations regarding market variables ($\phi_n=0$), it is possible to obtain a closed-form solution for $K_a(t)$. In particular, we obtain a formula for $K_a(10)$ which can be evaluated using a pocket calculator.

We start by reinstating the derivative on the left hand side of (A5.1.2):

$$K'_a = I_a - \delta K_a .\qquad\text{(E5.17.1)}$$

Integrating from 0 to τ gives

$$K_a(\tau) = K_a(0)e^{-\delta\tau} + \int_0^\tau I_a(t)e^{-\delta(\tau-t)}\, dt .\qquad\text{(E5.17.2)}$$

Next, we reinstate the derivative on the left hand side of (A5.1.1):

$$\lambda'_a = (r+\delta)\lambda_a - \beta(1-T^{de}) .\qquad\text{(E5.17.3)}$$

Under our expectation assumptions, the increase in the dividend tax does not move β (the expected short-run profit per unit of capital) from its initial steady-state value. Assuming that the increase in the dividend tax rate takes place at time τ (year 10 in this exercise), we can solve (E5.17.3) to obtain, for any $t \le \tau$,[32]

$$\lambda_a(t) = \beta(1-T_1^d)\int_t^\tau e^{-(r+\delta)(s-t)}ds + \beta(1-T_2^d)\int_\tau^\infty e^{-(r+\delta)(s-t)}ds , \quad (E5.17.4)$$

where T_1^d and T_2^d are the initial and new rates of dividend tax (0.1 and 0.2). From (E5.17.4), we find that

$$\lambda_a(t) = \frac{\beta(1-T_1^d)}{(r+\delta)} + \frac{\beta(T_1^d-T_2^d)}{r+\delta}e^{-(r+\delta)(\tau-t)} \quad \text{for } t \le \tau. \quad (E5.17.5)$$

Substituting (E5.17.5) into (A5.1.8) and then into (E5.17.2) gives

$$K_a(\tau) = K_a(0)e^{-\delta\tau} +$$

$$\frac{1}{2W^e\theta_a}\left[\frac{\beta}{(1-T^{se})}\left(\frac{1}{r+\delta}\right)\left(\frac{1-e^{-\tau\delta}}{\delta}\right) + \frac{\beta(T_1^d-T_2^d)(1-e^{-(r+2\delta)\tau})}{(r+\delta)(1-T_1^d)(1-T^{se})(r+2\delta)} - \frac{P_3^e(1-e^{-\delta\tau})}{\delta}\right].$$

$$(E5.17.6)$$

With $T_1^d=0.1$ and $T_2^d=0.2$, (E5.17.6) in conjunction with the data and parameter values in Appendix 5.1, implies that

$$K_a(10) = 0.9113 . \quad (E5.17.7)$$

(b)   In Table E5.17.1, step sizes and grid intervals decrease downward and to the right. Hence, the solution becomes more accurate in those directions, approaching the true value of $K_a(10)$, 0.9113, which we discovered in part (a).

Because first-order Taylor expansions form the basis of the linearizations in each dimension, the difference between values obtained from successive halvings of the step size decreases by a factor of about two.[33] For example, in the first column, the difference between the 1-step and 2-step solutions is 0.0018 (=0.9623 – 0.9605) while the difference between the 2-step and 4-step solutions is 0.0009 (=0.9605 – 0.9596). Similarly, in the first row, the differences between the 10-

---

[32]   In deriving (E5.17.4) we first use the integrating factor $e^{-(r+\delta)s}$ in (E5.17.3). This gives us a formula for $\lambda_a(t)$ as an integral expression over the period t to ∞. In obtaining this expression, we assume that λ_a grows at a rate less than $(r+\delta)$ as time tends to infinity. Finally, we split the integral at time τ, using the property of integrals that $\int_a^b f(x)dx = \int_a^\tau f(x)dx + \int_\tau^b f(x)dx$.

[33]   See Exercise 3.7

Table E5.17.3

The Effect of Grid Choice and Step Number on
the Computed Capital Stock of Sector A at Period 10*

No. of steps	Grid				
	A	B	C	D	G
1	.9623	.9407	.9323	.9233	.9199
2	.9605	.9392	.9310	.9226	.9192
4	.9596	.9384	.9303	.9222	.9187
8	.9591	.9381	.9300	.9219	.9185
∞	.9586	.9377	.9297	.9217	.9183

* The true value of K(10) is .9113

and 20-interval solutions and the 20- and 40-interval solutions are 0.0247 (=0.9623 – 0.9376) and 0.0129 (=0.9376 – 0.9247), respectively. This suggests that Richardson's extrapolation is applicable. For example, extrapolating from the (1,10) and (2,20) results, gives a good approximation to $K_a(10)$, namely 0.9099 (=2(0.9361) – 0.9623).

From the initial 1-step, 10-interval solution, accuracy increases most rapidly by increasing the number of finite-difference grid points. This indicates that the error introduced by the finite-difference approximation overwhelms that of the Johansen linearization. In fact, doubling the grid density improves the solution by more than increasing the number of Johansen steps to infinity.

(c)   After the shock of the announcement of the tax change and its implementation in year 10, the system will be back almost to the steady state at late years like 90. Since high-order derivatives of the model's variables will be close to zero there, it might be desirable to move grid points to an earlier time where the derivatives are large. One possibility would be to shift the point from year 90 to year 5; this is done in grid B in Table E5.17.2. Continuing the rearrangement produces the other grids shown in the table. We expect the results for $K_a(10)$ to become more accurate as more of the grid points are concentrated in the early years.

Simulations of the effects of the announced change in the dividend tax were carried out with each of the grids in Table E5.17.2, producing the results shown in Table E5.17.3. Again, results are shown for several numbers of Johansen steps. By reading down the columns of

Table E5.17.3, it can be seen that using a non-uniform grid does not harm convergence when the number of iterations is increased. Secondly, the table demonstrates that rearranging a limited number of grid points has produced a solution almost as accurate as increasing the density of a uniform grid by a factor of eight.

Exercise 5.18   *Some illustrative simulations*

In this exercise we ask you to look at some results from the intertemporal general equilibrium model. We have chosen simulations which illustrate (i) how results can be changed by differences in assumptions concerning expectations, (ii) how results arising from intertemporal optimization of investment depend on intraperiod general equilibrium calculations and (iii) how intertemporal investment optimization affects the results generated by the intraperiod general equilibrium models.

(a)   Figure E5.18.1 provides graphical representations of the results from the intertemporal model for effects of an announced change in the divided tax (T^d) from 10 to 20 percent to be implemented in year 10. The results were generated under two sets of expectation assumptions: perfect foresight $(\phi_n=\phi_x=1)$, and fixed expectations with respect to market variables but perfect foresight with respect to policy variables $(\phi_n=0, \phi_x=1)$. The simulations were run using ten finite-difference intervals placed according to column G in Table E5.17.2 and the shocks were imposed in one step. The charts show the percentage deviations for selected variables from their base-case values at each point of time. The paths marked "P" are for perfect foresight $(\phi_n=\phi_x=1)$ and those marked "F" are for fixed expectations $(\phi_n=0, \phi_x=1)$

Comment on the results in Figure E5.18.1. Why does perfect foresight (P) tend to produce damped responses compared with fixed expectations (F)?

(b)   Figures E5.18.2 and E5.18.3 provide graphical representations of results for the effects of announced changes from 0 to 10 per cent in the sales tax rates applying to goods A and 2 to be implemented in year 10. The simulations were conducted under the assumption of perfect foresight $(\phi_n=\phi_x=1)$. Again, we used ten finite-difference intervals placed according to column G in Table E5.17.2 and imposed the shocks in one step.

Comment on the two sets of results and compare them.

Figure E5.18.1
Effects of an announced increase in the dividend tax

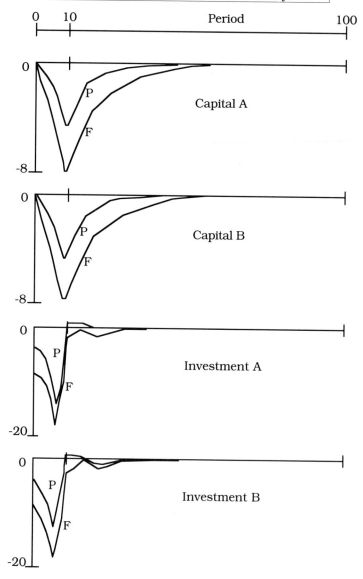

Figure E5.18.1
(continued)

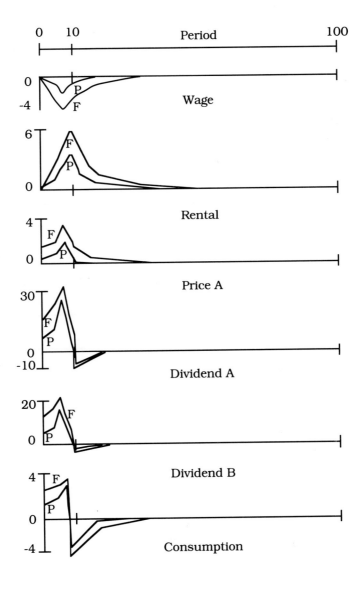

Figure E5.18.2
*Effects of an announced increase in the sales tax on
good A under perfect foresight*

All graphs show the percentage change in a
variable from its base-case value in each year.

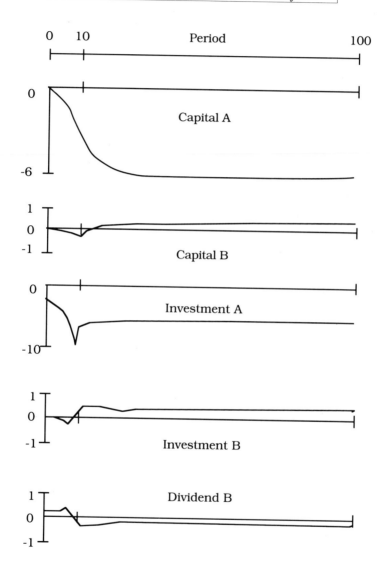

Figure E5.18.2
(continued)

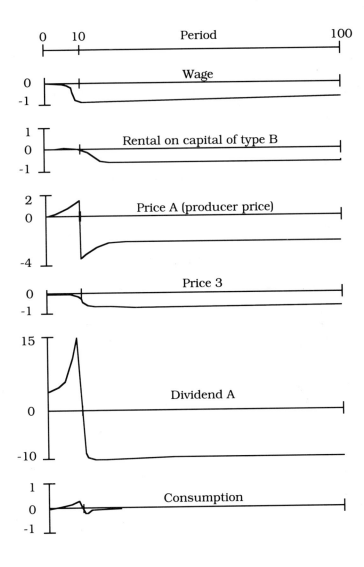

Figure E5.18.3
*Effects of an announced increase in the sales tax on
good 2 under perfect foresight*

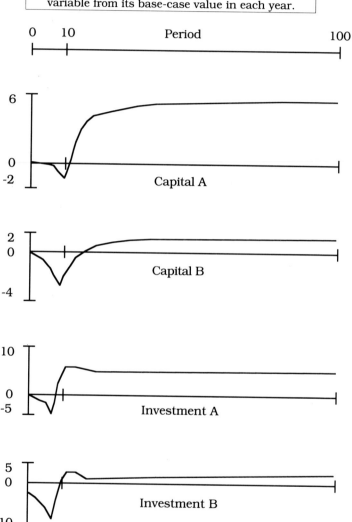

Figure E5.18.3
(continued)

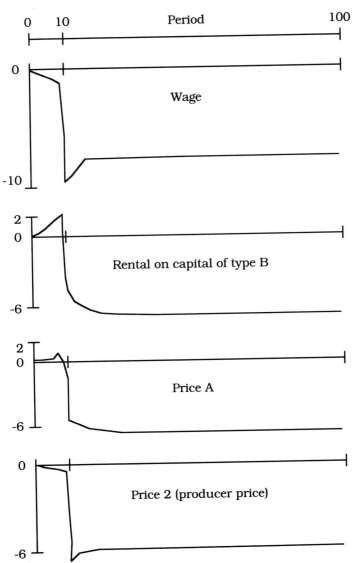

... (continued)

Figure E5.18.3
(continued)

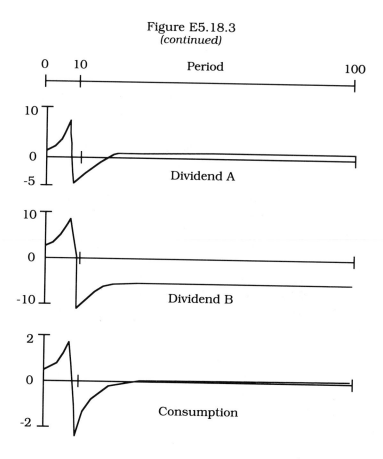

Answer to Exercise 5.18

(a)   The striking feature of Figure E5.18.1 is that perfect foresight with respect to prices and wages attenuates the response of the model by about 50 percent. This effect occurs even in period zero: investment falls less than half as much under perfect foresight as it does under fixed expectations. The simulations are so different because as the capital stocks decline in the general equilibrium setting, their rental values rise. Firms with foresight understand this and do not let their capital stocks deteriorate as fast as those expecting rental values to be unchanged. From this we conclude that adding general equilibrium effects can change the results from the investment models substantially. If agents have rational expectations, a partial equilibrium investment model will, in this example, overstate the responses of investment and capital stocks by 50 percent.

Another feature of the results is that many of the variables change substantially in the interval before the tax is implemented. This demonstrates that intertemporal optimization by investors can have a substantial effect on the economy even before an anticipated event occurs.

Finally, the two sets of results show that differences in the paths of the intertemporal variables (investment and capital) have significant consequences for ordinary general equilibrium variables such as prices and wages.

(b)   The intraperiod general equilibrium effect of the tax on good A is to raise the purchasers' prices of the good and lower its producer's price. This makes investment in sector A less attractive, causing its capital stock to decline.[34] In the long run, the capital stock in sector A falls by about 6 percent.

The decline in sector A has effects throughout the economy. It frees up labor that was employed in sector A, causing a drop in the wage rate. Lower wages benefit sector B by lowering its investment costs. Hence, I_b increases and K_b rises over time. This drives down the rental price of capital B. With both wages and the rental price of capital falling, the producer prices of goods 1, 2 and 3 must fall.

Before the tax is implemented, D_a increases. This comes about because investment drops in anticipation of the tax, leaving more earnings to be distributed as dividends (see also Exercise 5.5(d)). Once the tax is in place, however, smaller dividends are paid and D_a drops below its base-case value. The present value of the change in the dividend stream is negative — the tax results in a windfall loss to owners of the firm.

An interesting result in Figure E5.18.3 is that in the long run the increase in the tax on good 2 causes both capital stocks to rise. In Figure E5.18.2, the increase in the tax on good A caused capital of type B to rise but that of type A to fall. The source of the two increases in the capital stocks in Figure E5.18.3 is the labor intensity of sector 2. A contraction in sector 2's output leads to a substantial drop in the wage.

---

34 Apart from sign, the paths of sector A's investment and capital stock are similar to those analysed in Exercise 5.5(d) and displayed in Figure E5.5.5. There we were concerned with an announced increase in a firm's output price. Here we are concerned with an announced decrease.

This lowers investment costs for both sectors A and B, causing investment to rise and both capital stocks to grow. Finally, growth of the capital stocks causes the rental price of capital produced by sector B and the price of good A to fall. In the end, sector A has gained, producing slightly higher dividends, while sector B's dividends have fallen considerably.

Appendix 5.1   The Intertemporal Model: Equations, Variables and Trial Data Set

The Equations

(i)   Dynamic Equations

The model contains four sets of dynamic equations linking different points in time. Two are sector A's equations of motion, and two are sector B's. Together they govern the evolution of λ_a, λ_b, K_a and K_b. Since each equation holds over each grid interval, with N intervals there are 4N dynamic equations in all.

$$\left[\lambda_a(t+h)-\lambda_a(t)\right]/h = (r+\delta)\lambda_a(t) - \beta(t)\left[1-T^{de}(t)\right], \quad (A5.1.1)$$

$$\left[K_a(t+h)-K_a(t)\right]/h = I_a(t) - \delta K_a(t) . \quad (A5.1.2)$$

$$\left[\lambda_b(t+h)-\lambda_b(t)\right]/h = (r+\delta)\lambda_b(t) - \rho^e\left[1-T^{de}(t)\right], \quad (A5.1.3)$$

$$\left[K_b(t+h)-K_b(t)\right]/h = I_b(t) - \delta K_b(t) . \quad (A5.1.4)$$

(ii)   Boundary conditions

The model has four boundary conditions: the two initial capital stocks, $K_a(0)$ and $K_b(0)$, and the two steady-state multipliers, λ_a^{ss} and λ_b^{ss}. The capital stocks can be obtained from observable data, but the multipliers must be calculated using the equations below:

$$\lambda_a^{ss} = \beta(1-T^{de})/(r+\delta) , \quad (A5.1.5)$$

$$\lambda_b^{ss} = \rho^e(1-T^{de})/(r+\delta). \quad (A5.1.6)$$

(iii)   Intraperiod equations

Each period's submodel consists of the 26 equations listed below. Since these hold at each grid point, a grid of N intervals will have 26(N+1) intraperiod equations.

Short run profit on a unit of K_a:

$$\beta = \left(\frac{1-\epsilon_a}{\epsilon_a}\right)\left(\frac{\epsilon_a P_a^e}{w^e}\right)^{1/(1-\epsilon_a)} w^e . \quad (A5.1.7)$$

Investment by sector A:

$$I_a = \frac{1}{2w^e\theta_a}\left(\frac{\lambda_a}{(1-T^{de})(1-T^{se})} - P_3^e\right). \quad (A5.1.8)$$

Output of sector A:

$$X_a = (L_a^P)^{\epsilon_a}(K_a)^{1-\epsilon_a} . \quad (A5.1.9)$$

Labor demanded for production in sector A:

$$L_a^P = \left(\frac{\varepsilon_a P_a}{W}\right)^{1/(1-\varepsilon_a)} K_a \ . \tag{A5.1.10}$$

Labor demanded for investment by sector A:

$$L_a^I = \theta_a I_a^2 \ . \tag{A5.1.11}$$

Pretax dividends of sector A:

$$D_a = P_a X_a - W L_a^P - \left(P_3 I_a + W L_a^I\right)(1-T^s) \ . \tag{A5.1.12}$$

Investment by sector B:

$$I_b = \frac{1}{2W^e \theta_b}\left(\frac{\lambda_b}{(1-T^{de})(1-T^{se})} - P_3^e\right). \tag{A5.1.13}$$

Labor demanded by sector B:

$$L_b^I = \theta_b I_b^2 \ . \tag{A5.1.14}$$

Pretax dividends of sector B:

$$D_b = \rho K_b - (P_3 I_b + W L_b^I)(1-T^s) \ . \tag{A5.1.15}$$

Labor demanded by sector i, $i \in \{1,2,3\}$:

$$L_i = \frac{1}{\gamma_i} X_i \left(\frac{\rho \varepsilon_i}{W(1-\varepsilon_i)}\right)^{1-\varepsilon_i} \ . \tag{A5.1.16}$$

Capital B demanded by sector i, $i \in \{1,2,3\}$:

$$K_b^i = \frac{1}{\gamma_i} X_i \left(\frac{W(1-\varepsilon_i)}{\rho \varepsilon_i}\right)^{\varepsilon_i} \ . \tag{A5.1.17}$$

Zero-pure-profit condition for sector i, $i \in \{1,2\}$:

$$X_i P_i = W L_i + \rho K_b^i \ . \tag{A5.1.18}$$

Zero-pure-profit condition for sector 3:

$$X_3 P_3 = (1+T_s^3)(W L_3 + \rho K_b^3) \ . \tag{A5.1.19}$$

Labor market equilibrium condition:

$$L = L_a^P + L_a^I + L_b^I + L_1 + L_2 + L_3 \ . \tag{A5.1.20}$$

Capital B market equilibrium condition:

$$K_b = K_b^1 + K_b^2 + K_b^3 \ . \tag{A5.1.21}$$

Consumption spending:

$$C = W L(1-T^w) + (D_a + D_b)(1-T^d) + LS \ . \tag{A5.1.22}$$

Government spending:

$$G = T^d(D_a + D_b) - T^s \left[P_3(I_a + I_b) + W(\theta_a I_a^2 + \theta_b I_b^2) \right] + T_s^a P_a X_a$$

$$+ T_s^1 P_1 X_1 + T_s^2 X_2 P_2 + T_s^3 P_3 X_3 / (1 + T_s^3) + T^W WL - LS \ . \quad (A5.1.23)$$

Market equilibrium for good i, i ∈ {A,1,2}:

$$P_i X_i (1 + T_s^i) = \alpha_C^i C + \alpha_G^i G . \quad (A5.1.24)$$

Price deflator:

$$\zeta = \frac{X_a P_a (1 + T_s^a) + X_1 P_1 (1 + T_s^1) + X_2 P_2 (1 + T_s^2)}{X_a \bar{P}_a + X_1 \bar{P}_1 + X_2 \bar{P}_2} . \quad (A5.1.25)$$

(iv)   Expectations

Next, there are six sets of equations which determine investors' expectations. These hold at each grid point. On a grid of N intervals, there will be 6(N+1) equations in all. They are:

$$W^e = (W)^{\phi_n} (W^x)^{1-\phi_n} \ , \quad (A5.1.26)$$

$$\rho^e = (\rho)^{\phi_n} (\rho^x)^{1-\phi_n} \ , \quad (A5.1.27)$$

$$P_a^e = (P_a)^{\phi_n} (P_a^x)^{1-\phi_n} \ , \quad (A5.1.28)$$

$$P_3^e = (P_3)^{\phi_n} (P_3^x)^{1-\phi_n} \ , \quad (A5.1.29)$$

$$T^{de} = (T^d)^{\phi_x} (T^{dx})^{1-\phi_x} \ , \quad (A5.1.30)$$

$$T^{se} = (T^s)^{\phi_x} (T^{sx})^{1-\phi_x} \ . \quad (A5.1.31)$$

Variables and Trial Data Set

Tables A5.1.1 and A5.1.2 list the model's variables and parameters together with values used in our simulations discussed in Exercises 5.16 and 5.17. The values in Table A5.1.1 are the base-case values used in the Johansen linearization. Because they are steady-state values they can be used at each grid point. Our selection of exogenous variables is shown in Table A5.1.3.

Table A5.1.1
Variables in the Intertemporal General Equilibrium Model

Symbol	Definition	Value
K_a	Capital stock A, specific to industry A	1.0
β	Short run profit on a unit of K_a	0.25
λ_a	Marginal value of K_a	1.5
K_b	Capital stock B, nonspecific	10.0
ρ	Rental price of a unit of K_b	0.25
λ_b	Marginal value of K_b	1.5
K_b^1	Type B capital used in industry 1	3.177778
K_b^2	Type B capital used in industry 2	4.622222
K_b^3	Type B capital used in industry 3	2.2
W	Wage rate	1.0
L	Total labor supply	5.0
L_a^P	Labor used in production by industry A	0.25
L_a^I	Labor used in investment by industry A	0.042593
L_b^I	Labor used in investment by industry B	0.425926
L_1	Labor used by industry 1	0.264815
L_2	Labor used by industry 2	3.466667
L_3	Labor used by industry 3	0.55
P_a	Price of good A, basic value	1.0
P_1	Price of good 1, basic value	1.0
P_2	Price of good 2, basic value	1.0
P_3	Price of raw capital goods, purchasers' cost	1.0
X_a	Production of good A	0.5
X_1	Production of good 1	1.059259
X_2	Production of good 2	4.622222
X_3	Production of raw capital goods	1.1
I_a	Investment by industry A	0.1
I_b	Investment by industry B	1.0

continued

Table A5.1.1 (continued)

Symbol	Definition	Value
D_a	Dividends paid by industry A	0.121667
D_b	Dividends paid by industry B	1.216667
C	Private consumption	5.404500
G	Government spending	0.776981
T^w	Tax rate on wages	0.2
T_s^a	Sales tax rate on good A	0.0
T_s^1	Sales tax rate on good 1	0.0
T_s^2	Sales tax rate on good 2	0.0
T_s^3	Sales tax rate on good 3	0.0
LS	Lump sum payment	0.2
T^d	Dividend tax rate	0.10
T^s	Investment subsidy rate	0.10
γ_1	Technical change variable, industry 1	0.620403
γ_2	Technical change variable, industry 2	1.240806
γ_3	Technical change variable, industry 3	1.0
ρ^x	Exogenous expectation, rental price	0.25
W^x	Exogenous expectation, wage rate	1.0
P_3^x	Exogenous expectation, raw capital price	1.0
P_a^x	Exogenous expectation, price of good A	1.0
T^{dx}	Exogenous expectation, dividend tax rate	0.10
T^{sx}	Exogenous expectation, investment subsidy	0.10
ρ^e	Actual expectation, rental price	0.25
W^e	Actual expectation, wage rate	1.0
P_3^e	Actual expectation, raw capital price	1.0
P_a^e	Actual expectation, price of good A	1.0
T^{de}	Actual expectation, dividend tax rate	0.10
T^{se}	Actual expectation, investment subsidy	0.10
r	Interest rate	0.05
ζ	Price deflator	1.0

Table A5.1.2
Parameters in the Trial Data Set

Symbol	Definition	Value
δ	Depreciation rate	0.10
θ_a	Investment parameter, industry A	4.259259
θ_b	Investment parameter, industry B	0.425926
ε_a	Labor exponent, industry A	0.5
ε_1	Labor exponent, industry 1	0.25
ε_2	Labor exponent, industry 2	0.75
ε_3	Labor exponent, industry 3	0.5
α_C^a	Share of private consumption, good A	0.080887
α_C^1	Share of private consumption, good 1	0.171360
α_C^2	Share of private consumption, good 2	0.747753
α_G^a	Share of government spending, good A	0.080887
α_G^1	Share of government spending, good 1	0.171360
α_G^2	Share of government spending, good 2	0.747753
ϕ_n ϕ_x	Weighting parameters in expectations equations. Values are varied between simulations, see Exercise 5.16	
$\bar{P}_a$ $\bar{P}_1$ $\bar{P}_2$	Base period purchasers' prices used in the denominator of the price deflator, see equation (A5.1.25)	1.0 1.0 1.0

Table A5.1.3

Exogenous Variables

Symbol	Description	Symbol	Description
K_a	Sector A capital (period 0 only)	γ_i $\scriptstyle i=1,2,3$	Technical change variables for industries 1, 2 and 3
K_b	Sector B capital (period 0 only)	ρ^x	Exogenous expectations, rental price
L	Total labor supply	W^x	Exogenous expectations, wage rate
G	Government spending	P_3^x	Exogenous expectations, raw capital price
T^w	Tax rate on wages	P_a^x	Exogenous expectations, price of good A
T_s^i $\scriptstyle i=a,1,2,3$	Sales tax rates on goods A, 1, 2 and 3	T^{dx}	Exogenous expectations, dividend tax rate
T^d	Dividend tax rate	T^{sx}	Exogenous expectations, investment subsidy
T^s	Investment subsidy rate	ζ	Price deflator
r	Interest rate		

Author Index

Adams, P.D.	155,186
Adelman, I.	154,155,243
Alaouze, C.	155,230
Allen, R.G.D.	155,219
Anderson, N.	85,110n,116
Armington, P.S.	85,142n,153, 155,224,225
Arrow, K.J.	85,124n
Australian Bureau of Statistics	21,24
Bacha, Edmar L.	87,see also Taylor
Barna, T.	23,24
Benjamin, N.C.	154,155
Bergman L.	153,155
Berndt, E.R.	85,134n
Birkhoff, Garrett	280,282,292 331n,344n
Bisschop, Johannes	5,6
Bjorck, A.	85,110n,116
Black, S.L.	83,87,160,195
Blanchard, Olivier Jean	281,282,286n
Boadway R.	155,195
Borges, A.M.	154,155
Bovenberg, A.L.	79,85
Bowles, S.	5,6,77n,82,85, 96,124n,126n,134n, 135,144n,156,220, see also Dixon
Bright, I.A.	158,see also Murphy
Brooke, Anthony	5,6
Brooker, R.J.	158,see also Murphy
Brown, F.	156,196
Bródy, A.	23,24
Bryson, Arthur E. Jr	280,282
Caddy, V.	156,220
Cardoso, Eliana A.	87,see also Taylor
Carter, A.P.	23,24, see also Leontief
Chenery, H.B.	23,24,85,124n
Clark,P.	23,24
Codsi, George	5,6,85,102n
Cohen, A.M.	85,110
Conte, S.D.	85,110n,113
Cox, D.	153,156,157,218
Cronin, M.R.	156,196,197
Dahlquist, G.	85,110n,116
de Boor, Carl	85,110n,113
de Melo, J.	149,153,154,156
Deardorff, A.V.	153,156,196
Deaton, A.	85,148
Decaluwé, B.	154,156
Dervis, K.	149,153,154,156,196
Devarajan, S.	154,155
Dixon, P.B.	2,3,5,6,13,14,15,16,23,24, 76n,77n,79,82,83,84,85,87, 96,113,124n,126n,128n,134n, 135,144n,153,154,157,160,180, 195,199,208,218,230,240,242
Dorfman, R.	23,24
Drud, Arne	2,5,6
Duchin, F.	23,24
Fair, Ray C.	282,338n,339n
Fischer, Stanley	281,282,286n
Flannery, B.	282,see also Press
Fox, L.	282,348
Francis, J.	159,195, see also Stern
Frisch, R.	82,85
Fullerton, D.	154,157
Gayer, A.D.	5,6
Geeves, W.D.	158,see also Murphy
Ginsburgh, V.	2,6
Gossling, W.F.	23,24
Goulder, L.H.	154,155
Grais, Wafik	5,6
Gregory, Robert Todd	87,113,114
Gruen, F.H.	86,128n,159,208
Hadley, G.	22,24
Hanoch, Giora	85,126n
Harberger, A.C.	82,85
Harris, R.	153,156,157,218
Harrison, G.W.	154,158
Hayashi, F.	282,289n,330
Henderson, Y.K.	154,157
Higgs, P.J.	155,157,186
Ho, Yu-Chi	280,282
Houthakker, H.S.	82,85,86,96
Hudson, E.A.	86,134n,154,157
Intriligator, M.D.	82,86
Isaacson, E.,	282,345
Johansen, L.	73,79,83,84,86,109
Johnson, P.R.	159,195
Jones, R.W.	82,86,153,157
Jorgenson, D.W.	85,86,134,153,154, 155,157,158,216,220
Kamien, Morton I.	280,282,288
Katzner, D.W.	86,132n,138,142n
Keller, H.B.	282,345
Keller, W.J.	79,83,85,86
Kelley, A.C.	153,158
Kendrick, David	5,6,77n,82,85, 96,124n,126n,134n, 135,144n,see also Dixon
Kimbell, L.J.	154,158
King, A.	154,157

Lancaster, Kelvin   82,86
Lange, G.M.   23,24
Lawrence, D.   158,208
Leitmann, G.   280,282
Leontief, W.W.   1,2,5,6,17,19,21,22,
                 23,24,38,40,44,70,71
Lipton, D.   282,336
Lluch, C.   158,193
Lysy, Frank J.   87,see also Taylor
Marsden, J.S.   155,see also Alaouze
Martens, A.   154,156
McKay, L.   158,208
McLaren, Keith   282,289n
Meade, J.E.   82,86
Meeraus, Alexander   2,5,6
Mercenier, J.   153,158
Miller, Merton   282,286n
Minhas, B.S.   85,124n
Modigliani, Franco   282,286n
Muellbauer, J.   85,148
Murphy, C.W.   158,208
Parham, D.J.   159,220
Parmenter, B.R.   5,7,23,24,76n,82,
                 83,84,85,128n,153,
                 154,157,158,160,180,
                 195,242,see also Dixon
Pearson, K.R.   2,3,5,6,7,85,102n
Petri, P.A.   24,see also Leontief
Phlips, L.   86,148
Piggott, J.   153,154,158
Polenske, K.R.   23,24
Poterba, J.   282,see also Lipton
Powell, A.A.   83,86,87,128n,148,
                 157,158,159,160,193,
                 208,242,see also Dixon
Press, W.   281,282,333,334
Pyatt, Graham   5,6
Rimmer, R.J.   153,157,195
Roberts, S.M.   281,283,334,336
Robinson, S.   149,150,153,154,155,
                 156,190,194,220,243
Rostow, W.W.   5,6
Rota, Gian-Carlo   280,282,292,
                       331n,344n
Rutherford, Thomas Fox   2,5,7
Ryland G.J.   159,220
Sachs, J.   282,see also Lipton
Sams, D.   154,160
Samuelson, P.A.   23,24
Sanderson, W.C.   153,158

Sauvy, Alfred   7,17
Scarf, Herbert E.   2,7,153,159
Schumacher, B.   159,195,
                      see also Stern
Schwartz, A.J.   5,6
Schwartz, Nancy L.   280,282,288
Scobie, G.M.   159,195
Sevaldson, P.   159,216
Shipman, J.S.   281,283,334,336
Shoven, J.B.   153,154,157,159
Shumway, C.R.   159,208
Skolka, J.V.   23,24
Solow, R.M.   23,24,85,124n
Srinivasan, T.N.   153,159
Staelin, C.P.   83,86,159,196
Stern, R.M.   153,156,159,195,196,230
Strang, Gilbert   283,301n
Summers, L. H.   282,283,289n,330,
                     see also Lipton
Sutton, J.M.   76n,82,83,84,85,128n,
                 157,180,see also Dixon
Taplin, B.K.   158,see also Murphy
Taylor, John B.   282,338n,339n
Taylor, Lance   79,82,83,84,87,160,195
Teukolsky, S.   282,see also Press
Tewarson, Reginald P.   87,117n
Tinbergen, J.   160,220
Treddenick, J.   155,195
United Nations   21,25
U.S. Department of Commerce 21,25
  Bureau of Economic Analysis 21,25
Vetterling, W.   282,see also Press
Vincent, D.P.   5,6,13,14,15,16,76n,82,
                 83,84,85,87,128n,154,157,
                 160,180,208,see also Dixon
Vlastuin, C.   158,208
Waelbroeck, J.   2,6,153,158
Warr, P.G.   153,160
Weiss, R.D.   160,220
Whalley, J.   153,154,156,157,159,196
Wigle, R.   153,157
Wilcoxen, Peter J.   154,158,160,283,
                      340,342n,359
Williams, R.A.   158,193
Williamson, J.G.   153,158
Wood, D.O.   85,134n
Young, David M.   87,113,114
Zalai, E   153,155
Zeitsch, J.   155,see also Alaouze

Subject Index

absorption 252,255

absorption matrix 20,25-7

ad valorem tariff rate 95

adjustment costs
– see investment cost function

aggregation problem (relating to composition of an industry's output) 199-200,204

agricultural land 218

agriculture 199

algorithms 151

applied general equilibrium modeling – nature of 1

arbitrage equation 283,285-6,316

Armington – his treatment of imports in CGE models 142,151,224

Australian economy
ORANI model of 1
technical change in 13-15

balance of trade identity
in linearized models 166,240-1

balanced expansion (of the economy in DMR model) 247,249

balanced growth
in intertemporal models 295

base case
for an intertemporal model 359

basic prices or values 28-9,189,231

boundary conditions 299,300,304, 333-4,343-4,377

calibration 151
of CET supply system 208-210
of coefficients of input-output model 54-65
from published data 36-7
of import demand equations in DMR model 219-24
of Stylized Johansen model 98-100
of import/domestic substitution equations in DMR model 229-34

capital accumulation constraint 287,318,331

capital gains 284,287,309, 316-7,320,321-5,327

capital/labor substitution 220

CES function 151,212-3,216-7,225
– see also production function

CET function – see production possibilities frontier

circularity
need to avoid in interpreting simulation results 256-7

closure(s) 81
of DMR model 161,179
of Stylized Johansen model 104-8
in intertemporal models 357
standard ORANI closure (of DMR model) 179,246-51
with respect to capital stocks (in DMR model) 237-8
with respect to labor market (in DMR model) 237-8,240-2

Cobb-Douglas function
– see utility function; production function

coefficients compared with parameters 150

combinatorial approach (to solution of applied GE models) 2

commodity composition of output 199-210

competing imports 25

composite commodities 161

computable general equilibrium
– see applied general equilibrium...

computer software
flexible, use of 87
– see also GEMPACK

computing strategies versus algorithms 151

concave function 132n

condensed system
– see Johansen model

constant returns to scale 133
in DMR model 218,249
in input-output model 72
in Stylized Johansen model 89,91,106-7

construction price of capital 184

consumer price index 241

consumption function 246

control variable
in optimal control problems 288

cost function – see translog unit cost function

costate variable
  and stock market data   330-2
  discontinuous changes in   300-1
  in optimal control problems   288
  – see also multiplier
costs of adjustment
  – see investment cost function
CRESH function
  – see production function
CRETH function
  – see production possibilities
       frontier
demand function
  household   89-91,143
  input – see input demand functions
depreciation   240
development economics
  use of input-output in   20,23
difference approximation
  forward   341-2,347
  central   346-7
  central, on an uneven grid   347
  second-order   346
diminishing returns
  in intertemporal models   325-7
  to scale   218
displacement analysis   77
disposable income   246
distribution of income   243
dividend function, example of   325,
                                       330-2,351,353
dividend tax experiment
  analytical solution   363-5
  phase diagram analysis   305-9
dividends   284-5
  and market value of a firm   286-7
  present value of   285-6
DMR (Dervis, de Melo and
       Robinson) model   149
  closures of   179
  equations of   162-8
  other notation appearing in the
       levels equations of   172
  other notation appearing in
       percentage-change
       equations of   173-8
  parameters required for per-
       centage-change form of   180
  supplementary data file for   181
  variables of   169-71

earnings function   289
  constant returns to scale in   291
  derivation of   289-91
eigenvalues
  in intertemporal models   301-4
elasticity of transformation
                                       128,133,201
eliminated variables   101-2
Engel's aggregation   144
Engel's law   96
environmental economics
  use of input-output in   20,23
equations of motion   290,316,
                                       325-6,333,342,377
Euler method for solving non-
  linear equations   110-24,331-4,361
exchange rates   153
exchange shortages   149
expectations   355-6
  rational   355
  – see also rational expectations
  sample formation mechanisms 379
export demand elasticities   151,195-9
  sensitivity of results to   195,199
export subsidies   236
export supply   204,210
exportable products (in DMR model)
                                       161,199-207
extrapolation
  in multi-step Johansen solution
       – see Euler method...
  Richardson's   115-6
Fair-Taylor algorithm   338-40
final demands
  in DMR model   191,253
  in input-output models   39-40
finite difference method   340-8
  grid spacing   361-7
  numerical accuracy   362
  use with Johansen's method   342,
                                       345-6,357-9
first-order conditions
  for cost minimization   91,125-7
  for revenue maximizing   132,202
  for utility maximizing   91
fix price – see rationing
forecasting (versus policy analysis)
                                       79-80

foreign saving 265

GDP (gross domestic product)
in the Stylized Johansen model
92-3
in DMR model
from the expenditure side 252-4
from the income side 252,254-5
change due to terms of trade
deterioration 261

GEMPACK software 102-3

government expenditure function 246

gross operating surplus 186

Hamiltonian function 288,318,331

homogeneity
of 1st degree of real endogenous
variables (in DMR model)
with respect to real
exogenous variables 247,249
of degree zero of real variables (in
DMR model) with respect
to absolute prices 246-8
of translog unit cost function
134-5,140
of consumer demand function 144

'horse stories' 17

IAESR at University of Melbourne 1

idle capacity 237-8

IMPACT Project 1

import demand functions
under rationing (in DMR model)
224-9

import/domestic substitution
224,229,230

imports
at purchasers' prices 29-30
basic values of 26
matrix, computation of
from published data 36-7

income distribution 243

increasing returns to scale 218

indexation of wages 240,242

indirect allocation of imports 32-4,189

information set
and expectations 284
changes in 293,299

initial solution
of the Stylized Johansen model 97

initial value problem 333-4

input demand functions
in DMR model 162-3,211-9
in basic input-output model 71-2
in Stylized Johansen model
89,92,95
from CES production function
124-6
from CRESH production function
126-8
from nested Cobb-Douglas/CES
production function 143,145-6
from nested Leontief/CES
production function 142-5
from translog cost function 134-6

input-output accounting
– see input-output table(s)

input-output coefficients
for wine-cloth economy 8,10

input-output data 19,25-7
and the initial solution
of a Johansen model 97
in DMR model 150,186-91
use of 87,97,98-100
use of to set coefficients
in DMR model 191-4
in input-output models 54-65
– see also make matrix; absorption
matrix; input-output table(s)

input-output model(s) 19
and national income identity 41
as CGE models 70-2
commodity prices in 40,47,54,71
equations of 38-41
open static version of 38-41
producer optimization in 70

input-output multipliers 65-7

input-output table(s)
allocation of imports in
direct 32-4
indirect 32-4
commodity by industry 28-34
industry by industry 35-7
for Norway 216
role of fixed coefficients in 70-1
treatment of imports in 25-6
treatment of multi-
industry products in 41-5
treatment of multi-
product industries in 41-5
valuation of flows in
at basic values 28-9,189,231
at producers' prices 31
at purchasers' prices 28-31

integrating factor   284-5,302,317

international economics
  use of input-output in   45-8

international trade   149

interpreting results   256-67

investment   149,151,265
  allocation of across industries
    in DMR model   165,239-40
  financing of   286
  firm's objective function   277,
283,286

investment cost function   289
  adjustment costs   291,296,
314,316,349
    curvature properties   289
    derivation   287,291

isocost lines   71

isoquant
  of Leontief production function   71

Johansen linearization
  – see Johansen-style computation

Johansen model
  condensed system   99-103
  Stylized   88-109,249
    solutions of   105
    theoretical structure of   88-90

Johansen-style computation   161,236
  numerical accuracy of   361-3,366
    – see also linearization error
  use with finite difference method
342,345-6,357-9
  defined   73-9,87,150

key sector   69

Korea, DMR (Dervis, de Melo and
    Robinson) model of   149-50

labor/capital substitution
  – see capital/labor substitution

labor/labor substitution   216,220

large change (in Johansen
  solution) – see multi-step...

Leontief function
  – see production function

life-cycle consumption model   277

linearization error   78-9,81,109-24
  – see also Johansen-style...

make matrix   20,25-7

margins
  defined   36
  matrix, computation of
    from published data   36-7

market clearing equations
  in basic input-output model   38
  in DMR model   164-5,237-8
  in Stylized Johansen model   90

markup pricing   242

markup(s)   26-7
  treatment of in basic values
    input-output tables   28
  treatment of in input-
    output models   49-54
  treatment of in purchasers'
    prices input-output tables   29-31
  – see also margins

material/material substitution   216

material/primary factor substitution
216

mathematical programming
  approach to applied GE modeling   2

mobility of factors   237-8

multi-product industries   128-32,199

multi-step Johansen computation
79,110-124,210,231,233

multiple shooting   336-8

multiplier
  analysis, limitations of   69-70
  and stock market data   289n
  current value   289
  in optimal control problems   288
  in steady state   320-1
  input-output   65-7
  intertemporal interpretation   286-7

national accounts   253

negative gross operating surplus   186

Newton's method   335,337-8

non-competing imports   25
  at basic values   28-9
  at purchasers' prices   28-31

notation
  in DMR model   182-6
  in intertemporal general
    equilibrium model   380-2
  in Stylized Johansen model   88-9

numeraire   93,96
  role in intertemporal models   360

numerical analysis 110,113,115

occupational mobility 238

optimal control 278,288

ORANI closure 179-80,246-51

ORANI model 1,99,128n,199,240,246

parameters
  of the structural form 97

parameters compared with
  coefficients 150

percentage-change form
  method of deriving 124-48
  of Stylized Johansen model 94-5

phase diagram
  construction 292-304

policy analysis 79

Ponzi scheme 286

power rule (in linearization) 94

powers of taxes, tariffs and subsidies
  95,185,236,244

price indexes in DMR model 241

price transmission elasticity 199

primary-factor-augmenting technical
  change 185,219,247

producers' prices 31

product rule (in linearization) 94

production function
  Cobb-Douglas 88,92,96,108,124,
    139,212,218,222-3
  CES 124,128
  CRESH 126
  Leontief 142,194,213-4,216-7
  nested 134,142-6
  separable 142-3

production possibilities frontier
  CET 128-33,151,200-9
  CRETH 128-9,133

production possibilities set
  in wine-cloth economy 9

purchasers' prices 28-31

pure theory of international trade
  198

quotas (in DMR model)
  151-2,225-6,228-9

rates of return 239

rational expectations
  significance of 355

rationing
  of imports (in DMR model)
    151-2,225-6,228-9

real wages
  in wine-cloth economy 12-3

regional analysis
  use of input-output in 20,23

rental price of capital 184,242,266

rents arising from import quotas
  226,228-9

response of DMR model
  in the standard *ORANI* closure to:
    an exchange-rate shock 246-9
    equal percentage shocks in
      all real exogenous variables
        247,249
    an increase in the
      marginal propensity to
        spend 247
    10 per cent primary-factor-
      augmenting technical
      change plus 10 per cent
      increase in real wages
      plus 10 per cent reduction
      in all capital
      availabilities 247
  in the standard DMR closure
    to a fall in the price of
    the major export commodity
      256-67

results, interpreting 256-67

returns to scale
  – see constant returns to scale

Richardson's extrapolation, in
  intertemporal models 344

risk premium
  in investment models 279

saddle path stability
  – see stable path - uniqueness

sales taxes 26-7
  in basic-values
    input-output table 28-9
  in purchasers' prices
    input-output table 28-31
  treatment of in
    input-output models 49-54

saving (in DMR model) 265

savings supply function 277,
  352,360-1

scale – see constant returns to scale
Scarf algorithm   2
secondary production – treatment of
        in input-output tables   35-6
separable function   142,213,218
Shepard's lemma   135-6,138
shooting   334-6
short run profit function
        – see earnings function
small country assumption   195
solution of applied GE models
    computer packages for   2,3,4
    – see also *GEMPACK*
solution(s)
    for DMR model   258,260,274-6
    for Stylized Johansen model   105
    for wine-cloth economy   14
stability, of intertemporal models 303
stable path   293
    uniqueness   293,298-301,304,326
    with diminishing returns   325,327
state variable   288,300,304,339
stochastic optimal control   280
structural form   80,90,93-6
Stylized Johansen model   88-109,249
    – see also Johansen model
subsidy
    commodity-specific   236
    general   236
    'power' of   236
substitution elasticities
                96,116,124,216,220
sum rule (in linearization)   94
supply equations
    from CET production possibilities
        frontier   129,132-3,200-6
    from CRETH production possi-
        bilities frontier   133
symmetry of unit cost function   140
tariff   153,253
    commodity-specific   236
    general   236
    'power' of   95,244
    term, in GDP computation   261

taxes (in DMR model)   149
Taylor's series
    translog function as   137,141
technical change   8-16,185,219,
                            247,252-3
    and employment   13-7
    social consequences of   13-7
terms of trade
    fall in, in DMR model   256-67
test simulations   152,246-51
testing intertemporal models 357,361
trade policies   153
transformation effect   133
transformation elasticity
                128-9,133,201,210
translog unit cost function   133-41
transmission elasticities   196,198-9
transversality condition   286,293,
                299-300,316,318,334,341
truncation error   342,345-6,362-3
    – see also finite difference method
two-point boundary value problem
                                    334,338
typicalization of a database   186
unemployment   237-8
unit cost function – see translog...
utility function
    Cobb-Douglas
                88,91-2,96,108,192,212
        separable   142-3
wage indexation   240,242
Walras' law   93,355
wine-cloth economy   7-17
World Bank   2,149
zero input-output flows   186
zero pure profits
    in basic input-output model   71
    in capital creation   236
    in DMR model   163-4,182,234-6
    in exporting   235
    in importing   236
    in Stylized Johansen model   90